THE PROPER BOSTONIANS

THE
Proper
Bostonians

CLEVELAND

AMORY

Parnassus Imprints
Orleans, Massachusetts

For CORA

CONTENTS

*With a frontispiece of Mrs. "Jack" Gardner, as painted by John Singer
Sargent in 1888; front endpaper map "A Bostonian's Idea of the United
States of America" by Daniel K. Wallingford; back endpaper montage
of cards and invitations.*

THE PROPER BOSTONIANS

CHAPTER ONE

THE HUB

There is a story in Boston that in the palmy days of the twenties a Chicago banking house asked the Boston investment firm of Lee, Higginson & Co. for a letter of recommendation about a young Bostonian they were considering employing. Lee, Higginson could not say enough for the young man. His father, they wrote, was a Cabot, his mother a Lowell; farther back his background was a happy blend of Saltonstalls, Appletons, Peabodys, and others of Boston's First Families. The recommendation was given without hesitation.

Several days later came a curt acknowledgment from Chicago. Lee, Higginson was thanked for its trouble. Unfortunately, however, the material supplied on the young man was not exactly of the type the Chicago firm was seeking. "We were not," their letter declared, "contemplating using Mr. —— for breeding purposes."

That story is legendary but it is at the same time basic to an understanding of Boston and the Proper Bostonian. To the country at large the Proper Bostonian is not always easily identifiable. He does not necessarily live in Boston Proper. He may still live in the Beacon Hill area of his city, but he is more likely to be found in such socially circumspect Boston suburbs as Brookline, Chestnut Hill, Milton, Wellesley, Needham, Dedham or Dover—and way stations from Pride's Crossing to Woods Hole. He is not especially individual in appearance. Although outside observers have claimed to be able to tell the

Proper Bostonian male by waistcoat, and the Proper Bostonian female by hat, these marks are not foolproof. Neither is his speech an infallible sign. The actor, Leo Carroll, engaged in learning how to speak for his role of George Apley, in the play based on John P. Marquand's novel of a latter-day Proper Bostonian, found no less than thirteen recognized Boston Brahmin accents. The broad "a" and the stern omission of the "r," generally regarded as typically Bostonian, is not an invariable rule. Actually the Proper Bostonian is more inclined to speak with a clipped "a." He says not Haa-vaad for the college he loves so well, but Hah-vud. He may leave out the "r" in a word like marbles, but he doesn't say maa-bles; he says mabbles. In a word like idea, he has even been known to add an "r."

Once identified, however, the Proper Bostonian is a very well-defined type—more so, it would seem, than the Proper Baltimorean, the Proper Philadelphian, or the Proper person of any other city. His basic character traits are almost unmistakable. This is undoubtedly because, as the Lee, Higginson story suggests, Boston Society has always devoted a great deal of attention to his breeding. The Proper Bostonian did not just happen; he was planned. Since he was from the start, in that charming Boston phrase "well-connected," he was planned to fit into a social world so small that he could not help being well-defined. He is a charter member of a Society which more than one historian has called the most exclusive of that of any city in America, and which has charter members only. It used to be said that, socially speaking, Philadelphia asked who a person is, New York how much is he worth, and Boston what does he know. Nationally it has now become generally recognized that Boston Society has long cared even more than Philadelphia about the first point and has refined the asking of who a person is to the point of demanding to know who he was. Philadelphia asks about a man's parents; Boston wants to know about his grandparents. According to the Boston Chamber of Commerce, Boston is 2,350,000 people. Boston Society, according to the Boston *Social Register,* is 8000 people. Yet to the strict Proper Bostonian this volume, which admits only one Jewish man and, in a city now 79 percent Catholic in population, less than a dozen Catholic families, is considered impossibly large. Too much attention to it is regarded as a mark of social insecurity, and several Boston Society leaders have never allowed their names to be listed at all. One Somerset Club bachelor always referred to the *Register* as a "damned telephone book" and regularly protested its size by making it a practice, upon receiving his annual copy, to tear it in half and return it to its New York headquarters.

Actually this man, in his rough division of the *Register,* was not going far enough. Operating on the basis of those Families which it has come to regard as First Families—only a few dozen in all—Boston Society is fundamentally far less than half its 8000 Social Registerites. Out of the total number of Bostonians, few are called and fewer still are chosen into this fundamental Boston Society. Not content with excluding some million Bostonians of Irish background, as well as many hundreds of thousands of Bostonians of Italian, Jewish, Polish and other backgrounds, it also cheerfully excludes another several hundred thousand or so of persons whose backgrounds are as undeniably Anglo-Saxon as its First Families' own and yet, because of imperfectly established connections with a First Family, can never hope to become Proper Bostonians.

This figurative handful, the First Family Society of the Proper Bostonian, would be interesting enough if it had done nothing more, through all the years of its existence, than hold its social fort against all comers. But it has done considerably more than this. Despite its numerical insignificance it has set its stamp on the country's fifth largest city so indelibly that when an outsider thinks of a Bostonian he thinks only of the Proper Bostonian. When Thomas Gold Appleton a century ago used the phrase "Cold Roast Boston," he was a Proper Bostonian speaking only of other Proper Bostonians. But the phrase has lasted, not alone for Appleton and his friends and their descendants, but for Boston itself. In the same way, one small poem which had its genesis in the social aspirations of just two Boston Families has become

what is probably the closest thing to a social folk song any city
ever had. Originally patterned on a toast delivered by an anonymous "Western man" at a Harvard alumni dinner in 1905, it
was refined in 1910 by Dr. John Collins Bossidy of Holy Cross
to be recited, apparently for all time, as follows:

> And this is good old Boston
> The home of the bean and the cod,
> Where the Lowells talk to the Cabots,
> And the Cabots talk only to God.

The stamp of the Proper Bostonian on his city has stood the
test of time. The personality of Boston remains the personality
of the Proper Bostonian—not only to such alien critics as the
editors of the *New Yorker* and *Time* magazines, and to count-
less authors of fiction from Worcester to Hollywood, but in fact.
Boston's Irish population may be in control of the city's government, but not for nothing are they referred to as "the poor,
downtrodden majority." Boston as a city still moves almost as it
did in Emerson's day, when he described it as locomoting as
cautiously as a Yankee gentleman "with his hands in his pockets." In 1945 an up-and-coming court removed the still exist-
ing ban imposed in 1637 on the "Boston Jezebel," Miss Anne
Hutchinson, but only a year later, in 1946, as Boston was making elaborate plans to be the City of Tomorrow, the park commissioner, engaged in planning a modern parking space under
Boston Common, noted rather sadly that if any of the old-time
property owners of Beacon Hill wished to take advantage of the
ancient and immutable statute permitting them to graze their
cows on top of the Common, he would still be powerless to do
anything about it.

To the Proper Bostonian such things are part and parcel of
Boston's charm. He has always had much less interest in what he
still firmly regards as "his Boston" becoming any City of Tomorrow than he has had in keeping it the City of Yesterday.

Above all, he is proud of the fact that, regardless of its changing political complexion, Boston is still undisputedly America's Family City. The Proper Bostonian has always used this word not in the sense of one's immediate family but in the Oriental fashion to mean one's clan or all those of the same name who have the same ancestors—and it is not necessary to go to Boston's Chinatown to find that this is the sense in which Boston as a whole uses the word today. There are many drugstores in the city, some of which have no intention of ever yielding to the advent of the soda fountain, which have been in the same Family for well over a hundred years. Even such newfangled contraptions as the swan boats which during the summer ply the waters of the Public Gardens at ten cents a ride for adults and five cents for children have already been under the same Family ownership for seventy-five years. Virtually every tree in the Gardens and on the Common is marked with its Family name, both in Latin and in English, and the Boston *Transcript* was always known for publishing, in every Wednesday evening edition, the most complete genealogy column in existence.

There is little question that the Proper Bostonian, willingly or not, has taught other Bostonians to regard Family consciousness as the key to upward gravitation in the Boston social scale. To some extent he has even influenced the naturally democratic Irish population of his city in this regard, so that they have become known for graduating through Family stages from "Shanty" Irish to "Lace-curtain" Irish, and finally to "Venetian-blind" Irish, and to look rather askance at those a rung below them on the shamrock path. Others have been influenced more strongly. One Society editor of a Boston paper, weary of First Family snubs, not long ago spent a full year filling out blanks and tracing her ancestors through eleven generations to satisfy the exacting requirements of the Society of Mayflower Descendants. For some years the president of the Massachusetts Society of Colonial Dames has found that her position necessitates going to such an un-Bostonian extreme as the maintenance of a full-time social secretary in her own home, and even the august New

England Historic Genealogic Society, the oldest of such organizations in the country, has a regular monthly "social hour." Reverence for a Family crest has become a Boston tradition, and while officers of the New England Committee on Heraldry have from time to time attempted to make clear that coats-of-arms have "nothing to do with social position," Bostonians of varying backgrounds have not hesitated to assume them. The late Mrs. Mary Baker Eddy, beloved founder of the Christian Science Church, was merely following a well-recognized trend when she awarded herself a Scottish crest and had it carved in mahogany in the vestibule of her Commonwealth Avenue home—only to have to scrape it off when representatives of the McNeil Family in Scotland came to this country to challenge her right to the crest. Proper Bostonian leadership has been notably slipshod on the whole question of coats-of-arms. Many years ago the merchant William Appleton made a businesslike study of the problem and came to the conclusion that only eight Boston Families, Appletons included, were entitled to crests. Dissatisfied with this, since the Lowells were not included, the late poetess Amy Lowell went into the matter on her own and figured out that thirteen Families was the correct figure. Only the present Charles Francis Adams would seem to have shown becoming modesty in the debate. Branding as spurious the Lowell crest at that time being carved in Harvard's Lowell House, he declared that to his knowledge only two Families, not alone in Boston but in all of New England—the Winthrops and the Saltonstalls —were worthy of the honor of arms-bearing.

If he has led others astray on his purple path, the Proper Bostonian is blithely unconcerned with the fact. He remains the Man of Family Supreme. So close is his identification with his ancestors that in answer to the simple question, "How long have you been in Boston?" such a man is likely to reply, "*I*'ve been here since 1730," or 1700—and he really thinks he has. He has immense pride in his forebears and he includes all of them. The portraits of past black sheep hang on his walls along with those of his stern-faced ancestors whose ways were more tried and true. In a Boston Bowditch home today may be found the portrait of Habbakuk, town drunk of Salem, side by side with that of his son, Nathaniel, the celebrated navigator and mathematician. The Proper Bostonian feels that if certain of his ancestors were distinguished, so much the better, but they do not have to have been. His Family tree, at least in his own mind, is rooted so firmly it needs no ornaments on its branches. When after a dignified Proper Boston courtship of seven years the poet Henry Wadsworth Longfellow married into the Appleton Family, the Appletons felt very pleased about it—for the Longfellows, of course. The poet wasn't, after all, a Bostonian at all, having been born in Portland, Maine. When one of the Boston Forbeses married the daughter of philosopher Ralph Waldo Emerson, the Forbeses began to feel very kindly toward the strange man from Concord; his daughter soon became, in the Proper Boston manner of speaking, "a Forbes." Some years ago a New York girl who had married into a Boston First Family and who had, in customary fashion, named her first child after her husband, spoke of naming her second son after her own brother. In great agitation a dowager of the First Family came to see her and said, "I hear you are naming your son Alfred. I have been back over the Family tree and I cannot find a single record of anyone of that name." For the young wife to protest that she, too, had a Family was useless. In the Boston sense she had none.

Oliver Wendell Holmes the elder, poet and doctor, posing for himself the question, "What do I mean by a man of Family?" once defined the Proper Bostonian idea in no uncertain terms:

> Four or five generations of gentlemen and gentlewomen; among them a member of his Majesty's Council for the Provinces, a Governor or so, one or two Doctors of Divinity, a member of Congress, not later than the time of long boots with tassels. . . .

Dr. Holmes declared that Family portraits and Family books both definitely had their place, and that so too did a "blazoned" crest on the Family silver—"the same in worsted, by a maiden aunt." He concluded:

No, my friends, I go (always, other things being equal) for the man who inherits family traditions and the cumulative humanities of at least four or five generations. . . . I go for the man with the gallery of family portraits against the one with the twenty-five-cent daguerreotype.*

At an early age the late Henry Cabot Lodge was once moved to ask his grandfather about his ancestors. "My boy," he was told sharply, "we do not talk about Family in this country. It is enough for you to know that your grandfather is an honest man." The remark had such a profound effect on Lodge that he never forgot it. He was soon to find, however, that his grandfather was almost alone in Boston in such ancestral impiety. When Lodge became a senator, his Massachusetts colleague, Senator Samuel Hoar, told him—"with great satisfaction," Lodge recalled—that he had discovered that through a mutual ancestor, the pastor of Salem's first church, they were both descended from a sister of Chaucer.

No Boston First Family party is complete without some discussion of genealogy. One of these parties, traditionally a Thanksgiving or Christmas affair, is apt to be so large that many of the guests, though relatives, will be strangers to each other; if afterwards one speaks of not connecting with someone he means, in the Boston manner of speaking, that though he saw the person and even may have spoken with him, he did not place him on the Family tree. For many years the Lowell Christmas night parties, landmarks of Boston's First Family gatherings, would have tested even the antiquarian who occupied himself for a quarter of a century compiling the official Lowell Family genealogy. The Bowditch Family met the problem squarely as recently as 1936 by supplying every guest present with a ten-generation genealogy, a pamphlet designed in loose-leaf form

* *The Autocrat of the Breakfast-Table*, by Oliver Wendell Holmes (Boston: Houghton Mifflin) © 1858, 1882, 1886 and 1891.

with extra space provided for keeping the work up to date. Occasionally a crisis occurs at one of these parties as when Calvin Coolidge was elected President and a Boston Coolidge dinner was thrown into an uproar of discussion to determine what exact relation was this man from far-off Vermont. To get this distinguished Family talking about anything was in itself no mean achievement—the Society journal *Town Topics* once described Boston Coolidges as "scions of silence"—but fortunately among those present was Julian Coolidge, professor of mathematics at Harvard, who is a very precise man. After a moment's thought he came up with his answer, "Calvin is my seventh cousin once removed," he said. He was later proved correct.

The dynastic proportions of Boston's First Families are staggering. One way of measuring these proportions is in the class lists of Harvard, to which most sons of First Families have naturally gravitated. A son of the present Senator represents the ninth successive generation of Saltonstalls, all descendants in the male line, to attend the college, as follows: Nathaniel, 1659; Richard, 1695; Richard, 1722; Nathaniel, 1766; Leverett, 1802; Leverett, 1844; Richard, 1881; Leverett, 1914; and Leverett, 1939. The Wigglesworths have sent to Harvard no less than eight Edward Wigglesworths alone, while Dr. George Cheever Shattuck and Dr. Richard Warren represent, respectively, the fifth and sixth generations of Boston Shattucks and Warrens who have attended the Harvard Medical School. The First Families have indeed always been noted not only for the recurrence of the same first name but also for the recurrence of the same profession. In the Lowell Family there were three generations of Judge Johns, beginning with one appointed by George Washington. Among the Cabots there have been seven successive generations of Samuels, the last three of whom have been manufacturing chemists. In the Quincy Family were four generations of Josiahs, three of them being mayors of Boston. For a hundred years there have been Augustus Lorings and Moorfield Storeys and other imposing names in Boston's legal profession.

A present member of the Homans Family declares that when she says Dr. John Homans she may mean her great-grandfather, her grandfather, her father, her brother, her nephew or her cousin—all of that name and all physicians. Besides this name confusion First Family genealogy is further complicated by the overlapping of generations. On the testimony of one writer, whose mother was a Cabot, it "sometimes happened that a Cabot girl would be a great-aunt before she was born."

First Families in Boston have tended toward marrying each other in a way that would do justice to the planned marriages of European royalty. Historian John Gorham Palfrey, commenting on the homogeneousness of New England life, once declared that a purer strain of English blood existed in New England than in any English county. Boston's best have determined to keep it that way. With the exception that no Saltonstall has ever yet married a Lowell, intermarriage among First Families has occurred in large proportion in almost every generation. Old Colonel Henry Lee, an impeccable First Family man, phrased the matter gently:

> Lees, Cabots, Jacksons and Higginsons knew each other well . . . and had a satisfying belief that New England morality and intellectuality had produced nothing better than they were; so they very contentedly made a little clique of themselves, and inter-married very much, with a sure and cheerful faith that in such alliances there can be no blunder.*

In one Cabot family out of seven children who married, four married Higginsons. In a Jackson family of five, three married Cabots. In a Peabody family of four boys and two girls, two of the boys and a girl married Lawrences. In one family of Boston Shaws there were eleven children. Nine married members of other Boston First Families, one died at the age of seven months, and the eleventh became a Catholic priest. Yet even this intimate marriage circle has often proved too large. There is

* *Memoir of Colonel Henry Lee,* by John T. Morse, Jr. (Boston: Little, Brown) © 1905.

scarcely a First Family in Boston without a record in its background of a marriage of cousins. When George Cabot, the first great Cabot merchant, married a Higginson, it was a double first-cousin alliance. The late Henry Cabot Lodge's great-grandparents also were double first-cousins. Nathaniel Bowditch, rated one of the most illustrious ancestors on any First Family tree, married a first cousin as his second wife. Charles Bulfinch, Boston's greatest architect, Helen Choate Bell, Boston's best known Society wit, Lawrence Lowell and Endicott Peabody, Boston's two outstanding educators, all chose cousin spouses. Only in the case of Lowell was the relationship even as far removed as a second cousin. Among Peabodys and Hunnewells the marrying of cousins has become almost a tradition; the Hunnewell genealogy is said to have become so complicated through such alliances that it has never been satisfactorily worked out beyond 1892. One Peabody who married her cousin explained cousinly romance as almost inevitable in a Society as closely knit as Boston's, where "we had so many Family parties and picnics and all that sort of thing." Recently when two young First Family cousins became engaged a Boston matron put her official stamp of approval on the young girl's intentions. "Isn't it nice," she said, "Faith isn't marrying out of the Family."

Boston's First Families have been notably strict in their rules on the adoption of children. There have been cases in which elder members of a Family have dissuaded a childless couple from adding offspring of unknown parentage to the Family tree. In one case a couple who wished to adopt a son were forced, after considerable urging, to compromise on the selection of two daughters instead. Children of these would not then carry on the sacred name. Generally accorded special mention in the history of the Battle of Boston Eugenics is the long-suffering scion of a First Family who was prevented from marrying the girl of his choice because of her inferior social position. The parents went so far as to declare they would publicly disinherit him if he added such an unworthy strain to their proud line.

Resolutely, nonetheless, the young scion courted his girl in the slow but steady Proper Bostonian manner, and upon the death of his parents married her—thirty years later.

Along with the Family idea the Proper Bostonian has stamped a provinciality upon his city which has through the years shown few signs of decreasing. So long as Anglo-Saxon gentlemen stuck together, one writer has phrased it, the Bostonian felt that his world could not go wholly to the dogs. His world, of course, was Boston. "We all," wrote Dr. Holmes in the last century, "carry the Common in our head as the unit of space, the State House as the standard of architecture, and measure off men in Edward Everetts as with a yardstick." Viewed in this later time, Holmes' choice of Edward Everett could scarcely have been more ironic if he had planned it; a giant among Proper Bostonians of his day, Everett is now nationally remembered almost solely for his part at the ceremonies at Gettysburg on November 19, 1863, in which he delayed Lincoln's two-minute Gettysburg Address by an oration lasting exactly two hours. But Holmes also expressed a more durable idea. It was he who gave local newspapermen their beloved short word for Boston when he declared that firmly planted in the minds of all true Bostonians is the idea that Boston is the "hub of the solar system." However difficult it is to defend this hub thesis from a purely scientific viewpoint, there are Bostonians only too glad to try it, and one Boston lady not long ago made a stirring attempt. At a meeting of the New England Poetry Society the talk had turned to sea shells, and the chairman of the meeting had taken the trouble to demonstrate that the spirals in all shells went in the same direction. To the Boston lady this was interesting, but no more so than a fact of nature she had learned in the horticultural line. "Do you know," she said with quiet pride, "that all lilies that grow north of Boston point south and all lilies south of Boston point north."

At one time a valiant attempt was made to explain Boston provinciality as being due to the city's location. Boston was a place in the corner, not on the main line to anywhere in particular, and thus was contrasted to the positions of New York, Philadelphia, Baltimore and Washington, which, it was said, stood like separated houses on a country street, not far enough apart to prevent the occupants from holding neighborly relations with one another. Unfortunately this explanation was made many years before the advent of fast modern methods of travel and is severely dated. Now it is clear that Boston's lack of interest in other cities is made of sterner stuff, and that stuff, it would seem, is nothing more or less than the impressive stamp of the character of the Proper Bostonian upon the character of his city as a whole. The Proper Bostonian is not by nature a traveler. In an earlier day he made his Grand Tour, always with particular emphasis on England—for London alone was enough like Boston to suit him—and of late years he has been pushed by wars and other circumstances to various parts of the globe, but basically he remains adamant in his lack of geographical curiosity outside the suburbs of Boston. The Beacon Hill lady who, chided for her lack of travel, asked simply, "Why should I travel when I'm already here?" would seem to have put the matter in a nutshell—also her compatriot who, arriving in California and asked how she came West, replied, "Via Dedham." Josiah Bradlee, a well-known merchant of his time, though no First Family man, was merely following Proper Bostonian leadership when he spent in his lifetime of eighty-two years but one night outside Boston, and that one at a distance of some ten miles. Today this leadership is in the hands of such a distinguished Proper Bostonian as Charles Francis Adams, whose business requires his presence in New York every week or so but who makes no bones about the fact that, though a man in his eighties, he prefers to ride a milk train back to Boston rather than spend a night in a New York hotel. Of all Boston's First Families the Forbeses, long-time resident of the select suburb of Milton, have always been particularly well known for their love of home and hearth. In the summer they go to Naushon, their own island off Boston's south shore where there are, in contrast to other Boston summer resorts, not just all Bostonians, but all Forbeses. When Cameron Forbes was appointed governor-general of the Philippines many years ago, his brother Ralph was congratulated. "I don't know," said Ralph, "it's kind of tough on Cam. He won't know what's going on in Milton any more."

The ordinary Bostonian has been taught by the Proper Bostonian to give the West a wide berth. When, in 1935, industrial designer Daniel K. Wallingford, who had already published a map entitled A New Yorker's Idea of the United States, moved to Boston and took up residence there, he received so many letters from people asking him to immortalize the Bostonian's viewpoint that he shortly came up with his Bostonian's Idea of the United States. Minnesota-born Wallingford felt keenly Boston's geographical limitations in respect to the West and in his work the Great Lakes are carefully noted as "fresh water" and under a large blank area marked "Western Prairies" appears the line: "Dayton, Kansas City, Toledo, Helena, Tulsa, Indianapolis, Milwaukee, and other such cities are located in this territory." The Midwest has apparently always been Boston's bane. "A grand reservoir for our excess population," declared a young Boston clergyman when the region was first being settled. A more modern story grew up around two sisters from Burlington, Iowa, who came to Boston to marry Bostonians. Declaring they were from Iowa, they once received the astonishing rebuke, "In Boston we pronounce it Ohio." Today a Boston businessman who is forced to travel in the West a good deal proudly declares he always keeps his watch on "Boston time" and computes the difference. In so doing, of course, he is following a travel tradition long established by the true Proper Bostonian. The man who perhaps best blazed this trail for him was the late Barrett Wendell. Called the Brahmin of Brahmins, Wendell once visited the Blarney stone in Ireland. He did not kiss it, he reported, but instead touched it with his umbrella and kissed that. For his own country, however, he showed not even this deference. Addressing Sir Robert White-Thompson, whom he always described as his "dearest of English friends," Wendell wrote from Kilbourne, Wisconsin, under date of July 3, 1884, as follows:

> *Dear Colonel Thomson:*—For the first time in four years I am on my travels, or something very like it. . . . The truth is that this Western country of ours is terribly uninteresting. It is very fertile, but very flat. The landscape is as monotonous as landscapes can be. The towns are brand new, and very ugly. The cities are the colossal works of men who as a rule know how to make money but not how to spend it. And though here and there you find oases in this desert—such as a small club in Chicago, which is in every respect all that a club should be—the whole atmosphere is very depressing to a man who is not too busy to stop and think. Accordingly, I am rather depressed.*

In sharp contrast to his attitude toward the rest of the country is the Boston position, enforced by the Proper Bostonian, in regard to visitors to The Hub. Woe to the stranger who gets off at the Back Bay Station, or even one who proceeds to the South Station or the Park Street subway exit, without the feeling that he has come to a shrine. The bend of the knee and the doff of the hat are a part of the picture. "I come," wrote the novelist William Dean Howells of his first visit, "as the passionate pilgrim from the West approached his Holy Land in Boston." Howells, of course, was welcome. So, too, was the Boston woman who, reluctantly transplanted to another part of the country, returned to be asked how she liked being home again. Having been well taught in the Proper Boston school she was taken aback. "Like it?" she said. "Why I never thought of it that way. Liking Boston is like saluting the flag."

The Proper Bostonian has no chamber of commerce approach to his city. It is not for him to talk it up. He expects his visitor to come, see, and be conquered. The stranger must give evidence that he has the same sort of awesome respect for what he sees that his hosts have always had. Rare is the visitor who has

---

* *Barrett Wendell and His Letters*, by M. A. DeWolfe Howe (Boston: Atlantic Monthly Press) © 1922.

not, at one time or another, had the feeling that he is a man
under suspicion. He would like to laugh at the city and break
the ice, but he usually feels he cannot. Boston has been taught
by the Proper Bostonian to take itself seriously, and the city
which an English traveller once described as "proud to be a
chill on the hot surface of American strenuosity" is not easy to
laugh at. Earl Derr Biggers, who later became famous as the
author of Charley Chan, recalled that his first newspaper job
was writing a column in Boston. "Writing a humorous column
in Boston," he declared, "was a good deal like making faces in
church; it offended a lot of nice people, and wasn't much fun."
The cartoonist Gluyas Williams puts it another way. Though
born in California, he has made his home in Boston for some
thirty-five years. "Oh, your Bostonian will laugh all right," he
asserts, "only not when you expect him to."

A Proper Boston institution is, of course, rarely a laughing
matter. When General Sherman Miles was assigned to command the First Corps area and came to Boston during World
War II, he searched at some length for a place to live. Finally he
located a second-floor apartment over an office at the corner of
Beacon and Charles Streets, a building in the best, though increasingly commercial, section of the city. To a lady at dinner he
confided his finding, at the same time frankly confessing he was
not too keen on the idea of living "over the corner drugstore."
Coldly the lady set him straight. "General Miles," she said, "the
National Shawmut Bank is *not* the corner drugstore."

Of all his institutions, the Proper Bostonian has perhaps had
most difficulty in enforcing, on both the fellow inhabitants of
his city and his visitors, his high regard for Harvard University.
Since all First Family sons repair there, he wishes it to be recognized as the only college there is, but since the great majority
of Bostonians have little or no connection with it, and since Boston has half a dozen other colleges as well—not to mention the
fact that Harvard is located not in Boston at all, but in Cambridge—this is a difficult task indeed. Nonetheless the Proper
Bostonian has done his best, and to be elected to membership in

Harvard's "Corporation," a self-perpetuating group of Bostonians who run the University—and who in recent years have managed to include one or two New Yorkers in their number —is a Bostonian honor not to be compared with anything else. The late Bishop Lawrence, himself a member of the group, once stated that a Bostonian might speak disparagingly of the House of Bishops or the College of Cardinals but not of the Harvard Corporation. Probably the notable story of the university as a focal point of local pride is that which occurred some years ago during the Taft administration in Washington. A visitor to Harvard sought to see the late Lawrence Lowell, then president of the university. Having been called to the nation's capital on a matter of business, Lowell could not be seen. The visitor was stopped by a secretary in the outer office. "The President is in Washington," she said, "seeing Mr. Taft."

The combined effect of Boston's lack of enthusiasm for crasser cities and its insistence upon homage at home has not been without its natural reaction. John P. Marquand, a Somerset Club man himself though the author of several novels severely critical of the ways of the Proper Bostonians, has declared that all Americans have a sneaking fondness for the city, shocked though he admits they may be by its austerities and its Puritanism. If this is true, certainly many Americans have kept this feeling of fondness to themselves. To the salesman Boston and its environs have long been known as the graveyard circuit; it has been said that no worse fate can befall a travelling man than to have to spend a Sunday in that city. The New York businessman, referring to the cool breeze which blows in from Boston Harbor to end each summer hot spell, and the special express which leaves the South Station for New York at five o'clock each weekday, has a stock expression for the unsophisticated little city north of him. "The best things about Boston," he says, "are the east wind and the Merchant's Limited." People of the Midwest have been known to repay in kind the all but official Boston attitude toward them. The late Mrs. Henry Adams, discouraged at the reception she and her friends had once received in that part of the country, wrote home that Ohio people in particular seemed to her "sensitive" about "Boston folks." The present Mrs. Charles Francis Adams believes that this anti-Boston bias may well have its roots in the none too savory reputation of Boston hospitality. A leader in Washington Society when her husband was Secretary of the Navy, she has a sister who is a ranking Philadelphia hostess and thus has some basis for a comparison with other cities. "When a stranger comes to town here," she declares, "we say, 'Heavens, we've got to do something about so-and-so.' Other cities seem to like to do it."

On a national scale Boston's notices are rarely good ones. Whenever an event occurs, such as the banning of a popular book or the election of a mayor who, at the age of seventy-one, faced the possibility of forty-seven years in jail, Boston pays dearly for the cold shoulder it has the reputation for extending to the rest of the country. In between times commentators in other cities are never averse to taking pot shots in its direction just to keep themselves in training. "Ever delightful Boston," editorialized the New York *Sun* some years ago for no particular reason, "so sure of its excellence in little things as well as great, and so pleased with its destiny of being better than other cities are." Ex-Governor Ellis Arnall of Georgia, discussing the shortcomings of his own state in a recent book, put in a few remarks about Boston for good measure. A "festering mud puddle" he called it, and "America's Tobacco Road." Even Boston-born Lucius Beebe, returning to his native land for the Boston opening of the play, *The Late George Apley,* in November, 1944, could not forbear noting in the New York *Herald Tribune* a doubtful impression of the place:

> A combination of sleet and rain peculiar to the Hub descended from a sodden sky. Galoshes were common currency in Dartmouth Street. The Boston papers were devoted principally to genealogical exchanges between politicians of Gaelic antecedents. Across a murky Charles River the ample electric signboard of the National Casket Company beckoned through the

gloom. In the Algonquin Club elderly codgers snoozed over slim copies of the *Illustrated London News*. The New Haven trains were variously and very late, and the carpet from the restaurant of the Ritz had gone to the cleaners and not been returned. There were no lemons in town, and no Chesterfields either, and New Yorkers making the perilous overland journey were advised by phone to bring their own. . . . In a word, Boston was possessed of all the hilarious overtones of Liverpool on a Sunday evening in March.

Despite the dubious distinction he has won for his city the Proper Bostonian is still in his own domain regarded in almost all cases with respect and in some instances with actual affection. His private life is almost inviolate. On the Society pages of his papers his treatment is deferential in the extreme, and today the New York type gossip column is nonexistent in any Boston paper. It has been said that Walter Winchell would have starved to death if he had lived in Boston. "Except for charity," says Mrs. Fiske Warren, for three generations a First Family leader, "no reporter has ever crossed my threshold." A present-day Society editor recalls that as a cub reporter she had once inserted in an article she was writing an item to the effect that Boston's Harvard Club was stocked, to the exclusion of any other brand, with Fairy Soap. Though her reporting was accurate, she was called to the managing editor's office and told that the paper had a policy of "not saying things like that about nice people." In the library of the Boston *Herald* the envelope containing the clippings of Miss Eleanor ("Sissy") Frothingham, Boston's most colorful First Family debutante of recent years—who turned nightclub torch-singer and later married a saxophone player—is clearly marked for the benefit of any brash reporter: NOT TO BE REFERRED TO AS A GLAMOR GIRL.

This seeming abdication of journalistic responsibility cannot entirely be explained by the fact that the Boston newspapers are largely controlled by the Boston banks, which are in turn dominated by Proper Bostonians. There is also a sizeable amount of evidence to support the thesis that the ordinary Bos-

tonian rather looks up to the Proper Bostonian and is not inclined to laugh at him. Referring to the least endearing of
various first Family traits—such as the bluntness of Cabots, the
frostiness of Lowells, the tactlessness of Adamses, the perversity
of Forbeses, the irascibility of Higginsons, the frugality of Lawrences, etc.—the late lawyer James Byrne once said that to him
there was nothing humorous about it. The son of an Irish con-
tractor, Byrne worked his way through Harvard tutoring sons
of First Families and became the only man of his background
and religion ever honored with membership on the Harvard
Corporation. "It is strong stock," he said, "that can produce the
same traits of character in generation after generation. No, I
don't laugh at it."

If the Proper Bostonian has stamped on his city its stigma of
narrow provinciality and general cold roastness, it seems to be
also generally recognized that on his back still falls a large share
of the burden of carrying on the cultural tradition which in various fields once made Boston known as the Athens of America.
The Cabot who has long been the moving spirit of the ill-famed
Watch and Ward Society, active in book-banning and theatre
censorship, may have let this tradition down. But at the same
time three other Cabots were making up for it by being hard
at work heading the boards of trustees of the Boston Symphony,
whose fame is every Bostonian's pride and joy, the Judge Baker
Foundation, which has become nationally known for its work in
juvenile delinquency, and the Boston Athenaeum, which is in
many respects the country's outstanding private library. Boston
as a whole knows that its First Families are not yet incapable of
producing able citizens. The late Cabot doctor brothers Richard and Hugh, the former known as the father of medical social
service and the latter a distinguished surgeon also known for
social service, were standout examples of this, and today Boston
Cabots continue to dominate *Who's Who* in a measure as im-
pressively as they dominate the *Social Register*. There are no
less than ten of them listed in the 1946-47 volume.

In Boston the member of a First Family lives in a world of

special privilege. For him the minor inconveniences of life are all but by-passed. If he lives on Beacon Hill he will probably have a view of the Common or perhaps a fenced-in park of his own, such as on fashionable Louisburg Square, where the twenty-two so-called proprietors or homeowners have practically no responsibility to their city at all, own the entire square outright, and meet annually to tax themselves for the upkeep of their park and the care of their street. If he lives in Back Bay, he will doubtless be on the "water side" of Beacon Street or the "sunny side" of Commonwealth Avenue; the other side of these streets would be, for him, the wrong side of the tracks. Outside his home, he may even have a special kind of sidewalk to distinguish his residence. So-called "rich men's sidewalks," they are small areas of glazed brick laid in fancy patterns instead of the ordinary Boston rough brick or cement walks. Ames Corner, located at the north corner of Commonwealth and Dartmouth Streets, is one of these; dangerously slippery as the corner is in wet weather, it has been allowed to remain as a sort of Boston monument to a man who was once officially connected with seventy-five of the country's railroads. If the Proper Bostonian is one of the many who have moved to the suburbs, he will be "protected" by rigid zoning laws of his own making and may not have a numbered street address at all. That is part of his privilege.

Everywhere the Proper Bostonian goes in his city he is likely to find that the magic of the Family Name pronounced will open virtually all doors, admit to the best clubs, and even see to a wide variety of special attentions. One of these special attentions began as a mere matter of the changing of a street name and ended by affording historians with a complete saga of Boston social protocol. Originally Belknap Street on Beacon Hill was divided by cross streets into three parts which faithfully represented three grades of social stature. In the upper part were some of the city's finest houses, owned by wealthy First Family Bostonians. In the middle part were residents of long standing but of humbler position, while the lower part was occupied almost entirely by colored people. After enduring the situation for some time, the Proper Bostonians of Belknap Street petitioned the city government to change the name of their portion of the street to Joy Street. The middle group, seeing the way the wind was blowing, next asked to have their portion renamed. When this request was also granted, the colored people began to feel the slur. Finally they too put in their request to be a part of Joy Street and the name Belknap was abandoned altogether. It has not been used since.

Trains have changed schedules, stores have changed hours, and courts have changed statutes—all for the First Families. There are people in Boston today who remember the picture of Judge John Lowell, squire of the suburb of Chestnut Hill, who, often late for the 8:25 commuter's special, never missed the train. While a trainful of commuters complained in vain, it was never 8:25 to the engineer until the Judge was aboard. As for Boston's stores, the more exclusive of them have long catered to the whims of First Families irrespective of the fact that other customers are notoriously freer spenders. In the days before government regulations made such practice illegal, it was not unusual for a store to allow a First Family to run a bill for as much as two years without attempting collection beyond the usual formal statement of account rendered. Harrison Gray Otis, nineteenth-century king of Boston Society, had early set a high standard for this sort of privilege when, in 1830, on the day fixed for the organization of Boston's present-day city government, he sent word to the members of the city council that he was ill and wished them to convene at his Beacon Hill residence. A few members protested that a municipal inauguration should not be held in a private home, but an invitation from an Otis was a command performance, and held it was.

To the courts—or rather to one particular court, the Massachusetts Supreme Court—the First Families have always repaired for the most remarkable of their privileges. Through its interpretations of their so-called "spendthrift" trusts Boston's First Family fortunes have long been tied up beyond the reach of any power save possibly, as one financial writer put it, the Communist International. Beneficiaries under these trusts, regardless of their age or business acumen, cannot sell or dispose of their rights to the income. This type of restriction is sanctioned by the courts of most of the United States; but the Massachusetts judges have gone a long step further in permitting the principal to be put beyond the reach of creditors of the heirs designated to receive it. The power of the trustee, as long as he is by court definition a "prudent" man, is close to absolute. He rules not only until an heir becomes of age but in some cases all the heir's life. In time of First Family fortune stresses trustees have been known to be able to keep all money away from creditors; then, when such storms have blown over, they have been able to turn on the golden faucet once more. Almost all these trustees are themselves First Family men and they have usually made sure that the trusts they handle are re-established before the Rule Against Perpetuities could be invoked to put them out of business. The total power and resources of Boston's Family trusts have never been figured, but some years ago one of the city's trustee officers alone paid three percent of Boston's total tax levy.

Most of Boston's First Families owe their lives of privilege, at least to some extent, to these trusts. The Lowell and Lawrence trusts, united by a Lawrence marriage on the part of the late Augustus Lowell, are particularly formidable affairs. So, too, is the Sears trust. This was established by Joshua Montgomery Sears, a Boston merchant who was so busy making money in the West Indies trade he didn't take time out to get married until he was in his sixties. On his death in 1857 he left a son, Joshua Junior, who was then two years old. Only a very small part of young Joshua's inheritance, however, was left fluid, just enough, on a day-by-day estimate of the trustee, for bringing him up and educating him. The rest of the estate was thoroughly tied up and was shrewdly manipulated so as to increase and multiply until the boy matured. When this happened, the mature Joshua awoke to find himself a wealthier man than even his father might have imagined. At the age of twenty-one he became Boston's largest taxpayer.

No Boston Family, not even the Searses, find generous representation in the various encyclopedias of wealth that have from time to time been published in the twentieth century. In *America's Sixty Families*, published in 1937, the Winthrops were listed as No. 22, and James Jackson Storrow of Lee, Higginson & Co. rated No. 57, but the Winthrops made their money largely in New York banking, and Mr. Storrow won his position through his ability as an individual entrepreneur. The real significance of Boston's trusts lies not in their size but in the fact that they have enabled Boston's First Families to defy economic laws and the cherished American maxim of shirtsleeves to shirtsleeves in three generations. When the match king, Ivar Krueger committed suicide and Lee, Higginson & Co., which had backed him to the hilt, went into liquidation to the extent of some $25,-000,000 of his worthless stock, the late Lawrence Lowell alone lost $194,412. But the bulk of the Lowell Family trust funds, invested in Grade-A bonds, were still intact, and neither the late Lawrence nor any Lowell since was ever to feel the necessity of getting out and shouldering a pick and starting all over again. When Leverett Saltonstall was having campaign photographs taken on his Needham farm, the pictures of the Senator doing some off-hours work in his garden were regarded as the first evidence of shirtsleeves in the Saltonstall Family in not three, but nine generations. "The great family trusts," *Fortune* magazine declared in 1933, "stand between the Bostonians and the activities of contemporary life like the transparent but all too solid glass which separates the angel fish of an aquarium from the grubby little boys outside."

In view of all their privileges it is not surprising that Boston's First Families have, on occasion, been forced to do battle for their birthright. There have been instances in which this struggle has been carried to court—when ordinary Bostonians have seen fit to become Proper Bostonians by the simple procedure of having their names changed, and have faced not only a judge but the irate Family itself. In contrast to trust cases, however, which seem to have been concluded with monotonous regularity in favor of First Families, court decisions in these name cases have gone both ways. A man who wanted to become an Amory was refused permission when a sizeable proportion of the members of that small but gamely vigilant Family appeared in court to register protest. In another case, five members of a family named Hogan—one of whom, a stenographer, gave as her reason that she was "in pursuit of happiness"—were unsuccessful in asking to have their name changed to a hyphenated name ending with Homans. They had found, arrayed in court against them, not only Boston Homanses but also a representative of the Society for the Preservation of New England Antiquities.

Surprisingly enough, the reverse decisions—those allowing name changes—seem to be on the record against the most prominent Boston Families of all, including Adamses, Appletons, and even Cabots. One Cabot case stands out above others as a classic of Boston Society. In this the judge allowed the plaintiff, a man named Kabotznick, to assume the honored name, apparently not foreseeing that his decision was also going to work a hardship on the Lowells. He was shortly reminded of this fact by an anonymous newspaper poet. Re-wording Boston's social folk song, the poet wrote:

> And this is good old Boston,
>   The home of the bean and the cod,
> Where the Lowells have no one to talk to,
>   'Cause the Cabots talk Yiddish, by God!

CHAPTER TWO

THE "FIRST" FAMILIES

Contrary to the general impression they are never loath to give outsiders, the First Families of Boston are not those whose forebears came over on the *Mayflower*. Only one *Mayflower* passenger ever lived in Boston at all. She was Mary Chilton, who later moved to Boston and for whom the city's most socially desirable woman's club was named. The *Mayflower* was never concerned with Boston's Puritans. It took Pilgrims to Plymouth and, from the social standpoint, the Pilgrims of Plymouth and the Puritans of Boston were horses of two very different colors. Plymouth, settled in 1620, was made up of people who were proud of the fact that hardly a one of them had more than a few drops of Old English blue blood in his veins. Boston, settled in 1630, was in comparison a definitely aristocratic undertaking, financed to the extent of a sum equal to five million dollars, and made up largely of upper-crust merchant adventurers. Relations between the two colonies were never overly cordial. When in 1645 the Pilgrims asked Governor Winthrop and his Bostonians to help them against the French, Winthrop agreed, provided the Pilgrims would bear all expenses. This of course the Pilgrims, not being a rich community, could not do, and the undertaking fell through—except that the Bostonians promptly went down and began a profitable trade with the French. Finally in 1691 Boston, as the Massachusetts Bay Colony, absorbed Plymouth altogether.

Besides not being *Mayflower*-descended, Boston's First Families of today are, with few exceptions, not those Families which rose to prominence early in the city's history. Almost all today's Families enjoy thinking of themselves as such, but they are, strictly speaking, no more entitled to the thought than they are to the coats-of-arms many of them have freely adopted. The Puritan Fathers were no democrats—"If the people be governors," asked John Cotton, "who then shall be governed?"—and they treasured their class distinctions—a man had to be worth a thousand dollars for his wife to wear a silk scarf—but they also believed in economic regulations which, along with those imposed by the jealous rulers of the colony in England, had the effect of forbidding the rise of lasting high Society dynasties. Plenty of Puritans made money, and good money, in timber, ships and fishing, but few were able to found Families in the enduring Boston sense.

There are many examples of such social fade-outs. A score or more can be seen from a comparison of the roster of names who made up the extremely social Ancient and Honorable Artillery Company, which was formed in 1637, with any listing of the most prominent Boston Families of today. Almost none have, in the Society sense, survived at all. Robert Keayne, a tailor in England who rose to become Boston's first great Society merchant, left the longest will in New England history but not one long enough to entitle his descendants to a place in the social picture of a later time. Thomas Boylston, the richest man in Colonial Massachusetts, who was worth $400,000 at the time of the Revolution, has left his name on Boston's chief uptown commercial thoroughfare, but there are no Boylston descendants in Boston's *Social Register* of today. Paul Revere is a striking case. He was rich, lived to be eighty-three, joined a dozen clubs, organized the first Scottish Rite Masonic Lodge in Massachusetts, married twice and had eight children by each wife—yet not one of his many descendants today cuts a social swath in keeping with the aspirations the famed midnight rider and silversmith had for his Family.

Hutchinsons and Gores, Royalls and Vassalls, Dudleys and Pinchons, Brimmers and Bromfields, once names to conjure with in Boston Society circles, have all fallen by the wayside. Some of these early-day Families died out from natural causes. Other whole Family groups were among the thousand Loyalists who left for Halifax, and did not return, when the British evacuated Boston in the Revolution. But these facts alone do not explain so many fade-outs. Many a Family, rising early, lived too well to last. They spent their money instead of leaving it for their descendants. The Hancocks did this, or rather one Hancock, John, did it all by himself. His Uncle Thomas had made the money before the Revolution, and John spent it, half a million dollars—a huge fortune for those times—in just ten years after the Revolution. In that period, as King of Boston Society, he lived on a social scale that included the wearing of solid gold buttons and the snubbing of George Washington. But when he died in 1793 he left no will at all, and even his house, Beacon Hill's famed Hancock House, once the pride of Yankee Society, was unable to ride the storm. It was torn down for taxes in 1863, Boston thereby losing what has been called the finest example of Colonial architecture in all the thirteen colonies.

The affairs of Hancock's estate were so hopelessly complicated that they dragged on legally well into the twentieth century, and generations of Proper Bostonians were thus provided with a lasting textbook example of the wisdom of stern wills, trust funds, and other ways of nipping extravagant heirs in the bud. But if the Hancock case was not enough, there were always the Otises to go by. Here was extravagance on a truly horrid scale. Social arbiter Harrison Gray Otis, who took up Boston Society where Hancock left off, wore gold-laced hats and the costliest waistcoats in town. He ate four meals a day, starting with a breakfast of *paté de fois gras*. He built three homes in all, one on Beacon Street so large it accommodated not only himself but three of his married children, each family having a private sitting room with plenty of room for their own guests as well as an entire floor of their own for ballroom entertaining. Such children, of course, were not likely to think of salting away much of the Otis fortune for the rainy days which fell upon future Otis heirs, and they did not. Speaking for the Boston Otises of today, the present Mrs. Harrison Gray Otis puts the matter frankly. "We don't live on Otis money," she says, "any more." Speaking of another Boston Family, the Quincys, formidable throughout the city's past history, today's lone *Social Register* representative of that Family, an artist by trade, is not at all bitter about the fact that his forebears gave little attention to the accumulation of wealth for future heirs. He refers to his Family in the past tense not without actual pride. The Quincys, he feels, were aristocrats of the Southern tradition, rather than of the Boston school.

"All through Boston history," says a veteran Boston author, "when a Family loses its financial stability, it has a way of beginning to disappear." This man, whose own wife was a member of one of the once-pinnacled but now all but extinct Families, is the first to admit that it is a difficult matter indeed to find records of any such stability back in the early days of Boston's history. It is necessary to wait patiently for the coming of the real Boston Family-founder, the nineteenth-century merchant prince. Whether in shipping, in railroading, in textiles, in mining, or in banking, he is the stout trunk of almost every First Family tree. Today's Boston Families know him well because it was he who made them "Firsts." There is scarcely a Family that does not owe its position in the city's Society to the money he made and saved and left in the spendthrift-proof trusts for them. Outside of Boston, from the publicity standpoint, the merchant fared poorly because he made the mistake of flourishing in his dingy counting room at the same time Boston's literary lights were setting the social world more or less ablaze in Society-studded salons. But given his due, he at least makes possible the tracing of a remarkably clear pattern of First Family history.

The pattern is this. Practically every First Family which has lasted in Boston social history can be divided into two periods —its A.M., or ante-merchant period, and its P.M., or post-merchant period. In the A.M. it is only important, from the social standpoint, that the Family be in recognized existence. What the Family forebears were doing in the hundred and fifty years from 1630 until 1780 or so makes little difference—there was not much doing anyway. Neither the accurate identification of the first bearer of the name to "come over"—the Lees and the Holmeses have never satisfied themselves on this point—nor where the Family originally settled—Boston's Gardiners came from Maine, its Hallowells from Pennsylvania—are important considerations.

After the Revolution, or better still, after the War of 1812 and lasting roughly through the Civil War, in the great Family-founding days of the nineteenth century—somewhere along the line—there must be the merchant prince, the real Family-founder. Then comes the P.M. period, in which it is important that the Family either never spend more than the income of the prince's fortune or, if they are determined to do so, then produce other merchants to make up the necessary stability.

The chief variation on this theme is a matter of marriage. Families have been known, without any merchant prince of their own, to become "Firsts" in Boston by one or more significant marital alliances with those more fortunate in this regard. Since Boston Society has always had a reputation for giving short shrift to impoverished clans, wise intermarriage has been proved virtually essential for any Family which wished to remain a "First" and yet showed signs of weakening stability—when too many members of it started going in for poorly paid, non-mercantile pursuits. The Holmeses were one Family which faced this problem squarely. Abiel Holmes, father of the first Oliver Wendell Holmes, poet and doctor, was a minister. For his first wife he had married the daughter of the president of Yale. When this wife died, however, he chose as his second wife the only daughter of the Honorable Oliver Wendell, a prosperous Boston merchant, and it was this alliance that enabled young Holmes, as he frankly expressed it, to "live like a gentle-

man" while he was studying abroad. When young Holmes himself came to marrying, he chose as his bride Amelia Lee Jackson,
daughter of the Honorable Charles Jackson, and thus consoli-
dated the Holmes situation with a fair share of Jackson wealth.
His son, the distinguished jurist Oliver Wendell Holmes, also
married a merchant daughter, a girl proudly described by her
father-in-law as "a very helpful, hopeful, powerful, as well as
brilliant woman."

Even the three most prominent of Boston's early-day Families, the Winthrops, the Adamses and the Saltonstalls, finally
became engulfed in the nineteenth century's lasting commercial
Society. The Winthrops, unable to keep up with the fast marital
pace set by their original Governor John—who was married
four times, and all to women of wealth—finally went into banking, though in New York, which accounts for their small representation in Boston social circles today. The Adamses held out
for seven generations but finally bowed to the inevitable when
Charles Francis Adams I, the diplomat, married the daughter of
Peter Chardon Brooks, Boston's first millionaire. The Saltonstalls, for all the fact that their first Richard was a nephew of
the lord mayor of London and was a genuine knight, and that
his son was called "the Worshipful Mr. Saltonstall" by the
people of Ipswich, would hardly be the Family in Boston they
are today if they had not produced something besides mere lawyers and men of public service. At last, after the middle of the
nineteenth century, they produced a man who went after the
job of Family stabilizing in a determined manner. First he
married a widow who had inherited not one but three Boston
fortunes—an Appleton fortune from her husband, a Silsbee fortune from her father, and a Crowninshield fortune from her
mother—then he went out and made a fourth fortune on his
own as a mill man. It was undoubtedly not this man to whom
the author of the official Saltonstall history was referring when,
in a speech in 1890, he declared: "May my right hand forget
her cunning and my tongue cleave to the roof of my mouth ere

I forget my forefathers, and all they endured in their simple lives, in their cold houses and churches, with few comforts and fewer luxuries. . . ." *

This First Family pattern is strikingly evident in the case of the Cabots, socially Boston's First of Firsts. They are probably the best example extant of a Boston "Old Family" not being what people generally think of such Families as being. No relation to the explorers, John and Sebastian, they have never been able to establish a recognized connection with the French Chabot Family, whose coat-of-arms they have nonetheless adopted. They not only missed the *Mayflower* but they missed her by some four generations. They came not from England at all, but from the Isle of Jersey. The date was 1700. And they settled, not in Boston, but in Salem.

Once established, however, the Cabots lost no time—first in Salem and then in Boston—in clamping themselves on the top layer of Yankee commercial Society with a bulldog hold they have never since relinquished. "The Cabots," a *Fortune* writer declared recently, "have never been remarkable for personal distinction, but rather for shrewd business sense, family solidarity, and ability to marry money." This verdict is harsh; in any case, what money Cabots did not marry, they made. They are generally credited with having produced more merchants than any other two Families in Boston's history. From the time of the firm of J. and A. Cabot, which emerged from the Revolution as the richest concern in New England, to some six Cabot firms listed in Boston's last published Blue Book, Cabot merchants have been active in virtually every field in which Proper Bostonians have been able to make fortunes. George Cabot ran away from Harvard, went to sea as a cabin boy, and went on to have a fabulously successful career and become the country's first Secretary of the Navy. John Cabot, grandson of one of the original Cabot brothers who came over in 1700, established the country's first cotton mill outside of Boston, at Beverly, in 1787.

* *Famous Families of Massachusetts,* by Mary Caroline Crawford (Boston: Little, Brown) © 1930.

The first of a long line of Samuel Cabots came down from Salem as soon as he foresaw the tremendously expanding shipping trade which would follow the War of 1812. In November of 1812 he married the eldest daughter of Boston's most success- ful shipping merchant, Colonel Thomas Handasyd Perkins, promptly moved into his father-in-law's house and soon became a partner in his firm. He died a millionaire, which has become almost a habit of Cabots ever since.

Whether or not Boston is, as most historians have claimed, basically a nineteenth-century town, few will dispute that its Society is rooted, apparently forever, in that century's rampant industrialism. The Families which rose to prominence early, and managed to hold their position, only did so, it seems, be- cause they were able to produce a merchant at the crucial time. A Weld, for example, was one of the richest men in Governor Winthrop's troupe; then for six generations the Welds passed into obscurity only to emerge, in the nineteenth century, with two great merchants in a row, first a shipping man and then a railroader, which gave this Family a social stability it has never lost. The Shaws also were prominent early, and they remained so, but it took a great Shaw merchant to put the Family in what might be termed the permanent deep freeze of social position in Boston. The Lowell Family are a good illustration of the fact that men like judges appointed by George Washington and poets like James Russell are not enough to make a Boston First Family. Without Francis Cabot Lowell, who made possible the successful introduction of the power loom in this country, and John Amory Lowell, who married a Cabot cousin and further concentrated the Family's wealth with a notable mercantile career, the Lowells would not enjoy the social security they do today. It does not please a Boston Lowell to think that his lordly position in the Boston hierarchy rests on crass commercialism; he points instead to the latter-day generation of the Family, which included such notables as the cigar-smoking poetess Amy, the astronomer Percival and the architect Guy, and he declares that his position rests on higher things. But Lawrence Lowell, former president of Harvard and brother of Amy and Percival, would have none of such folderol. Only a few years before his death he spoke of the matter to his friend, the late George Cabot, in his blunt, outspoken way: "I'm getting rather worried about the Lowell Family, George. There's nobody in it making money any more."

The rise of Boston's nineteenth-century commercial Society upset many a cherished Puritan applecart. In particular, it showed a remarkable open-mindedness on the part of Boston's ministers. From the Puritan fathers who fined Robert Keayne, the city's first merchant, for making too much profit, and made him publicly lament his "covetous and corrupt heart," it is some distance to the words Father Taylor, Boston's noted sailor-preacher, bestowed on Colonel Thomas Handasyd Perkins, when he espied him seated in his church one Sunday: "Boston's merchant princes! Do you want to see one of them, boys? There he sits, look at him!" The records of the church relate that thereupon the entire congregation arose and, struggling for positions of better vantage, the people fixed their eyes on the great merchant while the minister continued: "God bless you, sir! When you die angels will fight for the honor of carrying you to heaven on their shoulders."

Father Taylor, like the good sound Republican he was, regularly prayed for the election of good sound businessmen to public office. When a man named Briggs was running for governor he closed a memorable church service on the Sunday before the election with the following supplication:

O Lord, give us good men to rule over us, just men, temperance men, Christian men, men who fear Thee, who obey Thy commandments, men who—but, O Lord, what's the use of veering and hauling and pointing all 'round the compass? Give us George N. Briggs for Governor! *

* *Old Shipping Days in Boston.* State Street Trust Co., Boston, © 1918.

The next day Briggs was elected. There was a new spirit in Boston. No minister worth his salt was going to quibble over technicalities with a trade that was making Boston the center of the world. When Captain Kemble returned from a three years' voyage on a Sunday and kissed his wife on his front doorstep he had been put in the stocks for profaning the Lord's day. Now, on another Sabbath, when Black Ben Forbes, the youngest captain in the China trade, also returned from three years at sea, he was able to rout banker Henry Higginson right out of church and hustle him down to the bank to deposit $30,000 in doubloons to the account of Perkins & Co.—and no one said a word. The latter-day idea of the Puritan Sunday was dawning, an idea which may be said to have reached its peak when, in 1920, during a campaign against Sunday movies and golf, Boston manufacturers argued that workmen "who had no sport Sunday do their best day's work Monday."

One of the early Emerson ministers—the philosopher came, on his father's side, from a line of eight successive generations of them—had always prayed daily that none of his descendants might become wealthy. Now times had indeed changed. Everywhere the so-called "holy-stewardship" of business was being preached and lectured about. When to this was added a sort of holy trusteeship of the profits involved, Boston's First Families were well on their way to what had all the earmarks of eternal stability. The most popular lecture of the period was one entitled "Acres of Diamonds." In this the lecturer, Rev. Russell H. Conwell, expressed the hard-fisted philosophy of the real Yankee:

Money is power. Every good man and woman ought to strive for power. Tens of thousands of men and women get rich honestly. But they are often accused by an envious lazy crowd of unsuccessful persons of being dishonest and oppressive. I say, Get rich! Get rich! *

* *The Hero in History*, by Dixon Wecter (New York: Scribner's) © 1941.

The good Dr. Conwell was taken at his word. First came the merchants from "down Salem way," on the move up to Boston to carve their niches in Boston society—a Cabot, a Derby, a Sears, an Endicott, a Peabody, a Crowninshield, and many others. All represent First Family names today, and yet all were men who, if not actually pirates, were at least vikings in their methods. If they were above the triangular traffic of Colonial days—when rum was taken to Africa, slaves from Africa to the West Indies, and molasses from the West Indies back to Boston —they were not averse to an occasional sally into the opium trade. To ease their New England consciences, rum was technically known as "West Indies Goods"; the label, "Groceries and W.I. Goods," was a familiar one on Boston's Merchants' Row. Admittedly, this was a mere gesture. But no gesture was what is generally recognized as the landmark of the Bostonian conscience, when, on a day in October, 1853, Boston's greatest clipper builder, Donald McKay, launched his *Great Republic,* up to that time the largest merchant ship ever built, to the crack of a bottle of plain water.

The money was there, conscience or no conscience. In only five voyages Joseph Peabody's ships paid duties alone aggregating $587,000. What the total profits on these five cargoes were is not revealed, but they were comfortable. The Peabodys were the town's Royal Family, and at one time the saying was current that it was "Peabody, or nobody" in Salem. The merchant George Cabot once confided to a friend he had made $130,000 profit on a single ship, while Captain Codman, in a year's cargo of tea run by one ship, cleared $100,000. The nineteenth-century dollar was no twentieth-century facsimile, and these sums were fortunes indeed. They were incredibly large when compared with the salaries of those days. Nathaniel Bowditch, son of the mathematician and navigator, was only lured from his beloved Salem to come to Boston and take over the presidency of the Life Insurance Co. by being offered what was then considered the princely stipend of $5,000 a year. Fortunately for their descendants the Bowditches had other irons in the fire. In

Boston's golden age of Family-founding it was no time to be working for a salary. If you couldn't get in on the ground floor in shipping or making things, there was always the speculating road to fortune—never in the wild manner, of course, but always in the shrewd, calculating manner of the Yankee horse-trader—in Continental securities made safe by Hamilton's funding system, or in real estate of known value. "My great-great-grandfather," relates an irreverent member of a First Family today, "never believed in the word 'speculation' at all. But there was such a fashion for buying up farm mortgages in the wild West, he was finally persuaded to take on one. Knowing him, no one was surprised when his 'farm' turned out to be six square miles in the center of Chicago!"

Three of Boston's merchants, led by Harrison Gray Otis, founded at least a part of their Family fortunes in a typically calculating real-estate venture closer at hand—and all at the expense of John Singleton Copley, the portrait painter. Otis, member of the committee to procure the site for Massachusetts' new State House, is said to have had advance knowledge that Beacon Hill was to be chosen and in any case did secure for himself and his two partners Copley's Beacon Hill estate at a fantastically low figure. Copley, away in England at the time, tried for years to repudiate the sale and accused not only Otis but his agent, Samuel Cabot, of all manner of chicanery. Unfortunately for him he found practically all of Boston's blue bloods arrayed against him, and he never got anywhere. The fifteen acres "stolen" from him, in the Beacon Hill State House area, were soon worth several times the amount he received from all his paintings during his lifetime, and Copley, who died virtually penniless, never ceased to castigate those whom he called the "better people of Boston" for the rough treatment they had given him. His son, visiting Boston, claimed that even the wives of the merchants were so interested in their dollars they were not averse to "starving their servants in their own homes."

Men who went about building Family fortunes by making things had a wide latitude. The first Jacksons made nails. The

Ameses made shovels. The early Ayers made patent medicines, later ones made sarsaparilla. A Gray made rope. A Stone made soap. The Brewers, coincidentally enough, were distillers. Two brother Lorings made stationery; a third brother went to Malaga, Spain, and made his mark shipping raisins back to Boston. In the textile business the most picturesque characters of the day were the brothers Lawrence, Amos and Abbott, who started store clerking at the age of thirteen and fifteen respectively. Both dyspeptics in their later days, and parsimonious always, they were nonetheless true Horatio Algers of Boston's Golden Book. "Their vigilance in looking after their debts," declares one writer, "secured their success." On the sea, it seemed, everything turned to gold, or at least silver, for the benefit of the Boston merchant. There was a saying about one man that if he sent a shingle afloat on the ebb tide bearing a pebble, it would return on the flood, freighted with a silver dollar. When John Lowell Gardner, father-in-law of Boston's Mrs. "Jack" Gardner and generally considered the last of the East India merchants, died in 1884, he had been so uniformly successful in his ventures that one of his sons, engaged in unscrambling his estate of five million dollars, was moved to remark: "If you had started Dad at the foot of State Street with nothing on, by the time he had reached the Old State House he would have had a new suit of clothes, spats, a derby hat, a Malacca cane, and money in his pocket."

The Indies apparently liked anything with a Boston label. Frederic Tudor got rich by selling them ice; so did the fabulous "Lord" Timothy Dexter of Newburyport, who sold them, according to actual records, warming pans and mittens. The fact the natives used the warming pans for skillets never bothered Dexter, and he kept up his lucrative trade for many years. One of Colonel Perkins' ships made a sort of sideline of collecting sea otters; at the end of the season they sold them to natives for forty dollars a pelt. Occasionally on the return trips of some of these ships something would go awry. But almost as often, apparently, the versatility of Boston's merchants managed to save

the day—and the Family. The young merchant Joseph Tuckerman, returning from a voyage in the midst of the panic of 1837,
was greeted as he made his way to his home by his father throwing open his window and shouting, "Joseph, we are all ruined."
It was true, as Joseph's cargo of Eastern merchandise brought no
bids at all. Only a little while later, however, young Tuckerman
had an opportunity to ride on a train propelled by the "Johnnie
Bull," the famous locomotive imported to this country from
England. At once realizing the value of iron for railroads, he
entered the iron business and recouped the Tuckerman fortune.

A notable triumph over adversity occurred in the Eliot Family. Samuel Eliot, father of Harvard's President Charles, had
been a successful merchant in the East India trade but later, involved in a commercial house failure, he lost his entire fortune.
"From ample wealth, honorably used, he sank—or rather rose,"
declares a biographer, "to a still more honorable poverty." Fortunately this poverty was not to be of long duration. His father's
reverses occurred late in the year 1857 and Charles, not being a
merchant himself, did the next best thing in the First Family
tradition, and in October, 1858, married Miss Ellen Derby Peabody, granddaughter of Elias Hasket Derby, once rated the largest shipowner in the world. He then built two adjoining houses
in Cambridge, and moving with his wife into one of them, established a home for his parents in the other.

The acknowledged king of the merchant princes was Colonel
Thomas Handasyd Perkins. He not only launched Boston's
Perkins Family along with his ships but, since his company later
merged to make the all-powerful Russell & Co., was also indi-
rectly responsible for the launching of a sizeable proportion of
all Boston's merchant Families. Cabots and Lodges, Forbeses
and Cunninghams, Appletons and Bacons, Russells and Coolidges, Parkmans and Shaws, Codmans and Hunnewells, as well
as several others, all owe something of their fortunes to the

great "Long Tom," as he was first called in Salem. Typical of many of the men who made Boston Families "Firsts," he was the son of a wine seller who began his career as a boy before the mast and ended by building a business reaching from Rio to Canton. Offered the post of Secretary of the Navy by George Washington, he politely refused the position saying, with no exaggeration, he owned a larger fleet of vessels than that possessed by the Navy and believed it was more important for him to continue to manage his own property.

Life for future Family-founders trained by Perkins was no bed of roses. Clerks were often worked eighteen hours a day and they were told what to do in monosyllables or at best short, terse expressions, a habit of speaking the Perkins Family has proudly maintained to the present day. One clerk left for future Bostonians a revealing picture of work at Perkins & Co. when he recalled being employed one cold winter day counting the barrel staves that came out of a schooner. Falling in between the vessels and the dock in water full of floating ice, he barely saved his life. "When Mr. Perkins came down and found me wet through and trembling with cold, he did not say a word," the clerk wrote. "My pride was so touched by his indifference I remained until darkness allowed me to leave." It was little wonder such clerks wanted to leave the counting room for the sea as soon as possible —and also that they became rapidly skilled in the Yankee art of knowing the value of a dollar. One young man on going to sea was asked by a number of his Proper Boston friends to bring back certain Chinese goods for them. All except one gave him the money for the purchases. When the ship returned he gave his friends their goods, except for that one. On being asked by that person why there was nothing for him, the young man promptly explained that, upon anchoring at Calcutta, he had placed all the orders for the purchases on the ship's capstan with the money carefully laid on each memorandum—and that of course the memorandum which had not been weighted down had blown away.

There were two ways to become a merchant prince in the Perkins school of hard knocks. One was to go to sea and learn to be an actual sea captain; the other was to enter the counting room and learn to be a supercargo, a position which had nothing to do with the running of the ship but which entailed sailing on the vessel and assuming complete charge of the commercial concerns of the voyage. Rising along either path was not by any means just a matter of having a Harvard accent and knowing how to polish the right apple at the right time. For Boston at least, there was a real democracy at work in the founding of Family fortunes, and "getting in through the cabin window," as the expression was, was a rare thing. Young Dan Bacon, from a well-to-do Cape Cod family rode down to the sea on his family's white horse, and hired someone to ride the horse back. He founded the Bacon fortune. But there were other captains from far humbler circumstances who also did nicely for themselves and their descendants. One boasted he had only three days of schooling in his life. "The first day," he said, "school didn't keep; the second day the teacher was sick, and the third day I played hookey." In the supercargo line, there was a Cabot who married the boss's daughter, but there was also John Murray Forbes, who at sixteen swept floors for his supper, and at twenty was close to being a millionaire.

No other Boston First Family fortune spread-eagles the nineteenth century in quite such remarkable proportions as that of the Forbeses. For one thing, they had two fortune builders, Robert Bennet Forbes the sea captain, as well as his brother, John Murray Forbes, who chose the supercargo route. For another thing, young John Murray was far from being an ordinary supercargo. Arriving in China at the age of seventeen, he soon won the respect of the great Chinese merchant Houqua, a man worth $26,000,000 in 1830 and of a Chinese Family which, though no longer active in trade, is to this day one of the richest in that country. Before he had grown a beard young Forbes was conducting all of the elderly Houqua's correspondence and was at the same time chartering and loading ships on his own; his services commanded ten per cent of the profits of the trade. At twenty he was bald but he was pretty close to his first million.

Like the good Proper Bostonian he was, Forbes returned home to his city to get married, but, as a biographer rather ingenuously relates, "now that he had a wife, it was more than ever necessary for him to make a good income," and after a month he went back to China, without his wife, and stayed three years more. Once more returning, he foresaw the decline of Boston shipping and turned his attention, and the money he had made, to railroads. This field had already been pioneered by Forbes' patron, Colonel Perkins, who had constructed in 1826 what is generally considered the first railroad in the country—a line operated by horsepower and used to haul stones from the Quincy quarries to make Boston's Bunker Hill monument. After Forbes, other Boston railroad builders like the Ameses, who made a national scandal out of their "Family financing" of Union Pacific, were to go farther in this field. But Forbes, in his own way, did well enough. He bought first the Michigan Central, later the Burlington and Missouri, and out of this latter developed the Chicago, Burlington, and Quincy. Steering his properties through panics and political troubles and even the Civil War—during which he took time out to go on a secret mission to England for his friend Abraham Lincoln—he made profits which even according to present-day Forbeses, notably reticent on the subject of Family finance, were enormous.

In his declining years Forbes still felt no urge to retire on his laurels. Instead, through his son William, he befriended early in the 1870's a tall, eager-eyed Scottish professor who ran a school in Boston for training teachers of the deaf and in out-of-school hours was always tinkering with an invention in which he had great faith. Forbes also had faith in it, and with the success of that professor, whose name was Alexander Graham Bell, the third John Murray Forbes fortune became closely identified. Forbes' son William later became president of the American Bell Telephone Company.

In 1898, at the age of eighty-five, Forbes died; but his life remains as the mark of a First Family merchant playing the nineteenth century at par. It was no coincidence that a few years ago *Life* magazine chose to photograph, as the living symbol of the city's inherited wealth, the Beacon Hill home of Allan Forbes, a leader of the Forbes Family and head of Boston's State Street Trust Co. One of the pictures showed Forbes in overalls cleaning his sidewalk with a broom. While the other pictures brought the banker the usual number of letters beginning with "You have a kind face . . ." and ending with a request for money, the sidewalk-sweeping pose attracted a remarkable number of genuine fan letters. Forbes was particularly impressed with one letter from an exterminator formerly with the U. S. Public Service Department, which began as follows:

> My dear sir,
>   I am glad that you Big men are interested in getting streets clean in Boston. We little men don't dare to say anything or Pols would Boycott us. I am a Public Ratcatcher in 6 New England states. Boston has more rats, mice than any city up here in East. In South we use 30 Days and 6 Months convicts to clean up sts. They do a good job. Why not Boston. . . .

In the matter of the telephone the Forbes Family went beyond the usual pattern of Family-founding. Several other Boston Families made fortunes out of the telephone company but they are not necessarily First Families. They were too late. John Murray Forbes was a First Family man on two counts. He was a bona fide supercargo shipping merchant to start with and he was also a railroad builder in the recognized merchant era. That he was also a "telephone man" was, in the social sense, strictly incidental. For, shortly after the Civil War—the death in 1878 of John Lowell Gardner, last East India merchant, is a sort of generally regarded curfew—the recognized merchant era came to a close. All of a sudden, as it were, the Golden Gates to Boston's First Familyland clanged shut, and, generally speaking, they have remained shut ever since. Even the word "merchant," in the Old English sense it had up to that time always been used —as a man who, in Dr. Johnson's definition, "trafficks to remote countries"—died out in the Boston language. When it came to be used in the sense of a general trader, domestic or foreign, as it is today, it was no longer a word to be used in connection with founding a First Family. Neither Harvey Parker nor Eben Jordan, for example, two Maine boys who came to Boston with a total worldly wealth of about a dollar each and went on to found, respectively, Boston's most famous hotel, the Parker House, and New England's largest store, Jordan, Marsh & Co., were able to found First Families. They were near enough to the "right" era but their business made them the "wrong" type of merchant in that era. Men like Andrew Preston of United Fruit, whose ships sailed the seven seas, or "Napoleon" William Wood of American Woolen, a true devil-take-the-hindmost industrialist, were, on the other hand, the "right" type of merchants, but they came too late and were in the "wrong" era. By the time their fortunes were founded they discovered the gates were shut and the bars were up—and Boston Society has big gates and strong bars.

"Most of the best Boston Families were founded by shipmasters," Captain John Codman, himself a shipmaster and founder of the Boston Codmans once declared, and Thomas Gold Appleton, of the merchant Appletons went him one better. "Every real Boston Family," he said, "has a sea-captain in its background." That these statements are not literally true is obvious from the roster of Boston's best which derive from railroads, textiles, and such. But again it is noteworthy that almost all the latter derive from the sea era. When the sea captain and the "real" merchant were gone, the era was over. It is also noteworthy that the railroad or textile industrialist was never quite on a par with the real merchant. He was never, for example, a merchant prince; that title was reserved exclusively for the men whose offices were on the wharves. One of the most famous snubs in Boston society annals was delivered by old Colonel Perkins, king of the princes, to one of the Lawrence textile brothers. The latter had been attempting to see him one day on Merchants' Row on a matter of business. Turning abruptly to a third person, Colonel Perkins pointed a finger at Lawrence, a man known to all Bostonians of his day, and haughtily inquired, "Who is that man who keeps following me around?"

Arbitrary as Boston's social deadline many seem to outsiders, it is vital to the preservation of the First Family tradition. The present-day Proper Bostonian is a man keenly sensitive to the charge that his Society is one based on money alone. People have been saying that for a long time. Even before Boston was founded Captain John Smith, exploring the Boston area from Jamestown in 1614, gave it as his opinion that no other motive than riches would ever draw people there. More than two hundred years after Boston was founded a pamphleteer was still beating the same sort of drum when, in 1846, he declared:

> It is no derogation, then, to the Boston aristocracy that it rests upon money. Money is something substantial. Every body knows that and feels it. Birth is a mere idea which grows every day more and more intangible.*

Smith might have gone unanswered. No Proper Bostonian recognizes the good Captain John, or the initial date of Jamestown's founding either; American history begins with Plymouth, and that is that. But the pamphleteer, and the persistent charges which followed, would some day have to be answered. In good time they were, when along about the 1870's the Proper Bostonian closed the gates to any more First Family-founding. All right, he said in effect, our Society does rest upon money. But he said then, and he will still insist today, that it was money made at the right time in the right way.

A background of romance is apparently necessary to the founding of any Society. The Proper Bostonian of today takes the same pleasure in linking himself to men like Perkins and his

* *Our First Men, A Calendar of Wealth, Fashion and Gentility* (Boston: Privately printed, 1846).

captains as the Southern gentleman takes in tracing his ancestry back to Lee and his generals. They are his glamour boys of the Good Old Days, and from them his Society gets its romantic flavor. There is a curious parallel, too, with the South in the matter of titles. Boston, like Kentucky, had its "colonels." Both the elder Perkins and his son were colonels. Lees, Lymans, Higginsons and other Families have merchants in their backgrounds whose names were always prefixed with that rank, though one Higginson, the donor of Boston's Symphony Orchestra, was never allowed to proceed beyond the rank of major to avoid confusion with a colonel cousin. A Peabody even became a general, while a Sears, who actually did have some regular military standing—having the task of once a year leading a corps of cadets to conduct the Governor and the General Court from the State House to the Old South Church—was forced to content himself with being only a captain.

But such things were a necessary part of the romance. The flavor of the sea is a living tradition in Boston. Amid motor trucks and freight trains Boston's Atlantic Avenue still maintains what a recent historian calls a "frigate-like" dignity in memory of the days of the packets and the clippers. As if he had planned for the permanence of the Society that formed there, Charles Bulfinch, architect of Boston's State House and its most elegant Beacon Hill mansions, had himself designed India Wharf's solid-looking brick block of thirty-two stores with their counting rooms overhead. In these, it has been said, the Proper Bostonian of today still sees his old-time merchants like a scene from a Thackeray novel, dressed in stocks and long coats, against a background of brocades and silks, watching with cold but fatherly eyes for their ships to come in and shaking their hard but honest fists under each other's side whiskers.

The Proper Bostonian closes his eyes and basks in it all. There is a charm to the picture. As a youngster Captain Black Ben Forbes had gone to school under old Miss Doubleday; too lame to go skipping about and maintain discipline with the ordinary hickory stick, she taught her pupils to the tune of a long fishing rod, which she could apply to the more recalcitrant members of her class without ever leaving her seat. As an old man home from the sea, Ben Forbes, the Old Commodore, who was called "the embodiment of physical aristocracy"—tall and slender, with mahogany-tinted skin and a head of white hair—built himself a house with portholes instead of windows on the top floor. In the cellar of his house he built himself a complete closed-in room, reached only by following a long narrow passageway through an opening in the brick—a room so well concealed it was only discovered by members of the Forbes Family within the past few years, some three quarters of a century after the sea captain's death.

Black Ben had a right to such idiosyncrasies. On the high seas he and his fellow captains would live on like knights of old in the memories of descendants of the Society they founded. There are legends, of course, about these men—a Hemenway captain was such a good pilot it was said he could "take a ship up a mountain, gather a freight of cool air and return on time with his eyes shut"—but there are also facts. At Fayal, where three generations of the good old Boston Family of Dabney had been American consuls, there was a smallpox epidemic; the port was closed to the ships of all nations—except those of Boston. At Whampoa a Boston captain arrived with a slow ship and found to his consternation that only the fastest vessels were getting any freight. He promptly bet the captain of the fastest English clipper in port he would beat him home. The English captain at once accepted, but the Yankee had made sure his bet was public knowledge with the result that he was able to fill his ship with freight at good prices. He lost the money he had wagered but the extra freight he was able to carry more than made up the difference. Another Britisher once pointed to the Stars and Stripes flying over a Boston ship and remarked that it wasn't a flag that "has braved for a thousand years the battle and the breeze." "No," was the dry Yankee response, "but it has licked one that has."

There was even romance in the counting rooms. The Boston

merchants, for all their money making, were setting a standard of integrity that has lasted to the benefit of Boston business to the present day. The Proper Bostonian is proud his Society is founded on men who, in an era when written agreements were a rarity, were men literally as good as their word. The merchant Russell Sturgis, once asked if it was true that not a single written agreement had ever been recorded in all the immense transactions betwen the Chinese merchant Houqua and Boston's Russell & Co., said promptly that it was not. He had found, he declared, one evidence of a written agreement. Still preserved by the Sturgis Family, it is a slip of rice paper a few inches long bearing the inscription, "Forty thousand dollars. Houqua."

Present-day Boston Families like the Appletons and the Coolidges treasure statements of merchant integrity as issued by their Family-founding forebears. An Appleton compared the mercantile honor of the day with the honor of a woman. It was "as delicate and fragile," he said, and it would not "bear the slightest stain." A filial Coolidge, speaking of his merchant father, writes:

> Mr. Coolidge never went astray . . . did not content himself with obeying the rules of the technical code of mere mercantile honesty but preferred rather to carry down-town with him the honorable spirit of a gentleman . . . The result was that not so much as even a mark of interrogation was ever set against any act of his.*

The "spirit of a gentleman" remains of great importance to the Proper Bostonian. He wishes no truck with the modern idea of "deals" carried on with the aid of a few drinks and a hotel suite. "A Boston gentleman," said the late Rodman Weld, "never takes a drink before 3 o'clock or east of Park Street," by which he meant before the time of the stock-market closing or anywhere in the business district. West of Park Street, in the club and residential district, it was all right, of course, for gentlemen to get together "after hours." A nephew of Weld's once

---

* *The Autobiography of T. Jefferson Coolidge* (Boston: Houghton Mifflin) ⓒ 1923.

came to him, claiming that in the law office where he was working, he was being made the butt of jokes by an officious partner
of the firm and disliked it so much he was determined to leave
the office. Weld looked at his nephew without sympathy. He
asked him only if he was learning something where he was.
When the nephew admitted as much, Weld declared, "If you
are getting what you want, why do you care whether you get it
from a gentleman or a cad? You are not going to his office for
his society but to be a better lawyer. You can associate with
gentlemen after six o'clock."

In that spirit the Proper Bostonian faces, for better or for
worse, the modern world of business. When two of Boston's
best-loved First Family firms, Kidder, Peabody and Lee, Higginson, went to the wall during the last depression, there was
some criticism of the way in which the liquidations were
handled, some people claiming that the lawyers of several of the
Families avoided total ruin for their clients by the timely turning of assets from husband to wife. There was never, however,
criticism of the individual integrity of any of the First Family
men involved. An accountant who after the storm went to the
Lee, Higginson vault with George Cabot Lee, senior partner of
the firm, was never to forget how "handsomely," as he put it,
Banker Lee threw everything he owned into the breach.

On occasion the Proper Bostonian may admit his Society is
basically a monied one. But no one will ever get him to admit
that it is not a Society founded in a day when there was more
romance to money making than there is today—because it was,
after all, a Society founded on the romance of the sea. When the
gates of Boston's First Family Society were closed, the "codfish
aristocracy" securely inside felt they could stand—and some of
their descendants would seem to feel they can stand today—and
repeat with Dr. Holmes the latter's verses written in 1873 for
the Centennial Dinner of the Proprietors of the Boston Pier:

Dear friends, we are strangers; we never before
Have suspected what love to each other we bore;

But each of us all to his neighbor is dear,
Whose heart has a throb for our time-honoured pier.

Who—who that has loved it so long and so well—
The flower of his birthright would barter or sell?
No: pride of the bay, while its ripples shall run,
You shall pass, as an heirloom, from father to son!

Let me part with the acres my grandfather bought,
With the bonds that my uncle's kind legacy brought,
With my bank-shares,—old "Union," whose ten per cent. stock
Stands stiff through the storms as the Eddystone rock;

With my rights (or my wrongs) in the "Erie"—alas!
With my claims on the mournful and "Mutual Mass.";
With my "Phil., Wil. & Balt.," with my "C., B. & Q.,"
But I never, no never, will sell out to you.

We drink to thy past and thy future today,
Strong right arm of Boston, stretched out o'er the bay.
May the winds waft the wealth of all nations to thee,
And thy dividends flow like the waves of the sea!*

* *Other Merchants and Sea Captains of Old Boston.* State Street Trust Co.
Boston. © 1919.

CHAPTER THREE

GRANDFATHER ON THE BRAIN

------◆◖●◗◆------

"I can still see my grandfather," declares Proper Bostonian Edward Jackson Holmes, "as if he were standing by my side."

For many years president of Boston's Museum of Fine Arts, Holmes is today a man in his seventies and the last in line of one of Boston's most noted First Families. Few Proper Bostonians can boast a grandfather as distinguished as Oliver Wendell Holmes, poet and doctor, and father of the late Justice Holmes —the present Mr. Holmes' uncle—but the fact that he remembers his grandfather so vividly is a characteristic trait of Proper Bostonians. Dr. Holmes died on October 7, 1894, at a time when Mr. Holmes was just twenty-one years old, and yet the poet is as alive in Mr. Holmes' memory as if he were still autocratting at the Holmes breakfast table at 296 Beacon Street as he did half a century ago.

Boston has long been known as a city suffering from what has been called "Grandfather on the Brain," a cult dating from the days when the grandfather-merchant, as the golden Family Founder, was the key figure of the whole Boston Society system and was entitled to an almost godlike respect. Dr. Holmes was no grandfather-merchant, but he and his father had both married merchant Family wives, and Dr. Holmes was not dependent on his income from poetry and medicine to hold his head high in Boston Society. The true shipping merchant was, of course, equally highly respected. With the passage of years, as the grandfather-merchant has become the great-grandfather-merchant, or even the great-great-grandfather-merchant, this "Grandfather on the Brain" malady has lost some of its virulence, but the respect to be accorded the Family Founder is still a powerful force. Even young Proper Bostonians know they would not be where they are today if it were not for him. Many are still living off the money he made, and those that are not owe to his prestige at least something of their position in Boston Society today. When the young Harvard sociologist George Homans was recently asked by his friend, Dr. John Forbes Perkins, Jr., to write something personal on the flyleaf of a book he had written, Homans chose the line, "From one degenerate son of old Massachusetts seafaring stock to another." The dedication was appropriate, and, having no wish to be degenerate, many of the current generation of Proper Bostonians have a praiseworthy desire to justify their position in Society and live up to the worthy ways of their grandfather-merchant, no matter how many generations back he may have been.

Unfortunately for such a desire, the present-day Proper Bostonian does not have a very clear idea of what this man he wishes to emulate was really like. It is not that the material on the subject is lacking in quantity. Every Proper Bostonian's library has, alongside the Bible, the Family genealogy, and the Complete Works of Emerson, at least one grandfather-merchant biography, as well as two, three, or even four volumes of his privately printed *Letters and Journals.* The trouble lies rather in the quality. Few of the biographers, with such notable exceptions as the late John T. Morse, Jr., who died at the age of ninety-six still practicing the art, and M. A. DeWolfe Howe, who in his eighties is still ably chronicling Boston's elite, have managed to treat their subjects with any objectivity at all. Too many of these works are written by members of the Family itself. One writer speaks rather sharply in his preface of being forced to perform the "filial duty" of telling his father's life, and his work seems to suffer accordingly. The late Lawrence Lowell, former president of Harvard, left a particularly heavy-handed account of his brother Percival, the astronomer; before writing it he declared, in the peremptory Lowell manner, that biography should be a matter of, not what a man was, but what he did. Even non-Family biographers, who may have wished to do more complete work, have felt the Family influence. Knowing that all of their statements must pass through rigorous Family censorship before publication, they have been reduced to producing what amounts, in sum total, to little more than a graveyard eulogy. The result has been what might be expected. First Families themselves have had trouble keeping their eyes open through such books, as evident from the fact that many a Boston First Family biography has been known to end up at Goodspeed's, Boston's best-known second-hand bookstore, with its pages still uncut.

The Lawrence Family in print might be regarded as typical. The late Bishop Lawrence many years ago obediently wrote the life of his father, a life which he portrays as eminently happy from every angle. Then, at the age of seventy-seven, the Bishop wrote his own life, entitled *Memories of a Happy Life*. When he died at the age of ninety-one, Rev. Henry Knox Sherrill, now presiding Bishop of the Episcopal Church, finished the job for him in a book called *Later Years of a Happy Life*. This, in a word, may be said to be what is wrong with so much of Boston biography—it is too happy. Amid as much economic, intellectual and domestic bliss as such books contain, no mortal—not even a bishop—could possibly emerge as a real person. As for a shrewd, horse-trading Yankee merchant, he does not have a chance. The good old days, in the final analysis, just couldn't have been that good.

The diaries and *Letters and Journals* of the period are almost equally unsatisfactory from the point of view of revealing the merchant's private life. The Great Man of the Family simply will not let his hair down. He tells, as he would to a casual stranger, everything that goes on about him—of his business, his politics, his religion, and especially of the guiding principles of his life—but he rarely mentions a failing, a foible, or a misstep, and even less often, how he feels on subjects of a personal nature. He is by no means modest; he is just irritatingly ret-icent. The late Alexander Woollcott probably put his finger on the all-time high-water mark of this reticence—and at the same time put even Boston's greatest First Family autobiographer in a class with the merchant-writers—when he declared how "shocked" he had been to plough through five hundred pages of *The Education of Henry Adams* without finding a single mention of Adams' twenty years of married life.

If slighted as a real-life personality, the grandfather-merchant lives on vigorously as a legendary character. From all the eulo-gies and the diaries, unsatisfactory as they are, he can be drawn as a sort of composite type. "A noble type," says the author Van Wyck Brooks, "severely limited." He may have been less exem-plary than his biographers would have his descendants believe but he was at the same time something more than the definition of American mercantile success as once given by a French writer —that all that was needed was "a good constitution and a bad heart." The Boston merchant's sayings alone prove him more than that; they have a ring to them which has given them—and him—permanent places in the Boston legend.

To the Proper Bostonian these sayings of his grandfather, or great-grandfather, handed down from father to son in the Bos-ton First Family tradition, are more than mere Boston bons mots. They are Family coats-of-arms, not emblazoned in Latin on letterheads, but spoken in Yankee English over the counting-room desk and actually worn on the field of honorable mercan-tile strife. They are a part of grandfather himself, and their guar-antee is as good as the Grade-A bonds grandfather salted away in the Family trust fund. "Business before friends," said old Amos Lawrence, and proudly made it his lifetime motto; he chose his wife, he once admitted, because she had "such a reci-procity of feelings, sentiments, and principles" with those of his own. "Idleness," declared the elder Colonel Perkins, "is the mother of mischief"; in ninety years of life he never knew the meaning of the word vacation. The time to be up, old David

Sears felt, was five o'clock; at such a time on the dot, six days a week, and fifty-two weeks a year, his private barber arrived at his house to shave him.

Boston's first millionaire, Peter Chardon Brooks, who made four million dollars in marine insurance, believed in cold baths and abstinence from hard liquor. "Cold water, inside and out," he used to say. A man who claimed he never willingly endorsed the obligation of a friend, he had perhaps the simplest success formula of the day for any young man wishing to get ahead. "Let him mind his business," he said. Old Robert Gould Shaw, who started at scratch and made a million, had his capsule formula, too. "Keep one's countenance open and one's thoughts closed," his motto ran; in his various business ventures he had partners from time to time but he examined every bill himself and always kept his own private books in his own handwriting. No true Boston merchant took any unnecessary risk. "Keep in shoal water" was a mercantile byword on Merchants' Row. This carried over to other fields as well. Jonathan Phillips set a standard for the future Proper Bostonian's love of understatement when, asked for a recommendation on behalf of his friend, William Ellery Channing, Boston's saintly Unitarian minister, he stated: "I have known him long. I have studied his character. I believe him capable of virtue."

Once in a while of course the Boston merchant, being only human, did miss the boat. John Murray Forbes, staying at a Chicago hotel in 1847, was offered land near the building for $1.25 an acre but he did not take it. In 1884 he figured that if he had put just the money he had paid for his stay in the hotel into that acreage it would have been worth about $12,000,000. One group of Boston merchants missed one of the nineteenth century's greatest opportunities when in 1853 with a chance to buy the New York Central Railroad for $9,000,000, they refused. According to a recent historian, the deal, which might have reversed the positions of New York and Boston as cities of the future, was turned down because it had been made by a man who, though a New Englander, was a Springfield man and hence

"a sort of foreigner" in Boston. By and large, however, Grand•
father and his homey precepts stood the test of time, and on several occasions when they have been ignored by grandfather's
descendants—as when Lee, Higginson & Co. allowed match king
Ivar Krueger, who later removed from them the sum of $25,•
000,000, the use of its Oval Room to deliver a "How to Succeed"
lecture to the young men of its firm—the consequences have
been known to be unhappy.

Nowhere is there better evidence that the grandfather-merchant sayings are still an influence on present-day Proper Bostonians than along Boston's State Street, banking and investment center of the city. Loyal Proper Bostonians remember
when Wall Street was merely "the State Street of New York,"
and here time-tested blue-blood firms have carried on under a
score of professional trustees—almost half of whom seem to have
had fathers who were professional trustees before them—with
Grandfather's nuggets of wisdom solemnly chanted. Boston
business empires still rise and fall on sayings like John Murray
Forbes' dictum: "Get the business first, fuss over details later."
Another Forbesism was that only a stock with an established
rock bottom, one proved by a previous market crash, was a
proper investment; then, even in the event of another crash,
you could always wait patiently for it to rise again. One Boston
merchant coined the famous State Street maxim, "Never more
than ten percent in anything." Another declared that a good
investor ought to be able to "feel it in his bones" when money
was going to get tight. A good investment was one "as safe as
Lee's vaults," dating from what the old merchant Harry Lee
always regarded as the crowning achievement of his life—the
building of Lee, Higginson's safety deposit in the 1850's. Old
Henry Cabot had no use for preferred stocks. If a company was
any good, he used to say, he wanted its common stock; if it
wasn't, he wanted none of it. Setting a pattern for Boston provincialism in the money mart, old Philip Dexter once observed, "I
never invest in anything I can't see from my office window."
Through the years such cherished mercantile maxims have

probably had much to do with the fact that Boston's securities market stands to this day second only to New York as the country's richest—and second to none as the most conservative. The Proper Bostonian now plays the great Wall Street game, but he still plays it close to his vest, and the most thriving of his firms are those which have remembered such a modest grandfather-merchant adage as that of old John Lowell Gardner, last of the East India crew. "The only difference between a successful man and a failure," Grandfather Gardner used to say, "is that the successful man is mistaken only two times out of five, and the unsuccessful man is mistaken three times out of five."

The grandfather-merchant left behind for future Proper Bostonians some notable glimpses of himself as a man devoted to self-improvement. The merchant T. Jefferson Coolidge, firm trunk of the Boston Coolidge tree and descended through his mother from Thomas Jefferson, left one of the most lasting of such glimpses in what he describes as his "Day Book." He kept it, he declared, "to relieve the unhappy member of the Massachusetts Historical Society, to whom may be allotted, after my death, as is usual in the Society, my biography," but actually his little book goes farther than supplying mere biographical details. Early in life, he reveals, he found that money was the only "real avenue" to social success in Boston. Accordingly, he first goes to work as a clerk for Perkins & Co. and soon goes on from there to marry an Appleton and enter the textile business. Later Minister to France, he was indeed a social success, but this is by no means the end of his self-improvement.

Coolidge is the true Boston Puritan, the Puritan who will never admit that he is one. He records at length an attempt at vegetarianism, which he embraces significantly enough not just because he had read about it in Benjamin Franklin's autobiography but because he had at first hand observed it as being of salutary aid in the matter of the fierce temper of his friend, Francis Cabot Lowell, the textile king. "I had taken it up," he writes, "not as Franklin did, as a duty, but to see if it would improve my mind and my temper." Seeing no favorable results in six months, he is relieved to give it up. Again he imitated Franklin in the matter of keeping a chart on which he enumerates, each evening before going to bed, the various sins he has committed on that day. But while the jovial Franklin had topped his chart with what he considered the necessary virtues to be followed—Temperance, Silence, Order, Resolution, Frugality, Industry, etc.—it is significant that the stern Coolidge reminds himself only of the vices to be avoided. He chooses Pride, Want of Chastity, Temper, Meanness in Money Matters, Cowardice, and Envy, and then for a full year rigorously keeps his daily chart. "But I found," he laconically records at the end, "as with my vegetarianism, that it did me much less good than I expected."

Several of Boston's First Families cherish individual grandfather legends of their own, and many of these have a peculiar charm to them which is not evident from mere diaries or day books. The Jackson Family goes all others one step farther, however, in a notable great-grandfather story, told of the Honorable Charles Jackson, who, as a young child, was given the opportunity of meeting George Washington, a house guest of his father. Shortly before the meeting, the story is told, the father took the child aside and told him he wanted him always to remember the moment which was about to come. The child promised he would, but when the moment came, in the Jackson living room, with Washington affectionately patting him on the head, young Charles suddenly looked up and said, "You will have to speak the truth, Sir, in this house." It is in the First Family grandfather tradition that all Jackson biographers have clung to this story, finding its charm in no wise diminished by the facts that the cherry tree incident and Washington's remark, "I cannot tell a lie, Sir," were first heard some seven years after the President's death, having been added, as an imaginative afterthought, to the fifth edition of Parson Weems' biography.

At least one Boston Family grandfather story has stood the test of time in such fashion that it seems to belong more to the problems of today than to the nineteenth century. This concerns the Codman Family, or more particularly Captain John Codman, a Boston sea captain of unusual talents. Taking on a new crew in New York on one of his voyages, he discovered the first day out that the crew refused to scrub the deck. Remarkably enough for those days they had a written labor contract, and scrubbing the deck, they declared, was not in this document. "Well," asked Codman cheerfully, "what is?" A sailor quoted the contract verbatim: "To make sail, steer the ship, hoist the anchor". . . etc. "Very good," said Codman, still cheerful. "Then you can let go the anchor thirty fathoms and we will keep hauling it and dropping it again until you gentlemen are satisfied." According to the story, the crew saw the point at once and promptly fell to scrubbing the deck. It is not surprising that in the years since Captain John's success in labor-management relations many a Boston Codman has been associated with politics. A present leader of the Family was recently the only First Family Beacon Hiller in Mayor James M. Curley's inner council. He campaigned vigorously for the Irish-Catholic mayor, long anathema to the blue bloods, and at the latter's last election was promptly rewarded with the post of fire commissioner.

Considering the fragmentary knowledge he has had to go on—a saying here and a legendary story there—the latter-day Proper Bostonian would seem to have had marked success in reproducing reasonably accurate grandfather-merchant facsimiles. There is scarcely a First Family in Boston which has not at one time or another boasted at least one worthy chip off the old block. In the Gray Family the founder of what is now one of the bluest of Boston's many blue-blood law firms was a true grandson of his merchant prince grandfather, William Gray. Old Billy, as he was called, moved to Boston with a quarter of the ships of Salem under his flag and a well-developed flair for taking his time. "I'll think on't" was his favorite expression, and it was said he never made a hurried decision in his life. Writing of Billy's grandson, who was born March 24, 1828, a biographer relates that he inherited his grandfather's lack of hurry in all things and "remained a bachelor until June 4, 1889." In the Lowell Family the late Lawrence, former president of Harvard, was a teacher by profession but he always remained a merchant grandson at heart. He ran Harvard as a business proposition, as his grandfather had run the Lowell textile empire. His favorite personal possessions were two twenty-dollar gold pieces which his grandfather had given him and which he wore to his dying day attached to his shirt as cuff-buttons. His grandfather had married a cousin, and Lawrence married a cousin. As a boy at Harvard his grandfather had been known as an extremely pontifical young man, who took for his Commencement thesis the weighty subject, "Whether Prosperity and Increase of Wealth Have a Favorable Influence upon the Manners and Morals of the People." Grandson Lowell took himself with gravity throughout his life, and though his work, *The Government of England,* published in 1908, is regarded as a classic in its field, his prose style was of such a formidable nature that it troubled even his staunchest admirers. His grandfather's obituary was written in the line, "He seemed to have a firm confidence in his own judgment," and Harvard's president seems to have gone to some lengths to preserve the tradition. At the drop of a hat he would reassert his stand on any decision in his own life, and as late as 1940, a friend noted, he was still defending "with an ingenuity that was almost convincing" his father's position in voting for Bell instead of Lincoln in 1860.

Lowell's basic philosophy was grandfather-merchant inherited. "Truly," he wrote, "the future has less to fear from individual than from cooperative selfishness." He had the merchant's traditional distrust of artistic pursuits which was shared by another merchant grandson, Endicott Peabody, founder of Groton School. Of Peabody's regard for artists a biographer has written:

Basically he distrusted artists as a genus. Something Puritan in him told him that, in spite of his love for them often as individuals, they were a folk who have unreliable relationships

with the world, the flesh, and the devil, with a consequent
weakening of moral fiber. At best, he felt, artists are interpre-
ters, and while interpretation is well enough in its way, it is not
on a plane with genuine accomplishment.*

University president though he was, Lowell too might have
been described by those lines. Unfortunately Harvard's leader
was fated to have a sister who was a distinct artist, the poetess
Amy. He did his best to understand her and be loyal—"I'll say
anything I want about my sister," he once told his secretary,
"but by Jove I won't allow anyone else to"—but after reading
her life of the poet John Keats he told her frankly that while he
found it "better than I expected" he was sure that if he had
known Keats he would not have liked him at all. It is ironic that
it was Amy, and not Lawrence, who left the happiest picture
of grandfilial devotion in all the Lowell Family, which she accomplished in just four lines of her poem, "The Painted Ceiling":

> My Grandpapa lives in a wonderful house
> With a great many windows and doors,
> There are stairs that go up, and stairs that go down,
> To such beautiful slippery floors.†

While biographers have dutifully attempted to reveal Boston's Family-founding merchants as dryly witty men in the Calvin Coolidge tradition, this has been a difficult task indeed with
men who apparently counted their words as carefully as their
change. Of one merchant it is written that he never spoke "an
unnecessary word" in his life. Of another whole group of Boston's nineteenth-century best it is related: "To receive a bow or
'Good morning' from one of these men, as, tall and erect and
with manly step, they walked down State Street and along Commercial Street to their counting-rooms, was something not to be

* *Peabody of Groton*, by Frank D. Ashburn (New York: Coward McCann) ©
1944.
† *A Dome of Many-Coloured Glass*, by Amy Lowell (Boston: Houghton Mifflin)
© 1912.

despised by any one." But unlovable as these traits of character may seem to the outsider many a good Boston merchant Family has proudly carried them on as a permanent part of the city's grandfather tradition. Clipper-ship Families like Hoopers and Perkinses, Cunninghams and Frothinghams, Hemenways and Hunnewells, are known to be no wasters of words on minor social amenities. No Boston Lyman, for example, has ever established a high reputation for humor, particularly in matters concerning Boston or a Lyman. Emerging from the Boston opening of the play *The Late George Apley*, a Cunningham approached a Lyman and said hesitatingly, "Very amusing, wasn't it?" "No," said Lyman severely, "very exaggerated," and passed on.

Boston's well-known Lodges are descended from merchants on both sides of the Family, going back as far as the city's Family-founding merchants go. The late Henry Cabot Lodge's father was a particularly decisive Bostonian. One evening he looked at his son with displeasure. "That big boy is five years old and cannot read," he announced. "It is time he went to school." That is the way things have apparently always been done in the Lodge Family; the next day the boy went to school. At another time the elder merchant, walking on a dark street with his son, was accosted by a tramp. He knocked the man down. "I think that fellow had a knife," he said. It is little wonder the son, later the deadly foe of Woodrow Wilson and the League of Nations, inherited his often-described "cool and distant" manner from such a background. One of the late Senator's grandsons, on the other hand, present Senator Henry Cabot Lodge, Jr., is generally credited with attempting to overcome his so-called "Little Boy Blue" inheritance by door-to-door campaigning and other conscientious efforts to unbend. When told he doesn't seem at all "like a Lodge" he takes it as a compliment, and his brother John, present occupant of the Connecticut Congressional seat recently vacated by Clare Booth Luce, wears the name with equal ease. Both of the "new Lodges," it might be noted, were very definitely in the Boston grandfather rut to start with. Their father died when they were both young, and they were reared by a quaint combination of mother and grandfather.

Senator Leverett Saltonstall also had no mean tradition of Family austerity to contend with. His father, the late Richard Middlecott Saltonstall, was always called "Sir Richard" and regularly rode a huge horse around the Boston suburb of Chestnut Hill like a knight on a charger with a red carnation in his buttonhole and a derby on his head. Once routed out of bed by some children playing a nightly prank, he sprang to his window and shouted across to his neighbors, the Lees, a noted Chestnut Hill war cry: "Shall I come down with my man and my gun?" Recognizing bad politics when he saw it, the present Senator started out early to live down some of this Family tradition. By 1938 he was making the remarkable claim to the voters of Massachusetts that his grandfather was a "poor man" since he had been forced to sell part of his wine cellar to send his son to Harvard. Apparently, the voters were convinced, and today even Saltonstall's political opponents wonder at the adroit manner in which the son of Chestnut Hill's "Sir Richard" has managed to become "Lev" from one end of Boston to the other. As proof of Saltonstall's acceptance by the Hub's Irish population, Boston *Globe* political analyst Joseph Dinneen cites the fact that the Senator is, "by virtue of an obscure ancestor found somewhere in his family tree," a member of the Charitable Irish Society, oldest and most august fraternity for Sons of Erin in America.

Among several of Boston's First Families there have been instances in which one distinct trait of character has been handed down from the original grandfather generation to the present. In one, the Lawrence Family, the trait of abstinence can be followed from the very beginning. It starts with old Amos Lawrence, elder of the two brothers Lawrence who founded their Family fortune in the textile business, and is still going strong. Amos believed that success in any form of endeavor depended on this trait. Writing, in later days, of his early life as a clerk, he declares:

> We five boys were in the habit every forenoon of making a drink compounded of rum, raisins, sugar, nutmeg, &c. with biscuit,—all palatable to eat and drink. After being in the store four weeks, I found myself admonished by my appetite of the approach of the hour for indulgence. Thinking the habit might make trouble if allowed to grow stronger, without apology to my seniors I declined partaking with them. My first resolution was to abstain for a week, and, when the week was out, for a month, and then for a year. Finally, I resolved to abstain for the rest of my apprenticeship, which was for five years longer. During that whole period I never drank a spoonful, though I mixed gallons daily for my old master and his customers. I decided not to be a slave to tobacco in any form, though I loved the odor of it then and even now have in my drawer a superior Havana cigar, given me not long since, by a friend, but only to smell of.*

Not all Lawrences by any means have exercised such self-denial as this, but in the matter of smoking at least they have taken Amos at his word. The late Bishop Lawrence, grandson of Amos, recalled that as a boy he had been offered a horse and carriage if he would not smoke until he was twenty-one. At that age he settled for $1200 instead of the horse and carriage and, in his own words, "always put off smoking until tomorrow." In his seventies, advised by a friend to take up the habit to counteract his increasing nervousness, he went directly to the doctor of the Harvard football team and placed the decision in his hands. He was relieved to find the latter of the opinion it would do him more harm than good. To this day neither of Bishop Lawrence's two sons nor any one of his five grown Lawrence grandsons has

* *Famous Families of Massachusetts*, by Mary Caroline Crawford (Boston: Little Brown) © 1930.

taken up smoking in any form, thus tracing back five full generations to Amos.

In some cases where First Families in Boston were fortunate
enough to have two nineteenth-century merchant grandfathers
at the same time, the Families have been actually split by the
difference in personalities into two distinct twentieth-century
branches. The Lawrences had not only Amos, but his brother
Abbott as well, an equally famous textile king who later became
minister to England. Amos was the more practical man, known
not only for abstinences, but also for his hard common sense.
Abbott was a more rounded man, who did not hesitate to give
up business for diplomacy, and was also more charming. In the
Boston vernacular Amos was "steady," Abbott "unsteady," and
Boston Lawrences are still divided by Boston Society on that
basis, depending upon which grandfather they trace to. Boston
Forbeses are even more sharply defined. Those which descend
from Grandfather John Murray, the merchant, are familiarly
known as "long-tailed Forbeses," while those descending from
Robert Bennet, the sea captain, are "short-tails."

This division, too, hinges on the completely different personalities of the two great brothers Forbes. John Murray was a
true merchant. At the end of a day in which he had filled in his
own hand thirty-one pages of his account book, he could write a
letter ending, "Y'rs in great haste hunger and all uncharitable-
ness, having been here at my desk since 8½ AM, now 6 PM, living upon crackers . . .", but he had definite ideas on how life
should be lived outside his counting room. He never had a house
in town and, from refusing to allow his trotting horses to have
their tails cut to insisting that his children take "a happy view of
life and death," he was a firm believer in nature in the raw. He
bought several homes in Milton and the entire island of Naushon, off Cape Cod, which is to this day populated exclusively
by his descendants. Here all true "long-tail" Forbeses enjoy
vacations in a civilization unspoiled by modern conveniences
and go in for such diversions as birdwalks, sheep-herding, and

horseback weddings. John Murray himself set the pattern for the uninhibitedness of his branch of the Family when, a man in his eighties and in the dead of winter, he used to drive to and from Milton to Boston in an open sleigh, an apron tied about his waist and a peaked hood over his head, looking for all the world, as one of the Family recalls, like a member of the Ku Klux Klan.

John Murray's brother, Robert Bennet, on the other hand, was a lovable old salt who had less definite ideas of life and nature and believed in general conformity. He, too, had a home in Milton but he took little interest in the growing Bohemianism of his brother's branch of the Family and did not consider it a travesty on nature when a son saw fit to dock his horse's tail or even move into town. Where his brother prided himself on purchasing one shapeless felt hat a year, Robert Bennet was the best-dressed vestryman of King's Chapel. Little by little his descendants in the Family, the "short-tails," have become known as the "high-collar" Forbeses, while the "long-tails" have been forced to submit to the "low-collar" sobriquet. A grandson of Robert Bennet is today a Boston fashion plate; of a grandson of John Murray, on the other hand, the story is told that he went to court a girl one winter day in his bare feet, explaining that he was trying to get through to the spring without buying a pair of shoes. The girl, dissatisfied with the explanation, refused to let him into her house and shortly chose another husband.

If Boston were located in West Virginia it is possible that such grandfather differences might have assumed the proportions of a Family feud. But Families like Boston Lawrences and Forbeses are hardly the feuding type. To outsiders they present a united grandfather front. Cameron Forbes, former governor-general of the Philippines and recognized Forbes Family patriarch, is a long-tailed, low-collared John Murray man. When it came to the preparation of his autobiography for *Who's Who*, however, he had no wish to slight publicly the short-tailed, high-collared branch of his Family and tactfully chose to refer only to his maternal grandfather, Ralph Waldo Emerson. After such a delicate bit of intra-Family diplomacy, it would be unkind indeed to make an issue of the fact that, among 40,145 members of the latest edition of that volume, Proper Bostonian Forbes alone found it necessary to list a grandfather at all.

CHAPTER FOUR

GOD AND MAMMON

————◆◀◆▶◆————

Once upon a time there lived in Boston a lean, hawk-eyed merchant by the name of Honorable William Appleton. Though the Family-founding sire of the Boston Appletons and a maternal grandfather of both Senator Leverett Saltonstall and the late Bishop William Lawrence, he is not as well remembered today as certain historically more colorful souls of his day. This is a pity. For Appleton rendered a lasting service to all future generations of Proper Bostonians. In his introspective writings he left a frank, intimate picture of his merchant life which, when compared with the elegiacs compounded about him by biographers of the day, makes crystal clear the remarkable discrepancy between the Boston grandfather of fiction and the Boston grandfather of fact.

A biographer of the day, for example, declares:

> We have no misgivings in holding up such a life before the young men of New England, as worthy of honor and emulation. In the lengthening roll of those princely merchants whose unsullied integrity has established the commercial credit of Boston, whose munificence has endowed its institutions of learning, charity, and religion, and whose honorable lives have been among its noblest ornaments, the name of William Appleton . . . deserves no second place.*

In the diary of his own son-in-law, T. Jefferson Coolidge, however, the merchant is revealed in a rather different light.

* *Memoir of Hon. William Appleton*, by Rev. Chandler Robbins (Boston: John Wilson & Son) © 1863.

78

Here Appleton is declared to be "despotic" and "nervous" and a man who "made himself most uncomfortable to his sons-in-law, Amos A. Lawrence, F. G. Dexter, and myself." Summing up the man Coolidge states: "I think I never knew him to do an unkind thing, and never heard him say a kind word."

Who, then, can be believed? The biographer is obviously a member of Boston's Graveyard Eulogy School, while young Coolidge seems to be a man with a rather sharp in-law axe to grind. For an answer to this riddle present-day Proper Bostonians are indebted to Susan M. Loring, granddaughter of the Honorable William and a sister of the late Bishop Lawrence. In 1922 Mrs. Loring resurrected and privately published in Boston a small volume entitled *Selections From the Diaries of William Appleton*. Though the book was published only for the benefit of Appleton's descendants, these *Selections*, along with certain additions from Appleton's other writings, can be pieced together to form a portrait which reveals the Boston grandfather-merchant in what must have been at least close to his true colors.

Appleton, who lived from 1786 to 1862, kept his diary for almost fifty years, up to within two weeks of his death, and in contrast to other diarists of the period, he wrote in an appealing, off-guard manner, undoubtedly without the least suspicion that even a filial granddaughter would put the work to posthumous use. All through the diary there is evidence of the characteristic Proper Bostonian struggle going on in his mind between his worldly desires and his religious convictions. Appleton loves money. He loves to make it and, above all, he loves to save it. Once asked in later years if he was not worried his children would spend all he had so carefully kept, he replied simply he was not—that if they had as much fun spending it as he had saving it they would be happy indeed. But Appleton is also a religious man. He believes in God and in furthering God's kingdom on earth; in fact, his greatest wish is to be remembered after his death as a Man of Good Works rather than a money maker *per se*. The diary thus becomes more than a diary; it is a novel of suspense. The merchant's worldly desires, though often earnestly resisted, cannot be overcome, yet his religious convictions, though often baffled, keep returning to the fray. The issue remains in doubt to the very end of his life.

At the outset Appleton shows his mettle by scorning the American Horatio Alger tradition of being penniless to start with. Boston merchants ordinarily went in heavily for this tradition. In later years almost all of them fell to vying with one another for the distinction of having started with the least capital; they got it down to a dollar or two and even, in the case of Appleton's own uncle, as slender a sum as a dime. But Appleton himself is too accurate a financier to indulge in this sort of thing. He went into business at the age of twenty with, he says, seven hundred dollars he inherited and "two hundred I drew in a Lottery." After just seven years in the business of importing and exporting various types of goods he finds, by 1814, he is worth $60,000. In that year, he writes, "I engaged in a Matrimonial Speculation, the whole result of which is not ascertained." Four years later, after his persistent dyspepsia has necessitated travels and a long absence from business, he is satisfied on this score:

> My good Wife is happy and deservedly so; she is all that any reasonable man could wish, ever finding friends and so fortunate as to have no enemies. I have been better satisfied with her the last year in troubles and anxieties than in prosperity; she has strong powers of mind not brought into action on common occasions; take her all in all, her husband and friends have cause to be proud of her.

By 1822 his random jottings show the Great Conflict in his mind:

> I attended Church at St. Paul's this morning and heard an interesting sermon . . . on self examination. My feelings were that from time to time I would . . . endeavour to correct my faults by acknowledging them to myself . . .

But he admits that he remains occupied with business to the exclusion of all else:

> My mind is very much bent on making money, more than securing temporal friends or lasting peace. . . . I dined this day with Mr. Nathan Appleton, a party of twenty-two. I seldom have a pleasanter time, but almost always find I have something to regret when I pass the day in a large party.

A month later, he is worse:

> I feel that I am quite eaten up with business; while in Church, my mind with all the exertion I endeavoured to make, was flying from City to City, from Ship to Ship and from Speculation to Speculation . . .

Until finally:

> I am so much excited by my business concerns that I have very little pleasure . . .

Ten years later, by 1832, he is both unsatisfied and satisfied:

> I am not very well satisfied with myself; my prejudices are very strong. I feel as if others who are in a degree dependent on me should be governed by my feelings more than I ought. I have considerable to contend with, but I ought to soar above trifles. As to my dealings with others I am quite satisfied with myself; I have no temptation to make a hard bargain, except the pride of having done better than others. I do not feel anxious to make money for the sake of having it, and should as soon spend my whole income as not if I could do it with a belief that it would do more good than harm.

At the same time, rating himself as worth $330,000, he cannot forbear a factual report of his attainments:

> My property has increased every year since I have been in business except the year 1829. . . . My success in business is un-

common, no man in Boston of the Age, I am forty-five, has made as much, and only one, David Sears, possesses as much probably . . .

His increasing indigestion, which causes his doctor to put him on a diet of dyspepsy crackers and milk, as well as the high price of labor—girls in the factories at Lowell getting two dollars and a half a week "besides their board"—are problems which occupy him much. Six years later he is again summing himself up:

More than half a century have I lived: almost without parallel in the smiles of Fortune, in wealth, Wife, children, etc. So much for me has been granted by kind Heaven, what have I done for my fellow beings? Very little beyond my own connections; my Wife, children, Mother & Sisters have not been neglected but beyond my immediate circle very little has been done to promote the cause of religion, and strange to say that with a full conviction of the error, I continue to be engrossed in the cares of this World, a desire to increase a fortune now large, more than six hundred Thousand dollars and one Hundred times more than I expected at twenty years old ever to possess. My present intentions are to lessen my business, try to bring my mind to dwell on things of more importance, to associate more with religious persons . . .

When it comes to giving away his money, even to the Church, however, he admits this is not easy:

Most gladly would I increase and multiply my contributions, if I could only find objects that I could entirely approve, and be satisfied that larger bestowments would do good, and not harm. To give to individuals does not always benefit them; and even to give to churches sometimes takes away from the energy and efforts of their members.

The death of a son who, though only twenty-four and never in good health, had already accumulated "from his own earnings" a fortune of over $100,000, causes Appleton to declare:

His death changed most of my plans of business. It is indeed a sad event to part with such a son, but it is the will of Heaven and I would not acknowledge myself so selfish as to wish him back again to contend with this sinful world.

On a trip to New York in 1841, on board a boat caught in a violent gale, he reveals the Proper Bostonian's approach to the problem of disaster:

. . . our boat with many goods on deck broached to, laid on her side for some time; much alarm and danger; I remained in my berth feeling I could do no good on deck, and if we were to be lost I might as well go down in the boat as to be drowned outside . . . I endeavoured to recollect if there was anything I had left in an unfinished state, but as to my Worldly affairs, I had nothing that required my particular attention. We arrived at New York at eight o'clock.

In 1847, at Saratoga Springs, he does his Boston best to enjoy a vacation, but it is not easy:

The time passes pleasantly, but with much sameness: drink Water, eat Breakfast, lounge, talk, dine, hear the Band play, take tea, go to the drawing room to see the young people dance and end the day. Thus the days passes until Friday, 23rd, when we left . . .

Two years later the death of a friend makes a deep impression on him, also the man's will:

May 9th. Mr. —— died this Morning. I have long known him; a very correct man in his intercourse with others; apparently with no fixed religious views; he lived with little happiness and died almost unthought of. 11th. Mr. —— interred. Went to the House, opened the Will; a strong commentary on the saving of money for relatives, in seeing the dissatisfaction expressed by Most persons . . .

In 1850 he writes of a typical dinner party of the day. So firmly rooted is Boston Society by this time—and so little has it changed since—that it might be observed that a present-day First Family dinner party could well include every one of these names. For once Appleton forgets his diet—but not the price of the Bouquet:

> Party of twenty at dinner,—James Lawrence, Chas. Perkins, Ed Perkins, N. Thayer, F. B. Brooks, A. Otis, John Lowell, Jr., S. Eliot, T. H. Perkins, Jr., T. G. Appleton, Mr. Dwight, Chas. Amory, Chas. Lyman, P. Grant, Mason Warren, Dr. Hooper, Wm. A., Jr., Mrs. A. & Harriet. Dinner well served by three blacks and our two servants; it consisted first of cold Oysters, then sherry wine offered; brown and white soup, followed by Oyster Pates, Hock wine offered; boiled and baked Fish, Pass the wine; next, boiled Turkey, roast Mutton, Veal with Peas and Ham; Sweet Bread and Croquettes; then Wine and Roman Punch. After Course, two pair Canvas-Back Ducks, two pair Grouse, Wood Cocks and Quails, with Salad;—Blanc Mange, Jelly, Baked and Frozen Pudding, etc., etc., with Ice Cream, Grapes, Pears, Apples, Oranges, & Ornamental Sweets from the Confectioner; a Bouquet for Centre costing twenty-five Dollars. This is our third Party this month. So much for the Fashion of the day; fruit and flowers placed on table before dinner & remain during the whole time.

Again he is plagued by dissatisfaction. This time another of his sons and his daughter, later Mrs. Coolidge, have given him cause for complaint:

> Went to church; at the Communion, not satisfied with myself; this was from getting my mind fixed on a letter I had rec'd and answered in the morning, & not finding my Son at church. I feared he was getting wrong feelings on Religious Subjects, and in my fears for him I was lost to all good impressions. We had with us at dinner most of our family. Mr. Jefferson Coolidge, who has lately become engaged to Hetty, was of our party. I think well of him, but did not approve of the engagement on account of their age; both being less than twenty years old . . .

Elected to Congress in 1851, he keeps his own counsel, as was his lifelong custom. "Though his voice was never heard in debate," a Washington observer writes of him, "yet he exerted a weighty influence, and most successfully promoted the interests of those whom he represented." After serving two terms he is defeated for a third—"not," Appleton himself writes, "because my friends had lost respect or confidence in me, but because they differed from me in political expediences." Later he is elected for not only a third but a fourth term.

During the panic of 1857 no church service is able to take his mind off his affairs. This he dutifully regrets:

. . . attended St. Paul's Church, Communion; regret much to find myself so much agitated as to the business of the past week that I could not keep my mind from it during the devotions of the day; poor miserable beings, we are . . .

In 1860 his wife suffers a heart attack. According to son-in-law T. Jefferson Coolidge, Mrs. Appleton was throughout her life entirely dependent on her husband. "I doubt," he records, "if she could have formed any opinion without knowing his." When she is taken ill Appleton writes of her in his usual manner, considering the situation from all angles:

It is sad, very sad. I have almost from the commencement of our married life contemplated from my Age & broken Constitution that when we separated I should be first called— (it may be so)—and from the time I was making my first Will in 1816 She was first considered; I then gave her the half of the property I might have, and in all the changes since I have ever thought of her comfort and independence when I was gone and provided accordingly. This is the first serious illness she has had during our married life of forty-five years within a few days. We, during that period, have had many, many blessings. We have lived happily (I think) as the World goes, but I would not be understood to say we always thought alike and that difference of opinion was always expressed in as mild and considerate terms as it should have been. There was never a want of love, confidence, or respect. She always leaned on me, I always loved her dearly and never doubted her affection for a moment; were I to say there was never a Word passed that was not in harmony, my children, should this come to their eyes, would not give me that credit for sincerity that I wish from them . . .

Three months later his wife is dead. But Appleton reorganizes his affairs in his decisive manner, sells his place in Brookline for $23,000—"about the cost of the buildings," he reports—and in 1861 is back on the subject of his digestion again:

Rode to Brookline in the morning with Mrs. S. Appleton, & to Dorchester in the afternoon—much troubled with bird I ate for dinner. 22nd. Good night, ate oatmeal gruel and small chop for dinner, nothing else for the day . . . I eat less than would be thought possible and live . . .

But even at the age of seventy-five he still has his Great Conflict to contend with:

I must be busy. I don't know how to stop . . . I love best to do that which is the most difficult. That which others would not undertake pleases me most . . . If my natural insight enables me to see farther than most men in certain directions, my nature also compels me to make use of this endowment . . . I can't help seeing openings for profit, neither can I help availing of them. I pray God to keep me from being avaricious, and proud of my success; but I cannot bear the shame of falling below my own powers and being left behind by those who are not my equals.

Only a few months before his death he is back at the old stand:

We are going rapidly into paper currency. Prices of all kinds of stock will advance materially; I cannot avoid taking an interest in the prices and speculations; I am endeavouring to show the younger part of the Merchants that an old man of seventy-five has energy left; at the same time I am thinking what I shall do with the profits on the Salt Peter & Pepper I have bought & sold. I shall give part to the public & the balance to my distant relatives . . .

The issue of the Great Conflict remains in doubt to the very last, beyond his diary, which ends three weeks before his death. Finally, a friend has written, he dropped "the instruments of his Earthly service, meekly laid himself down, folded his hands upon his breast . . . and fell asleep." But a member of the merchant's own family has recalled still one more line. Appleton was asleep but he was not yet dead. He woke once more and "with his very last breath," it is related, dictated "in scarcely intelligible accents" a codicil to his will—and this was concerned with the disposition of the sum of five thousand dollars apparently hitherto neglected. Then, and only then, does Appleton die.

It would be hard to deny that there is not at least some of Honorable William Appleton, merchant of Boston, in every Proper Bostonian of today. But it should be remembered that Appleton's diary was never intended as a public record, and it should not be read as one. It was a private document; he was not even sure that his Family would read it—as witness his line about wishing to be honest about his wife before his children "should this come to their eyes." The merchants kept their inner thoughts on such subjects as their Great Conflict to themselves, and it is in this spirit that such latter-day merchant grandsons as Harvard president Lawrence Lowell, Groton headmaster Endicott Peabody and Bishop William Lawrence bravely carried on. All these men became public figures by the very nature of their position in Boston Society, but they retained the right to keep their own counsel. Lowell said his prayers out loud, and visitors to his home recall that he would come downstairs to breakfast in the morning saying the last of them, but this was not for other people's benefit. It was simply because he was not a man to allow religion to slow him down in getting on

88   THE PROPER BOSTONIANS

with the affairs of the day. "I am not sure," said Endicott Peabody, "I like boys to think too much. A lot of people think a lot
of things we could do without. Manifestly the world is full of
evil that we all encounter as we go along. Nobody denies that.
But why emphasize it as we go along?" Bishop Lawrence used to
state proudly that he was "no theologian." In his diary which
he kept with a reticence which argued that he felt it might come
to other eyes—his own sister was responsible for the publishing
of Appleton's diary—there was not a single note of introspection.
His religious convictions were deep but so simple that they
might be summarized along the line that God was good to
Bishop Lawrence and Bishop Lawrence was, in turn, grateful to
God. Once asked by a grandson what to say in a speech the boy
was to make on a philosophical subject, the Bishop who, even
in his ninety-second year, always began his speeches with "a
squaring of the shoulders," wrote the boy nothing of philosophy
but a stern line about posture: "Collect yourself with the
thought, 'Am I standing firmly, easily and naturally?' for if you
are not firm on your feet your audience will feel it and think
that what you have to say is weak."

The grandfather-merchant had shown the way to be firm on
one's feet and be tough. He was tough not only in his business
methods but in his physical activity, and this physical activity
took the place of philosophy and analytical thinking. Physical
failings were untenable thoughts. Appleton was outspoken
about his dyspepsia, but though failing fast in health he took on
a fourth term in Congress at the age of seventy-four. At the
age of seventy-five Captain John Codman felt he was "going
soft" and rode a horse from Boston to New York in the middle
of winter to prove to himself he was not. In the same way Lawrence Lowell, in his last illness just a month or two before his
death, broke away from those watching him long enough to
make the Esplanade and try to walk. He had felt that all he
needed was one of his customary four-mile-an-hour constitu-
tionals to put him back in shape. His cousin, who had run after
him and in whose arms he collapsed still could not convince

him he would never take one of those walks again. John Murray Forbes was never seasick a day in his life. "All such suffering from that cause," his wife, who was a poor sailor, once sadly admitted, "John termed weak-mindedness." Compare this to Endicott Peabody's attitude in the Groton School infirmary— one which has been described by an eyewitness as "a curious combination of sympathy for the sufferer and incredulity that anyone should be troubled by weakness of the flesh."

Peabody was probably the toughest physical specimen ever produced by the Proper Bostonian breed. Schooled in England, he set marks of strength and endurance that English boys marvelled at. In this country his first job was founding the first Episcopal Church in Tombstone, Arizona. He left six months later —"The East," he wrote, "is the place for an Eastern boy"—but he was there in 1882 when the town was admittedly the toughest mining-camp in America, and he acquitted himself well. According to the Tombstone *Epitaph* he was "mighty live for an Easterner" and the paper went on to say, "When it comes to baseball, he's a daisy." At Groton his physical activity was legendary. Of exercise, a Groton master once said, he made "a sacrament." He is reported to have gone thirty-two years without ever failing to do for one day what he had made up his mind was to be that day's duty. Then he was forced, against his will, to take a vacation. Up to almost the last day of his life he exercised with his boys during recess and earlier in the morning, by himself, with dumbbells. At the age of eighty-four a visitor who called on him and attended a late dinner in Boston with him returned to Groton at midnight and noted Peabody seemed to "regret" the four hours and forty-five minutes of sleep he was about to have before rising the next morning in time to get "some things done" and then listen to a broadcast of a speech by Hitler scheduled to begin at five-thirty.

To this day the Proper Bostonian feels he is letting down the grandfather-merchant tradition if he shows any signs of weakening in old age. Peabody was not a startling exception. "Seventy-seven years old," declared Bishop Lawrence in his

Memoirs, "feel as I did at fifty or sixty, but not able to do as much at a stretch and of course do not run except short distances." The "except short distances" was no exaggeration. The Bishop liked to move right along, even up stairs, and it took an attack of whooping cough at the age of eighty-five—of which a friend recalled that it "delighted" him to be the oldest person on record to have the disease—to make him use the elevator his family had installed in his four-story home. Boston First Family men scorn elevators. They travel in automobiles only reluctantly and they do not take taxi-cabs. They walk. Bostonians today can set their watches by the early-morning comings and late-afternoon goings of such present-day First Family Society leaders as Godfrey Lowell Cabot, Charles Francis Adams, and Neal Rantoul. All men in their eighties, they regularly walk all winter long from their Back Bay homes to their downtown offices and back again—a distance of some four miles. Cabot, nearing ninety, likes an extra stroll around lunchtime and has averaged close to five miles of walking a day ever since he can remember.

To retire from business is, in Boston First Family Society, a suspect action. The Proper Bostonian of advanced years may not be fortunate enough to have any more business, but if he doesn't he pretends he has and whiles away his mornings at least at directors' meetings, in the Family trust office, or at some other place where he is still an active part of the world. Failing all these, he takes up a hobby in a stern business-like manner. One First Family man became a renowned collector of Chinese porcelain, which he somehow managed to turn into a paying proposition. Another raised, and of course sold, orchids. Still a third, at what would be outside Boston recognized as a reasonable retirement age, took up the study of medicine at Harvard Medical School. He never intended to practice, but he firmly intended to keep busy. "There is no period of a man's life in which he has a right to put himself on the shelf," a Proper Bostonian once admonished the late Josiah Quincy. "There are but two persons who have the right to lay you aside—your doctor and the sexton."

Retiring from business is like giving in to the Boston winter; it reflects on a man's character. Even wearing too heavy an overcoat is taboo. Leathery old Augustus Lowell, father of Harvard's Lawrence, on the testimony of his own daughter, never wore an overcoat in his life. The Proper Bostonian does not willingly go to Florida, Arizona or California except perhaps once in his life to satisfy his curiosity as to such effete ways of life. If made to take a winter vacation he is likely to go to a cabin in Maine or Vermont and rough it for a while. One of Boston's elder Cutler brothers, president of the Old Colony Trust Co., discharged from the Army as a brigadier-general after World War II, was virtually forced South for a winter, but he solved the difficulty by taking a bicycle trip through Louisiana. On his best day, he recorded, he pedaled sixty-two miles.

Always a practical man, the grandfather-merchant left the matter of the total record of his earthly existence to other hands. Inwardly, as in the case of William Appleton, he may have had doubts on this score, but outwardly he maintained to the end a completely calm front to be handed down to his sons and grandsons. His worldly course, he was convinced, he had pursued in a forthright, honest, and manly way, and that was all that mattered. If he made what others might feel was a little too much money, he himself felt he was meant to make that much. "God," said one merchant, "made me a rich man." This same man wrote as confidently on subjects such as *The Original Sin and the Trinity* as he did on *Labor and the Tariff*. The business journal of Boston's first millionaire merchant, Peter Chardon Brooks, a journal which unlike Appleton's diary is evidently intended for the edification of the public at large, abounds in complacent religious reflections and comments. There is a rock-like self-satisfaction in all public utterances of these men—so much so that it is almost impossible to find in the career of any one of them any outward indication that if he had his life to

live over again he would have chosen to make a single important change in his course of action. In the light of future knowledge he might have changed a decision here or an idea there,
but in his final reckoning he was sure that at the time he made
that decision or embraced that idea he had done so to the best
of his ability. When his ledger was ready to be closed for the
last time he knew it would balance—just as it had always bal-
anced.

The Proper Bostonian of today owes much to this calmly
confident front his grandfather-merchant maintained to the
outer world. He, too, preserves the front, in little matters as
well as in larger spheres. One First Family man, for example,
will shortly round out a full fifty years of going every summer
to the same island in Maine for his vacation. He maintains it
is the best vacation spot in the world and his friends find it difficult to argue with him on the point since he has never been
anywhere else. In the larger sphere, this calm front is useful
even in the facing of death. Inheriting the idea that if he had it
all to do over again he would change nothing, the Proper Bostonian never desires any extra time to set his record straight.
His record is already straight, and death in its own good time
can be looked forward to as actually desirable. The nineteenth-
century Boston gentleman Edmund Quincy phrased it for him
a hundred years ago:

> Death, it seems to me, should be regarded as the greatest of
> earthly blessings—the accomplishment of our previous state of
> semi-spiritual existence. I enjoy this life highly—few more so;
> and few have more circumstances to make it pleasant to them;
> but it seems to me nothing to be compared with death as a
> thing to be desired.*

The grandfather-merchant even went so far as to teach his
descendants, by his own example, the correct way to end one's
life. The last few days in the life of Nathan Appleton, cousin

* *Later Years of the Saturday Club,* by M. A. DeWolfe Howe (Boston: Houghton Mifflin) © 1921.

of William and also a successful merchant, were outstanding in this regard. Just four days before his own death his daughter, the wife of the poet Henry Wadsworth Longfellow, had tripped on a lighted taper at the foot of the stairs of her home, and though the poet had tried to smother the fire by jumping to wrap her in a rug, the immense steel hoops under her skirt had prevented the fire's being smothered and she had been burned to death. On a Saturday the merchant went to her funeral, at the same time being advised by his doctor he had himself but two days to live. A friend who came to see him after the funeral said he would return on Monday. The merchant, who by this time had begun arranging for his own funeral, told him quietly that this would be unnecessary as he would not be alive on Monday. At this the friend became worried that the merchant's mind had been affected by so much bad news and told the doctor as much. When the merchant died, however, as he said he would, on Sunday morning, the friend later recalled what his last words to him had been, two days earlier. "I am not afraid," the merchant had said. "To tell you the truth I believe I am not afraid of anything."

To the end the merchant maintained his Yankee independence. One man, it is recorded, died with his fist doubled up at his nurse because she wanted him to lie in a different position from that which he insisted was the position he wanted to die in. Captain Robert Bennet Forbes shortly before his death appeared to be waiting for something. When someone asked him what it was, he answered, "I have gone down to the docks, and I am waiting for the old ferryman to carry me over." The death of the elder Colonel Perkins was characteristic. As his end approached, all entreaties on the part of his family to make him realize death was near appeared to fail. Finally his sister begged him at least to take to his bed. "Certainly not," he replied with decision, "I have always proposed to die dressed and sitting in my chair." An hour later he did.

Perkins' son, the younger Colonel Perkins, provided one of the most notable of all the merchants' exemplary departures.

Once called Boston's best-dressed man, he had been rather a gay blade in his time, and on his deathbed was approached by a friend who gave him, rather hesitantly, the advice that he would do well to repent his sins if he wanted to go to heaven. Perkins thought little of the idea. In two sentences he delivered what will undoubtedly remain as the all-time Proper Bostonian statement on the question of the hereafter.

"I am about as good," he declared, "as Gus Thorndike, Jim Otis or Charlie Hammond, and almost as good as Frank Codman. I shall go where they go, and there is where I wish to go."

CHAPTER FIVE

THE BOSTON WOMAN

———— ◄●►► ————

The one quality with which the female of the Proper Bostonian species has most impressed outsiders—once they are safely
beyond the stage of merely staring at her antiquated hat, her
stout shoes, and her generally severe exterior—is her incredible
vitality. Many years ago a frail young clergyman from some
effete hinterland west of Boston was invited to come to the city
to deliver a series of lectures. During his stay he was run ragged
by the elderly head of the women's committee of the church
which had engaged him and became, to his embarrassment, so
exhausted he did not know how he could find the strength to
complete his work. Feeling that the woman's religion must be
the source of her energy and believing he would benefit from
hearing her express this source to him, he spoke to her frankly.
"Madam," he said, "may I ask what it is that has given you the
strength to do all that you do?" The woman regarded his anxious, worn countenance for a moment with some displeasure,
then replied stiffly, "Victuals, sir, victuals."

Actually it is more likely that the woman was prescribing
for the needs of the young man himself rather than parting
with the secret of her own energy. The Boston woman is not by
nature an extraordinarily large eater and she is by no means as
physically well fortified in appearance as, for example, the typical suburban clubwoman regularly cartooned by Helen Hokin-
son in the *New Yorker* magazine. But she is energetic and she
wears her low-heeled walking shoes for a purpose. It is almost
impossible to travel around the Back Bay-Beacon Hill zone

without being impressed with the number of Boston's "low-heelers"—a familiar term for First Family ladies—who, many of them being of remarkably advanced years, regularly ply the streets from dawn to dark, and often long after dark, in a resolute manner. Yet when these women stop at their favorite Boston beaneries—such as the Brittany Coffee Shop or the Old English Tea Room—it is usually merely to sip a cup of tea and take a bite or two of an English muffin and then move on again.

Psychologists have long been interested in this problem of the phenomenal activity of the Boston Amazon, and knowing they must look deeper than the moderate caloric intake of these women, many have come to the conclusion that energy, pent up by the Puritan inhibitions of Boston life, will, like truth, out in the end. One Boston psychiatrist, whose mother-in-law was a Cabot, recalls that he·used to sit and argue with her on this subject. He was never able to get far with his research,.however, because, though a woman in her eighties, she would fret like a race horse as the argument increased in intensity and swing her leg so impatiently that he was reduced to staring in wonder at her excess energy. First Family women are known Boston over for their determination to "fill their life," as the expression is, regardless of their age. A wealthy Wellesley widow turned seventy took up painting. She enjoyed it but found it too sedentary an occupation to use all her time, and recently turned eighty, took up sculpture as well. Lilla Cabot Perry, another First Family artist of note, did her best work when approaching her ninetieth birthday and, painting five hours every day at that age, used to say she felt sure she was getting better all the time.

Many of Boston's most active women of today seem to feel they must make up for time lost as a result of an overly restricted Victorian girlhood. "We used to be perfectly asinine most of the time," perky First Family spinster Katharine Homans declares. "We'd spend whole afternoons sitting in bay windows and watching people walk up and down Commonwealth Avenue." During World War II Miss Homans, in the neighborhood of seventy and with a distinctly frail appearance, spent her Mondays and Fridays running ward errands for four hours a day in the Massachusetts General Hospital, her Tuesdays travelling all over town for Boston's Family Welfare Society, and her Thursdays at the Red Cross. The owner of a country place of thirty acres with only a part-time gardener, she liked to keep her Wednesdays and Saturdays "open," as she called them, for gardening, but she also sandwiched in regular work at the heart clinic of another Boston hospital and at the same time managed to keep up with the almost compulsory pursuits of all true Proper Boston women—lectures, concerts, indignation meetings, etc.

In some ways the most remarkable First Family hyperthyroid cases are those of two of Boston Society's most charming characters of today, Mrs. Augustus Hemenway, a sister of the late Bishop Lawrence, and Miss Minna Hall. Friends since debutante days, both are now approaching ninety but continue to lead such active lives that they think nothing of a two- or three-mile walk if they have nothing else to occupy their time. Mrs. Hemenway is a year older than Miss Hall, but the latter has the distinction of being the only living member of an organization formed by one of the elder Boston Lowells, known as The Society of Those Still Living in the House They Were Born In. Miss Hall's home in Brookline antedates her by a scant ten years. Fifty years ago, together with Mrs. Hemenway, she founded the Massachusetts Audubon Society, which dedicated itself against the then prevalent fashion of women wearing egret feathers in their hats; today both women are still severe critics of any feathered hats they encounter on Boston streets. The solicitude of these two friends for each other's health is touching, tinged as it is with an entirely unconscious rivalry. "Minna is so busy these days," Mrs. Hemenway will tell a fellow member at an Audubon meeting, "I'm really afraid she's overdoing," while Minna, for her part, cornering a friend at Symphony, will express concern over how tired Harriet Hemenway must be with all her gadding about. "Harriet's a gadder," she declares firmly, "she just doesn't know when to stop."

With such examples before them it is little wonder that Boston women are known for growing old with zest. Few mind giving their exact ages and many take great pride in their advancing years. Gray hair is not something to be delayed by cheap artifice; it is something to be looked forward to. Life, for the Proper Boston woman, begins at no mere forty; it is more likely to be sixty. Then she can wear her queen-mother hair-do, her inherited hat, and her ankle-length fur coat with the righteous air of knowing she is safely past the draft age of fashion for good. "I love growing old," Susan Hale of Boston's illustrious Hale Family once wrote to a friend. "Each year I come to is the most exciting yet." At the time she wrote she was seventy-four, ill and deaf, but this mattered little to her. "Life," said Julia Ward Howe, who spent a large part of her ninety-one years as a Beacon Streeter, "is like a cup of tea, the sugar is all at the bottom." The author of the *Battle Hymn of the Republic* caught what might be called the true spirit of the Boston woman when, at the age of eighty-seven, she wrote in her diary:

> I pray for many things this year. For myself, I ask continued health of mind and body, work, useful, honorable, remunerative, as it shall please God to send; for my dear family, work of the same description with comfortable wages.

That the First Family ladies of Boston have a tradition of hardihood behind them is undeniable. The very first woman to land in Boston, who came over with Governor Winthrop and his party in 1630, set the pace at the earliest possible moment when she jumped from the bow of the boat onto the beach in order to gain the distinction of being the first ashore. Outliving her husband by fifty years, she supported herself by keeping open house for Harvard students at an inn on Beacon Street and lived to be a hundred and five years old. At the age of a hundred and three she had her portrait painted lest her example of fortitude be lost on future generations of her sex. Fortunately, it was not. It was no easy thing to be a Puritan wife and follow such a schedule as that laid out by one of New England's leading First Family ministers of his day. In his journal for 1719, he notes:

> Oct. 30. I marry.
> We begin to keep house.
> My proposed order:
> 1. At 5 get up and go into my study.
> 2. Pray and read in the Original Bible till 6 and then call up the family.
> 3. At 6½ Go to Family Prayers and only the Porringer of Chocolate for Breakfast.
> 4. At 7 go in to my study till 12½ and then do something about the House till 1 to dinner.
> 5. Dinner at 1.
> 6. At 2 Dress and go about till Candle Light, except Wednesday after Dinner, do something about the House: Saturday after Dinner visit Dr. Sewall's till 2½ and then Home.
> 7. At Candle Light and Study to 9½ at 9½ go to Family Prayers and so to Bed: N.B. I eat no supper.*

This sort of thing had undoubtedly something to do with the development of the Boston woman's character, which was to rise to such heights in time of stress. "With your shield, or on it," the Spartan mother used to say to her son knowing that, with the heavy shields Spartan warriors carried, flight was impossible and her son would either return to her victorious or be carried home dead. Echoing this cry, the First Family mother of four good Boston Burnham sons watched them march off to the Revolution with their father and shouted from her doorway: "Never let me hear that one of you was shot in the back." Needless to say, none of them was; coming from such a home, the Army was the Life of Riley to the Burnham boys. Curiously enough, all during the early-day trials and tribulations of Boston, the Boston woman exhibited the same resoluteness of character whichever side she was on. During the Revolution, if a

---

* *Famous Families of Massachusetts*, by Mary Caroline Crawford (Boston: Little Brown) © 1930.

Patriot she scorned to touch a drop of Black Market tea—
though no true Boston woman before or since has ever been
known to be able to get by five o'clock without it—if a Loyalist
she was utterly fearless in facing deportation and confiscation
of her property. Few Loyalist women who later were able to
return to Boston were ever known to change sides. "My grandmother," James Russell Lowell once observed, "was a Loyalist
to her death and whenever Independence Day came around,
instead of joining in the general rejoicing, she would dress in
deep black, fast all day, and loudly lament our late unhappy
differences with his Most Gracious Majesty."

In the golden Family-founding days of the nineteenth century
the Boston woman also played a vigorous role, both as merchant
mother and sea-captain wife. The mother of Boston's greatest
merchant, the elder Colonel Perkins, was early left a widow
with eight children to be brought up. Her husband, however,
had been engaged in a small export business dealing in furs and
imported hats, and the young widow did so well at carrying it
on that letters often came to her from Holland addressed to
Mr. Elizabeth Perkins—the highest possible compliment. The
mother of another man who became one of Boston's most successful merchants had fifteen children to look after as well as
all the housework to do. In a diary of later years the merchant
recalled the picture of his anxious mother stirring the uncov-
ered well on their place with a long stick to see if one of her
children she had lost track of had by chance drowned himself.
He wrote that his mother was always "greatly relieved" when
her stick scraped freely over the bottom of the well. Robert
Bennet Forbes, the sea captain, had a particularly sturdy
specimen of a mother. Sailing with her young children to join
her husband in France, she wrote on the ship, a full five weeks
at sea after leaving Boston, a factual account of her difficulties:

We have just seen five vessels, perhaps privateers to our sorrow. We have been under water most of the time . . . The
cabin and my stateroom have been so wet as to compel me to

bail out the water constantly. Many days we lived in darkness, or only seeing by the light of a dim lamp. At night I am often obliged to have the boys in my bunk, theirs being wet. I was only seasick three weeks.*

Married early, girls often went to sea side by side with their husband ship captains. At the age of nineteen one wife, sailing from Boston to San Francisco, had her husband suddenly stricken blind with brain fever, and with no other officer on board who understood navigation, was forced to take charge of the ship. Calmly studying in spare moments out of books brought to her from the ship's cabin, not only navigation but also medicine—so that she could care for her husband—she brought the ship around Cape Horn and put into Frisco on time to discharge the cargo. For fifty nights, it is recorded, she never left the deck. One sea captain, whose ship had foundered on a shoal in the China Seas and was being torn to pieces by breakers, ran to his cabin to get his wife. He found her seated on a sea chest dressed in his pants and the mate's coat and vest and ready for any emergency. All she wanted, she told him, was a hat. Amazed, her husband found her one and watched her take a pair of scissors, coolly and quickly cut off her hair close to her head, and put on the hat. "There," she asked cheerfully, "don't I look like a boy?" Together they went on deck, and his wife's calmness, the captain later maintained, was the only thing that restored order among the panic-stricken crew and made the eventual rescue of all of them possible. On still another memorable voyage Mrs. Joseph Coolidge, nineteenth-century matriarch of Boston Coolidges, was sailing as a passenger on a ship commanded by Captain Dumaresq, often called the prince of Boston sea captains. Dumaresq, finding his ship being chased by pirates who appeared to be gaining, graciously deferred to Mrs. Coolidge the decision as to whether, if the pirates caught them, they should allow themselves to be captured or whether he should blow the ship up. "Blow her up," said Mrs.

* *Canton Captain,* by James B. Connolly (New York: Doubleday Doran) © 1942.

Coolidge abruptly and then went on deck, despite remon-
strances from the captain, for a better view of her race for life.
This race was only won when the pirates, for no apparent reason, abandoned the chase.

With her physical hardihood established, the Boston woman
of the nineteenth century went on to greater things. It seems
impossible to realize now, but there was a time in Boston when
females were not admitted to lectures. When the Boston Lyceum series of lectures was inaugurated early in the nineteenth
century, however, its promoter had an idea. "I will attach a
locomotive to this Lyceum," he declared, "which shall *make it
go.*" His locomotive was the Boston woman, and it is doubtful
if anyone has ever given a more accurate description of the female of the Proper Bostonian species. She did, of course, make
the Lyceum series go, and regular attendance at lectures has
ever since been a ritual in her life. She has always had her favor-
ites—the traveler Burton Holmes is now working on his third
generation of Boston women—but through the years she has
welcomed to her podium with open ears any author of whatever
note and, particularly in these latter days, all manner of international experts. She has made her city a recognized Garden of
Eden on the American lecture circuit, and the intense seriousness with which she attends any and all offerings has become
proverbial. A brief sample of this was demonstrated during
World War II when the Boston author John P. Marquand was
on the platform. Marquand, who has been married twice, told
his audience he had "one son in the Seventh Army and another
in diapers." One lady could not refrain from questioning this.
"Mr. Marquand," she asked, "where is Diapers?"

Margaret Fuller, Boston's great feminist of the nineteenth
century, was a strong dose in the prescription which has made
the Boston woman's character of today. An extremely plain
woman who talked in a nasal voice and had a habit of constantly
opening and shutting her eyes, she had nonetheless great personal magnetism—the most, Emerson once said, of any woman
he ever knew. She began by teaching a class of the twenty-five

women she considered most "cultivated" in Boston the art of "mental refinement," and went on from there to refine Boston womanhood on a larger scale. "It is a vulgar error," she once said, "that love, *a* love, is to woman her whole existence. She is also born for Truth and Love in their universal energy."

The Boston woman learned from this sort of thing a zeal for reform which was not long in expressing itself. Women, not men, were the moving spirit in one noted meeting of the day which had no less an object than Universal Reform. If the Proper Boston merchant held sternly aloof from Brook Farm, the country's most distinguished experiment in communal living—what else could he do with an organization which had Nathaniel Hawthorne for head of its finance committee, a man who had never met a payroll in his life?—his sisters, and in some cases, even his wife, did not. First Family women were from the start a real force in the experiment, and if foredoomed to general failure, the Farm succeeded in giving women one ultramodern landmark in emancipation—the establishment of the first nursery school known in America.

As a general thing, wife-reformers of the nineteenth century did not disturb the tranquillity of the Proper Boston marriage as they have been known to do in later days. This seems to have been at least partly due to the remarkable equanimity of the merchant-husbands involved, who were evidently able to take such things, along with their occasional financial reverses, in stride. One of these merchant-husbands, asked how he felt about the manifold activities of his wife, a well-known reformer of her day, replied briefly that he attended the closer to his own business the more his wife attended to other people's. But the question seems also to have been solved by the fact that many a First Family woman, feeling the urge for reform at an early age, chose for her mate, not a merchant at all but a very different type of man. A young Cabot girl with a reforming bent, for example, married Theodore Parker, a veritable firebrand of reform. Parker, who once devoted an entire sermon to the topic "The Temptations of Milkmen," and who ate no breakfast, but instead started each day by reading five books of the Bible, would have been a match for any wife-reformer. So, too, would have been his friend, George Ripley, founder of Brook Farm. Ripley once stated with some pride that his marriage was "founded not upon any romantic or sudden passion" but instead "upon great respect for her [his wife's] intellectual power, moral worth, deep and true Christian piety and peculiar refinement and dignity of character." Wendell Phillips, the abolitionist, though a son of Boston's first mayor and a First Family man, was still another young bridegroom far removed from the merchant-husband when he admitted that his wife invariably preceded him in the adoption of the various causes he advocated. Leaving his London boardinghouse one day to attend a convention where he was to deliver an address, he went out the door with the parting words of his young wife ringing in his ears: "Wendell, don't shilly shally." Wendell did not. Though the convention was a World Anti-Slavery meeting and had nothing to do with women at all, Phillips ended by delivering the first speech ever made by a man in advocacy of the rights of women.

Along with her reform, the Proper Boston woman has always played a leading part in church activities. The real strength of Boston's First Family churches has apparently always lain in the female head of the women's auxiliary, always the vigorous type of blue-blood feminist, rather than in her male counterpart who, as the impeccable warden or vestryman, may be the nominal leader of the congregation but actually is likely to content himself with passing the collection plate and keeping a weather eye out that the current preacher doesn't get himself out on a limb with any socialistic tommyrot. Denominationally most of the Boston churches started out by being Congregationalist, once the established faith of New England. Then, in the nineteenth century, the Emersons, Channings, Eliots and Lowells brought Unitarianism to a high position of favor among the First Families. Little by little, however, a practical low-church Episcopalianism began to make severe inroads on Boston's home-grown Unitarianism. Many a First Family woman turned with joy to the more definite ritual of this Episcopalianism, which included kneeling for prayer—Unitarians bend and make "slight obeisance" but do not kneel—and belief in the divinity of Christ. Sometimes she brought her husband along with her; sometimes First Families were split on the question. When the handsome young bachelor Phillips Brooks came to Boston in 1869 from Philadelphia, it was the Boston woman who soon made a social as well as an ecclesiastical lion out of him. With ringing rhetoric from his Trinity Church pulpit Brooks soon had even such staunch Unitarian feminists as the daughters of James Russell Lowell and Dr. Oliver Wendell Holmes proudly referring to him as "our bishop"; since Brooks had been born a Unitarian, his success was singularly important in placing Episcopalianism on a par with Unitarianism in the fight for the No. 1 religion of Boston's best.

This struggle has by no means abated, and it is the Boston woman, who relishes such things, who has kept it in focus in the Boston Society picture. Episcopal ladies still regard the God of the Unitarians, as He was once characterized, as "an oblong blur," and delight in such stories as that told of the mother of Harvard's president Eliot who, addressing a friend who had just become an Episcopalian, asked incredulously, "Eliza, do *you* kneel down in church and call yourself a miserable sinner? Neither I nor any member of my family will ever do *that!*" For their part the Unitarian ladies do not find it hard to remember the days when even the great Brooks was characterized as "an Episcopalian—with leanings toward Christianity" and when Emerson made his telling definition of Boston Episcopalianism as the best diagonal line that could be drawn between the life of Jesus Christ and that of the Boston merchant Abbott Lawrence. When Harvard turned from Unitarianism and went non-sectarian—its Divinity School was once described as consisting of "three mystics, three skeptics and three dyspeptics"— it was, of course, a triumph for the Episcopalians. So was the growth of the First Family fed Episcopal Church Schools which

under the leadership of such men as Endicott Peabody of Groton
have always been staunchly Episcopalian. But Boston's Unitarian ladies are a strong breed and, if now outnumbered, they still
show no signs of submitting to social domination by the upstart
Episcopalians. From such sturdy Unitarian redoubts as historic King's Chapel, home of Curtises, Coolidges and in-town
Cabots, or Chestnut Hill's First Church, home of Lees, Higginsons, Saltonstalls and out-of-town Cabots, they are still ready to
carry the fight to all comers. Chestnut Hill's church is a social
match for any church in America of any denomination. So exclusively aristocratic in tone is its congregation that the church's
annual meeting is always a "formal" affair, with all women present in evening dresses and all men in tuxedos. Only one member of the church is recognized as underprivileged even by
Chestnut Hill standards but there is no question of any embarrassment from this angle. Probably the only church in which no
collection plate is ever passed, the First Church handles its finances by a First Family finance committee which decides on a
proportionate annual assessment for each family in the parish.

The most recent highlight of this Unitarian-Episcopalian
struggle was the case of Dr. Phillips Endecott Osgood. A man in
his middle sixties, for many years Boston's outstanding preacher,
Dr. Osgood in 1945 rocked all of Proper Boston to its heels with
his announced intention to divorce his wife and marry his secretary. An Episcopalian who preached in the wintertime at Boston's in-town Emmanuel Church and in the summer at Emmanuel Church in Manchester-by-the-Sea, he was a First Family
Episcopalian stand-by. Shortly after his change in marital plans,
however, Dr. Osgood resigned from the Episcopal Church "for
theological reasons" and joined the Unitarian Church, in which
he was shortly offered a high appointment. Historians were
thus afforded an opportunity to compare the reactions of both
Churches almost at once under the same storm. Unfortunately
the Proper Boston woman of any denomination looks upon divorce with such disfavor that the test was inconclusive. Dr. Osgood soon resigned his Unitarian appointment, and he became

to Boston's Unitarian ladies as well as to their Episcopalian sisters simply Dr. "Wasgood."

It is characteristic of the Proper Boston woman that, whether Episcopalian or Unitarian, in a city which has the largest per capita Catholic population in America she barely recognizes Catholicism. She has equally little contact with Christian Scientists; her Boston may be their home, but with the exception of an occasional reading of the *Christian Science Monitor*, generally regarded as the best newspaper in Boston, she is in no way concerned with the faith. As for other Protestant sects, the late Henry Coit, first headmaster of St. Paul's School, probably spoke her mind as well as his own when he felt it necessary to rebuke a woman whose son, for some reason, showed inclinations toward becoming a Presbyterian. "Never forget, my dear," he said gently, "that in the life to come the Presbyterians will not be on the same plane as the Episcopalians." The Oxford Group, with its early emphasis on public confession, has had particularly hard sledding among traditionally inhibited First Family ladies. Off to a good start with the conversion of the daughter of Episcopal leader Bishop Lawrence, it had more difficulty in an attempt to duplicate this feat on another leading First Family Episcopalian. At a banquet the woman was given the seat of honor next to Frank Buchman, founder of the movement. After dinner an enthusiastic young Grouper rushed up to her and demanded to know what she thought of his leader. Receiving a haughty Episcopalian stare and an abruptly unfavorable verdict he was crushed—but only for a moment. Then, looking the lady over, he declared firmly, "Madam, you wouldn't have liked Jesus Christ or St. Paul."

In her own home it did not take the Proper Boston woman long to emancipate herself from her early nineteenth-century position. Where once she had played a yes-dear second fiddle to her merchant-husband, even in the domain of ordering meals and hiring servants, she soon fought fire with fire and became an executive in her own right. Today in most First Family homes in Boston it is impossible to say who is the more dominant character. If the male still assiduously retains his prerogative of keeping his bankbook to himself and holding his wife to a household budget of his own making, the female brooks no interference in the actual running of the home. Bishop Lawrence, in the description of his mother in his *Memoirs,* left a revealing picture of the First Family Boston housewife. Mrs. Lawrence, her son wrote, was a woman of such physical stamina that he had once seen her lift a sideboard which two men refused to touch. She never showed any anxiety in her face or in her actions. Once in a while, however, she would come down with what she described as a sick headache, in the treatment of which she took little stock in the advice of her doctor. Like all good Proper Bostonian Families the Lawrences had, of course, their Family Doctor, but the latter used to say he was called, in time of sickness of some member of the family, only to see what medicine Mrs. Lawrence would advise him to give—and then give it. To the assembled Lawrences at breakfast each morning Mrs. Lawrence would always ask, in the manner of a general addressing a group of staff officers, "Now what is the order of performances today?" Mrs. John T. Sargent, a near contemporary of Mrs. Lawrence, put into a memorable line the Proper Boston woman's pride in her executive capacities. "I can't do things myself," she used to say, "but I can manage those who can."

The Proper Boston woman's sphere of managerial activity is a large one. One curious example of this may be found in her pronunciation of the name of S. S. Pierce, long the city's First Family grocery. Founded many years ago by the Boston Pierce Family, who used the pronunciation "Purse" to distinguish themselves from lesser Pierces, the store soon found the appellation inconvenient for business reasons and announced they wished to be S. S. Pierce—pronounced Pierce. The Boston woman would have none of this, however, and though today Walworth Pierce, present head of the firm, is Pierce to his friends as well as his business acquaintances, no First Family lady ever refers to the store as anything but S. S. Purse. In the matter of the New Haven Railroad, another cherished First Family institution, one Proper Boston woman also showed her mettle. Some years ago, after an unfortunate collision had taken place on the line, she wrote to the president of the railroad and reminded him of the fact that her daughter regularly rode one of his trains; she wished him to speak personally to the engineer about driving carefully. The president wrote back that, much as he would like to do so, it would be impossible for him to make contact with each of his company's thousand or more engineers. Once more he received a letter, the lady taking issue with him on the point. "Furthermore," she added in sharp postscript, she had herself noticed on a recent trip on the railroad that "your man in Providence"—evidently referring to the baggage collector at the station—"is almost constantly in a draft."

Whatever her complaint, and to whomever addressed, the Proper Boston woman expects preferential treatment and immediate action. Remarkably enough, she usually receives it. Many of these women would undoubtedly be inveterate letter-to-the-editor writers were it not for the fact that their names would be published; this, of course, with the exception of the late Boston *Transcript,* would be an unthinkable breach of propriety, and First Family ladies today usually confine themselves to major issues, which they take up on a private basis direct with the top. During World War II Miss Rose Standish Nichols, noted Beacon Hill spinster, did not hesitate to write directly to Admiral King in Washington complaining that his subordinate, Admiral Halsey, who had just referred to the Japanese in his customary colorful manner, was "a disgrace to the Navy." He was, she declared, "not a gentleman." Admiral King not only answered Miss Nichols politely but also told her he had referred her letter to Halsey and said he would appreciate hearing from her what the latter's reply would be. Unfortunately for King's curiosity, this reply was not all it might have been. Even Battling Bill was apparently awed by the Boston spinster. In a letter which contained not so much as a gosh, he told Miss Nichols merely that he had been misquoted.

Basically unembarrassable, the First Family lady is so secure in her position in Boston that she has no fear of looking ridiculous. With rarified aplomb she does not hesitate to carry in public an assortment of bundles which would bring a blush to the cheek of her upstairs maid, and she faces with complete indifference such feminine tragedies as being caught with a run in her stocking or wearing her galoshes on a sunny day. Rules are made for others, not her. She jay-walks freely on Boston streets and in a crowded store, while never pushy in the vulgar sense, she does not hesitate to go direct to the department head for service, rather than wait her turn in line. Carefully brought up never to raise her voice, she rarely lowers it either. In a public place where others are talking in low tones she feels free to carry on a conversation with a friend in the same well-bred but clearly audible pitch she would use in her own drawing room.

The difficulty of controlling such women even for short periods of time was illustrated some years ago when the wife of a prominent Boston surgeon, a woman in her upper sixties, determined to get herself a driver's license. Out on the road, taking her test with a young instructor, she was doing nicely when, climbing a steep hill, she was suddenly ordered by the instructor to stop the car and turn around. It was a routine part of the test but the woman drove on as if she had not heard. Again the instructor repeated his order. At this the woman turned and gave him a sharp glance, then said, "Young man, nobody but a fool would turn around here." The instructor, deciding he had met his match, let her continue up the hill and around to the inspection station. Without another word having passed between them, the woman was handed her license.

Nowhere does the First Family lady show the more forbidding side of her nature more clearly than within the sacrosanct confines of the Chilton Club. Far from being merely one more of Boston's many women's clubs, the Chilton is the real social "must." In the Proper Boston woman's parlance "everybody in

Boston" belongs to it, everybody being understood to mean a select five hundred, or about one-tenth of one percent of the city's feminine population. Seemingly patterned on an English men's club rather than the usual American informal type of women's club, the Chilton is in reality Boston's female Somerset—almost equally archaic and in some respects as austere. There are three entrances to the club, one for members only off Commonwealth Avenue, one for members and guests off Dartmouth Street, and one for delivery people and servants off an alley. No member of the press is ever admitted, even from the alley, and Society editors, apparently on pain of not even being permitted to stand outside, are not allowed to mention club activities at all. If a debutante tea takes place in the club they are supposed to write merely that a tea was given and not say where. Submission to such ruling is, of course, merely one more evidence of First Family power in Boston. But Chilton Club power extends even beyond Boston. Legendary in the club is the story of a New Yorker who arrived, by the guest entrance, late one afternoon to give a lecture. Having little time to change her clothes before being due to talk, she asked for a room to dress in and telephoned downstairs for her dinner to be sent up. Just as she had completed her toilet she heard a knock on the door, which she opened to admit, not the expected waiter, but the manager of the club, a formidable woman of the Old School. The latter surveyed the lecturer for some moments in stern silence, then abruptly turned on her heel with the ultimatum, "You are far too well to have dinner served in your room."

Near by the Chilton Club and ranking not far from it as a social haunt of the Proper Boston woman is the ancient and honorable Exeter Street Theatre. The oldest continuously operating movie theatre in Boston, it was built originally as a church and still has regular Sunday morning services. Boston's First Family ladies, who scorn Hollywood and all its works, are nonetheless enticed to this mausoleum-like structure by reason of the fact that its proprietor, a cultivated woman with a degree and an accent from the University of London, features foreign films

and runs her business in the homey way she knows all Proper
Boston women love. She calls all her regular patrons by name,
knows what night they generally want to come and where they
wish to sit. She never buys a picture without seeing it first; when
her patrons telephone her and ask if they should come—which
is general practice—she tells them whether or not she thinks
they will have a good time. If they come against her advice, she
makes clear that they are on their own. The chances are they
will enjoy themselves, for, an astute analyst of the Proper Boston woman's character, she would rather hold over a second-rate
import than show a Hollywood Western, a slapstick comedy, or
anything "off-color."

Bookstores all over Boston reflect this homey touch First Family ladies love so well. Not for nothing is Boston's most successful book chain called the Personal Bookshop, an outfit with a
score of stores two of which, in the Beacon Hill area, face each
other on opposite sides of the same street. Many of these Boston
bookstores, including the famed Old Corner, Lauriat's and Jordan Marsh, given standing orders by their feminine customers,
select a number of books each month, which they know will suit
a certain customer's taste, and send them to her. For many years
one store has been filling such an order from a Chestnut Hill
dowager for "nice novels about nice people." To another bookseller a lady described what she wanted as "books about the kind
of people I would have to my own house to dinner." Deploring
the moral laxity of modern authors she went further and stated
she wanted only the works of authors who knew when to "close
the door." Decent people, she felt, closed the door to their own
bathrooms and bedrooms, and decent authors should know
enough to do the same. A former Proper Boston woman, now
living in California, wrote her bookstore she was homesick and
wanted everything they had about Boston. Another expatriated
dowager asked for "anything you think I should know about."
Now living in Maine, she has felt out of touch with her former
home in the center of the world. After some debate the store
recently sent her two books about the atomic bomb. Woe to the

bookseller who trusts blindly to advance publicity and sends such discerning clients books merely because he knows they are going to be popular. Some years ago, in the heat of a Christmas rush, a salesman sent a Proper Boston woman a copy of *Kitty Foyle*. He received a prompt telephone call in which the lady told him curtly she wouldn't allow that kind of book in her kitchen. "I had my husband take it down to the furnace," she said, "with my fire tongs." From this sort of book burning, it might be noted, it was only a step for many of such First Family ladies to be on the "side of decency" in the recent furore over Boston book banning.

The herd instinct among Proper Boston women has long been the delight of established Boston institutions and the bane of those wishing to break into the select circle. Such institutions may even be individuals. From head to toe—from the hairdresser who for twenty years has been going from one Proper Boston home to another as "the" hairdresser, to the chiropodist who for three decades has been "the" chiropodist—First Family ladies attend to their personal needs in the secure company of their social equals. For an entire generation, apparently in the belief that there were no good barbers anywhere else, Proper Boston mothers even from distant suburbs took their sons to Boston's ancient Hotel Vendome to have their hair crew cut in the approved pre-Harvard fashion. Today it is not unusual for such a distant suburbanite to make a special trip in town to a tiny old-fashioned bakery, where her mother went before her and where she is sure to see her friends, just to procure such a small order as a half dozen cocoanut cakes for tea. A restaurant suddenly becomes "popular" in Boston—popular, of course, in the restricted sense—not because it serves good food or has an inviting atmosphere, but because some First Family social leader has "discovered" it, brought her friends, and made it, as the saying is, a "ladies' and gentlemen's place to eat."

Generally speaking, so restricted is the Proper Boston woman's patronage that to her Boston might well be a town of a few thousand people instead of a city of a million. When shopping in such a city as New York, where, as she puts it, "no one cares *who* you are," she is particularly unhappy. The more chic and modern the store the more irritated it makes her. Almost certain to be too ostentatious to suit her Puritan taste, it is likely to be "cheap," a word she uses for New York in general, though not of course in the monetary sense. One lady, returning recently from a New York shopping spree, reported indignantly to her Boston lunch club that though she had introduced herself to a department head of Bonwit Teller as Mrs. —— of Boston, she had been met with a blank stare—"as if she'd never heard the name in her life." Another matron demonstrated how far out of the swim of modern living the Proper Boston woman often finds herself, when, on a short trip during the postwar meat shortage, she stopped at a diner for the first time in her life. Pointing to the meat sandwich being consumed by the man next to her she told the man at the counter she wished one like it, whatever it was. The man stared at her for a moment, then called through the slide in a triumphant voice, "Hey, Joe, come out here and get a load of a dame who's never seen a hamburg!"

The store the Proper Boston woman knows best in her city is R. H. Stearns. For half a century its first-floor glove counter has been the meeting place of First Family ladies, and the length of time a woman has spent waiting here for her friends is a fair barometer of her social standing. Founded a hundred years ago by the original Stearns, a genial old-time merchant, the store remained in the hands of his son until the latter's death in 1939. The present chairman of the board has been with the company for more than forty years and a personnel survey held some time before World War II disclosed that, of his eight hundred-odd employees, more than two hundred had served the store in some capacity for twenty-five years, and twenty of them for over fifty years. One of these half-century salesmen was a man who knew without being reminded the stocking sizes of more than five hundred Boston women. Such a phenomenal memory is not a requisite for a Stearns' salesman, but an increasingly respectful familiarity with all First Family ladies, and with their marriages and intermarriages, is an almost sure road to advancement in the store.

Hardly more than a pigmy compared with such large up-to-date Boston stores as Jordan Marsh and Filene's, Stearns nonetheless does close to a ten-million-dollar-a-year business in a homey atmosphere which has never abandoned the nineteenth-century grandmother in catering to the twentieth-century debutante. Its present chairman, now a man in his seventies, runs his store like a well-bred Boston Family. He lives on Beacon Hill, walks across the Common each morning—usually without an overcoat even in the winter—and arrives well before eight o'clock. Each evening at 5:30 closing time he walks through all eleven floors of his store saying good night to his clerks and whatever customers may have remained to that time. He is not quite certain how his store ever cornered Boston's social market as completely as it has but, knowing his Proper Boston woman well, he doesn't intend to lose her trade—and unnecessarily increase his overhead—by indulging in such fripperies as lushly décored windows, French-accented manikins, mirrored-wall dressing rooms, etc. Stearns has none of these things. But all during World War II, alone of New England stores, it never forgot that war casualty, the "stylish stout," and still today bravely displays, along with sleeker trends, all manner of old-time merchandise, including pearl chokers, Queen Mary hats, cameo brooches, high-necked, long-sleeved nightgowns, etc.—and business thrives.

The penchant for Victorian clothing is an integral part of the Proper Boston woman's character and is apparently as immutable as anything else about that character. Some years ago the father of a girl who with his wife had been present at graduation-day festivities and a dance at St. Mark's School found his daughter in tears after the affair. "I wish Mother would look like a New York mother," the girl sobbed. The father resolved to speak to his wife on the subject. The mother, Boston diarist Edith Forbes Perkins, records the event for posterity. She did indeed buy a "fashionable bonnet" shortly after the affair to please her daughter, but she declares: "Never shall I forget that bonnet—it was a soft gray felt with cherry ribbons, *not a bit like me!*"

This attitude is typical. Whether she is or not, the Proper Boston woman is not loath to think of herself as fundamentally drab and she does not wish her appearance to interfere with her Puritan pleasure. While this modesty has its charm by way of contrast with the *haut monde* peacocks in some other cities it also has its dangers in producing a type of woman who is not only indifferent to, but in extreme instances actually looks down upon, femininity itself. The Proper Boston woman dresses, as a man dresses, for all day and she shops the way a man shops, as quickly and efficiently as possible. She speaks of "doing" stores the way, when travelling, she is likely to speak of "doing" cities. "We have done Rome, Florence, Pisa, and Leghorn," the indefatigable Susan Hale once wrote proudly home to her Boston friends, "all in five days." In the same spirit the Boston woman enters a store, knowing exactly what she wants and out to get just it and nothing else. It is a bold salesgirl who tries to make a sale to such a woman by telling her "everybody is wearing" this or that. To the Proper Boston woman what other people are wearing, particularly the young people, means less than nothing. One Boston salesgirl, significantly not at Stearns but at one of the specialty shops in the Ritz-Carlton district, recently recalled a First Family matron's remark on being shown the latest spring fashions. "Don't you dare sell me anything like that," the woman told her sharply. "I don't like butterfly clothes, and" —she added after a telling pause—"neither does my husband."

The day of days for the Proper Boston woman comes twenty-six times a year—every Friday all winter—at Symphony. Here she blossoms in all her glory, for Symphony—one never speaks of it as "the" Symphony but always just as "Symphony"—is not only Culture with a capital "C" but it is also Society with a capital "S." There is also Symphony every Saturday night, to which some First Family ladies do come, bringing their husbands with them, but the only concerts that really matter for First Family

femininity are held on Friday. "Friday afternoons," former
Proper Bostonian Lucius Beebe has written, "assume the aspect
of holy days dedicated to the classics and a vast craning of necks
to be certain that the Hallowells and the Forbeses are in their accustomed stalls." To be a true Symphony patron one must be a
"Friend" of the orchestra—in other words, a contributor to the
orchestra's annual deficit as well as a regular attender at the concerts. For many years Major Henry Lee Higginson, who founded
Symphony in 1881, made up this deficit himself, but he was
finally persuaded to share the privilege with others of Boston's
best. Ever since the Major gave in, Boston's First Families have
thrown their Yankee caution to the winds, loosened their purse
strings and vied for the soul-satisfying distinction of digging
deep in the cause of Boston Culture. Once a year Symphony's
program announces not only the complete list of Friends but
also publishes an Honor Roll of all those who have attended the
orchestra under each of its regular conductors, from Sir George
Henschel in 1881 to the present Sergei Koussevitzky, who began
conducting in 1924. Significantly there are over a hundred
women, and only fifteen men, on this Roll.

Outsiders who visit Symphony for the first time rarely remember much about the music, however widely acclaimed Boston's
orchestra has been, but they never forget the spectacle of the
audience. The Proper Boston woman has a busy day on Friday.
She has a Chilton Club lecture and a Chilton Club lunch but
she is never late, and seldom early, for Symphony. For more than
half a century, attired in her sensible coat, her sensible hat and
her sensible shoes, she has entered the hall promptly at 2:25 and
swept serenely to her seat in a manner that defies description. If
she forgets her ticket it is no tragedy. A large proportion of
patrons regularly do this, but they have been so resolutely
marching toward the same seats for so many years that no usher,
even in a packed hall, would dare attempt to stop them. "You
must go," writes guide-book author Eleanor Early, "to see old
Boston on parade." But there is no hurry—Symphony will wait
for you:

When I was a small child, a Symphony audience looked exactly as it does today . . . This phenomenon had been going
on then for a long time, and it may last forever. I think that
when this year's debs are another day's spinsters, they will save
all their perfectly good clothes and they will wear them to Symphony on Fridays. They will arrive in the family's old car . . .
And they will smile gently at the men who did not marry them.
Although they may look bored, they will be quite happy. And
their shabbiness will be in the traditional manner. For this is
the Boston legend.*

* *And This Is Boston!*, by Eleanor Early (Boston: Houghton Mifflin) © 1938.

CHAPTER SIX

BELLES AND GRANDES DAMES

—————◄►————

While the history of Boston Society has been largely concerned with a rather forbidding type of femininity—as witness the widespread story of the woman who on entering a New York store said, "I come from Boston, I'm a Unitarian, and I wear drawers. Now you know the kind of hat I want"—it would be unjust not to take note of the fact that there have been at least a few women, in each era of Boston Society, who would rank with the charmers of any city. One of the first of these was responsible for starting the most famous brother-feud in Boston social history.

Known simply as "the widow Gore," she was the outstanding beauty in Boston's gay post-Revolution days and she lived in style in a mansion on Beacon Street. One afternoon in the 1790's two Lee brothers, sons of old Captain Joseph Lee of Salem, determined—unfortunately at the same time—to pay their respects to her. Joseph, the elder, approached from one direction, walking down Beacon Street, while Thomas, the younger, approached from the other direction, up the street. Resolute like all Boston Lees, so occupied were the brothers with thoughts of Mrs. Gore that they did not see each other until, at almost exactly the same moment, Joseph set foot on the upper side of the widow's doorstep and Thomas set foot on the lower side. Then, and only then, they looked up. They glared at each other in silence, then abruptly turned away, each the way he had come. Never again did either of the two brothers come to see the

widow Gore. And they did not speak to each other for approximately fifty years.

On his deathbed, in 1845, Joseph sent for Thomas. "Hello,
Tom," he said.

"Hello, Joe," said Thomas.

According to a present-day Lee historian, that was all the conversation there was, and "that, in characteristic Lee fashion,
ended the long feud." In view of the none too satisfactory ending, however, and in fairness to the widow Gore, it might be
pointed out that her spell over Thomas Lee at least might be
considered not to have ended until fifteen years later—a spell of
sixty-five years in all. Then, in 1860, as founder of Chestnut
Hill's First Church, Thomas chose a bell for the church chapel
with the remarkable inscription, "Let Brotherly Love Continue."

In other stories of the feud, some historians discount the part
played by the beautiful widow altogether, claiming that Boston
First Family brother-feuds are such a common occurrence that
Mrs. Gore deserves little credit for starting one. Two brothers
Fay, for example, carried on a notable feud for a reason no one
has ever been able to pin down. Both merchants, they sat back
to back in the same office for thirty years without ever speaking
to each other. When business affairs demanded communication,
they dictated letters to one another through a stenographer. On
social occasions, meeting at the Somerset Club, they spoke to
each other only through a third party. Yet women played no
part at all in the affair, both Fay wives being fast friends
throughout the thirty years.

One woman never slighted by Boston social historians and to
whom is unanimously accorded the honor of being the most
famous belle ever boasted by the city, is Emily Marshall. Chest-
nut-haired and described by one historian as "perfect in face and
figure," she flourished some time after the widow Gore, in the
days of the 1820's and 30's, and was a young lady of such unusual charm that it was actually a mark of distinction, among
the beaux of the day, not to be in love with her. Her followers

included virtually every bachelor of prominence in the city and in her daily mail—the first "fan mail" of its sort in America— she often received as many as a dozen sonnets from admirers, known and unknown. A typical one of these follows:

> Elegance floats about thee like a dress,
> Melting the airy motion of thy form
> Into one swaying grace; and loveliness,
> Like a rich tint that makes a picture warm,
> Is lurking in the chestnut of thy tress,
> Enriching it, as moonlight after storm
> Mingles dark shadows into gentleness.
> A beauty that bewilders like a spell
> Reigns in thine eyes' clear hazel; and thy brow
> So pure in veined transparency doth tell
> How spiritually beautiful art thou—
> A temple where angelic love might dwell.
> Life in thy presence were a thing to keep,
> Like a gay dreamer clinging to his sleep.*

Cabmen of the day, waiting for Emily, were often so spell-bound with her that they would forget to open the doors of their carriages and merely stand gaping at her. William Lloyd Garrison, one of Boston's most illustrious radicals, was known to admit that he went to a church presided over by "a reactionary" just to see her. As for the minister who in 1831 married Emily to the mayor's son, William Foster Otis, he, too, was struck with her. He declared after the ceremony that while he had always previously doubted the power of women like Mary Queen of Scots to make men die for them, he now felt, after seeing Emily at close range, that there was something to such stories. "After seeing Emily," he wrote, "I understand that some women—perhaps one in each century—could really exercise such a power."

In contrast with other belles of high Society in her day Emily was notably modest and usually dressed with what, for those times at least, was extreme simplicity. A description of her wed-

* *Romantic Days in Old Boston,* by Mary Caroline Crawford (Boston: Little, Brown) © 1922.

ding, as left by her sister-in-law, is evidence that it did not take
extra trimmings to make Emily stand out as a bride:

> The bride . . . was unaffected and modest. Her dress was
> beautiful, a white crepe lisse with a rich line of silver embroi-
> dery at the top of the deep hem. The neck and sleeves trimmed
> with three rows of elegant blonde lace. Gloves embroidered
> with silver, stockings ditto. Her black hair dressed plain in
> front, high bows with a few orange blossoms, and a rich blonde
> lace scarf beautifully arranged on her head, one end hanging
> front over her left shoulder, the other hanging behind over her
> right. No ornaments of any kind either on her neck or ears,
> not even a buckle. I never saw her look better.*

Unfortunately Emily Marshall Otis lived less than five years
after her marriage. A martyr to the primitive surgery of the day,
she died at the age of twenty-nine immediately after the birth of
her third child. One of her great-granddaughters, Lydia Eliot
Codman, who is today active in First Family social circles, was
the city's most famous belle of the early 1900's and takes great
pride in her descent from the woman who, in the words of Boston historian Josiah Quincy, "as completely filled the [Boston]
ideal of the lovely and the feminine as did [Daniel] Webster
the ideal of the intellectual and the masculine."

With Emily's death her place as chief charmer of Boston society passed to another Otis wife, Mrs. Harrison Gray Otis, Jr.
Still referred to by Boston Otises of today as the "notorious,"
she was a large bouncing woman, with none of Emily's good
looks but with verve enough to corral an impressive list of admirers, including Henry Clay. Her maiden name was Eliza
Henderson Boardman and, as the daughter of one of Boston's
most successful East India merchants, she travelled widely as a
young girl and dented the Societies of Paris, London and
Vienna, as well as Boston. Early left a widow with five children,
she inherited enough money from her husband, together with

---

* *Famous Families of Massachusetts,* by Mary Caroline Crawford (Boston:
Little Brown) © 1930.

a hundred and fifty thousand dollars from her merchant-father, to build a large Beacon Hill home and transform herself without delay from a belle to her own idea of a great lady. She is credited with being the first woman who ever waltzed in Boston —to the intense displeasure of her father-in-law, who pronounced the newfangled dance "an indecorous exhibition." She also rebelled against the idea of ladies not being allowed to go where they wished on foot, even after dark. Liking to walk, she made a habit of walking home after parties accompanied by a servant named John. John was evidently capable of handling any and all trouble on such trips, including that once offered by a beau who felt that if the young widow could walk home alone with John she could as well walk with him. Pressing his point one evening, he approached the pair saucily. Mrs. Otis turned to her servant. "John," she directed, "knock that man down." Upon which, the story goes, John did, and the young widow was ever after left unmolested on her nightly excursions. She never remarried, though it was not for lack of offers. During the Civil War, then a lady shading sixty, she still had enough of her buoyant charm to sell kisses for charity at a price of five dollars each, a mark which still stands for present-day Boston debutantes to shoot at.

Mrs. Otis' chief distinction in social history rests on her establishment of the salon as an American Society institution. Though an author herself, with a novel entitled *The Barclays of Boston* to her credit, her salons were not primarily literary. Instead, in assuming the leadership in what was soon to become the Society woman's national sport of treeing celebrities, she showed a hitherto unprecedented catholicism of taste. One of her Thursday soirees was a triple-headed affair which included, it is recorded, "President Fillmore, Lord Elgin, and an Indian Chief." Besides her "Thursdays" Mrs. Otis also vigorously at-homed at her "Saturday afternoons," in which, mindful of her own ever-increasing figure as well as being a general rebel against the heavy eating of the times, she prided herself on her "skimpy" refreshments. She gave her guests cocoa and cakes instead of what was then considered "the thing" to serve—full-course meals topped off with great steaming bowls of hot stewed oysters.

Taking the cue from Mrs. Otis—much as she on occasion shocked them—other more conservative hostesses also took up the nurturing of the Society salon, though on a more definitely literary plane. After Boston's stern hostesses of the nineteenth century had entered the field of salon-keeping in earnest, men like Emerson, Holmes and Longfellow needed no male support to make them immortal. A contemporary of Mrs. Otis and also the daughter of an East India merchant, Mrs. George Ticknor carried literary lionism to giddy heights when she set herself up in a home which had a parlor downstairs for the entertaining of nouveau writers and a library upstairs for the truly elect. "I have never seen any Society equal to what was there," declares a commentator of the Ticknor salons, "quiet cordiality shading off into degrees of welcome, high-bred courtesy in discussion and courtly grace of movement . . . greatly honored were those who had access to her house." *

Not only a recognized position in Society but also advanced years have always been requisites for Proper Boston salon-keeping. One must be, in other words, a grande dame. Mrs. James T. Fields, who was still teaing authors in her parlor in her eighties, was one of these. Another was Julia Ward Howe, who was so successful at summoning celebrities for the New England Woman's Club that she had a forty-year term as president of that organization. Still others were elderly women like Mrs. Edwin Whipple, who made her thirty years of "Sundays" a Boston institution, and Louise Chandler Moulton, whose "Fridays" lasted almost as long and were after her death continued by the Boston Authors' Club. Her idea of perfect happiness, Mrs. Moulton used to say, was sitting by an open fire with an author and a piece of sponge cake.

Today Mrs. Fiske Warren, a woman in her upper seventies,

* *Romantic Days in Old Boston,* by Mary Caroline Crawford (Boston: Little Brown) © 1922.

carries on this cakes-and-ale tradition with her regular salons
for the New England Poetry Society. Some twenty years ago
she succeeded Amy Lowell as president of this organization. To
be invited to join, and hence become a salon habitue of Mrs.
Warren, a poet must have had a book of poems actually published, not just privately printed, or else have had a poem appear in the *Atlantic, Harper's,* the *Saturday Review of Literature* or the *Christian Science Monitor.* Significantly the brands
of poetry as published by the *Saturday Evening Post* and the various women's magazines are not recognized. Mrs. Warren herself has never published a poem in this country but has appeared
in English magazines, which makes her even more highly regarded. A woman of rare charm, she dedicates herself conscientiously to her salons and her writing and at the same time has
managed to become Boston's most renowned collector of sea
shells and all manner of bric-a-brac. She seldom leaves her an-
tique-studded Beacon Hill home at all—never, if she can help
it, for purely social engagements. She feels that if even once in a
while she were to go clandestinely to a friend's house for a lunch
or dinner, other friends would hear of it and soon too much of
her time would be taken from her artistic pursuits. All who have
attended Mrs. Warren's salons agree that they are a part of Old
Boston unduplicated anywhere else—where Harvard professors,
poets, and the better-bred Beacon Hill Bohemians distribute
themselves gingerly around a large living room, among fragile
sea shells and almost equally fragile chairs, sip tea and sherry,
and engage in low-voiced discussions of poetry, philosophy and
kindred subjects.

The Proper Boston woman has always shown great enthusiasm for discussions and the pure and simple art of talking. In the
old days there was once a vogue of holding what were called
"converzationes." In these literature, religion and even politics
—but never scandal or fashion—were discussed in highly for-
malized gatherings. Unfortunately they soon became too formal,
and even in a city like Boston they were fated to die of their own
weight. At about the time of their passing, however, there rose

to power in the city a lady named Helen Choate Bell. A slight woman with titian hair and clear-cut features she was Boston's greatest talker, the most famous Society wit in the city's history, and until her death in 1918 at the age of eighty-eight she reigned supreme over the city's smart set. Her father, Rufus Choate, was in his day one of Boston's best-known lawyers. Of this man an admirer and professor at the Harvard Law School declared that while there are plenty of people in the world who are never at a loss for *a* word, he was never at a loss for *the* word—and Mrs. Bell, as his daughter, was liberally endowed not only with Choate affluence but also with Choate wit. Early in life in the Proper Boston tradition she married her cousin; soon, however, she was left a widow and she lived most of the rest of her life with a married sister in a small house on Beacon Hill's Chestnut Street. But her life was a full one. "Her charm," the late Henry Cabot Lodge, one of her many disciples, once wrote, "was as potent when she was eighty as in the heyday of youth. It was impossible to knock at any door in the vast literature of imagination and not find her at home."

Often called the Complete Boston Woman, Mrs. Bell loved "coziness"—she used to say—and friends, books and music, and above all, talk. To be a bosom friend of hers was to be as far "in" in the Society of the day as it was possible to get, and one could be pushed beyond the pale by one barb of her repartee. A notable example of the latter occurred in the case of a young Harvard man much invited about during one winter of the early 1900's. Little by little hostesses began to tire of him and finally one was moved to ask frankly in the Proper Boston manner, "Does he know anything?" "Know anything!" shot back Mrs. Bell, "why he doesn't even *suspect*." Like most wits, however, Mrs. Bell was evidently better in person than she appears in the light of cold print. She never wrote for publication in her life; she was a talker pure and simple. But she had a remarkable facility for making even the dullest of her devotees feel that they themselves were witty. "As you talked with her," a friend once declared, "you knew that she was the most brilliant woman in

the world, and you felt that you were a close second." Another
wrote that she was unaffected and, while an omnivorous reader
and possessed of a keen memory, never displayed "raw knowledge." The favorite word for Mrs. Bell's bons mots among
Boston's pearl-choker set who still remember her is "delicious."
Unfortunately few of these delicious stories, once quoted and
requoted up and down Beacon Hill, have been able to keep
their flavor with the passing years, and an entire generation of
Proper Bostonians has grown up to whom even Mrs. Bell's name,
once a First Family household word, is unfamiliar. The only one
of her sayings which might be said to have lasted in the sense of
Bartlett's *Familiar Quotations*—though it did not make it—is
her aphorism on the subject of the automobile: it was Mrs. Bell
who said that it would soon divide mankind into two classes, the
quick and the dead.

But in any fair analysis Mrs. Bell as a Boston grande dame
deserves a high place in Boston social history for at least one
reason. She stands almost alone among generations of First Family pseudo-intellectuals as an inherently honest woman. Many a
Proper Boston woman has always pretended to love Nature
because Emerson loved Nature and Thoreau loved Nature and
one simply must love Nature. She joins a garden club, hires a
gardener to manicure a garden and enters her daffodils in the
annual daffodil show of the Massachusetts Horticultural Society—while all the time she knows inside herself she infinitely
prefers her darkened Victorian drawing room and her fireside
tea to anything about the great outdoors. Mrs. Bell would have
none of such hypocrisy. She refused to have anything to do with
gardening and even avoided trips to the country whenever she
could. "Talk of the carpet of nature! " she scoffed. "Give me a
three-ply Chestnut Street garage." To a friend departing for the
woods and fields she said, "Go kick a tree for me." On another
occasion out driving past a field of asparagus she commented to
a companion how queer it looked. "I always thought," she said,
"the cook braided the ends." Proper Boston women, no matter
how much they may actually dislike travel in France and French

literature, are brought up to like it—so liked it must be, second only of course to travel in England and English literature. But Mrs. Bell frankly expressed revulsion at all things French. "The French," she once said, "are a low lot. Give them two more legs and a tail and there you are! I think they have an original nastiness that beats original sin."

In comparison with so many Boston hostesses who have always pretended to like house guests but all too often disliked the very idea of them, Mrs. Bell was the soul of honesty. House guests interfere with the cut-and-dried routine of the running of the Proper Boston household, and they also break down the Boston Society hostess' beloved formality of "by the clock" entertaining. Mrs. Bell knew this well and though she spent most of her life in her sister's home, she refused to pass as much as a night anywhere else. Once refusing an invitation she declared she had always been pursued by "fear of waking up dead in some strange house." In her last years when she had a home of her own, she was not afraid to make her position clear on this point. "An empty nest is best," she gave as a motto for her guest room, and a letter to a friend stands as a testimony to her integrity:

> I wrote to Miss —— to ask her to visit me. I told her not to come if it was hot and not to come if it was rainy. In fact, I gave her such a narrow margin of weather that I hope she won't be able to come at all.*

As a salon-keeper Mrs. Bell was a standout. People who were invited to her house recall that she had great ability to bring out wit in the lions of the day by acting as a foil for them. She could also put on a show of her own, from comedy to tragedy. She could sparkle with witticisms at her dinner table and afterwards, though no singer—"I have but two notes in my voice," she used to say—she would sit at the piano and recite moving passages of poetry, weaving in the verses with a few chords, and reduce to tears the same audience that had laughed only a short

* *Mrs. Bell,* by Paulina Cony Drown (Boston: Houghton Mifflin) © 1931.

while before. One man who signed himself "G.S." and who was especially devoted to Mrs. Bell declared in a letter to the *Transcript* after her death that she was unique "even in the generation that had Mrs. Julia Ward Howe, the Carys and Cabots, the genius of the Sturgis family, the beauty of Shaws and Parkmans, of Sears and Lymans, the distinction of Mrs. Agassiz, the friendship of Anna Cabot Lodge, the loveliness of Mrs. James T. Fields, and the hospitality of Mrs. Dorr." Surely Proper Bostonian pride could go no farther. Mrs. Bell herself might have scorned such indiscriminate praise. She was never too fond of her title as the Complete Boston Woman. Once she was teased to the point of irritation about being left alone with a young man at a party. "What did you do," she was asked, "recite poetry to him?" "Ha," snapped Mrs. Bell. "I know men too well for that. I made him recite poetry to me."

For a Boston Society which has never lacked for grandes dames to have to admit that its greatest was not a Bostonian at all but a New York import is a stern story indeed. Furthermore this greatest of grandes dames was a lady who persisted in regarding herself as a sort of dedicated spirit to wake up Boston. The daughter of a New York dry-goods merchant named David Stewart, she was christened Isabella. In the year 1860 she married John Lowell Gardner, son of the last of Boston's East India merchants, and moved to Boston. From then until her death in 1924 at the age of eighty-five Isabella Stewart Gardner proceeded to do everything that Proper Boston women do not do, and then some. "In a Society," wrote Lucius Beebe, "where entertaining Major Higginson at tea and sleigh-riding on the Brighton Road on Sunday afternoon were the ultimate public activities endorsed by decorum, she soon became far from anonymous."

Mrs. Gardner didn't drink tea; she drank beer. She adored it, she said. She didn't go sleigh-riding; instead, she went walking down Tremont Street with a lion named Rex on a leash. She gave at-homes at her Beacon Street house and received her guests from a perch in the lower branches of a mimosa tree. Told that "everybody in Boston" was either a Unitarian or an Episcopalian, she became a Buddhist; then when the pleasure of that shock had worn off she became such a High-Church Episcopalian that her religion differed from Catholicism only in respect to allegiance to the Pope. Advised that the best people in Boston belonged to clubs she formed one of her own named the "It" Club. In Boston one coachman was enough for anybody, but Mrs. Gardner soon showed she wasn't anybody. She kept two footmen as well as a coachman and rarely drove out in her carriage without all three of them in full livery. Warned that a woman's social position in Boston might be judged in inverse ratio to her appearance, she spent thousands of dollars a year on the latest Paris fashions. She saw Cabots and Lowells leave their jewels in their safe-deposit boxes; she picked out her two largest diamonds, had them set on gold wire springs and wore them waving some six inches above her hair like the antennae of a butterfly. Mrs. Gardner even told risqué stories and told them in mixed company—at the same time, her bout with Buddhism behind her, each Lent with much fanfare she piously atoned for her misdeeds by scrubbing the steps of the Church of the Advent and sending out black-bordered invitations to Holy Communion.

Such a splash in the still waters of Boston Society could hardly be ignored. Mrs. Gardner's notices, both public and private, were by no means wholly favorable, but the New York Society Journal *Town Topics* rallied to her side in a notable defense:

Boston society consists of fossilized conventions; Mrs. Gardner has not failed to spurn them. Boston society consists of antique genealogical distinctions and exclusive standards; Mrs. Gardner has not failed to break down social barriers and evidence her belief in society as a vehicle for the cultivation of art, music, and intellectuality and to create a social renaissance. Beyond her wealth and her social position, she has exercised a certain personal hypnotism in the ranks of swelldom.

Hypnotic was the word for this woman. She had a way with her. Plain of face to the point of homeliness and short of stature, she had a strikingly curvaceous figure and attracted artists by the score, most of whom offered to paint her merely for the pleasure of doing so. When she finally chose John Singer Sargent to do her portrait, she once more showed her scorn for Bostonian propriety by having him paint her in a black low-necked dress with a rope of pearls around her waist and a black shawl drawn tightly around her hips. Exhibited at the gentlemanly St. Botolph Club in the winter of 1888-89 the picture caused so much comment that her husband had it removed and declared it would never be exhibited again as long as he lived. So far as it is known this is the only occasion he or anyone else ever told Mrs. Gardner what to do. "To dominate others," writes her biographer and present-day executor, Morris Carter, "gave Mrs. Gardner such pleasure that she must have regretted the passing of slavery."

Nonetheless as time went by, almost despite herself Mrs. Gardner assimilated certain unmistakable traits of the Boston Society in which she made herself Queen Bee. Not one of her huge diamonds but a small gold watch charm was her favorite jewel; she had it made from a ten-shilling piece she had once received from the London *Times* for covering an opera—the only money, she was fond of saying, she had ever earned. She poured out hundreds of thousands of dollars for her art collection and thousands for her clothes, but in the Proper Bostonian fashion she became increasingly careful of her small change. She thought little of paying Paderewski three thousand dollars to play at a tea for herself and a friend, but there are First Family ladies in Boston today who remember she would never allow more than one chop per head for a luncheon and that other phases of her entertaining were on a similarly slender scale. Boston entertaining has always been formal, and Mrs. Gardner made it if anything more so. "I hate people dropping in," she used to say, and people did not. All her life she allowed her friends to take hardly more liberties with her than her ac-

quaintances. All Boston knew her as "Mrs. Jack" but nobody
called her anything but Mrs. Gardner. In her high and mighti-
ness she actually out-Bostoned Boston itself. *C'est mon plaisir*
was her often-expressed motto, and her *plaisirs* were many and
varied. On her shopping tours she never left her carriage and
took quite for granted the store-to-street scurrying of salesmen
anxious to satisfy her idea of curb service. In wintry weather
she often had her coachman, regardless of pedestrians, drive
right on the sidewalk to the door of her home to spare her the
inconvenience of crossing the snow. One of her *plaisirs* even
carried beyond her lifetime. In her will her heirs are summarily
instructed to attend Church services at least twice a year—on
Christmas and on her birthday.

Mrs. Gardner's private life was not altogether a happy one.
Her only child died, five years after her marriage, at the age of
one. She had many male admirers but few friends of her own
sex. Many Proper Boston women would have nothing to do
with her, and though stories of her personal interest in young
musicians and artists were sometimes exaggerated by her admitted enemies, First Family governor Roger Wolcott went so
far as to forbid his wife to accept any invitation from her. In
1898, shortly after her husband died, Mrs. Gardner suffered a
nervous breakdown, and upon her recovery she was advised by
her doctors to take up a hobby. For such a woman this was a
daring prescription. The hobby she took up has probably never
been equalled in scope by any grande dame in America before
or since. It involved the erection of a complete Florentine palace
on the marshes of Boston's Fenway, in the upper reaches of
Back Bay. Mrs. Gardner bought the palace abroad and it was
shipped piece by piece on her order to this country. In the years
it took to complete the structure she was on hand every day she
was in Boston to take part in every operation. Sixty years old,
she brought her lunch and took her noon hour. She contributed
her ten cents for the oatmeal to be put in the drinking water.
On one occasion she took an axe and hewed a heavy beam to
show a workman just how she wanted it hewn. When the

walls of the palace court were ready for painting, she ordered a pail of white paint and a pail of pink paint to be brought to her. Then climbing the staging to the very top with a pail in each hand, she proceeded to begin the smearing of the walls, dipping her sponge from pail to pail. She refused to climb down until she had given her painters a full example of the exact effect she was after—that of pink Italian marble. Wherever she was working she always had a trumpeter close by her. When she wished to summon her workmen, the trumpeter would trumpet, one toot for the architect, two for the steam-fitter, three for the plumber, etc. One day a plumber was dilatory in responding to his toot. Mrs. Gardner fired him on the spot, then called his firm and ordered him replaced within the hour on pain of transferring the entire contract to another firm.

Mrs. Gardner built her palace to house her art collection. She had made a lifelong calling of this and was no amateur. Never lacking for money—she inherited $2,750,000 from her father in 1891 and several millions more when her husband died in 1898—she had through the years picked up a highly rated general and early Italian collection, including what many regard as the finest Titian extant, the huge "Rape of Europa." In contrast to other eminent Society collectors she was rarely swindled. When she attended auctions abroad, realizing that she was well-known as a wealthy American, she devised an elaborate series of signals to pass between herself—who to all appearances was not bidding—and her agent who kept himself anonymous. One of her favorite devices was to hold a handkerchief to her mouth and let it drop when she wanted her man to stop bidding. Playing this drop-the-handkerchief game in Paris she procured "The Concert" by Vermeer for six thousand dollars. In the National Gallery at Washington there are three Vermeers for which Andrew Mellon's buyers paid, respectively, the sums of $290,000, $350,000 and $400,000. A remarkably low proportion of Mrs. Gardner's total collection has ever been challenged as to its authenticity. Unfortunately, however, because of the strict terms of her will, the spurious items can never be removed—indeed nothing in her palace may ever be relocated, as much as from one wall to another.

Though she always intended her palace to be a public museum after her death, Mrs. Gardner used it as her home during her lifetime. When the government, however, which in those days did not permit art treasures of a hundred years or more vintage to enter the country duty-free—as they do today—demanded that she pay $150,000 in back duty, Mrs. Gardner became enraged. She felt that since her home was to be a museum, she should have better terms. To this the government's answer was that her palace was hardly a public affair. In the course of the dispute Mrs. Gardner finally made her home her idea of "public"—she opened it from 12 to 3 two weeks a year, Thanksgiving week except for Thanksgiving day and Holy Week except for Good Friday—but the government still got its $150,000. Nowadays Fenway Court is open to the public from 10 to 4 on Tuesdays, Thursdays and Saturdays, and Sunday afternoons from 1 to 4. In 1946 it attracted more than 85,000 persons.

Mrs. Gardner mellowed with advancing years, and with a wry gulp Boston's First Family Society swallowed her, but to this day it has never wholly digested her. Stories of Mrs. Jack's excesses, once the spice of every Proper Boston sewing circle, are rarely heard today, but a few tales persist. One is the story of her final days. Mrs. Gardner, it is said, could not even die without drama and had the last rites administered to her on several occasions before the end finally came. The legends of her baths have also outlasted the years. During hot weather Mrs. Gardner had a habit of ordering her custodians and servants to leave her courtyard, after which she would take to her fountain and sit for long periods of time, striking elaborate poses. According to the stories, these poses were much enjoyed by the custodians and servants who, instead of disappearing altogether, regularly retired only to a safe distance behind the pillars and statuaries. Still another story is the one of the Mrs. Gardner "nude." This is a real cross to bear for the employees of her museum. Mrs. Jack chose to have a pastel of herself painted by Whistler. She also wanted it hung beside another Whistler— and so it does, forever, since no picture may be changed. Unfortunately the other Whistler is a painting of a young lady without clothes, and its proximity to Mrs. Jack, combined with the stories of her eccentricities, has caused much confusion. "You would be surprised," says museum director Morris Carter sternly, "at the number of people who come in here with just one idea. All our staff have instructions to tell people that there is no nude of Mrs. Gardner here or anywhere else."

Such troublesome post-mortems can never take from Mrs. Gardner the fact that she was Boston Society's greatest grande dame. No one has ever approached her either in prominence or in her remarkable hold over the imagination of all types of people. Abroad even kings looked with favor on her. Sargent liked her so well he painted her half a dozen times; on one occasion to prove the power of her personality he did a portrait of her with the face left blank. Humbler people also took to her. An author in Florida wrote a novel about her and a lady from the Midwest, coming East for the first time, declared she had but two wishes—to see the Atlantic Ocean and Mrs. Gardner. On at least one occasion this popularity was put to an acid test. Driving out late one evening in the midst of a particularly violent Boston street-car strike, Mrs. Gardner found her carriage halted in the middle of an angry crowd. Her three men in their livery were of little assistance. Suddenly a figure loomed up and a heavy hand was laid on her carriage. A deep voice boomed inside, "Don't be afraid, Mrs. Jack, I'll see you through all right." With this the figure proceeded, as if by magic, to wave the crowd aside and make a path for the queen. Safely through, Mrs. Gardner leaned her head outside and spoke to her Galahad whom she still could not see in the darkness. "May I ask to whom I am indebted for this courtesy?" she asked. "Certainly, Ma'am," said the figure, leaping lightly from his post and touching his cap. "John L. Sullivan."

As far as her relations with Boston Society were concerned,

Mrs. Gardner's night of nights occurred on January 1, 1903. This was the date she held the grand opening of her palace for the benefit of that Society which had for forty-three years deferred the distasteful task of crowning her their queen. Tired of waiting, Mrs. Gardner had become fully prepared to crown herself. A lesser woman might have been baffled by the necessity of testing the acoustics of her music room as it would be when filled with people and yet keeping this room—as indeed she had the entire museum—a surprise awaiting the actual opening. Not, however, Mrs. Jack. Getting in touch with the director of the Perkins Institute for the Blind, she stated her case and procured a full-size audience of boys and girls for an afternoon concert. Only one incident occurred to mar the proceedings. It was a wintry day and the children had all worn rubbers; upon entering the palace each neatly placed his own pair in a spot a little apart from the others where he would be able to locate them on his return from the hall. During the tryout a caretaker, noticing the boots in what seemed to him needless disarray over the spic-and-span palace court, placed a piece of canvas on the floor and put all the pairs together on it. To the blind children returning from their concert, this rubber pile presented an almost hopeless problem. In later years Mrs. Gardner used to say that to her the most vivid thing about the opening of the palace was the time she spent that afternoon on her hands and knees pairing rubbers together and trying them on the blind children.

To many of the elders of Boston Society every detail of the Gardner party has remained vivid to this day. The curtain rose on the show at 10:30. That was the time specified on the invitation, and almost everyone invited congregated at the entrance of the palace together. Even the most die-hard of Mrs. Gardner's feudists were loath to miss a minute of an evening they had determined to spend from start to finish satisfying themselves firsthand on the score of Fenway Court. For three long years legends, like the palace itself, had been a-building. Would Mrs. Gardner's "Eyetalian palace" be, as her enemies had gossiped, a million-dollar myth and a nouveau riche night-mare? Or would it be real, as her friends of the It Club insisted, something that would be a latter-day shot in the arm for the culture of their city?

Characteristically Mrs. Gardner bided her time before per-mitting anyone to make the decision she, too, well knew they wished to make. At first her guests entering the lobby had ac-cess to just two rooms in the palace—the ladies' dressing room and the men's. The former, hung with light-blue brocades, con-tained a few modern paintings; in the latter were several etch-ings. There was nothing on which anyone could base even a snap judgment. Next the guests were escorted into the austere, pure-white music room. At the far end of this room, on a land-ing at the top of a horseshoe staircase, stood Mrs. Jack. Dressed in her smartest black gown, with her famed diamonds waving over her head, she was ready for her homage. The guests obedi-ently lined up, crossed the large room, climbed one side of the stairs, shook hands and climbed down the other. Then, except for the favored few Mrs. Gardner had chosen to remain on the balcony with her, everyone took seats while fifty members of the Boston Symphony conducted an hour-long concert. Finally Mrs. Jack was ready. At the conclusion of the music she gave a signal. At once a great mirror in òne corner of the music room was rolled back and guests could see the palace court. In the middle of a Boston winter the scene had a powerful effect on those present. It was, writes an eyewitness, "a gorgeous vista of blossoming summer gardens . . . with the odor of flowers stealing toward one as though wafted on a southern breeze." There was first "an intense silence broken only by the water trickling in the fountains; then came a growing murmur of delight, and one by one the guests pressed forward to make sure it was not all a dream."

The palace was now open for inspection, all except for the upstairs chapel, Mrs. Gardner's private holy of holies, and the Gothic Room, where the Sargent portrait which had caused so much shocked comment fifteen years before was still hidden

from prying eyes. Elsewhere the guests were free to wander at
will through the court, lighted by flame-colored lanterns from
the eight surrounding balconies, to the treasure-filled rooms,
lit by candles, of the three floors of the palace. As these rooms
filled with people it seemed to one historian as if "the Venetian
Renaissance had been reincarnated in twentieth century Boston." Somewhere, among Rembrandts and Raphaels, Whis-
tlers and Degas, each guest came to his own personal decision,
and the score was overwhelmingly in favor of Fenway Court.
That evening Mrs. Jack's palace took its place beside Bulfinch's
State House, the purple glass of Beacon Hill, Louisburg Square,
the Athenaeum, the Old Granary Burying Grounds and Symphony Hall as the seventh curio-wonder of the Proper Bostonian
World. William James, one of the honored guests at the occasion, was moved by the moral influence of the affair on Boston
Society. In a letter written to his hostess the following day, the
philosopher felt that a greater power than even Mrs. Jack had
called the turn at Boston's most memorable party:

> May I add, dear Madam, that the aesthetic perfection of all
> things (of which I will not speak, for you must be tired to
> death of praise thereof) seemed to have a peculiar effect on
> the company, making them quiet and docile and self-forgetful
> and kind, as if they had become as children (though children
> are just the reverse!) It was a very extraordinary and wonderful
> moral influence—expected by nobody, not designed, I am sure,
> by you, but felt, I am confident, by everyone today. Quite in
> the line of a Gospel miracle!*

Contemporaries of Mrs. Gardner on a far more modest scale
were Boston's three Palfrey sisters, Sarah, Anna and Mary.
Strictly speaking the Misses Palfrey were neither belles nor
grandes dames. They were not beautiful and they did not keep
salons or build museums, yet in a sense they did more than this.
In their respective lifetimes of ninety, eighty-four and seventy-

---

* *Isabella Stewart Gardner and Fenway Court,* by Morris Carter (Boston:
Houghton Mifflin) © 1925.

eight years, they epitomized the Puritan spinster type of woman-hood perhaps better than she has ever been epitomized before, and in the Hall of Fame of Boston's First Family femininity they carved themselves permanent niches.

To do this was no easy task. The Palfreys lived not in Boston but in Cambridge. Their father, the New England historian John Gorham Palfrey, formerly lived on Beacon Hill, a place where all true Boston spinsters have always belonged, but he was forced to move his family to Cambridge when he became head of the Harvard Divinity School. His daughters never quite got over their expatriation but neither were they ever able, even after his death, to get up enough steam to move back again. "We're retired Boston gentlewomen," they used to say, "sleeping in Cambridge." Fortunately the legend of the Palfreys soon became far too large for Cambridge Society to keep to itself. The historian John Fiske once described Cambridge—outside of Harvard—as the one place in Boston where no one "gives a damn who you are," but everyone seems to have given a damn about the Palfreys. Not that many people, even in their heyday, were privileged to know the spinsters personally. The Palfreys carried the Proper Bostonian's traditional aversion to enlarging acquaintanceships to a notable extreme. Though they travelled extensively in Europe, in this country they only once went farther than Nahant, Boston's First Family vacation resort some fifteen miles from the city. This was a trip all the way to Gloucester from which they returned surprised and pleased to report that they had met "several nice people" they had never met before.

The Palfrey girls had two brothers, both of whom married. There was no question of such a step for the sisters, however. Their mother was firm. She did not wish her home broken up until after her death, and since she lived to be ninety-eight, at which time only the youngest of her girls was under seventy, the male problem took care of itself in time. All the Palfreys, once vivacious brunettes, had made their Boston debuts before the Civil War, and the middle sister, Anna, who was the comeliest of the trio and had a plump figure, had had a fair share of admirers, but as the years went by even Anna's attendants became discouraged. The Palfreys became for all their charm a little timid about men. Harvard College, in the shadow of which they spent their hallowed lives, was ever a problem. When after the Spanish War some Cuban students were invited to attend the college, the sisters repaired in haste to ask the advice of their friend, President Eliot, as to whether or not he thought it would be safe for them to remain in their home—because, they said, "We hear the Cubans are very passionate people." When Sarah took up riding a cycle, her two juniors were so ashamed they promptly made her an apron which tied around her waist and hung so low that her ankles were made secure from possible peering eyes of Harvard boys. At this time Sarah, who is generally accorded the honor of being the first woman in Boston to ride a cycle of any sort, had just turned seventy-five.

"Aunt Sarah," as she was always called, was the queen of the Palfreys. Anna was prettier and Mary had what is described as a "regal beauty," but Sarah was the true charmer. The great-aunt and person for whom Sarah Palfrey Cooke, Boston's noted present-day tennis player, was named, she was a trim spry little soul who never weighed more than ninety pounds and yet tripped around Cambridge and Boston, on or off her cycle, with the greatest abandon. Her sisters were active but she was a dynamo. She painted vigorously, spoke four languages fluently, published poems in Latin as well as English, and was never averse to entering a controversy on any subject, by mail or in person. Not primarily a wit, she is credited with several sayings that have a place in the Boston legend. The most notable of these was her dictum on the state of wedlock of which, though as confirmed a spinster as her more modest sisters, she heartily approved. "Marriage," she said, "breaks down the natural barrier between the sexes."

Her sisters dead, at the age of eighty-eight Aunt Sarah went to Europe all alone, shortly before World War I, for what she declared was her "last look around." She came back to this country to take up during her final illness the study of Hebrew. When a friend remonstrated with her for the effort this involved, she said that she had always intended to take up the language and had put it off far too long as it was. "I wish to be able," she said with some finality, "to greet my Creator in his native tongue."

CHAPTER SEVEN

FAMILY NO. 1

When shortly after World War II Boston was planning a reception for General Eisenhower and arrangements were being made for the General to pass a night in one of the City's private homes, only one place was even seriously considered. This was a house at 177 Commonwealth Avenue. While there are more elaborate private homes in Boston's Back Bay, No. 177 is nonetheless Boston's address of addresses. In the entertainment of General Eisenhower it took immediate and unquestioned precedence over all other addresses in the same way its owner, Charles Francis Adams, a private citizen who has never held public office in Boston, took immediate and unquestioned precedence over all officials for the occasion. The Governor of the Commonwealth of Massachusetts might ride in triumph with the Chief of Staff in the big parade, the Mayor of the City of Boston might present the warrior with the keys to the city, but when it came right down to giving General Ike bed and board good old "Charlie Ad," or "The Deacon," as his friends variously call him, was the one and only choice. Now in his eighties and patriarch of all present-day Adamses, he is, in a City of First Families, Boston's acknowledged First Citizen.

As a Family the Adamses occupy a unique position in Boston's social hierarchy. From the pure Society standpoint they rank below the Cabots, to whom alone is accorded the honor of talking only to God. From the socio-intellectual standpoint they must be considered a step below the lordly Lowells who have, in recent years at least, outshone them in the fields of arts and sciences. From the socio-economic standpoint they are not in the running with the Forbeses, who are usually considered the symbol of Boston's inherited wealth and have a way of holding on to their money the Adamses have never learned. Nonetheless, the Adamses remain Boston's Family No. 1—and no questions asked or admitted.

The mere fact that an Adams was President of the United States before a Cabot had set up a shop in Boston, before a Lowell had manufactured either a textile or a poem, or before a Forbes had shipped to sea in the India trade, does not alone give them their exalted position. Neither does the fact that in the space of less than a hundred years they produced two Presidents, two Signers of the Declaration of Independence and three Ministers to England—a record that Cabots, Lowells and Forbeses all together cannot match. What places the Adamses on a pedestal above all other Boston Families has in reality little to do with either their early rise to fame or their early record of achievement. It is simply that the Adamses have gone on for well over a hundred and fifty years without having ever failed, for as much as a single generation, to come up with at least one man of outstanding eminence—and not just as men of eminence are so rated in Boston but as they are so rated on a national scale. Dixon Wecter, among the country's ablest social historians, unequivocally names the Adamses as the most distinguished Family in American history, and Wecter is a Texan who now makes his home in California.

Taking the Adamses all in all, Boston Society basks in the glory of their achievements and is entirely willing to accord present patriarch Charles Francis a sort of inalienable right to the city's First Citizenship. At the same time, while here and there a dowager may sigh, as one did recently, "Ah, the Adamses, *so* inhibited, *so* refined," Boston Society as a whole maintains certain reservations about their most illustrious single breed. Even at their best Adamses are not usually considered refined in the strictest sense of the word; at their worst they are regarded as socially defunct. James Russell Lowell had a line for the Family's proverbial tactlessness which is still a poignant phrase in the Proper Bostonian vernacular. "The Adamses," he said, "have a genius for saying even a gracious thing in an ungracious way."

Harsh as this remark may seem—especially from a member of a Boston Family which itself has never been known to carry off any blue-ribbon honors for civility—the Adamses have brought it on themselves. From the time of John Adams, who bluntly called John Hancock, Boston's first Society king, an "empty barrel," to the present-day Abigail Adams, who as a teen-ager in Boston's most fashionable debutante dispensary, Winsor School, is known as "a democratic girl," Adamses have been notably independent in their attitude toward Boston Society. Never kowtowers but prowd, cocky, cantankerous and intractable, they have met Cabots and Lowells, Beacon Hill and State Street, head on. When victorious in the fray they shook the Boston dust from their heels and moved on to Washington and higher things; when worsted they retired in good order to their so-called "Old House" in Quincy and wrote diaries and histories sternly critical of Boston and Proper Bostonians.

Quincy, the Adamses well knew, was on the wrong side of Boston's narrow-gauge social tracks. Yet for some four generations, until as recently as 1927—when their Old House, into which John Adams moved in 1787, was deeded to the public as a permanent Family memorial—they stubbornly refused to move to the neighborhood of Beacon Hill where they belonged. Even as a child of five Henry Adams could not help noting that there was something queer about being a Quincy boy. Later, in his *Education of Henry Adams,* he was to record that "though Quincy was but two hours' walk from Beacon Hill it belonged in a different world." As for the Boston of State Street, he wrote: "For two hundred years every Adams from father to son had lived within sight of State Street . . . yet none had ever been taken kindly to the town, or been taken kindly by it."

Henry, however, was putting it mildly. His brother Charles Francis Adams II, uncle of Boston's present patriarch, was not nearly so gentle. "Boston is provincial," he wrote. "It tends to stagnate." On Boston Society he was even more explicit. He found it "self-conscious" and "senseless" and a Society which seemed to have to pass through "a long period of cold storage." "I have summered it and wintered it," he declared, "tried it drunk and tried it sober; and, drunk or sober, there's nothing in it—save Boston!"

If they refused to court Society on the one hand, Adamses have always been known, on the other, for their almost equal obstinacy in regard to courting The People. Lacking the class-consciousness of the true blue-blood gentleman, they have at the same time evinced a lack of the common touch of the true red-blood politician. As more than one biographer of the Adams Family has noted, the word "we" is a rare one in the Family's vocabulary when it involves identification with the masses. Adamses are strictly "I" men. Generally speaking, they have been by the people and for the people, but not *of* the people. In the days of Presidents John and John Quincy an inch of a stoop was all the Family needed to conquer, but that inch was never forthcoming and neither John nor John Quincy could be re-elected for a second term. Today Charles Francis Adams, though he finds Boston's Irish "socially fascinating"—and is in return esteemed as a "good Yank" by them—still treasures his membership in the Somerset Club where he finds his closest friends. He readily admits that neither he nor any of his forebears have ever honestly attempted to learn what he, in the same manner one of those forebears would have used, rather wryly refers to as "the popular arts." In this respect it is noteworthy that the wives of Adamses have, through the generations, been singularly unhelpful to their husbands. Charming though she was, the first Abigail, wife of John, had her own wry way of referring to The People as "the mobility" and was hardly a political asset. No more so is the wife of the present Charles Francis who, though a woman of no little charm, is the Proper Bostonian type to her fingertips and a lady of considerable social gravity.

Their being thus, in a sense, neither fish nor fowl has never had the effect of making the Adamses an unhappy Family in Boston. Adamses have never had to stand either on the rather contrary verdict of Boston high Society or on the vagaries of popular acclaim. Adamses stand on their record. They are the only one of the First Families which has never been conspicuous on the wrong side of the ledger. In every other Boston First Family there have been men and women who were so pro-British or so pro-Southern, so anti-Lincoln or so anti-Wilson, that their activities stand as a dark reflection on the ability of these Families to cope with history on a national scale. Their present-day descendants are fated to read ancestral records with grimaces and decorously bowed heads. Not so the Adamses. They alone can hold their heads high, secure in the knowledge that hardly a single forebear ever failed, when the chips were down and his country called, to hew to the line of patriotism. One and all they put their country first and Boston, and often themselves, second. Furthermore, though often accused of seeking the limelight, no Adams since the time of John has ever basked in this light, once it came his way, in unseemly fashion. A typical case of exemplary conduct in this regard occurred as recently as 1929 when the present Charles Francis Adams took office in Washington as Secretary of the Navy. Since his great-great-grandfather had founded that Navy the moment was a historic one and the room was crowded with reporters and photographers. One of the latter asked the new Secretary to pose writing at his desk. Dutifully Adams sat down and glumly scribbled on a piece of paper while the bulbs flashed. Later the photographer retrieved the paper and read the line, "This is hell this is hell this is hell."

Like all other good Boston First Families the Adamses have their fair share of grandfather traditions and ancestral-duty complexes. Beyond this, however—and without any notable record of in-breeding or cousin marriages—they have also carried from generation to generation a remarkable similarity of physical characteristics. The so-called "Adams look" is an unmistakable one. Generally speaking Adamses are shorter than other Proper Bostonians but their look comes rather from their faces—their broad foreheads, sharply cut features, keen eyes and bulldog jaws. In an Adams face, it has been said, one can always see three things: intellectual power, iron will and calm determination. But Adams bodies, too, have given little cause for complaint. If one is an Adams he can almost take for granted the fact that he will live a long time. The maintenance of a severe standard of longevity is simply a part of the Adams tradition. Ferris Greenslet, able historian of the Lowell Family, noted rather sadly in his recent work, in which he made some comparison of Lowells vs. Adamses, that of the six most illustrious Adamses—John, John Quincy, Charles Francis I, Charles Francis II, Henry and Brooks—the average span of life was eighty-one years, whereas that of the twelve leading Lowells was only fifty-eight years. Since no Adams has ever been considered retired until he is in his grave, Adams hardihood has placed Lowells at a singular disadvantage in the Boston race for honors.

More than just being notable in man years per man, Adamses are also giants in man hours per day. In his eighties, even when "resting" at his country home in Concord, the present Charles Francis Adams does not get up at 6:45 every morning for any other apparent reason than that it is simply not in the Adams blood to lie abed in the early morning. In the Adams tradition he likes to "get something done" before breakfast, which he eats at 7:45. His great-grandfather John Quincy Adams, as Minister to Russia, also liked to get things done. In the middle of a Russian winter he made a habit of rising at three o'clock. Sometimes, he records in his diary, his fellow Americans would be just retiring, after an evening at the card table, as he began his day. Even then he complains that his time was too short: "If the day were of forty-eight hours instead of twenty-four I could employ them all so I had but eyes and hands to read and write."

Even the more minor of Adamsian character traits seem to

have come down undimmed through the years. Adamses, for example, have always had sharp tongues. Taciturn in social intercourse, they have never been known as witty people, but they have always had a way with the words they do part with. "Preserve your papers," old John Quincy told the members of New York's Historical Society a hundred years ago, "for some day," he roared pointing with his forefinger, "you may be assailed by the tongue of *slander!*" A young doctor present at the meeting declared in later years he doubted if a single person in the room would ever have forgotten the way Adams said that word "slander." Today Abigail Adams Homans, sister of Charles Francis, has become well known in Boston Society as a reparteeist simply on the basis of her Adams vigor of expression. Now nearing seventy, Mrs. Homans has mellowed to some extent, but she still has her moments. One of these came recently in the Ladies' Dining Room of the Somerset Club. A young man from Virginia was undertaking to describe the beauties of his native state in the fall. At length this proved exasperating to the ladies, and particularly Mrs. Homans. "Young man," she roared, spacing her words like whipcracks, "*hell* would be beautiful in October." Old John Quincy himself, Mrs. Homans' audience would have agreed, might have been proud of her that day.

The historian James Truslow Adams, whose work *The Adams Family* stands as a bible of Boston Adamses, has unearthed what is perhaps the most noteworthy of all Adams character traits and one which he believes has had almost as great an influence upon the Family's history as their continuous intellectual ability. This is their trait of self-dramatization. Since the time of John, the historian declares, Adamses have always imaginatively played the leading parts in whatever situations they found themselves and have always exaggerated in their own minds the odds against them to a remarkable extent. To an Adams, he shows, competition is no mere matter of chance:

A competitor is not merely a competitor; he is a malignant enemy, come from the Devil to destroy the noblest work of

God. Circumstances that may oppose their plans are not ac-
cidents; they are damnable efforts on the part of society to
thwart an Adams . . .*

While the historian declares he does not like to dwell on this
aspect of the Family he realizes its importance to any understanding of the Adamses as the one Boston Family which seems
to stem in most unadulterated fashion from the early Puritan
ministers. Their self-dramatization, he notes, has deified Adamses to dangerous proportions:

> In reading innumerable entries in the *Diaries* of John and
> John Quincy, as well as the *Autobiography* of Charles Francis
> and the *Education* of his brother Henry in the last generation,
> we are reminded of the *Diary* of Cotton Mather, whose vitu-
> perative vocabulary was even more copious, whose opponents
> were always "vile fools," "tools of Satan," and against whom
> the forces of society and of Hell itself were arrayed when any-
> one mildly disagreed with him. It is, indeed, an aspect of Puri-
> tanism, for if one is the elect of God what must, necessarily,
> one's enemies be? The inference to be made is of the simplest
> sort. To identify one's self with God is greatly to complicate
> one's social relations.†

From the practical standpoint nothing has complicated the
social relations of the Adamses more than the confusion result-
ing from the question of just what is an Adams and what is
not. To be a Boston Adams one must obviously be a Bostonian. James Truslow Adams, for example, historian of the Family though he is, has expressed himself as "quite satisfied" with
his own Virginia family of Adams and has made clear in the
first line of the preface of his book that he is not in the Boston
sense an Adams at all. But even in Boston the question is not
easy. As Boston First Families go, the Adamses are a very small
one today. Compared to a Family like the Boston Bowditches,
of whom a recent census revealed that there were no less than

---

* *The Adams Family*, by James Truslow Adams (Boston: Little Brown) © 1930.
† *Ibid.*

twenty-three individual families all tracing to the royal Bow-ditch ancestor, the navigator Nathaniel, the Adams royal strain is thin indeed. There are close to five hundred Adamses in the Boston telephone book and yet the families of royal Boston Adamses can be counted on one's fingers. Even the Boston *Social Register,* with its half-page roster of Adamses, is no infallible guide, since it contains several items of blended Bourbon strain.

Of late years Boston Adams confusion has been highlighted not only by the existence of two young men both of the name of John Quincy Adams and both of whom are in the royal line, but also by the existence of a Charles Francis Adams who is a prominent businessman but who is not royal at all. The former owner of the Boston Bruins hockey team, he is known to his friends as "Pop" but to strict Boston Society as "the wrong one," an appellation dating from the election of the royal Charles to the Tavern Club—when the royal name went up on the club bulletin board with the identification beneath it as "the right one." Some years ago Mrs. Charles Francis the royal Adams was called from bed in the middle of the night to answer her tele-phone. Since her husband is one of Boston's biggest financiers a late-hour phone call is no unusual occurrence in the household, but this particular one was. Her husband awoke to hear a re-markably short and severe conversation and, when his wife re-turned, worriedly inquired about it. "The Bruins' goal-guard," Mrs. Adams reported, "is in jail."

When the Proper Bostonian of today speaks of one of "The" Adamses, he actually means a member of only two tribes of the Family, for they are the only royal Adamses now left in the vi-cinity of Boston. One is the tribe of the late Charles Francis II and includes his two sons John and Henry and John's three children. The other is the tribe of Charles Francis III and in-cludes the present patriarch—who has dropped the "III"—his sister Abigail, two children of his late brother Arthur, together with his own son Charles Francis, Jr. and the latter's three children. Thus, in the final analysis, a royal Boston Adams to-day boils down to a baker's dozen. But such a typically ruthless Boston Society analysis does, of course, grave injustice to scores of one-time Boston Adams families now scattered all over the country, all of whom pyramid back, in genealogical sequence, to one of the nine children of the original Adams, a young farmer named Henry who came to Boston from England in the year 1636.

The date that Henry Adams chose to come over from England has a curious social significance, since it was also the year in which Harvard College was founded. Harvard and the Adamses were thus fated to start their triumphal march through Boston Society together, a march which is still proceeding strongly after more than three hundred years. More than this, however, it makes possible the measuring of the rise of the Adamses in their early generations by Harvard. From its founding Harvard spelled social prestige. Attendance at the college, and subsequent entrance into the ranks of the clergy, was in the seventeenth and eighteenth centuries: the only sure avenue to social success. It took the Adamses three generations to make Harvard —in the person of Joseph Adams, a farmer's son who became a minister—but once the Adamses had made Harvard, it took them only two generations more to make history. This they did not only in the person of John, another farmer's son who became his country's second President, but also in the person of John's cousin Sam.

Sam, the Man of the Town Meeting, and also of the Tea Party, has always been regarded in Adams history as a sort of custom-built offshoot on the recognized Adams assembly line of John—John Quincy—Charles Francis, etc. For one thing, Sam left behind him only daughters. For another, he was a popularist. He alone of all Adamses really did have the common touch— and was even rebuked for it by his cousin John who told him he was "too attentive to the public and not enough to himself and his family." Yet Sam managed this in the face of severe handicaps, even for an Adams. If John was plump, florid and vain and once described by Sir John Temple as "the most ungracious man I ever saw," Sam was no charmer either. His egg-shaped head gave him a humpty-dumpty appearance. When he gave a speech his hands trembled and his voice cracked. Socially, like John, he made the mistake of constantly tipping his spear in the social arena with "King" John Hancock. But the people turned to Sam. There is no finer testimony to the integrity of any Adams than the fact that Sam, as Boston's tax collector and an improvident man personally, was once in arrears to his city for a sum amounting to forty thousand dollars. No one ever seemed to question that Sam would some day pay it back, and pay it back he did, though his debts forced him to live to the day of his death in what he himself described as "honorable poverty."

The social story of John is a far happier one. Like his political life, however, which began with his undertaking of the unpopular task of defending the British captain tried for murder after the Boston Massacre, it was no easy road to start with. Shortly after leaving college he began courting, in the resolute Adams manner, a girl named Abigail Smith. Abigail's mother was born a Quincy and considered her daughter far above the normal reaches of John, the farmer's son. She did everything in her power to prevent the match, including burning a sizeable proportion of John's love letters, but John won in the end. In 1764, nine years after leaving college, he made Abigail his wife.

While never a political asset, Abigail was, from the day John married her, the biggest social asset any Adams ever had and is generally rated the most illustrious of all Adams wives. "No man has ever prospered in the world," she once wrote, "without the consent and cooperation of his wife," and from the social standpoint at least, John prospered mightily with this woman at his side. It has been Abigail's misfortune to be popularly remembered in social history by the fact that she once ordered Thomas Jefferson, when in Paris, to buy two pairs of corsets for her daughter—somehow assuming Jefferson would know the correct size. Actually, this was probably her only high Society *faux pas*. A nervous, sensitive girl, so delicate in health that as a child she never attended school at all, she moved in any Society circles smoothly and charmingly. Her *Letters,* most of them written to her "dearest friend"—the title by which she always addressed John—are a mine of material on the social life of the day. There were times of course, particularly on John's various diplomatic missions abroad, when a girl of her upbringing was bound to be shocked. Dining in Paris with her husband, Benjamin Franklin, and Franklin's good friend, the notorious Madame Helvetius, she winced when the latter put one arm around Franklin and another around John. Mme. Helvetius, Abigail sternly records, was *not* the kind of person she had ever before "met." At the Paris ballet she is actually wounded, and to her sister she writes from Auteuil under date of February 20, 1785, as follows:

> The dresses and beauty of the performers were enchanting; but, no sooner did the dance commence, than I felt my delicacy wounded, and I was ashamed to be seen to look at them. Girls, clothed in the thinnest silk and gauze, with their petticoats short, springing two feet from the floor, poising themselves in the air, with their feet flying, and as perfectly showing their garters and drawers as though no petticoats had been worn, was a sight altogether new to me.*

But later, after she had seen such dances repeatedly, Abigail learns to like them. And when separated from her husband she could write a very different type of letter. Once she wrote him with such passion that John immediately wrote back and told her to desist. What would the British think, he asked her, in cold roast Boston style, if they should capture a ship and confiscate the cargo and read one of her letters? Often he would punish her by not writing or by writing only commonplaces. Abigail could take just so much of this treatment. In one of her most noted letters, in September, 1778, she bursts forth in full fury against her Puritan spouse:

* *Familiar Letters of John Adams and His Wife Abigail Adams* (New York: Hurd & Houghton) © 1876.

In the very few lines I have received from you, not the least mention is made, that you have ever received a line from me . . . but I cannot take my pen, with my heart overflowing, and not give utterance to some of the abundance which is in it. Could you, after a thousand fears and anxieties, long expectation, and painful suspense, be satisfied with my telling you, that I was well, that I wished you were with me, that my daughter sent her duty, that I had ordered some articles for you, which I hoped would arrive, &c., &c.? By Heaven, if you could, you have changed hearts with some frozen Laplander, or made a voyage to a region that has chilled every drop of your blood; but I will restrain a pen already, I fear, too rash, nor shall it tell you how much I have suffered from this appearance of— inattention.*

Without Abigail John would undoubtedly have been, like most Adamses to come, a man of minor social activity. From her, however, he seems to have caught the spirit of the thing. As a young man of thirty-eight, meeting Lows, Scotts, Jays, Duanes and Bayards in New York, he seems to have forgotten he is socially a self-made man. "There is very little good breeding to be found," he writes. "I have not seen one real gentleman, one well bred man, since I came to town." As Vice-President he became worried about his title as President of the Senate. "When the President comes into the Senate, what shall I be? I cannot be President then. No, gentlemen, I cannot, I cannot. I wish gentlemen to think what I shall be." Assuming a coat-of-arms— which was later repudiated by his descendants—John found himself, on becoming President, variously dubbed "His Rotundity" and "Bonny Johnny." Once when the nature of aristocracy was being debated in the New York Constitutional Convention a speaker rose and said tauntingly: "I would refer the gentlemen for a definition of it to the Hon. John Adams, one of our *natural aristocrats.*"

John's answer is not recorded, but Abigail would have laughed the matter off. She had done her work well. To have

* *Ibid.*

made a "natural aristocrat" out of her farmer's son was no mean
accomplishment, and she took pride in it. At the same time,
though slightly baffled by its natural consequences—when
John failed to be elected for a second term—Abigail still stood
firm. "Every American wife," she once wrote in her later years,
"should know how to govern her domestics." Abigail was establishing the royal Adams line; in her world every American
wife had domestics, and that was that. On his own account, in
his rise to fame and social prestige, John too seems to have had
the royal Family urge. More than once he appears to have had
premonitions of establishing an Adams aristocracy. In a letter
to his wife in 1780 he declares:

> I must study politics and war that my sons may have liberty
> to study mathematics and philosophy. My sons ought to study
> mathematics and Philosophy . . . *in order to give their chil-
> dren* a right to study painting, poetry, music, architecture,
> statuary, tapestry and porcelain . . .*

The italicized portion, in view of the generations of Adamses
that were to come with Charles Francis and then Charles Francis' sons was prophetic indeed. First, though, there was to come
John Quincy.

John and Abigail had two other sons, who settled in Philadelphia and New York respectively, but it was on the shoulders
of John Quincy Adams that the royal mantle of the Adamses
fell for Generation No. 2. Boston social history is full of such
expressions as Puritan of Puritans, Yankee of Yankees, and
Bostonian of Bostonians, and in such a way John Quincy might
justly be called the Adams of Adamses. The ablest of all his
breed, and even for an Adams incredibly indefatigable in his
work habits, he has been accorded the highest I.Q.—165—of all
Americans in the Hall of Fame.

John Quincy's social quotient is a different story. For all his
sterling political qualities—his removal of just twelve office-
holders during his four-year term as President, and not one of

* *Ibid.*

them for "spoils," his refusal to accept a unanimously Senate-confirmed appointment to the Supreme Court because he said he was "unfitted" for the post, and instead, his humble return to Congress for eight successive terms until his death—he still manages to move through the pages of history as steadily and methodically, perhaps, but at the same time as coldly and in-humanly as a glacier. Where John had made Adams tactlessness a habit, John Quincy made it an art. Where John had been un-gracious, John Quincy was positively uncivil. He seems actually to have despised popularity. In a typically tactless remark in his later years he called an abrupt halt to what had been a mild upswing in the general feeling about him when he went out of his way to protest as an "insult to learning" Harvard's award of an honorary degree to Andrew Jackson, then the hero of the hour. Jackson, he said scornfully, could "hardly spell his own name."

The austerity of the John Quincy Adams legend is such that it is almost impossible to imagine him as a young man. A man who as a young diplomat rose at three o'clock and would not play cards when the stakes were "so high as to constitute gam-bling" is not easy to picture except as a grandfather. At the age of fourteen, however, John Quincy in Paris fell in love with a young French actress hardly older than he was. For seven years, he declared, he dreamed of her almost every night, though he admitted he had never once spoken to her or even seen her off the stage. In later years he stated, in his typical way, that he was thankful for this, because otherwise, he felt, he could not have helped declaring his love for her. "I learned from her," he wrote, "that lesson of never forming an acquaintance with an actress to which I have since invariably adhered and which I would lay as an injunction on all my sons." This was an injunc-tion which was further backed by another policy of John Quincy's, which was not to allow the Family carriage to be used for recreational purposes. If a son wished to attend the theatre he was obliged to walk from Quincy and back; this being a distance of some ten miles or more left little inclination for stage-door courtships.

The social behavior of this Proper Bostonian Adams of Adamses in the White House has certainly never been equalled by any President since. John Quincy had married in England an "internationalist," Louisa Catherine Johnson, a girl whose mother was English, whose father was American and who had spent all her early life in France. Even such training availed her little when it came to her trials and tribulations with her husband. As a social husband-pusher Louisa was no Abigail, but neither was John Quincy any John. No one ever pushed him, socially or in any other direction, in his life. He was, as his wife herself often admitted, "no mixer." His one contribution to Washington high life was the setting up of a billiard room in the White House—an action which shocked people but which gave him, as he played all by himself, a sort of "grim pleasure." He ignored all servants, and steadfastly refused to accede to his wife's wishes that he have a valet. Meanwhile, Louisa made the best of what she referred to as a "miserable" life. If she could not stop her husband from beginning a typical day with a reading of five books of the Bible, a pre-dawn hike of five miles and a nude, hour-long—significantly *against* the current—swim in the Potomac, while rude onlookers "laughed at his bald head popping up and down in the water," she did what she could with the remainder of the day. At her last "Drawing Room," it is recorded, she had the great new White House audience chamber thrown open for dancing—something which had never before happened at a Drawing Room in America.

The picture of Old John Quincy returning from the White House virtually penniless and finding every bit of real estate he owned, both in Boston and Quincy, mortgaged to pay his debts is not a pretty saga of Americana. Nonetheless, the role he was to play—going back to Congress for seventeen years until death, in the form of his second stroke, literally struck him dead on the floor of the House—fitted the grimness of his character far better than his diplomatic and White House life. There seems little question that he was actually happier in the part. The late Henry Cabot Lodge has preserved in writing a noted portrait of the old man's later years. According to Lodge, when Adams was seventy-seven he made a trip to New York where he shared a hotel room for the night with Dr. George Ellis, a prominent young Bostonian of the day. Ellis personally retailed to Lodge a description of the stay:

Mr. Adams would have no fire (it was November) but insisted on having the windows wide open . . . After talking some time Mr. Adams would say: "Now it is time to go to sleep and I am going to say my prayers. I shall say also the verse my mother taught me when a child. I have never failed to repeat it every night of my life. I have said it in Holland, Prussia, Russia, England, Washington and Quincy. I say it out loud and I don't mumble it either." Then he would repeat in a loud clear voice:

"Now I lay me down to sleep . . ."

At about 5 A.M. Mr. Adams would arise, and a wood fire being laid, would get from his trunk an old-fashioned tinderbox—he despised the recently invented lucifer matches—and would strike a light, kindle the fire and light his candle. Then he would strip, place a basin of water on the floor and sponge himself vigorously from head to foot. Then partially dressed, he would sit down by the fire, place the Bible on his knees, and holding the candle in one hand, expound a Psalm in the most vigorous manner.*

For the son of such a man to carry the Adams name forward in its third royal generation by virtue of his excellence as a diplomat would seem a defiance of the laws of heredity. It will be recalled, however, that John Quincy himself, not to mention his father before him, had also scored triumphs in this art. Unable to play diplomacy as a social game, by reason of their brusque manners, blunt tongues and general lack of *savoir-faire,* the Adamses practiced it instead of a profession, as dog-

---

* *Early Memories,* by Henry Cabot Lodge (New York: Scribner's) © 1913.

gedly determined as ambitious young lawyers entering the practice of law or new doctors entering medicine. The Adamses have apparently always known their own shortcomings, particularly when it came to manners and speaking. Rather than say the wrong thing, they said nothing. A curious little example of an Adams diplomatic triumph was won by John Quincy right in his own home, in the matter of his recalcitrant grandson Henry. Henry, going on seven, had rebelled one day against going to school and his mother could do nothing with him. Instead, he recalls, his grandfather, going on eighty, came quietly downstairs, put on his hat, put the boy's hand firmly in his, and walked him all the way to school. Henry was never to forget the way the matter had been handled:

> He had shown no temper, no irritation, no personal feeling, and had made no display of force. Above all, he had held his tongue. During their long walk he had said nothing; he had uttered no syllable of revolting cant about the duty of obedience and the wickedness of resistance to law; he had shown no concern in the matter; hardly even a consciousness of the boy's existence.*

John Quincy's son, Charles Francis Adams I, was to show the same kind of restraint in winning what has been called the most celebrated triumph in American diplomatic history—when he kept England, and France also, which most historians agree would have followed England, from siding with the Confederacy during the Civil War. Resembling his father strikingly in physical appearance, he was equally taciturn and has been called by a contemporary no more "companionable" a man. His self-control was close to absolute. One of his best friends wrote that he always believed him to be a man of warm affections and high temper but that, if he was, he "so concealed the one and controlled the other" that no one ever knew for sure. As Minister to England, in an English Society almost unanimously pro-

* *The Education of Henry Adams,* by Henry Adams (Boston: Mass. Historical Society) © 1918. (New York: Modern Library) © 1931.

Southern—its newspapers crying for war and its *Punch* car-
tooning Lincoln as a devil—Charles Francis stood almost
alone at his lonely post. But, as his own son Henry said of him,
if alone he was, he did not care. He had what Henry called a
singular "mental poise"—and also a "faculty of standing apart
without seeming aware that he was"—which enabled him, despite all difficulties, to stick to his job and see it through. Actually it is clear that he detested English Society. After six
weeks one finds him writing home that he had not been to "a
single entertainment where there was any conversation I should
care to remember," and he remained to the end, as Henry again
says of him, "one of the exceedingly small number of Americans" who was indifferent to dukes and duchesses and to whom
even Queen Victoria was "nothing more than a slightly inconvenient person."

By his marriage to Abigail Brooks, daughter of Boston's first
millionaire, Peter Chardon Brooks, Charles Francis I put the
Adams Family, for the first time in eight generations, on a firm
financial footing. No merchant, he had, in the Proper Bostonian
tradition, done the next best thing, the result of which was an
inheritance of some three hundred thousand dollars. It was a
social landmark in the Family's history. Charles Francis' sons
would be "free men." Never again would there be the spectacle
of an Adams returning from a lifetime of public service to find
Proper Bostonian "poverty" staring him in the face in Quincy.
When Charles Francis' own career was at an end, he would retire in style and enjoy to the full what has been called the only
recreation of all true Adamses—the writing, editing and publishing of Family papers. In turn he wrote the life and edited
the *Letters* of his grandmother Abigail; he wrote the life and
edited ten volumes of the papers of his grandfather; he wrote
his own *Autobiography*. In between, he brought his own fifty-
year diary up to date and finally edited twelve volumes of the
diary of his father. On the completion of the latter he declared: "I am now perfectly willing to go myself. My mission
is ended, and I may rest."

Not the least of his missions had been the leaving of no less than four sons, every one of whom was fated to carry the Adams name into its fourth and finest royal generation. The careers of these latter-day princes of the line were separate ones—including in the order of their age, John Quincy II in politics, Charles Francis II in business, Henry in literature and Brooks in history—but all were distinguished, and if every one of them had so much of Adams independence in him that he was also independent of his brothers, he was, still and all, an Adams. Indeed the similarity among the brothers is more striking than their noted accomplishments in their various fields. All were shy, all were sensitive, and all basically the inhibited Yankee type. All married well—John Quincy II and Henry a Boston Crowninshield and a Boston Hooper, respectively, Charles Francis II a wealthy New York girl, and Brooks a sister of Mrs. Henry Cabot Lodge—and all could have occupied the highest social positions they could have desired. Yet all were social rebels, not only against Society in general but against Boston Society in particular.

The eldest of the four horsemen, John Quincy II, father of the present Charles Francis Adams, was only a mild rebel. He made friends easily and was known as a "good fellow"—a rare social accomplishment for an Adams. But in a Boston Society ninety-nine and forty-four hundredths percent Republican, he became the leading Democrat in his state. And he rather confounded Boston's best by turning down the highest of all Proper Bostonian honors, the Presidency of Harvard. The youngest brother, Brooks, also staged only a mild rebellion. This took form in the publication of his book, *The Emancipation of Massachusetts*. All but forgotten today, it was in its time something of a bombshell, being in its approach an attack on Boston Society's beloved John Gorham Palfrey and his whole school of so-called "filio-pietistic" clerical historians. After Brooks' work New England history would never again be written by a school all too reminiscent of the Graveyard Eulogy School of biography.

There was nothing mild, however, in the frontal attack on Society as staged by Charles Francis II. The man who had tried Boston Society drunk and sober and found nothing in it save Boston was a severe critic of State Street Boston. Financially and outwardly successful in his work—his achievements included saving the Union Pacific from bankruptcy—he never found personal or social satisfaction in business. After his retirement he wrote scathingly of his connections in the commercial world, hugely enjoying the fact that such action enabled him to get in a few more words of his opinion of Boston Society, a Society which, as he well knew, was a businessman's Society through and through. "I have known, and known tolerably well," he records in his *Autobiography*, "a good many 'successful' men— 'big' financially—men famous during the last half century; and a less interesting crowd I do not care to encounter." Finding them, in the last analysis, a set of "mere moneygetters" and men "essentially unattractive and uninteresting," he declared: "Not one that I have ever known would I care to meet again, either in this world or the next."

The most famous of the brothers, Henry, whose *Education* stands as a classic of Americana, was always a rebel. On no other Adams, it has been said, did "the weight of the past settle so heavily" as it did on this greatest prince of its fourth royal generation. Henry, it might also be said, was close to being three quarters past tense to start with. He began his literary endeavors as a schoolboy by correcting the proof of his father's life of his great-grandfather, and he did not end them until the publication in 1918, after his own death, of his *Education*. As a boy Henry had rebelled against school. Returning from service as secretary to his father in London—where he had rebelled against English Society—he rebelled against Boston Society. He could not settle down in the city. Boston, he said, was full of his brothers. He did not want business and Boston had come to be business. The thought of life on Beacon Hill "lowered the pulsations of his heart." Offered a job teaching at Harvard, he refused it because, he declared, he knew "nothing of history,

less about teaching, and too much about Harvard." Instead
Henry went to Washington. Craving social success, he found it
in the capital. He became what he describes as a "young duke."
Then suddenly, almost despite himself, he returned to Boston
and started teaching history for "seven long years"—years which
he afterwards labelled as "failure."

Back in Boston Henry could never resist tossing barbs at all
that Boston Society held dear. When one of his students, the
late Henry Cabot Lodge, wrote him that he was considering
entering upon a career as a historian, Henry wrote back a reply
which failed to make a name for itself in the Athens of America:

> There is only one way to look at life and that is the practical
> way. Keep clear of mere sentiment whenever you have to decide
> a practical question . . . The question is whether the historico-
> literary line is practically worth following: not whether it will
> amuse or improve you. Can you make it *pay*, either in money,
> reputation, or any other solid value? *

Pointing out that such a line does pay as one of Boston's "most
respectable and respected" products, Henry commends such a
course to his noted pupil. Encouraging Lodge further, he mentions Prescott, Motley, Parkman and Bancroft as being men of
"no extraordinary gifts" and men who in any other field "would
not have been able to do very much in the world." As if such
mud-slinging at Boston's most beloved First Family scriveners
were not enough, Henry closes with a last ironic come-on:

> Further there is a great opening here at this time. Boston is
> running dry of literary authorities. Any one who has the abil-
> ity can enthrone himself here as a species of literary lion with
> ease . . . With it comes social dignity.

Henry never cared much for that "dignity," to which he so
often referred, of social Boston. But if he had no love for the
Boston Society of Beacon Hill he had even less for that part of

* *Early Memories,* by Henry Cabot Lodge (New York: Scribner's) © 1913.

Boston Society which he found residing in Cambridge. Unhappy in in-town salons and soirees he found himself equally
uncheered by the company of his confreres around Harvard.
"Several score of the best-educated, most agreeable, and personally the most social people in America," he wrote in his
Education, "united in Cambridge to make a social desert that
would have starved a polar bear."

The late Alexander Woollcott, who had been put out with
Henry for omitting to mention Mrs. Adams in his autobiography, claimed that it was characteristic of a man "who always
moved about the earth with something of the shrinking gait
of a professional violet crossing the ballroom floor." Actually,
however, rather than being characteristic, it is more probable
that Henry chose to omit mention of his wife in his autobiography because the book was not written until long after her
death and he simply preferred not to reopen the tragic chapter
of his life. Once one of Washington's most charming hostesses,
she became mentally ill and eventually committed suicide. That
Henry never recovered from her death is apparent. When the
ultimate in social success came to him, following the publication
of such of his works as his *History of the United States* and his
Mont St.-Michel and Chartres, he could not enjoy it. A social
rebel once more—this time by tragic circumstance—he spent
his last years in travel or virtually alone in his Washington home
where his well-known "brusqueries of manner" were a terror to
all but his intimates. An English visitor to Washington in these
years once declared that Henry was the one man in Washington "who called on no one and never left a card—not even on
ambassadors."

With the present Charles Francis Adams occupying a position
in the very bosom of Boston First Family Society, the revolt of
the Adams fourth generation would seem to have lost its steam
in the fifth. Where his father was a Democrat, Charles Francis

voted the Democratic ticket only through 1920 and then turned staunchly Republican, which he has been ever since. Where his father turned down the presidency of Harvard, Charles Francis eagerly embraced the position of treasurer of the University and held the job for thirty years. Where his great-great-grandfather had returned uncomplainingly from the Presidency of the United States to face his debts, Charles Francis says briefly of his two years as Mayor of Quincy: "I got $1000 a year. I couldn't afford politics."

At the same time, in the person of its present patriarch, there is no sign that Adams ability has died out in its fifth generation. Charles Francis has been rated an able Mayor of Quincy, an able Secretary of the Navy, and an extremely able Treasurer of Harvard. In his thirty years of handling the University's funds he escorted Harvard's endowment from twelve million dollars to a sum over a hundred and twenty million. He is the first of all Adamses to make a name for himself financially without incurring the wrath of State Street Boston. His list of directorships, numbering fifty-six different boards, is the most formidable one in the city today and a match for any other man in the country. One of Boston's long-time leading philanthropists, he is permanent president of Boston's Community Fund committee, and any large-scale charitable undertaking which takes place in the city is close to being suspect until it bears the regal letterhead endorsement—"Mr. and Mrs. Charles Francis Adams."

It is now, of course, high time for a sixth royal Adams generation to make its appearance on the Boston scene. Charles Francis is eighty. He cannot go on carrying the royal tradition indefinitely. He has no wish to be the last of the line and yet he well knows that there has in recent years been a discouraging tendency in the Adams Family to hark back, without—as the more illustrious Adamses always managed to do—at the same time bending forward. He has only one son, Charles Francis, Jr., who is a broker. While a necessary occupation in a Family whose financial empire is considerable, it is hardly one of proportions befitting a royal Heir Apparent. In the present patriarch's own generation his brother Arthur, who died some years ago at the age of sixty-nine, retired when he was thirty—sheer heresy for a royal Adams. The patriarch's cousins, John and Henry, of whom much was expected and who were sent out by their father Charles Francis II, to Lewiston, Idaho—where he had business connections and where he hoped they would "grow up with the country"—instead returned with startling rapidity to live near Boston and look after Family affairs.

It is just possible that there are too many present-day Adamses looking after Adams Family affairs. No one would deny Adamses the right to be Men of Family, but neither can anyone read the record of the breed without realizing that this right might also prove, in the end, the Family's Achilles' heel. Under the present patriarch there is still no danger. "My father," says Charles Francis Adams, Jr., "never talks much about Family. The day I first went to work he told me, 'I believe you've inherited a reputation for honesty—God help you if you lose it.' That was all he said."

Even the best of other Adamses, however, had the failing. Henry Adams in his later years, wandering and lost in the South Seas, found kinship even with the natives of Samoa. "They are tremendous aristocrats," he wrote. "Family is everything." Brooks Adams, last of the Adamses to live in the Old House at Quincy, had the Adams failing to a marked degree. As a young man he once had an experience with it which may or may not point a moral for future Adams generations. Brooks was turned down by the girl whom he had, after careful consideration, chosen to be his wife. At first he could not believe it. The girl could not understand whom she was refusing. Apparently, however, the girl did. She repeated her refusal. This time there was no mistake about it. Hastily Brooks Adams left the young lady's presence, never to press the matter again. But his departure included a last farewell.

"Why you perfect damn fool," he said.

CHAPTER EIGHT

WHOLESALE CHARITY

How clearly I remember reading when I was a boy the life of Amos Lawrence, the philanthropist. My employer gave me the book. I was sixteen years old. Mr. Lawrence was a great philanthropist who did big things in his time. He gave away more than one hundred thousand dollars to help mankind. I remember how fascinated I was with his letters. I can see as if the type were before my eyes now, how he gave away the crisp bills. Crisp bills! I could see and hear them. I made up my mind that, if I could manage it, some day I would give away crisp bills, too.*

Any Proper Bostonian of today might well be proud of that tribute, paid as recently as 1917 to one of Boston's most prominent Family-founding merchants. The speaker was John D. Rockefeller. While Boston's First Families have hardly been able to follow Amos Lawrence's example in such multiplied terms as Mr. Rockefeller, they have nonetheless done much to give their city a lasting reputation for charity on a wholesale basis. "There is not another city in the world," the New York *Herald Tribune* once declared, "which exhibits such constant benevolence." This praise for Boston, coming from New York, is high, and when added to the recent testimony of *The Nation*—that Boston was "the one place in America where wealth and the knowledge of how to use it were apt to coincide"—is impressive indeed.

* *Memories of a Happy Life,* by William Lawrence (Boston: Houghton Mifflin) © 1926.

At their peak production Boston's First Family merchants were founding not only their Families but also an average of one benevolent institution per year. In the thirty years from 1810 to 1840, for example, exactly thirty such institutions were established. Many of these are still in existence at the present time. In the middle of the last century, of the twenty-six rated millionaires living in or near Boston, almost all left behind them definite evidence of large-scale "good works." A pamphlet* published in Boston in 1846, summarizing the wealth of all men in Massachusetts worth $50,000 or more, had some kind words to say for practically all the millionaires. Of all the group together, a quarter were declared to be "more or less Benevolent," as follows:

No. of Rich Men in the State	1,496
Amount of property owned	$244,780,000
No. worth over one million dollars	18
" " just one million dollars	8
" " three fourths of a million dollars	10
" " half a million dollars	45
" " quarter of a million dollars	147
No. who began poor, or nearly so	705
No. who rec'd all, or the greater part, by inheritance or marriage	282
No. of rich Farmers	90
" " Manufacturers, (Cotton, Woolen, &c.)	53
" " Merchants (and Various Traders)	463
" " Lawyers (including Judges)	75
" " Physicians	31
" " Clergymen	12
" " Brokers (including some speculators)	46
" " Publishers	11
" " Editors	4
" " Shoe makers (and Dealers)	50
" " Tailors (and Clothes-Dealers)	10
" " Carpenters (and Ship-Builders)	15

* *The Rich Men of Massachusetts,* by A. Forbes and J. W. Greene (Boston: Fetridge & Co.) © 1851.

"	"	Masons	9
"	"	Butchers (and Provision-Dealers)	13
"	"	Distillers	14
No. ascertained to be more or less Benevolent			375
No. of Rich Old Bachelors			68

The figure of 375 "more or less Benevolent" out of the 1,496 total is a severe one. In computing it the writers of the pamphlet admitted to the application of a stern rule of thumb. Queen Victoria, they declared, gave $900,000 for relief of the Irish in the potato famine. Knowing the respective income of the Queen and that of a Boston laborer in their employ they stated that for the purposes of their pamphlet the latter would have had to give just eighty cents "to be precisely as benevolent as Her Majesty." They admitted using as a yardstick of benevolence another man they knew who had an annual income of twenty dollars and out of this annually gave fifty cents to charity. This man made it necessary, they claimed, for merchants like Nathan Appleton and Robert Gould Shaw to give, respectively, $37,500 and $50,-000 a year. Both of these men, being marked "benevolent" and "very benevolent," evidently passed even this acid test—a sterling tribute to the First Family merchant breed.

There can be little doubt that much of the merchant charity was given to settle the well-known ever-gnawing Proper Bostonian conscience. God may have made them rich men, as many believed, but few were sure enough of the fact not to put some earthly good works in their ledgers for added security in the final reckoning. One Boston merchant became so upset over his inability to stop worrying about a lost cargo on an overdue ship that, without waiting to hear the extent of his misfortune, he figured the total value of his ship and cargo down to the last dollar and gave that sum to the poor. Another Back Bay magnifico who, piqued by the high city tax rate, had moved out to the country—a practice which is still the bane of Boston's tax commission—recanted when faced with the local collector; he promptly assumed not only his own but all of his neighbors' taxes and paid the entire bill for the community. The son of Boston's great philanthropist, Amos Lawrence, and father of the late Bishop Lawrence, indulged in one of the most striking examples of Proper Bostonian conscience charity. It was in the days before the emergence of the Society for the Prevention of Cruelty to Animals and, a sensitive man, he could not bear the sight of old broken-down horses being bought and sold at Boston's Cattle Market each Thursday. He knew they would be put to work again and, to prevent this, he personally attended the market each week and bought the most pitiful cases; he would then lead these back to his home and have his gardener put them out of their misery. The kindheartedness which prompted his action did not prevent his establishing a huge burial ground for the animals under his grapevine trellis and proudly pointing out to his friends how he was killing two birds with one stone— putting animals out of their misery and at the same time considerably enriching his soil and increasing his crop of grapes.

In continuation of this conscience idea it has been noted that present-day First Family Society in Boston cannot really enjoy itself unless the proceeds of such enjoyment, over and above expenses, go for some charitable purpose. So recognized has become the custom of linking party-going with alms-giving that when the newly décored Hotel Somerset, old-time Society standby, recently held the gala postwar opening of its Balinese Room, guests were admitted by invitation only, and with reassurance that a part of their large entrance fee would go to the Girls' Club of Boston, Inc. According to one Society column the affair was "the most glamorous of the entire postwar season." Other hotels opening summer roof gardens, and even dance bands opening summer roadhouses, often abide by this tradition. "If you want to get the 'right people' in Boston out," an attendant at one of Boston's night spots recently remarked, "you've got to send them an invitation and tell them it's for charity. And," he added as a significant afterthought, "you'll probably never see any of them again until the next time you do it."

Today in Boston Society almost all dances for persons over

debutante age, and for which invitations are strictly limited, are benefit affairs. Such distinctly upper-crust steppings-out as the Waltz Evenings, which were started in Mrs. E. Sohier Welch's own living room, the Monday Art Openings, at which First Family debutantes are usually chosen to usher, and Mrs. John W. Myers' noted Morning Musicales, which has a waiting list of six hundred and for which First Family grandmothers have been known to will their tickets to grandchildren, are all charitable events. So, too, is the lecture series recently inaugurated by Mrs. William Dana Orcutt, wife of a prominent Boston author, called Boston's Mornings of Diversion. To the Proper Bostonian conscience it is enough that this kind of affair be for a charitable purpose; the actual charity is as immaterial as the charitable "take"—sometimes pitifully small. One hostess who never reveals the definite destination of her funds—her average guest being apparently satisfied with her general statement that the money goes to her "pet charities"—has been taken to task by a Society reporter, "We never have found out about the dough," she says, "how much or who gets." Even in the debutante department Boston's First Families must be comforted. "When your New England conscience rebels at a return to frivolity," recently counselled the Society editor of the Boston *Herald*, "remember that expensive parties put money into circulation and that thousands of people, including dressmakers, florists, wine dealers and caterers, are benefited."

Hand in hand with the conscience tradition there has come down in Boston a definite feeling for charity on a class basis. The example of one of Boston's earliest merchants who left his money to provide for persons reduced "by the Providence of God from Affluence to Penury"—and then, twenty-five years later, was again "by the Providence of God" called upon to "solicit his own charity"—would seem not to have been lost upon later generations of merchant Families. Of the eighteen Family trust charities in existence in Boston today six of them must still be administered, by the stern wills of the donors, on what amounts to a riches-to-rags basis. The largest of these, the David

Sears Charity, representing a sum of over $300,000, goes directly, in the words of its donor, "for the support of citizens or families who may have seen better days." The Boylston Relief fund is even more specific and must be administered, again in the words of its originator, for the relief of persons "reduced by the acts of Providence, not by indolence, extravagance or other vice."

Long-standing First Family institutions have benefited greatly by this kind of severely upper-bracketed charity. The Boston Symphony is of course one of these. Another, of far more ancient vintage, is the Boston Athenaeum, the city's "gentlemen's library." Still another is the Massachusetts General Hospital. This old-line blue-blood institution stands unique among hospitals in its sheep-and-goat division of private patients, having its Baker Memorial for persons with incomes of $7000 or less, and its Phillips House for persons with incomes exceeding $7000. The price of rooms and doctors' fees are scaled accordingly. In the Baker no doctor may charge more than $150 regardless of the nature of the operation he may perform or the number of times he may have to see his patient; in Phillips House he may charge what the traffic will bear.

But these institutions, favored as they have been by Proper Bostonian alms, are hardly more than beggars beside Harvard University. Boston Proper's prime example of patrician charity, Harvard literally overflows—all the way from its Sears Observatory to its Weld Boat House—with First Family benevolences. They have been in no small part responsible for making it the most heavily endowed institution of learning in the world. From even a casual study of its finances it is apparent that Boston's great merchants, along with establishing their Families at the "right" time, also gave their money to Harvard at the right time. A "Fund for Assisting Students," for example, established in 1838 with just $11,350 has grown simply by accruing interest, without the addition of any more capital, to be worth some half million dollars to the University today. But Harvard has not lacked for pin money in more recent times. The late Lawrence

Lowell, in his recent twenty-four-year tenure as president, personally gave the University more than two million dollars in Lowell money. Almost steadily through the years into Harvard's coffers has come Cabot money, Forbes money, Adams money, Peabody money, Appleton money—indeed some money from every First Family in Boston. It would undoubtedly be erroneous to assume that all the individual members of these Families, or even a majority of them, felt the "class angle" in their giving, but at least one who did was Boston's beloved Major Henry Lee Higginson. Never averse to giving advice to fellow philanthropists—which he did by writing such aptly titled articles as "A Word to the Rich"—Higginson was a lavish giver to his alma mater and once stated that not even the establishment of Boston's Symphony had given him more solid satisfaction than his generosity to Harvard. Writing to a cousin he reveals his feelings on the subject:

Dear ——:
Nobody knows his duties better than yourself—therefore I presume to admonish you. I want you, as the oldest and richest member of your family and mine, to give to the College $100,000, to be used in any way which seems best to you.

My reasons are that you, a public-spirited and educated gentleman, owe it to yourself, to your country, and to the Republic. How else are we to save our country if not by education in all ways and on all sides? What can we do so useful to the human race in every aspect? It is wasting your time to read such platitudes.

Democracy has got fast hold of the world, and *will* rule. Let us see that she does it more wisely and more humanly than the kings and nobles have done! Our chance is *now*—before the country is full and the struggle for bread becomes intense and bitter.

Educate, and save ourselves and our families and our money from mobs! *

* *Life and Letters of Henry Lee Higginson,* by Bliss Perry (Boston: Atlantic Monthly Press) © 1921.

The pattern of Proper Bostonian benevolence was early indicated by the writers of the pamphlet about the generosity of Boston's merchants. In a paragraph devoted to the merchant Moses Kimball the writers issue a characteristic warning. "Moses," they declare, "is benevolent, only let him alone. He must give just when, where, and how much his own separate judgment approves."

Moses was by no means an eccentric in this regard. John Murray Forbes in his will charged his heirs to use some of the millions he left them "within prudent limits" for charities which they could watch "under your own eyes." The merchant Augustus Hemenway gave his heirs a freer hand but begged them not to use a cent of the $100,000 in gold he left for charity "to make two paupers where there was but one before." Samuel Dexter, president of Massachusetts' first temperance society, could not bear the idea of any of his charitable donations ever going to drinkers. "Give me the money," he once said, "paid for the support of drunken paupers in the United States and I will pay the expenses of the Federal and of every state government in the United States, and in a few years beome as rich with the surplus as the nabob of Arcot." Dr. John Warren, one of the founders of the Massachusetts General Hospital, was also concerned with the problem of alcohol. His will left one hundred bottles of his best wine to his friend, the merchant William Appleton, recommending at the same time its use "only as a medicine and not during health."

Present-day Boston fortune-leavers show the same sort of individuality in their wills. Recently a Brookline man with the true Proper Bostonian love of "comfortable" size trust funds set up one at his death to provide an annual income of $5000 for the care and upkeep of his cat. A Wellesley widow provided an equal size fund for the care of a Mexican parrot. When the late Colonel William A. Gaston, former head of Boston's blue-blood Shawmut bank, died some years ago, he left an estate of six million with public bequests totaling only $6500; he explained this in his will by saying he had all his life been "a consistent giver to charity." The wife of a Boston Cabot may have felt the same way; in any event her will stipulated that each of her servants should receive the sum of five dollars. On the other hand, when one of the last of the so-called "Grand Old Men of Newbury-port" died a few years ago, he left his half-million-dollar fortune almost entirely to charity, leaving for his relatives only a few thousand dollars. He specified that this latter should be given at a ratio of twice as much for each male relative as for each fe-male. This male favoritism, in keeping with the Proper Bosto-nian lineage tradition, is not unusual. In just one year during its Tercentenary celebration Harvard raised a sum equal to half the total endowment of Wellesley College, and while private schools for boys as well as girls have felt a severe pinch in recent years, it is notable that the girls' institutions have had the harder time. In 1946 Beaver Country Day School, second only to Win-sor in social prestige, was actually threatened with mortgage foreclosure—to be saved in the nick of time when a determined band of Boston mothers, plying the Brookline streets in station wagons and button-holing even well-wishers who had never heard of the school for contributions as low as a dollar, raised the sum of $150,000 in just four weeks.

One reason for the Proper Bostonian's inclination to roll his own where charity is concerned is that it has always been consid-ered a cardinal sin of Yankeeism to be an easy mark. Benevo-lent as his conscience may make him, the Proper Bostonian would far rather be called a miser than a sucker. To his dying day Benjamin Franklin never forgot, as a boy in Boston, having paid too much for a whistle. For his charity he always wanted, in the Boston fashion, his money's worth. Going to hear the famed British Methodist Preacher, George Whitefield, one day on the Common, Franklin went with copper, silver and gold in his pocket. At first intending to contribute nothing, he soon de-cided to give up his copper; then another bit of the preacher's oratory induced him to part with his silver, and finally he gave even his gold. Franklin had made each decision himself and each in his own good time. He afterwards wrote that if the preacher had begun by asking him point-blank for money he wouldn't have given him a penny.

Ever since Franklin's time "easy does it" has been the motto of fund raisers in Boston. As a city Boston was the last to give in to the idea of all-inclusive Community Fund drives, not having done so until the last depression, and there are still many Proper Bostonians who feel such drives are a mistake and would rather continue support of their own individual—and carefully watched—so-called "goatfeathers," or hobby-charities. To them their purse is a touchy matter and comes untied only when the approach is correct. Knowing this, leaders of Community Fund and Red Cross drives keep what is called a "Special Gifts" list. A sort of Blue Book of Benevolence, it includes a large proportion of all Proper Bostonians and the regular house-to-house canvassers for the drives have nothing whatever to do with it. First Family doorbells are rung only by a special hand-picked crew. "It's undemocratic," declares a recent Red Cross chairman, "and our regular workers don't like not being allowed a crack at the big money, but we can't take a chance with their getting excited and using high pressure. You just can't high-pressure 'Special Gifts.' "

The late Bishop Lawrence always counselled against high pressure. "My rule," he wrote, "is never to allow a person to sign a pledge in my presence . . . If I should get it by personal pressure, I should never succeed with that man a second time." As the grandson of Amos Lawrence, Boston's greatest First Family philanthropist, it was fitting that the Bishop, a businessman at heart, should become Boston's greatest First Family fund raiser. He began as a boy at college raising money for Harvard's Hasty Pudding Club and he ended, as a man of ninety—"like a war-horse who again scents the smoke of battle," a biographer has written—raising money for a chapel for the Massachusetts General Hospital. He loved his work. "An invigorating avocation," he called it, one "more exciting than trout-fishing" and "you have all the fun of the gambler and do not gamble." Some causes the Bishop liked better than others. He found frankly "dull" the raising of $1,000,000 for Cambridge's Episcopal Theological School, and he hastened to complete the job in ninety days. On the other hand he enjoyed the raising of $8,800,000 for the Episcopal Church Pension Fund so much that he took a year off from his work as Bishop, procured himself a Wall Street office, and had what he called the happiest time of his life badgering Morgans, Vanderbilts, etc. for their money. From the late William K. Vanderbilt, he proudly reported in his notebook, he "got $100,000 in five minutes," which was unquestionably par for the New York circuit. An even more impressive testimonial came to him one day in the dining car of the New Haven Railroad on a trip back to Boston. A Bostonian who entered the car, knowing him by reputation and anxious to avoid an appeal which he felt sure would be forthcoming for some fund or other, moved up stealthily to the Bishop's table, dropped a five-dollar bill beside the sugar bowl, and disappeared back out of the car the way he had come.

Bishop Lawrence was a firm believer in the correct approach. He knew his Proper Boston woman as well as his Proper Boston man. Edith Forbes Perkins was so charmed by a "Letter to the Public" he had written to the newspapers asking for money for Harvard that she could not forbear noting in her diary that "the Bishop's appeal for the ten million dollars is like a poem, it's so lovely." Certainly millionaires, either in Boston or New York, had nothing to fear from the Bishop. If the millionaire is charitable, he declared as far back as 1900, he is "Christ's as much as was St. Paul, he is consecrated as was St. Francis of Assisi . . . Material prosperity is helping to make the national character sweeter, more joyous, more unselfish, more Christlike." It is doubtful if the conscience of the Puritan moneymaker was ever more comfortably embalmed.

An example of the incorrect approach to the Proper Bostonian was once used on the merchant John Murray Forbes. A woman charged her way into the Forbes' counting room and told him she had heard he had more money then he knew what to do with. She wanted some of it for herself and her son. Forbes was taken aback at her frankness. "Madam," he said sternly, "I will think of it." The woman was doubtful. "I'm afraid you won't do it," she said. It was then Forbes' turn to be frank. "I'm afraid I shan't," he said, and ushered her out. For a merchant like Forbes even the lending of money to friends was a delicate matter. His friend Robert Gould Shaw, at one time the most opulent merchant in his city, was one day stopped on the street by a younger friend who asked him for a loan of ten dollars. Shaw was willing on one condition—the man would have to agree not to "turn his face away" when they next met. A month ago, he said, he had loaned another friend a small sum of money and had since been cut by the man. "When I lend a man money," he declared, "and he is owing me, I want him to look me full in the face, as though nothing had happened. And then I shall be willing to lend him again."

In his money-giving the Proper Bostonian has often exhibited a passion for anonymity which has ranged from a simple desire to keep his name out of the papers to the extreme of not wishing even the recipients of his kindness to subject him to the embarrassment of thanks. Lawrence Lowell, suspected of giving Harvard's mammoth Indoor Athletic Building, gave it—if he did— so quietly that to this day no member of the Lowell Family is sure of the fact. For many years three First Family directors of Boston's Children's Hospital annually took upon themselves the task of making up the institution's entire deficit—a sum that amounted to as much as $20,000 a year for each of them—in such secrecy that even other members of the hospital's board did not know where the money was coming from. The head of a Boston textile concern who died several years ago was known for never having made a charitable donation by writing a check; whether his gift was a large donation to a public fund or a baseball ticket to the elevator boy, he wished his name in no way connected with it. Before Christmas each year he handed an itemized address list to a secretary in his office who then distributed to those named on it certain sums of money in blank envelopes. The secretary was instructed to say only that the money

was from a "gentleman friend." Word soon got around among
the man's Christmas circles, however, that those who made the
mistake of thanking their benefactor were striken from the list
for the next year.

"When I can do a good action and at the same time make
money," a latter-day Proper Bostonian once declared, "I find
that all my powers are moving in harmonious cooperation."
This type still exists in Boston along with that of the legendary
Trinity Church vestryman who, so the story goes, regularly
rented several "centrally located" Family pews on a yearly basis,
subletting them for shorter periods of time at a substantial
profit, and then regularly returned a tenth of this profit to the
collection plate each Sunday. Historically the best example of
the type was probably Peter Chardon Brooks, Boston's first millionaire. In his day Brooks was the happy choice for treasurer of
Boston's Washington Monument Society. Ten thousand dollars
had been raised for the monument but the sculptor was somewhat dilatory and by the time he had finished his work the sum
had accumulated in Brooks' golden hands to $17,000. Thus it
was possible to plan for an elaborate stand for the monument.
By the time this was done Brooks had even more to report from
his investments and in the end the venture practically paid for
itself. Brooks, who on his own admission never "willingly endorsed the obligation of a friend," nonetheless believed in large-
scale charity when it could be properly managed by trustees. On
an individual basis he was a stern man indeed. Throughout the
latter years of his life, at which time he was worth some four
million dollars, he reluctantly parceled out as a pension to an
elderly housekeeper who had at one time worked for him the
sum of one dollar a week.

Today's Boston Cabot Family have as high a reputation for
generosity as any First Family in the city. "Wherever there's a
cause there's a Cabot, and vice versa" has become a familiar
Boston saying. Godfrey Lowell Cabot, present-day patriarch of
Cabots, recalls that as a young boy he was brought up with the
idea that any extra money he had was money to be used for those

less fortunate than himself. His parents made him give to charity his very first "extra," an addition to his allowance that he received one Christmas. For many decades head of Godfrey L. Cabot, Inc., huge carbon black empire, he is today perhaps Boston's wealthiest man. Now going on ninety he estimates that by the time he dies he will have given to charity close to three million dollars. But there is probably no Proper Bostonian who hews to a sterner line of parting with his money in his own way. "Godfrey," a friend once remarked, "would give you his shirt if he thought you needed it and you hadn't asked for it. Ask him for something and, well, he sort of gets his back up."

The spectacle of a Boston Cabot with his back up—Cabots not being notably amenable people under the best of circumstances —would be a terrifying one to most solicitors for charity. On the Cabot record, moreover, there is at least one authentic story in which this was so. Stephen Cabot, younger relative of Godfrey and head of the Judge Baker Foundation, one of Boston's largest philanthropic organizations, tells the tale on himself. Walking across the Common one day he was accosted by a man obviously under the influence of liquor who boldly asked him for a quarter. Cabot looked at the man reproachfully. "My man, you've been drinking," he said. "I can't give you anything." Replied the man promptly: "Well, it would take a couple of drinks before I could ask a guy like you!"

In contrast to the Proper Bostonian merchants who usually adhered severely to the functional in their charities—a classic example being their allowing the Hancock House to be torn down for taxes—the Proper Boston woman has always gone in heavily for the sentimental. Mrs. Mary Hemenway, a merchant daughter, was so outraged at a group of her father's friends who had conspired to sell the Old South Meeting House, rendezvous of the Boston Tea Party, that she gave $100,000 to preserve it. A firm believer in the culture of the Indians, she regularly entertained representatives of such tribes as the Zunis at her home on Boston's North Shore, and spent the better part of her life attempting to have Indian corn made the country's national emblem. Rivalling Mrs. Hemenway in sentimental munificence has been Mrs. James Jackson Storrow, wife of a Lee, Higginson head who was a Boston "First Citizen" of the twenties. Some years after her husband's death Mrs. Storrow gave the Boston Park Commission the outright gift of a million dollars to have Boston's Charles River "beautified," a problem with which the Commission is still struggling.

It is noteworthy that both Mrs. Hemenway and Mrs. Storrow were able to go in for such largesse only upon the death of their husbands. Rarely is it the practice of Proper Bostonian husbands to open their books to their wives' scrutiny during their lifetime, and many a charitably inclined First Family wife has had such inclinations stifled until she was able to emerge on her own. Unless or until her husband died, the phrase "Not alms, but a Friend" coined by the late Proper Bostonian, Robert Treat Paine, for the use of Boston's Family Welfare Society, has often been stark necessity for her. Membership in Boston's old-line charitable sewing circles was actually forfeit if a woman failed to do a fair share of what was called "personal" work. Mrs. Elizabeth Dwight Cabot was a long-time leader of this kind of charity. In her work she always believed in bringing to the level of the poor what she frankly referred to as the "spiritual wealth" of those more financially privileged. Writing on this subject she declared:

> If we go to them [the poor] with hope and love in our hearts, with the offer of some better opportunities or some teaching in their ignorance, if we can win them to wise exertion, we do far more than help them to material improvement . . . God's justice and judgment has to be taught them, and whether love shows itself in teaching honesty and cleanliness and thrift or in sympathy, it comes to the same thing.*

* *Letters of Elizabeth Cabot,* by Elizabeth Cabot (Boston: Privately printed, 1905).

Long a favorite among such unmaterial gifts to the poor by Proper Boston women has been the donation of flowers. In vain did merchant Joseph Lee affix the slogan "Don't tie on the flowers—water the plant" to the Massachusetts Civic League. Boston women would have none of it. Early in Mrs. Elizabeth Dwight Cabot's charitable career she organized the Society for the Preservation of Wild Flowers in Brookline, a venture apparently designed to show that the only abundance that mattered, that of the Almighty, was available to everybody. Where Mrs. Cabot led, others followed. A member of the Fay family, for example, describes her mother-in-law's pet charity as recorded in a latter-day Fay diary:

> She had her own particular way of helping those less fortunate than herself. One of her great pleasures was to go out into the country, in the spring, and gather huge bunches of wild flowers—buttercups, clover, and daisies—and then drive out to the North End and scatter these flowers among the children she found playing in the streets.

The picture of Boston's Old Lady Bountiful, as she was called, primly dressed in black, with snow-white hair and a tiny muslin cap, plying with posies the streets of one of Boston's rougher districts, would seem, to say the least, a slightly dated one. But there is some evidence to support the fact that flowers from First Family ladies have been appreciated among Boston's less privileged even in more recent times. The late Mrs. Jack Gardner used to dress her Beacon Street windows with an almost constantly changing parade of floral arrangements. So evident was the gratitude in the faces of passers-by, she was fond of saying, that she never for a moment considered it anything but her bounden duty to continue it faithfully—and even did so during the trying days of her husband's last illness. More recently Mrs. Edwin S. Webster, outstanding Boston horticulturist, returning to her Commonwealth Avenue home which had been closed during World War II, revived her habit of putting an abundant display of flowers in the bay window of her house. With gratifying promptness anonymous cards and letters began to make their appearance, many being pushed under the Webster door by people who would not have dared to ring the bell. Mrs. Webster was thanked in glowing terms. Later exhibiting the evidence of the appreciation to a friend, she was moved to remark, "You know, I really feel I'm doing a great deal for those people."

In the story of one of Boston's most famous First Family charities, the Lowell Lectures, there is a flavor of real romance. These lectures were endowed more than a century ago by the merchant John Lowell who drew his will establishing them while broken by ill health and personal misfortune and as he sat on the banks of the Nile—literally as he wrote the document—"gazing in awe" at the old-world ruins of Thebes. The sum he left, a quarter of a million dollars, was up to that time with the exception of Philadelphia's Girard bequest the largest gift of its sort ever made by a private individual, and the will was drawn in the typically grand manner of the Family-founding merchant. Lecturers had to believe in "the divine revelation of the Old and New Testaments" and listeners were to be "neatly dressed and of orderly behavior." Every trustee of the fund must forever be a male descendant of his grandfather—"preferably one bearing the name of Lowell if among them anyone has the necessary qualifications." To their credit the Lowells, a Family which in one latter-day generation was able to produce a Harvard president, an astronomer, and an outstanding poetess, have always proved equal to the challenge, and today Ralph Lowell, president of the Boston Safe Deposit and Trust Co., represents the fourth generation from Merchant John to carry on the trusteeship of the fund. In their hands the original $250,000 has become, Lowell-fashion, $2,000,000.

The Lectures have always been notable for their bringing to Boston authorities of international repute, and the second chapter in the Lowell charity romance began early in their history with their inducing the great Swiss naturalist, Louis Agassiz, to come to Boston. Agassiz had once refused another invitation to come to the United States with a statement still puzzling to all true merchants—"I cannot afford to waste my time making money"—but for the Lowells he came. Shortly after his arrival the matriarch of the Boston Cary Family, a daughter of old Colonel Perkins, returned from church one Sunday. To her daughter Elizabeth, later president of Radcliffe College, she said in the direct Perkins manner, "I should like to know who it was who sat in the Lowells' pew this morning, for he is the only person I ever saw whom I should like you to marry." On learning the man was Agassiz, who had a wife and three children in Europe, she let the matter drop, only to pick it up again after a suitable interval when she also learned that Agassiz's wife had died suddenly. In the end Mrs. Cary, like most Proper Boston women, had her way. A social page for the day of April 25, 1850, records an important event in Boston's historic King's Chapel —the wedding of Mr. Louis Agassiz of Neuchâtel, Switzerland, and one Miss Elizabeth Cary, of Boston. The page further reads that "Lizzie looked lovely dressed in green silk, white camel's hair shawl, straw bonnet trimmed with white, and feathers on each side."

The final chapter of the saga concerns the third of Agassiz's three children by his first wife. All these children, brought over from Europe, had married into Boston First Families—a Shaw, a Higginson and a Russell respectively—and Alexander, the third of the children and the only son, had become a teacher at Harvard. Branching out from this he became interested in some copper mines purchased by his brother-in-law, Quincy Adams Shaw, in Northern Michigan. Searching for geological specimens on the shores of Lake Linden he came upon a prospector who showed him a nugget of copper he had found. Agassiz thanked the man, asked him where he found the nugget, and near where the man told him to search he discovered a likely looking vein of copper ore. Filing claim to the property, Agassiz hustled back to Boston, told his sisters Pauline Shaw and Ida Higginson the good news; then, all together, they founded on a distinctly social basis—not only among Shaws, Higginsons and Russells but also among Cabots, Paines, Grays, Gardners, Bowditches, Coolidges, etc.—a fabulous reviver of Boston First Family wealth, the Calumet and Hecla mine. For half a century, from 1871 throught the 1920's, the magic words Calumet and Hecla were Beacon Hill passkeys. The number of shares held in the mine was a fair index of a Family's Society page size, and the stock, issued at $12.50, rose to over a thousand dollars a share and paid to one of its entrepreneurs, Major Higginson, dividends alone of over four hundred percent of the original capital he had invested. The fact that it may today be purchased at a rather more modest figure is inconsequential. Most of Boston's First Families have long since liquidated their holdings in favor of less speculative—and less romantic—investments.

Irrespective of their romance and of the handsome way, through Agassiz and Calumet and Hecla, they have "paid off" to Boston's First Families, the Lowell Lectures are still very much of a going concern in Proper Boston. Currently given at the rate of a hundred a year, free to the public and broadcast over seven Boston radio stations, they have become a sort of textbook example in Boston's history of charities of the wisdom of wholesale beneficence on a private basis. An even older First Family charitable institution, on the other hand, the Massachusetts Humane Society, has provided a rather powerful example of quite a different kind.

Dating from 1785, the Humane Society was founded for the purpose of saving lives at sea. Originally it provided huts and lifeboats. Then, with the emergence of the Coast Guard, it turned to giving medals and money for acts of heroism and instruction in swimming with the cooperation of the State Y.M.C.A. At length overwhelmed with trying to give away its income surplus—from an original trust fund of $400,000—in such ever-narrowing spheres, it began in desperation giving money to any and all worthy causes, among them the Boston Lying-In Hospital. Finally it has turned itself over to becoming not only a charity but in the words of one of its historians, "frankly and gracefully dedicated to the most lavish, the most delicious, and the most memorable annual dinner known to the U. S."

Trustees of this remarkable Society admit that they have no longer anything to do but attend this dinner and, since there are eleven of them, pay for it every eleventh year. Officered by Charles Francis Adams, Francis Lee Higginson, T. Jefferson Coolidge and Leverett Saltonstall, the Humane men form what is perhaps the most impeccable social organization in Boston and, if they admit to being outdated as a charity, they will not admit to being outdated in their idea of how gentlemen should eat. A menu, served course by course in its entirety at the home of Charles Henry Joy in the year 1883, still stands as the Society's mark to shoot for, as follows:

Hidalgo Brown Sherry
Oysters
Royal Pale Sherry
Clear Soup
Latour Blanche
Boiled Chicken Halibut   Tomatoes
Pommery Sec
Boiled Capon, Chestnut stuffing   Truffles   Vegetables
Veuve Cliquot
Grouse with Fresh Mushrooms   Oyster Cutlets
Vol-au-vent
Chateau Margaux 1864
Ducks
Peter Dumesq Sherry
Cafe Parfait
Blue Seal Brandy
Frozen Pudding with Peaches
Old Ruby Port
Cheese
Madeira*
Dessert

*Daniel Webster 1795
Farquar
Benjamin Joy
Codman D.
Carolina

CHAPTER NINE

RETAIL PENURY

The distinguished lawyer Arthur Train once observed that the character of the true Bostonian was a combination of whole-sale charity and retail penuriousness. When one takes into account that the same authors, who a hundred years ago published a pamphlet bestowing bouquets on the Boston merchants for their large-scale munificence, could not resist at the same time handing the merchants all manner of brickbats for their personal economy, it is clear that the Proper Bostonian, merchant-blooded as he is, came by his reputation deservedly and that Mr. Train knew whereof he spoke.

The pamphleteers describe one merchant as a "lean and hungry" man; another, evidently a merchant unable to retire his thoughts from his counting room even after dark, as a man who "seldom sleeps o' nights." Still a third is a man who, though a "Rich Old Bachelor," will not consider allowing himself a housekeeper "since wages have o'erleaped a dollar a week." Of the millionaire John Bryant, of the shipping firm of Bryant and Sturgis, it is recorded: "Anybody who has ever had occasion to make change with Mr. Bryant will not be surprised at his acquisition of a fortune." One man who undoubtedly would not have been surprised with Bryant was a storekeeper who had occasion to make change with the Family-founding merchant John Parker. Incensed over an argument as to who was to pay an extra half cent in a large transaction, the storekeeper put a penny in a vice, broke it in half and gave Parker half of it. Taking the other half to the window of his Congress Street store, the man hung it on a string and kept it there for years as a warning to Parker and his ilk to stay away. Many a good old Boston merchant, however, regarded it instead as a mark of triumph and a sort of symbol of Yankee thrift.

For employees of these men there was no such thing as an expense account. In the conduct of their million-dollar businesses the head of the firm himself alone handled the purse strings and before he left his counting room each night every last dollar was either present or accounted for to his satisfaction. A ship captain of the firm of Bryant and Sturgis who just before his ship sailed went out on his own and bought a chronometer for $250 had to pay for it himself at the end of the voyage. His plea that the chronometer was essential for navigation fell upon deaf ears. "Could we have anticipated," an officer of the firm wrote of the incident, "that our injunctions respecting economy would have been so totally disregarded, we would have set fire to the ship rather than have sent her to sea." Richard Baker, Jr., who was later to become known as Boston's last "King of Merchants"—because it was said he could transact more business in a few hours than anyone else in a whole day—recalled that in his early life he had clerked in the firm of William F. Weld & Co. without a single raise in salary for nine years. Weld, who made sixteen million dollars and founded a Boston First Family which has been notably comfortable ever since, was evidently a veritable Scrooge of personal parsimony. The only present Baker received from him in those nine years of clerking was one Christmas gift of three dimes which were given, Baker remembered, with a note indicating that they were "in consequence of fidelity" and as "a mark of approbation."

To such merchants even life itself had a price ceiling on it. Travelling with his plantation manager to his plantation in Cuba old Augustus Hemenway was captured by pirates and held for ransom. All through a night, while his terrified manager pleaded with him to settle with the men at once, Hemenway calmly sat on a log surrounded by pirates, smoked cigars, and endeavored to beat down what he considered exorbitant demands for his safety. By the next morning the pirates were so unnerved by his calm and apparent readiness to die rather than be the victim of an overcharge that they were only too willing to lower their price. On that basis settlement was made. Hemenway agreed to remain as hostage and sent his man off for money—a trip that required several days. When the man returned the merchant paid the pirates and went on his way as if nothing had happened.

The merchants' hardness on their dollars carried over to other fields. Dr. James Jackson of the Boston Jackson Family, who with Dr. John Warren was later instrumental in the founding of the Massachusetts General Hospital, demonstrated that a professional man could be as mindful as any merchant of his account books. In his later years he recollected for a biographer his method of setting himself up in practice:

> I was very bold in my steps. I got a house as near State Street as I could find (Congress Street), so that I might be seen . . . I also had my wife's youngest brother Robert as a boarder at $3.00 or $3.50 a week. My wife's uncle, Mr. Samuel Cabot, my friend, lived in Milton, not rich but with a large family and he regarded it as his privilege to live with us as much as he pleased, mostly dining on very ordinary food. He added to our income on this account. My fees for this year, on the books, but good, amounted, I think, to $1800 or rather more. I think my whole expenses were about $1350. From this sum I considered half my house rent ($250.) fairly belonged to office rent, so that I have always regarded my proper home expense as $1100 and I have never known any man going among the Boston gentry who spent as little in his first year.*

Even in Boston's soon to be flowering field of literature the sound dollar mark of the First Family merchant was to have a place, though it was more often than not the mark of chill penury

* *A Memoir of Dr. James Jackson*, by James Jackson Putnam (Boston: Houghton Mifflin) © 1905.

for the authors concerned. "The solid men," declares Van Wyck Brooks, "believed in education." In their wholesale charitable manner they were highly in favor of book learning for, as Brooks puts it, their "sons and nephews, not to forget the meritorious poor." At the same time in their retail penuriousness these merchants found the idea of a son or nephew devoting himself wholly to such a pursuit as writing a difficult one to swallow. When John Perkins Cushing, adopted nephew of the elder Colonel Perkins, announced at the age of sixteen he wished to become a writer, his uncle who, it is recorded, had a strong distaste for this sort of nonsense promptly hustled the boy off to China in a Perkins & Co. boat. When Cushing returned at the age of twenty-three with seven million dollars to take his place along with John Murray Forbes as the richest New Englander of his generation, the Colonel had proved his point to the satisfaction of all concerned—including Cushing.

A few First Family scions were excused. Young Motley, son of a merchant, was one. But Motley, after a couple of attempts at novels, which were frowned on, settled down to writing history, which was of course good "solid stuff." The merchant grandson Parkman also wrote history, as did Prescott. But neither of these men enjoyed good health—they wouldn't have been much use shipping to sea in the India trade. For a perfectly healthy poet, however, the path was a thorny one. Thomas Bailey Aldrich, who coming to Boston early in life always described himself as "not genuine Boston, but Boston-plated," once proudly exhibited to the merchant he was working for a check for fifteen dollars he had received from *Harper's*. Told the money was in payment for a poem, the merchant roared, "Why don't you send the damned fool one every day?" James Russell Lowell, who was to become a First Family poet laureate, had a particularly difficult struggle with parental penury. At Harvard he received a letter from his father, about to go abroad, telling him he was to be paid an allowance of fifty cents a week from his brother Charles, such allowance to be raised to a dollar if he made Phi Beta Kappa. The letter concluded:

If I find my finances will allow it, I shall buy you something abroad. If you graduate one of the first five in your class I shall give you $100 on your graduation. If one of the first ten, $75. If one of the first twelve, $50. If the first or second scholar, $200. If you do not miss any exercises unexcused you shall have Bryant's *Mythology*, or any book of equal value, unless it is one I may specially want.*

It was little wonder that Lowell was to find Boston a city with "busyness in the blood" and its Society one in which "leisure is looked upon as the larceny of time that belongs to other people." The merchants left strictly to their womenfolk the placing of Boston's literary lions on their pedestals. John Murray Forbes endowed the literary Saturday Club—so-called Boston's "Mutual Admiration Society"—so thoroughly that up until recently members were supplied with free meals, but Forbes' son had married Emerson's daughter, and Forbes had himself been elected to the club—it was almost a Family affair. Old Colonel Higginson founded the Boston Authors' Club, but it is significant that the organization was for years referred to as "Higginson's last plaything." More typical was the banker who refused to allow Edward Everett Hale to open an account—despite Hale's pathetic plea that the forty-five cents he wanted to deposit represented the net profits from what he considered his best book—or the merchant who would not permit anyone to call him a merchant prince because he wished no truck with the "veneer of culture" with which he felt such a title might endow him. Too often, other bankers and merchants would have agreed, Boston culture was bad business. These bankers and merchants were men of robust prejudices and there were beginning to be too many books which "addled the minds" of the young. They were glad when Edgar Allan Poe left town. Poe was born in Boston but was never "a Bostonian"—and never would be so recognized by Boston Society. Agitator Wendell Phillips was a son of a Harvard president but was not admitted by the

* *James Russell Lowell,* by Horace Elisha Scudder (Boston: Houghton Mifflin) © 1901.

front door in the best houses on Beacon Street. When the time came to tie a rope around the neck of the radical editor William Lloyd Garrison, a "mob of gentlemen," it is recorded, did the trick—and would have hanged him but for the timely arrival of the police. "Sound" merchant-publishers all but blocked the movement to establish the *Atlantic Monthly*. They felt the anti-slavery plank in its prospectus would interfere with the established book market in the South, and only when the commercial success of *Uncle Tom's Cabin* had been proved did they give in and allow the magazine to begin publication. The payment rate for *Atlantic* authors no Boston merchant could have complained of—five dollars per printed page of seven hundred words.

Soundest of all the merchant publishers was the firm of Ticknor and Fields. Old George Ticknor, who married a merchant's daughter and became both a literary lion and a social arbiter at the same time, ran it in a manner indistinguishable from a shipping firm. He had a habit of demanding that authors whose manuscripts he had accepted appear in person. Once there they would be taken to an office in the rear of the building and solemnly paid off in gold pieces. This, Ticknor seemed to feel, gave them a better understanding of the value of a dollar—something they would never have learned from belles-lettres on a less business-like basis.

But Ticknor need not have troubled himself. The understanding of a dollar had already ingrained itself in Boston's core, and it is there to this day. Some of Boston's proudest firms have bowed to a free and easier era—notably the insurance company which up until World War I was still using sand for blotting paper and the textile concern which until about the same period refused to allow the purchase of scratch paper but insisted upon its employees taking the trouble to smooth out incoming envelopes and using the backs for that purpose—but economy is still State Street Boston's key word. An old-line firm of any kind which completely "does itself over" is likely to find itself regarded as one that's on the way out. When a First Family trust office was recently forced to move into a new building, it moved all right, but, to the despair of its New York interior decorator, brought along with it everything it felt necessary to grace its new surroundings—including roll-top desks, andirons, cuspidors, ship models, old prints, and even a stuffed fish. Boston's State Street Trust Co. actually prides itself on its nickname as "the George Apley of banks" and though it had given in to electricity, lights its main banking room with electrified versions of pewter whale-oil lamps; on its tables are pewter ink-wells dating to counting-room days. Some of New England's biggest business deals are still likely to be carried out in offices reached by archaic elevators where even the directors' board room is often bare of modern conveniences. Wages in these companies have, albeit reluctantly, moved with the times, but it is a curiosity of Boston's Old Guard firms that they are able to procure top-drawer directors to serve on their boards for fees well below prevailing remuneration in other cities. In some instances directors are still paid nothing at all, it being apparently regarded as such a high privilege to serve a "fine old firm" in this capacity that to receive a fee for going to a board meeting would be almost as unthinkable as taking pay for going to a First Family dinner party.

On a personal basis the inheritance of economy is a strong one among Proper Bostonians. First Family men vie with one another in telling tales of ancestral parsimony. For years two partners of Lee, Higginson & Co. had high reputations for being the nighest men in Boston of their day; one is credited with having fired on the spot an employee whom he saw having his shoes polished. "A man who can't shine his own shoes isn't worth much," he said. A more recent head of this firm, James Jackson Storrow, often called Boston's "First Citizen" of the twenties, used to look over the Lee, Higginson salesmen's chart periodically and pick out the low man. "You can't get rid of that man too soon to suit me," he would tell his sales manager. A present-day First Family trustee, George Peabody Gardner, tells a story on his wife's side of the family, of both her grandfather and father. Her grandfather at one time ran one of the largest cotton mills in New England and was one day accosted in his office by a man who owed him money. "Mr. Grosvenor," he said, shaking his fist, "you're the damnedest meanest man I've ever met." Ignoring the fist and pointing with pride to the only other occupant of his barren office, Grosvenor asked with his habitual stammer, "S-sir, have you ever m-met my son?" Still another Proper Bostonian relates a story of his cousin, one of the so-called "Grand Old Men" of Newburyport, a banker now in his nineties. During the merger of Newburyport's two banks some years ago it became necessary to clear out one bank completely. Together with his cashier, a man near seventy, the banker piled the contents of the safe-deposit vaults, including the entire assets of the bank, into four large suitcases; then, each of them carrying two of the bags, they boarded the train for Boston where they made arrangements to store the assets until the merger was completed. Later one of the banker's friends, hearing of this procedure and shocked at its danger, asked him why he hadn't handled it in the usual manner with an armored car. "A waste of money," was the brief reply. "Who's going to bother two old men with suitcases, anyway?"

No matter how wealthy he may be, the Proper Bostonian has such a constitutional weakness for "talking poor" that he has usually thoroughly convinced himself—if no one else—that he is poor, and he shops accordingly, wondering not only whether something he wants to buy is worth the price but also whether he, as a poor man, can afford it. He has his pet economies as he has his pet charities, and whether these take the form of driving a Ford car, of ignoring manicurists and other vendors of personal attentions, or of never permitting himself an "extra" on the Thompson's Spa blue-plate lunch, they are an integral part of his make-up. The late George Wigglesworth, father of blue-blood Congressman Richard Wigglesworth, gave the Massachusetts General Hospital several hundred thousand dollars in the course of his lifetime, but he never considered a pair of shoes worn out until he had had them re-soled three times. Tipping to the Proper Bostonian is a retail matter, having nothing to do with his beloved wholesale charity, and he is inclined to look upon it as an unnecessary shakedown. He has the reputation of being a strict ten-percenter in this regard, and it is significant that the hat-check girl at the Ritz Hotel cocktail bar, favored rendezvous of younger Proper Bostonians, has long since discarded other hat-check girls' time-honored practice of leaving only a neat display of quarters on their trays and of quickly hiding all dimes received. The Ritz girl is usually reduced to displaying her dimes—and hiding her nickels.

Boston's First Family Society, as founded by merchants with high regard for the value of a dollar, was hardly fated to be a Society of outlandish extravagance and it has never become one. In town the merchants built "mansions" but significantly the old-time New England definition of this word was any house with a back staircase. When by the very enormity of their wealth these merchants pushed Boston's scale of living several notches upward, there were always those ready to deplore such wickedness and beat a hasty retreat from the city's sinful ways. Russell Sturgis, merchant head not only of Boston's largest East India firm but also of London's Baring Brothers, returning from his last trip to the East had expected to live out the remainder of his days in Boston. Instead, finding prices too high for his liking, he immediately determined to take all his family back to the East. So irritated was the merchant with Boston and so quickly had he made his decision that his family were unable to get their luggage packed in time to take the boat he had planned—and only barely were they able to persuade him to agree to wait for them and their luggage and take the next boat. Sturgis never set foot in this country again. John Murray Forbes early in his career determined he would never own a house in Boston in his life, and he stuck to his decision. He bought a home in Milton and there he stayed, despite the difficulties the long commutation in those days imposed on a man who liked to be at his office at "7½" every morning. In Milton his six children were brought up the way he wished them to be brought up. "With their rich circle of acquaintance in Boston and with their probable wealth," he wrote, with some understatement as to the latter, "they would, if in the city, be liable to get injurious ideas of their own consequence and their own duties."

The merchants who moved to the country did not go in for show places. Generally speaking they built practical, durable, comfortable homes, and this has been the keynote of Proper Bostonian suburban architecture ever since. There are country estates in a few places around Boston, particularly on the North Shore and in Wellesley, which could hardly be classed as simple, but at the same time there is scarcely a home in the chief First Family theatres of operation—in Brookline, Milton or Dedham—which would bear comparison with the truly lush Society estates of Long Island, Lake Forest or Beverly Hills. Boston's millionaire banker Frederick H. Prince may today own what is one of the largest palaces in the East, Newport's "Marble House," into which the late Mrs. Oliver H. P. Belmont sunk several millions, but it is notable that banker Prince procured the estate, in August 1932, for what was the bargain-basement price for such an establishment—$50,000.

Plans for the founding of the most select of all Boston's First Family suburbs—that of Chestnut Hill, now considered a part of Brookline—were made, typically enough, by a group of merchants meeting in the middle of the last century in the counting room of Lee, Higginson & Co. Not a dollar was wasted and admittance to the community depended of course on one's being a Lee or a Higginson, a Cabot or a Curtis, etc. By 1854 Francis Lee, premier pioneer, was able to write: "There is every prospect of our getting up quite a pleasant little neighborhood . . . Saltonstall will live there, and I have commenced an attack on John Lowell, of whom I don't despair." Lee keeps as exact accounts in laying out his property as he would have in tabulating securities in his safe-deposit vault. "I counted out trees today," he writes again in 1854, "apples 18, pears 45, plums 10, quinces 8, cherries 32, making a total of 113 fruit trees; elms 10, ailanthus 8, oaks 4 and pines 3." Lee's description of his house, written to a friend, is a lasting commentary on the Proper Bostonian's idea of what a gentleman's country estate should be:

> I came out here at 2½ and after getting dinner drove up to our place. As I espied from afar . . . the long cozy stretch of barn and then peeping among the trees the pointed top of our own snuggery, I was delighted. It is *really* homely, a thorough English homestead, giving by its cozy, snug look an air of comfort to the whole place. I *know* you will like it.*

Another Chestnut Hillite built what he describes as "a pet of a house." In 1860 the Chestnut Hill Chapel was built, and while it is recorded that fourteen dollars was "with some difficulty" raised each Sunday for the minister's salary, no money was forthcoming for a janitor. Old George Lee himself, a present-day member of the Lee Family recalls, used to walk down the hill every Sunday morning with a big feather duster over his shoulder, open the Chapel, dust it and then ring the bell. Since this Chapel was the parent of Chestnut Hill's First Church of today, in which the congregation has reached a tone pitch of exclusiveness unmatched anywhere in Greater Boston, such industry was not unrewarded.

The idea of spending money for recreation has never been wholly accepted by the Proper Bostonian. While horse racing at Brookline's Country Club and drag hunts at the North Shore's Myopia Club have occasionally enlivened the picture, the common conception of Boston's First Family Society as one hard put to enjoy its off-hours would seem to be justified. The Proper Bostonian's Yankee-inherited frugality is not the whole story, but together with his Puritan-inherited disbelief in self-indulgence it has made him cut a decorously inconsequential figure as a Society "sport." A present-day Bostonian, now in his seventies, says that from the time he was a boy he loved fishing, but he hastens to make clear that of course he never had time to take

---

* *A History of the Chestnut Hill Chapel*, by Mary Lee. Boston. © 1937.

up the sport in earnest until he was fifty. When he did take it up he was relieved to find, he declares, that fishing was not "necessarily a lazy sport." Old Peter Chardon Brooks was late in life persuaded by wealthy New York friends to take up yachting as a hobby, but this did not prove to be Peter's dish. Regretfully he recalls in his diary the final chapter of his experiment:

> Took down my boathouse. I concluded, years ago, not to keep a boat any longer. I had no fondness for it myself, nor did I wish my children to have, for fear of accident, and the habit of idleness; and it caused a great deal of care. All these things I ought to have considered before I spent the money. I was in error . . . The boat disappointed me. I thought it would afford pleasure to us and our friends, but it did neither.*

The Proper Bostonian on his vacation has been the source of many a niggardly legend. The obvious resorts, the Newports and the Saratogas, the Palm Beaches and the Palm Springs, have never been for him. The only reason any Bostonian ever went as far as Bar Harbor, it used to be said, was that it was the nearest place he was able to find lobster at five cents a pound. Nahant, most venerable of First Family resorts and one all of fifteen miles from Boston, was originally "discovered" by the elder Colonel Perkins because, according to the stories, the Colonel was looking for a place to establish residence with as low a tax rate as possible. The essence of Boston Society self-containment, where the phrase "Cold Roast Boston" originated and where the late Henry Cabot Lodge fenced himself from his brother-in-law with barbed wire, Nahant grew to be a sort of symbol of Boston Society's idea of low-scaled high living. In early days on their cheerless rock-bound peninsula Boston's "Nahanters"—including at one time or another all of Boston's best—holed-in in simple stone cottages and proudly boasted they were free

* *Boston Unitarianism*, by O. B. Frothingham (New York: G. P. Putnam's Sons) © 1890.

from the "fury of fashion" at Newport. As time went by they managed to make of their Nahant Club one of the most exclusive summer clubs on the Atlantic Coast, at the same time keeping the entertainment afforded by that quaint little organization on a strictly penny-ante basis. The Club's Saturday Night "Dutch-treat" suppers, usually topped off by a round or two of early-evening croquet, were idyls of Proper Bostoniana which were brought to an end only by World War II when the General Electric Company took over the Club as a recreation home for its employees.

Some of Boston's best have never believed in the idea of spending money for recreation when they could be making it at work. Rufus Choate, distinguished First Family lawyer, used to take one three-day weekend each summer, which he felt was plenty of time off for anybody. "The lawyer's vacation," he once whimsically observed, "is the space between the question put to a witness and his answer." Not only Nahant but other First Family resorts bear out the idea that the Proper Bostonian, if he is going to be at all happy away from his work, must be comfortably uncomfortable. His mental ease depends not only upon some actual physical inconvenience—his hair-shirt complex—but also upon an extremely moderate per diem tariff. At "The Glades," South Shore haunt of Adamses, Ameses, Codmans, Searses and Saltonstalls, members of these Families can stay practically for nothing in various parts of a ramshackle old 1890 hotel which was bought at a bargain price many years ago. Naushon, the Forbeses' own island off Cape Cod and one which John Murray Forbes purchased for a song more than a century ago, is run by his grandson Cameron Forbes on such a careful basis that though he allows the servants in his "Mansion House" the privilege of electric lights, he permits candles only in the main part of the building. Emerson's phrase "plain living and high thinking" has long been the motto of vacationing Forbeses, but until they gave in to the idea of electric lights their servant problem was acute, and visitors noted that living was plain all right, but of necessity so devoted to such mundane tasks as cooking and dishwashing that not even the Forbeses had time or energy left for high thinking.

The Cabots of "Cabotville," North Haven, Maine, form what is perhaps the most striking example of a Proper Bostonian summer setup. This is a colony which includes four complete Cabot families in varying generations all crowded into Spartan-simple houses and all making use of one telephone in a farm-house more than a mile away. The only visible signs of luxury are a few small boats lying off the shore; never permitting such an extravagance as a dock, the Cabots procure these boats when they want them by a complicated system of running lines reaching out from the shore. Across a small stretch of bay and presenting a breath-taking picture of contrast with the colony is the summer estate of the Cabots' nearest neighbor, Thomas W. Lamont, chairman of the board of J. P. Morgan & Co. Lamont's New York friends, visiting him on occasion and viewing Cabotville from across his rolling lawns, find it difficult to believe his neighbors are really Boston's Almighty Cabots. Once convinced and well knowing the Cabots could if they wished live in as lordly estates as that of their host himself, these New Yorkers have been known to carry away with them an impression of Boston high Society as a sort of esoteric cult of St. Francis of Assisi—an impression which is by no means unpleasing to the cautious Cabots.

When force of circumstance has conspired to place the Proper Bostonian willy-nilly on the luxurious plane of living of his counterpart in other city Societies, he has usually shown himself at a distinct loss to understand such things. Some years ago a partner in one of Boston's leading law firms on his first trip to the West stopped off at a resort hotel in Tucson. Observing a sign which called attention to the hotel's shoe-shine service, whereby if he left his riding boots outside his door each night they would be returned all shined the next morning, he resolved to take advantage of the bargain throughout his stay. Today the man retains as his chief impression of the West the sharp pain of noting on his final bill an extra charge of $1.50 per night for the hotel's attention to his boots.

Such a man is a definite throwback to the Proper Bostonian of history. The early Adamses were always complaining of the "price" of Society, in New York, Philadelphia, Washington and even as far as St. Petersburg, Russia. The elder Colonel Perkins visiting George Washington at Mount Vernon couldn't sleep a wink, he recalls in his reminiscences, for marvelling at the luxuries which surrounded him. The merchant Jonathan Mason invited to visit Morrisania, grandiose home of Gouverneur Morris, was so shocked at "the profusion of plate, gold and mirror" that he was unable to eat. Even Harrison Gray Otis, Boston's outstanding merchant *bon vivant* who was able to eat his *pâté de fois gras* without qualms for breakfast, quailed at the gaiety of the Washington social life in which he became engulfed on his election to Congress. "I feel no disposition," he wrote to his wife whom he had typically sent back to Boston. "to take part in the bagatelle of the hour."

One of the minor phases of social life at the capital which made a lasting impression on Congressman Otis was his discovery that Washington had in his stables certain of his favorite horses which were at his order, according to Otis, "exempted from labor"—a truly shocking state of affairs to a Proper Bostonian and one which was taken by Otis in the same manner his latter-day descendants were to take what they considered the reckless expenditures of the New Deal. The personal approach of the Proper Bostonian to politics where it concerns finance has apparently always touched the retail-penury side of his character in no uncertain fashion. "I was against Franklin D. Roosevelt," declared a Proper Bostonian businessman in a noted interview, "from the day *he* abrogated the dollar contract on *my* dollar bill."

In some contrast to high Society femininity of other cities the Proper Boston woman has not let her man down in upholding the cherished First Family tradition of not spending money recklessly. She too was carefully nurtured in the department of economy of the Boston merchant school, and she has never been an amateur when it comes to talking poverty, regardless of her wealth. Some years ago one First Family lady was chided for this and called to the carpet by a friend. She was told she would have to admit, when she came right down to it, she had all the money she could possibly need for her own lifetime and her children's too. But the lady was still doubtful. "Well," she said hesitantly, "there are always grandchildren to think of."

Clothes, budgetary bane of women of lesser mettle, have never proved so to the Boston woman. A familiar legend is the story of the lady who, asked by an amazed visitor to Boston where Boston women get their hats, replied: "Our hats? Why, we have our hats." Like most Boston legends, however, there is something behind the story. For a woman to dress too smartly in Boston is to open herself to the charge that she is a social climber. First Family ladies view with alarm such evidence of the parvenue. A typical expression of contempt is the phrase, "She has everything she owns on her back." One Society editor, long inured to the habit of Boston women indulging in parsimony by ignoring all fashion trends and "making things do," claims she saw a First Family lady emerge from the Chilton Club dressed in a mandarin coat dating from the days of the Boston clippers and the China trade. Other editors have also struggled with the problem of reporting the party-going clothes of Boston's best. The custom has usually been to describe the lady's costume once or twice only and then if the costume continues to appear— as so often it does—to ignore the lady herself. One lately deceased grande dame, however, was such a Society standout she could not be ignored. Year after year on every formal occasion she appeared in the same white satin evening gown in which she had been presented at the Court of St. James's. One year the gown would be described as white, next as "off-white," then "oyster-white," and once more as "pearl-gray." Finally, exhausting their repertoire, the Society reporters would again go back to white and start all over again.

Many a Proper Boston woman even looks upon her entertaining as something to be handled with the utmost financial caution. For many years Boston's wealthy Curtis sisters, notably generous in charitable ventures, have been accustomed to top off sewing-circle luncheons held at their Beacon Hill home with chocolate éclairs neatly and thriftily cut in half. The wife of a Harvard professor made a sort of game out of economizing on her hospitality. From the financial point of view there was no necessity for her cutting any corners at all; her husband was a First Family man with a sizeable income to augment his salary, and she had simply chosen entertaining as her pet economy in the same manner she had chosen a certain hospital as her pet charity. She would go for as long as a year without doing any formal entertaining of any sort. Then with a rush she would hire in a phalanx of extra help, have her house cleaned from top to bottom, procure substantial quantities of food and liquor, and all in one twelve-hour period would take her turn as lunch-club hostess for her Boston friends, have her "Cambridge crowd"—her husband's faculty friends and their wives—to tea, and finish off with an elaborate dinner dance for her debutante daughter. Managing the whole affair with all the technique of an efficiency expert she would then call it a day—for another year.

One First Family merchant daughter built as a memorial to her father the first Episcopal church in Greater Boston which had no rented pews in it, and has maintained it with generous gifts ever since. In her own house, however, she has never permitted herself the luxury of screens, maintaining they are an unnecessary extravagance. When warm weather comes, and insects abound, she goes to bed early without turning on any lights. Another First Family home is completely without rugs; the lady of the house having never inherited any "good Orientals" refuses to spend money for any others. For many First Family ladies Pullmans are taboo. Irrespective of the length of their trip they prefer to save the money and sit out their journey in what they still refer to as "the common car."

For some years the outstanding example of First Family feminine frugality has been one of Boston's wealthiest widows. In the traditional manner she has been known to write a check for five thousand dollars for the Community Fund and at the same time maintain a swords-point relationship with her local grocer who had once made the mistake of filling her telephone order for bread with an extra-price loaf. Always demanding that her bills be itemized to the last penny, she refuses to write any check for under five dollars, shrinking not only from the cost of the check but also the price of the stamp. During World War II, unable to keep her large country estate satisfactorily stocked with servants, she moved into town to a hotel where she reached the ultimate in self-denial. Having decided the price of the hotel breakfast was exorbitant she made her own repast each morning on powdered coffee, bread saved from her previous night's supper, and two soft-boiled eggs from a supply regularly delivered to her by her chauffeur from her country farm. She cooked the eggs by the remarkable process of leaving them in her basin and running hot water over them for half an hour. When the news of this ritual travelled the hotel grapevine the manager graciously offered her the use of an electric plate. "No thanks," she said, entirely unabashed, "I'm no cook and I've always been afraid of those things."

In considering such instances of pecuniary diffidence among Boston's First Ladies emphasis should be laid on the fact that they have since girlhood been schooled in such ways by their menfolk, even in the matter of courtship. One Back Bay lady declares that the only present her husband ever brought her during the three years of their engagement was a copy of the Boston *Transcript* which he would pick up and deliver to her on his regular afternoon call. A New Yorker will never forget the initial gift from her lord and master. It came on her first wedding anniversary and was the obvious result of several long-distance phone calls she made to her mother during her first year in Boston; the present was a silver three-minute sandglass. At this she felt herself better off than a friend of hers whose husband had long promised her a trip to New York and a round of New York theaters. When the occasion finally came she discovered that her husband's idea of how to procure theatre tickets was to go to a turn-in agency and wait patiently until after the start of the play when the seat prices steadily decreased. Once having been forced to wait until the end of the first act to get a fifty-percent markdown, the woman asked her husband why they went at all. He could not see it that way—if they had stayed at home and not paid anything, he wouldn't have had the pleasure of beating the game.

The Proper Boston woman is merely a part of this great tradition; she has not gone beyond it. She may have started Boston's fashionable Beaver Country Day School in a Back Bay stable, and she may still choose to hold her elite Nucleus Club meetings in a room in a colored church at the foot of Beacon Hill—"It's convenient," one member explains frankly, "and it's very inexpensive"—but she is hardly in a class with the members of the Somerset Club, who have four floors of bedrooms above the main entrance and yet have no heat above the second floor, or the members of the Proper Boston male's most select lunch club, the "City Club Corporation." So called to distinguish itself from the 3000-member Boston City Club, the Corporation Club is kept to a strict 180-member maximum and candidates have been known to wait as long as fifteen years to get in—which they do through the downstairs washroom since, as distinct from probably any other club in America, that is the only members' entrance. Once in, they can enjoy luncheons consumed in barren surroundings but run on the unbeatable basis of all-you-can-eat for $25 a month. A steward who had served faithfully for twenty-five years was not long ago presented by members of the club with a gold watch, upon which he turned around and presented his benefactors with a silver coffee urn. Asked if the members had not been surprised with his return gift, he declared they had not. "You don't surprise those people," he said briefly. "They thanked me for the coffeepot like I thanked them for the watch."

On an individual basis it is doubtful if any Boston woman will ever be able to match what may well stand as the high-water mark of Proper Bostonian retail penury. This was set by an impeccable First Family man and senior partner in one of the city's most blue-blooded brokerage firms. Still at his desk today, a man in his eighties, he began to be troubled many years ago by increasing deafness. He refused to buy any sort of hearing device, however, because he declared they were too expensive. Knowing the man to be worth, at then prevailing stock-market values, somewhere between ten and twelve million dollars, other members of the firm felt his attitude was an unwarranted one. For years they hedged and hinted but to no avail. Then when the man reached the age of seventy they delegated a junior member of the firm to speak frankly with him on the subject. The senior partner was told that his usefulness to the firm had become impaired by his refusal to procure a hearing aid and that if he persisted in his attitude the matter of his retirement would be brought up at the next board meeting. Confronted as he knew he would be with still another mention of the expense of such an aid, the junior member was ready with his trump card—if the man wouldn't pay for it himself the other members of the firm would join together and give him one. Gruffly the senior partner agreed to buy his own.

Some time later the junior member of the firm was again in his superior's office, on this occasion to discuss a matter of business. To his amazement he could not seem to make himself heard. He found himself raising his voice higher and higher in his irritation. At last, pointing to the hearing aid, he shouted: "It doesn't seem to be working very well, does it?" "It works perfectly well," replied the senior partner. "It isn't turned on. The batteries cost like the devil."

CHAPTER TEN

DR. PARKMAN TAKES A WALK

To the student of American Society the year 1849 will always remain a red-letter one. In that year two events occurred at opposite ends of the country, both of which, in their own way, made social history. At one end, in Sutter's Creek, California, gold was discovered. At the other, in Boston, Massachusetts, Dr. George Parkman walked off the face of the earth.

The discovery of gold ushered in a new social era. It marked the first great rise of the Western *nouveau riche,* the beginning of that wonderful time when a gentleman arriving in San Francisco and offering a boy fifty cents to carry his suitcase could receive the reply, "Here's a dollar, man—carry it yourself," and when a poor Irish prospector suddenly striking it rich in a vein near Central City, Colorado, could fling down his pick and exclaim, "Thank God, now my wife can be a lady!"

Dr. Parkman's little walk did no such thing as this. It must be remembered, however, that it occurred some three thousand miles away. Boston is not Sutter's Creek or Central City or even San Francisco. There has never been a "new" social era in the Western sense in Boston's rock-ribbed Society, and it remains very doubtful if there ever will be one. The best that could be expected of any one event in Boston would be to shake up the old. Dr. Parkman's walk did this; it shook Boston Society to the very bottom of its First Family foundations. Viewed almost a hundred years later it thus seems, in its restricted way, almost as wonderful as the Gold Rush and not undeserving of the accidental fact that it happened, in the great march of social history, in exactly the same year.

The date was Friday, November 23rd. It was warm for a Boston November, and Dr. Parkman needed no overcoat as he left his Beacon Hill home at 8 Walnut Street. He wore in the fashion of the day a black morning coat, purple silk vest, dark trousers, a dark-figured black tie, and a black silk top hat. He had breakfasted as usual, and he left his home to head downtown toward the Merchants Bank on State Street. Dr. Parkman was quite a figure as he moved along. His high hat and angular physique made him seem far taller than his actual five feet nine and a half inches. He was sixty years old and his head was almost bald, but his hat hid this fact also. To all outward appearances he was remarkably well-preserved, his most striking feature being a conspicuously protruding chin. Boston Parkmans have been noted for their chins the way Boston Adamses are noted for their foreheads or Boston Saltonstalls are noted for their noses, and the chin of old Dr. Parkman was especially formidable. His lower jaw jutted out so far it had made the fitting of a set of false teeth for him a very difficult job. The dentist who had had that job had never forgotten it. He was proud of the china-white teeth he had installed. He had even kept the mold to prove to people that he, little Dr. Nathan Keep, had made the teeth of the great Dr. George Parkman.

Although he had studied to be a physician and received his degree Dr. Parkman had rarely practiced medicine in his life. He was a merchant at heart, one of Boston's wealthiest men, and he spent his time in the Boston manner keeping sharp account of his money—and a sharp eye on his debtors. He had many of the traits of character peculiar to the Proper Bostonian breed. He was shrewd and hard, but he was Boston-honest, Boston-direct and Boston-dependable. Like so many other First Family men before his time and after Dr. Parkman was not popular but he was highly respected. It was hard to like a man like Dr. Parkman because his manners were curt and he had a way of glaring at people that made them uncomfortable. Without liking him, however, it was possible to look up to him. People knew him as a great philanthropist and it was said he had given away a hundred thousand dollars in his time. The phrase "wholesale charity and retail penury" as descriptive of the Proper Bostonian breed had not yet come into the Boston lingo, though the day was coming when Dr. Parkman might be regarded as the very personification of it. Certainly he had given away large sums of money with wholesale generosity—even anonymously—yet with small sums, with money on a retail basis, he was penny-punctilious. "The same rule," a biographer records, "governed Dr. Parkman in settling an account involving the balance of a cent as in transactions of thousands of dollars."

Children in the Boston streets pointed out Dr. Parkman to other children. "There goes Dr. Parkman," they would say. People always seemed to point him out after he had passed them. There was no use speaking to Dr. Parkman before he went by. If you weren't his friend, Dr. George Shattuck, or his brother-in-law, Robert Gould Shaw, Esq., or a Cabot or a Lowell, or perhaps a man who owed him money—and then, as someone said, God help you—the doctor would ignore you. Dr. Parkman had no need to court favor from anybody. The Parkmans cut a sizeable chunk of Boston's social ice in 1849, and they still do today. Like other merchant-blooded First Families they were of course economically self-sufficient. They hadn't yet made much of an intellectual mark on their city, but a nephew of the doctor, Francis Parkman, had just published his first book and was on his way to becoming what Van Wyck Brooks has called "the climax and crown" of the Boston historical school. The Parkmans were in the Boston fashion well-connected by marriages. Dr. Parkman's sister's marriage with Robert Gould Shaw, Boston's wealthiest merchant, was a typical First Family alliance. As for Dr. Parkman's own wealth, some idea of its extent may be gathered from the fact that his son, who never worked a day in his life, was able to leave a will which bequeathed, among other things, the sum of five million dollars for the care and improvement of the Boston Common.

On the morning of that Friday, November 23rd, Dr. Parkman was hurrying. He walked with the characteristic gait of the Proper Bostonian merchant—a gait still practiced by such notable present-day First Family footmen as Charles Francis Adams and Godfrey Lowell Cabot—measuring off distances with long, ground-consuming strides. Dr. Parkman always hurried. Once when riding a horse up Beacon Hill and unable to speed the animal to his satisfaction he had left the horse in the middle of the street and hurried ahead on foot. On that occasion he had been after money, a matter of debt collection.

This morning, too, Dr. Parkman was after money. He left the Merchants Bank and after making several other calls dropped into a grocery store at the corner of Blossom and Vine Streets. This stop, the only non-financial mission of his morning, was to buy a head of lettuce for his invalid sister. He left it in the store and said he would return for it on his way home. The time was half past one and Dr. Parkman presumably intended to be home at 2:30, then the fashionable hour for one's midday meal. Ten minutes later, at 1:40, Elias Fuller, a merchant standing outside his counting room at Fuller's Iron Foundry at the corner of Vine and North Grove Streets, observed Dr. Parkman passing him headed north on North Grove Street. Fuller was later to remember that the doctor seemed particularly annoyed about something and recalled that his cane beat a brisk tattoo on the pavement as he hurried along. What the merchant observed at 1:40 that day is of more than passing importance, for Elias Fuller was the last man who ever saw the doctor alive on the streets of Boston. Somewhere, last seen going north on North Grove Street, Dr. George Parkman walked off the face of the earth.

At 8 Walnut Street Mrs. Parkman, her daughter Harriet and Dr. Parkman's invalid sister sat down to their two-thirty dinner long after three o'clock. Their dinner was ruined and there was no lettuce, but Mrs. Parkman and the others did not mind. They were all worried about the master of the house. Dr. Parkman was not the sort of man who was ever late for anything. Right after dinner they got in touch with Dr. Parkman's agent, Charles Kingsley. Kingsley was the man who looked after the doctor's business affairs, usually some time after the doctor had thoroughly looked after them himself. Almost at once Kingsley began to search for his employer. First Family men of the prominence of Dr. Parkman did not disappear in Boston—and they do not today—even for an afternoon. By night-fall Kingsley was ready to inform Robert Gould Shaw. Shaw, acting with the customary dispatch of the Proper Bostonian merchant, went at once to Boston's City Marshal, Mr. Tukey. Marshal Tukey did of course what Shaw told him to do, which was to instigate an all-night search.

The next morning the merchant Shaw placed advertisements in all the papers and had 28,000 handbills distributed. The advertisements and the handbills announced a reward of $3,000 for his brother-in-law alive and $1,000 for his brother-in-law dead. The prices, considering the times, were sky-high but Shaw knew what he was doing in Yankee Boston. Before long virtually every able-bodied man, woman and child in the city was looking for Dr. Parkman. They beat the bushes and they combed the streets. Slum areas were ransacked. All suspicious characters, all persons with known criminal records, were rounded up and held for questioning. Strangers in Boston were given a summary one-two treatment. An Irishman, it is recorded, attempting to change a twenty-dollar bill, was brought in to the police headquarters apparently solely on the assumption that no son of Erin, in the Boston of 1849, had any business with a bill of this size in his possession.

Every one of Dr. Parkman's actions on the previous day, up to 1:40, were checked. At that time, on North Grove Street, the trail always ended. Police had to sift all manner of wild reports. One had the doctor "beguiled to East Cambridge and done in." Another had him riding in a hansom cab, his head covered with blood, being driven at "breakneck speed" over a Charles River bridge. Of the papers only the Boston *Transcript* seems to have kept its head. Its reporter managed to learn from a servant in the Parkman home that the doctor had received a caller at 9:30 Friday reminding him of a 1:30 appointment later in the day. The servant could not remember what the man looked like, but the *Transcript* printed the story in its Saturday night edition along with the reward advertisements. Most people took the caller to be some sort of front man who had appeared to lead Dr. Parkman to a dastardly death. By Monday foul play was so thoroughly suspected that the shrewd merchant Shaw saw no reason to mention a sum as high as $1,000 for the body. Three thousand dollars was still the price for Dr. Parkman alive but only "a suitable reward" was mentioned in Shaw's Monday handbills for Dr. Parkman dead. Monday's handbills also noted the possibility of amnesia but the theory of a First Family man's mind wandering to this extent was regarded as highly doubtful. Dr. Parkman, it was stated, was "perfectly well" when he left his house.

All that the Parkman case now needed to make it a complete panorama of Boston's First Family Society was the active entry of Harvard College into the picture. This occurred on Sunday morning in the person of a caller to the home of Rev. Francis Parkman, the missing doctor's brother, where the entire Family Parkman in all its ramifications had gathered. The caller was a man named John White Webster, Harvard graduate and professor of chemistry at the Harvard Medical School. He was a short squat man, fifty-six years old, who had a mass of unruly black hair and always wore thick spectacles. He had had a most distinguished career. He had studied at Guy's Hospital, London, back in 1815, where among his fellow students had been the poet John Keats. He was a member of the London Geological Society, the American Academy of Arts and Sciences, and during his twenty-five years as a Harvard professor had published numerous nationally noted scientific works. His wife, a Hickling and aunt of the soon-to-be-recognized historian William Hickling Prescott, was "well-connected" with several of Boston's First Families.

The Rev. Parkman was glad to see Professor Webster and ushered him toward the parlor expecting that his desire would be to offer sympathy to the assorted Parkmans there assembled. But Webster, it seemed, did not want to go into the parlor. Instead he spoke abruptly to the minister. "I have come to tell you," he said, "that I saw your brother at half past one o'clock on Friday." The minister was glad to have this report. Since Webster also told him he had been the caller at the Parkman home earlier that day it cleared up the mystery of the strange appointment as recorded in the *Transcript*. Webster explained he should have come sooner but had been so busy he had not seen the notices of Dr. Parkman's disappearance until the previous night. The minister was also satisfied with this. Webster further declared that, at the appointment shortly after 1:30 which took place in his laboratory at the Medical School, he had paid Dr. Parkman the sum of $483.64 which he had owed him. This, of course, explained why the doctor had last been seen by the merchant Fuller in such a cane-tattooing hurry. It had indeed been a matter of a debt collection.

When Professor Webster had left, Robert Gould Shaw was advised of his visit. Shaw was intimate enough in his brother-in-law's affairs to know that Webster had been owing Dr. Parkman money for some time. He did not, however, know the full extent of Webster's misery. Few men have ever suffered from the retail penury side of the Proper Bostonian character as acutely as John White Webster.

The professor received a salary from Harvard of $1,200 a year. This, augmented by income from extra lectures he was able to give, might have sufficed for the average Harvard professor in those days. But Webster was not the average. His wife, for all her connections with Boston's First Families, was still a socially aspirant woman, particularly for her two daughters of debutante age. Mrs. Webster and the Misses Webster entertained lavishly at their charming home in Cambridge. Professor Webster went into debt. He borrowed money here and he borrowed money there. But mostly he borrowed from Dr. George Parkman.

Who better to borrow from? Dr. Parkman, man of wholesale charity, Proper Bostonian merchant philanthropist. He had given Harvard College the very ground on which at that time stood its Medical School. He had endowed the Parkman Chair of Anatomy, then being occupied by the great Dr. Oliver Wendell Holmes. He had himself been responsible for Webster's appointment as chemistry professor. There were no two ways about it. When Webster needed money the doctor was his obvious choice. As early as 1842 he had borrowed $400. He had then borrowed more. In 1847 he had borrowed from a group headed by Dr. Parkman the sum of $2000. For the latter he had been forced to give a mortgage on all his personal property. He knew he had little chance to pay the debt but he was banking on the generosity of the "good Dr. Parkman." A year later, in 1848, he even went to Dr. Parkman's brother-in-law, the merchant Shaw, and prevailed upon him to buy a mineral collection for $1,200. This was most unfortunate. The mineral collection, like the rest of Webster's property, in hock to Dr. Parkman and his group, was not Webster's to sell. By so doing he had made the doctor guilty of that cardinal sin of Yankeeism—the sin of being shown up as an easy mark. No longer was there for Webster any "good Dr. Parkman." "From that moment onward," says author Stewart Holbrook, "poor Professor Webster knew what it was like to have a Yankee bloodhound on his trail. His creditor was a punctilious man who paid his own obligations when due and he expected the same of everybody else, even a Harvard professor." *

Dr. Parkman dogged Professor Webster in the streets, outside his home, even to the classrooms. He would come in and take a front-row seat at Webster's lectures. He would not say anything; he would just sit and glare in that remarkable way

---

* "Murder at Harvard," by Stewart Holbrook, *The American Scholar*, 1945.

of his. He wrote the professor notes, not just plain insulting notes but the awful, superior, skin-biting notes of the Yankee gentleman. He spoke sternly of legal processes. Meeting Webster he would never shout at him but instead address him in clipped Proper Bostonian accents. It was always the same question. When would the professor be "ready" for him?

Dr. Parkman even bearded Professor Webster in his den, in the inner recesses of the latter's laboratory at the Medical School. He had been there, in the professor's private back room —according to the janitor of the building—on Monday evening, November 19th, just four days before he had disappeared.

The janitor was a strange man, the grim New England village type, a small person with dark brooding eyes. His name was Ephraim Littlefield. He watched with growing interest the goings-on around him. Following Webster's call on Rev. Francis Parkman, which established the farthest link yet on the trail of Dr. Parkman's walk, it had of course been necessary to search the Medical School. Littlefield wanted this done thoroughly, as thoroughly for example as they were dragging the Charles River outside. He personally led the investigators to Webster's laboratory. Everything was searched, all but the private back room and adjoining privy. One of the party of investigators, which also included Dr. Parkman's agent Kingsley, was a police officer named Derastus Clapp. Littlefield prevailed upon this officer to go into the back room, but just as Clapp opened the door Professor Webster solicitously called out for him to be careful. There were dangerous articles in there, he said. "Very well, then," said Officer Clapp, "I will not go in there and get blowed up." He backed out again.

The whole search was carried on to the satisfaction of even Robert Gould Shaw who, after all, knew at firsthand the story of Webster's duplicity via the mineral collection. And who was the little janitor Ephraim Littlefield to dispute the word of the great merchant Robert Shaw? As each day went by the theory of murder was becoming more and more generally accepted, but in a Boston Society eternally geared to the mesh of a Harvard A.B. degree the idea of pinning a homicide on a Harvard man—and a professor at that—was heresy itself. One might as well pry for the body of Dr. Parkman among the prayer cushions of the First Family pews in Trinity Church.

But Littlefield was not, in the socially sacrosanct meaning of the words, a "Harvard man." He was a Harvard janitor. Furthermore he was stubborn. He wanted the Medical School searched again. When it was, he was once more prodding the investigators to greater efforts. He told them they should visit the cellar of the building, down in the section where the Charles River water flowed in and carried off waste matter from the dissecting rooms and privies above. The agent Kingsley took one gentlemanly sniff from the head of the stairs and refused to accompany the janitor and the other investigators any farther. The others, however, went on. As they passed the wall under Webster's back room the janitor volunteered the information that it was now the only place in the building that hadn't been searched. Why not, the men wanted to know. The janitor explained that to get there it would be necessary to dig through the wall. The men had little stomach left for this sort of operation and soon rejoined Kingsley upstairs.

Littlefield, however, had plenty of stomach. He determined to dig into the wall himself. Whether he was by this time, Monday, already suspicious of Professor Webster has never been made clear. He had, it is true, heard the Webster-Parkman meeting of Monday night the week before. He had distinctly overheard the doctor say to the professor in that ever-insinuating way, "Something, Sir, must be accomplished." Just yesterday, Sunday, he had seen Professor Webster enter the Medical School around noontime, apparently shortly after he had made his call on Rev. Francis Parkman. Webster had spoken to him and had acted "very queerly." Come to think of it, Littlefield brooded, Sunday was a queer day for the professor to be hanging around the School anyway. "Ephraim," writes Richard Dempewolff, one of the Parkman case's most avid devotees, "was one of those shrewd New England conclusion-jumpers who, unfortunately for the people they victimize, are usually right. By putting two and two together, Mr. Littlefield achieved a nice round dozen." *

The janitor's wife was a practical woman. She thought little of her husband's determination to search the filthy old place under the private rooms of the Harvard professor she had always regarded as a fine gentleman. Her husband would lose his job, that would be what would happen. Just you wait and see, Mr. Littlefield.

Mr. Littlefield deferred to Mrs. Littlefield and did wait—until Tuesday, five days after Dr. Parkman's disappearance. On Tuesday something extraordinary happened. At four o'clock in the afternoon he heard Professor Webster's bell jangle, a signal that the janitor was wanted. He went to Webster's laboratory. The professor asked him if he had bought his Thanksgiving turkey yet. Littlefield did not know what to say. He replied he had thought some about going out Thanksgiving.

"Here," said Webster, "go and get yourself one." With that he handed the janitor an order for a turkey at a near-by grocery store.

John White Webster had here made a fatal error. The call he had paid on Rev. Francis Parkman had been bad enough. It had aroused the searching of the Medical School and had brought Littlefield actively into the case. But as Webster later admitted he had been afraid that sooner or later someone would have found out about his 1:30 Friday rendezvous with Dr. Parkman and felt that his best chance lay in making a clean breast of it. For this action in regard to the janitor's Thanksgiving turkey, however, there could be no such defense. If he hoped to win the janitor over to "his side," then he was a poor judge of human nature indeed. Harvard Janitor Ephraim Littlefield had worked for Harvard Professor John Webster for seven years—curiously the same length of time Professor John Webster had been borrowing from Dr. Parkman—without ever receiving a present of

* *Famous Old New England Murders,* by Richard Dempewolff (Brattleboro, Vt.: Stephen Daye Press, 1942).

any kind. And now, a Thanksgiving turkey. Even the deferentially dormant suspicions of Mrs. Littlefield were thoroughly aroused.

Janitor Littlefield had no chance to begin his labors Wednesday. Professor Webster was in his laboratory most of the day. On Thanksgiving, however, while Mrs. Littlefield kept her eyes peeled for the professor or any other intruder, the janitor began the task of crow-barring his way through the solid brick wall below the back room. It was slow work and even though the Littlefields took time off to enjoy their dinner—the janitor had characteristically not passed up the opportunity to procure a nine-pound bird—it was soon obvious he could not get through the wall in one day. That evening the Littlefields took time off again. They went to a dance given by the Sons of Temperance Division of the Boston Odd Fellows. They stayed until four o'clock in the morning. "There were twenty dances," Littlefield afterwards recalled, "and I danced eighteen out of the twenty."

Late Friday afternoon, after Professor Webster had left for the day, Littlefield was at his digging again. This time he had taken the precaution of advising two of the School's First Family doctors, Doctors Bigelow and Jackson, of what he was doing. They were surprised but told him since he had started he might as well continue. But they were against his idea of informing the dean of the School, Dr. Holmes, of the matter. It would, they felt, disturb the dean unnecessarily.

Even a half-hearted First Family blessing has always counted for something in Boston, and Janitor Littlefield now went to work with renewed vigor. Again his wife stood watch. At five-thirty he broke through the fifth of the five courses of brick in the wall. "I held my light forward," he afterwards declared, "and the first thing which I saw was the pelvis of a man, and two parts of a leg . . . It was no place for these things."

It was not indeed. Within fifteen minutes Doctors Bigelow and Jackson were on the scene. Later Dr. Holmes himself would view the remains. Meanwhile of course there was the matter of a little trip out to the Webster home in Cambridge.

To that same police officer who had been so loath to get himself "blowed up" in Webster's back room fell the honor of making the business trip to Cambridge and arresting the Harvard professor. Once bitten, Derastus Clapp was twice shy. There would be no more monkeyshines, Harvard or no Harvard. He had his cab halt some distance from the Webster home and approached on foot. Opening the outer gate he started up the walk just as Webster himself appeared on the steps of his house, apparently showing a visitor out. The professor attempted to duck back inside. Officer Clapp hailed him. "We are about to search the Medical School again," he called, moving forward rapidly as he spoke, "and we wish you to be present." Webster feigned the traditional Harvard indifference. It was a waste of time; the School had already been searched twice. Clapp laid a stern hand on his shoulder. Webster, escorted outward and suddenly noting two other men in the waiting cab, wanted to go back for his keys. Officer Clapp was not unaware of the drama of the moment. "Professor Webster," he said, "we have keys enough to unlock the whole of Harvard College."

Boston was in an uproar. Dr. Parkman had not walked off the face of the earth. He had been pushed off—and by the authoritative hands of a Harvard professor! Even the *Transcript,* calm when there was still a hope the Parkman case was merely a matter of disappearance, could restrain itself no longer. It threw its genteel caution to the winds. There were two exclamation marks after its headline, and its editor called on Shakespeare himself to sum up the situation:

Since last evening, our whole population has been in a state of the greatest possible excitement in consequence of the astounding rumor that the body of Dr. Parkman has been discovered, and that Dr. John W. Webster, Professor of Chemistry in the Medical School of Harvard College, and a gentleman connected by marriage with some of our most distinguished families, has been arrested and imprisoned, on suspicion of being the murderer. Incredulity, then amazement, and then blank, unspeakable horror have been the emotions, which have agitated the public mind as the rumor has gone on, gathering countenance and confirmation. Never in the annals of crime in Massachusetts has such a sensation been produced.

In the streets, in the market-place, at every turn, men greet each other with pale, eager looks and the inquiry, "Can it be true?" And then as the terrible reply, "the circumstances begin to gather weight against him," is wrung forth, the agitated listener can only vent his sickening sense of horror, in some expression as that of Hamlet,—

"O, horrible! O, horrible! most horrible!"

There is irony in the fact that proud, staid Boston chose the time it did to provide American Society with the nineteenth century's outstanding social circus. Boston was at the height of its cultural attainments in 1849. In that year a scholarly but hardly earth-shaking book by a rather minor Boston author, *The History of Spanish Literature* by George Ticknor, was the world literary event of the year and the only book recommended by Lord Macaulay to Queen Victoria. Yet just three months later, on March 19, 1850, Boston put on a show which for pure social artistry Barnum himself would have had difficulty matching. The Boston courtroom had everything. It had one of Boston's greatest jurists, Judge Lemuel Shaw, on its bench; it had the only Harvard professor ever to be tried for murder, John White Webster, as its defendant; it had promised witnesses of national renown, from Dr. Oliver Wendell Holmes on down; and in the offing, so to speak, it had the shades of Dr. George Parkman, perhaps the most socially distinguished victim in the annals of American crime.

Nobody wanted to miss such a sight. Trains and stages from all parts of the East brought people to Boston. They wanted tickets. Everybody in Boston wanted tickets, too. Consequences of revolutionary proportions were feared if they could not be accommodated. Yet what to do? There was only a small gallery to spare, it having been decreed in typical Boston fashion that the main part of the courtroom would be reserved on an invitation basis. Finally, Field Marshal Tukey hit on the only possible solution, which was to effect a complete change of audience in the gallery every ten minutes during the proceedings. It took elaborate street barricades and doorway defenses to do the job, but in the eleven days of the trial, to that little gallery holding hardly more than a hundred souls, came a recorded total of sixty thousand persons. Considering that the constabulary of Boston assigned to the job numbered just fifteen men, this feat ranks as a monumental milestone in police annals.

From the suspense angle the trial, which has been called a landmark in the history of criminal law, must have been something of a disappointment. By the time it began, despite Webster's protestations of innocence, there was little doubt in the minds of most of the spectators as to the guilt of the professor. A few days after his arrest a skeleton measuring 70½ inches had finally been assembled from the grisly remains found lying about under the professor's back room, and while the sum total of this was an inch taller than Dr. Parkman had been in happier days, there had been no question in the minds of the coroner's jury, of Dr. Holmes, and of a lot of other people, but that Dr. Parkman it was. The case against the professor was one of circumstantial evidence of course. No one had seen Webster and Parkman together at the time of the murder; indeed, during the trial the time of the murder was never satisfactorily established. But the strongest Webster adherents had to admit that it was evidence of a very powerful nature, as Chief Justice Shaw could not fail to point out in his famous charge to the jury, an address which lawyers today still consider one of the greatest expositions of the nature and use of circumstantial evidence ever delivered.

There were a number of pro-Websterites. Harvard professor though he may have been, he was still the underdog, up against the almighty forces of Boston's First Families. Many of the Websterites had undoubtedly had experiences of their own on the score of Proper Bostonian retail penury and were ready to recognize that Dr. Parkman had been so importunate a creditor that he had quite possibly driven the little professor first to distraction and then to the deed. They went to Rufus Choate, Boston's great First Family lawyer, and asked him to undertake the defense. After reading up on the case Choate was apparently willing to do so on the condition that Webster would admit the killing and plead manslaughter. Another First Family lawyer, old Judge Fay, with whom the Webster family regularly played whist, thought a verdict of manslaughter could be reached.

But Webster would not plead guilty. From the beginning he had made his defence an all but impossible task. He talked when he shouldn't have talked and he kept quiet when, at least by the light of hindsight, he should have come clean. On his first trip to the jail he immediately asked the officers about the finding of the body. "Have they found the *whole* body?" he wanted to know. This while certainly a reasonable question in view of the wide area over which the remains were found was hardly the thing for a man in his position to be asking. Then, while vehemently protesting his innocence, he took a strychnine pill out of his waistcoat pocket and attempted to kill himself, an attempt which was foiled only by the fact that, though the dose was a large one, he was in such a nervous condition it failed to take fatal effect. At the trial Webster maintained through his lawyers that the body he was proved to be so vigorously dismembering during his spare moments in the week following November 23rd had been a Medical School cadaver brought to him for that purpose. This was sheer folly, and the prosecution had but to call upon the little dentist, Nathan Keep, to prove it so. Tooth by tooth, during what was called one of the "tumultuous moments" of the trial, Dr. Keep fitted the fragments of the false teeth found in Webster's furnace into the mold he still had in his possession. Charred as they were there could be no doubt they had once been the china-white teeth of Dr. Parkman.

The spectators were treated to other memorable scenes. The great Dr. Holmes testified twice, once for the State on the matter of the identity of the reconstructed skeleton and once for the defense as a character witness for the accused. Professor Webster's character witnesses were a howitzer battery of First Family notables, among them Doctors Bigelow and Jackson, a Codman and a Lovering, the New England historian John Gorham Palfrey and Nathaniel Bowditch, son of the famed mathematician—even Harvard's president Jared Sparks took the stand for his errant employee. All seemed to agree that Webster, if occasionally irritable, was basically a kindhearted man, and President Sparks was thoughtful enough to add one gratuitous comment. "Our professors," he said, "do not often commit murder."

Credit was due Webster for his ability as a cadaver carver. He had done the job on Dr. Parkman, it was established, with no more formidable instrument than a jackknife. A Dr. Wood-bridge Strong was especially emphatic on this point. He had dissected a good many bodies in his time, he recalled, including a rush job on a decaying pirate, but never one with just a jack-knife. Ephraim Littlefield was of course star witness for the prosecution. The indefatigable little janitor talked for one whole day on the witness stand, a total of eight hours, five hours in the morning before recess for lunch and three hours in the afternoon. Only once did he falter and that on the occasion when, under cross-examination with the defense making a valiant attempt to throw suspicion on him, he was asked if he played "gambling cards" with friends in Webster's back room. Four times the defense had to ask the question and four times Littlefield refused to answer. Finally, his New England conscience stung to the quick, he replied in exasperation, "If you ask me if I played cards there *last winter,* I can truthfully say I did not."

In those days prisoners were not allowed to testify, but on the last day of the trial Professor Webster was asked if he wanted to say anything. Against the advice of his counsel he rose and spoke for fifteen minutes. He spent most of those precious moments denying the accusation that he had written the various anonymous notes which had been turning up from time to time in the City Marshal's office ever since the disappearance of Dr. Parkman. One of these had been signed CIVIS and Webster's last sentence was a pathetic plea for CIVIS to come forward if he was in the courtroom. CIVIS did not, and at eight o'clock on the evening of March 30th the trial was over.

Even the jury seems to have been overcome with pity for the professor. Before filing out of the courtroom the foreman, pointing a trembling finger at Webster, asked: "is that all? Is that the end? Can nothing further be said in defense of the man?" Three hours later the foreman and his cohorts were back, having spent, it is recorded, the first two hours and fifty-five minutes in prayer "to put off the sorrowful duty." When the verdict was delivered, "an awful and unbroken silence ensued, in which the Court, the jury, the clerk, and the spectators seemed to be absorbed in their own reflections."

Webster's hanging, by the neck and until he was dead, proceeded without untoward incident in the courtyard of Boston's Leverett Street jail just five months to the day after he had been declared guilty. Before that time, however, the professor made a complete confession. He stated that Dr. Parkman had come into his laboratory on that fatal Friday and that, when he had been unable to produce the money he owed, the doctor had shown him a sheaf of papers proving that he had been responsible for getting him his professorship. The doctor then added, "I got you into your office, Sir, and now I will get you out of it." This, said Webster, so infuriated him that he seized a stick of wood off his laboratory bench and struck Dr. Parkman one blow on the head. Death was instantaneous and Webster declared, "I saw nothing but the alternative of a successful removal and concealment of the body, on the one hand, and of infamy and de-

struction on the other." He then related his week-long attempt
to dismember and burn the body. Even the clergyman who
regularly visited Webster in his cell during his last days was not
able to extract from the professor the admission that the crime
had been premeditated. He had done it in that one frenzy of
rage. "I am irritable and passionate," the clergyman quoted
Webster as saying, "and Dr. Parkman was the most provoking of
men."

The late Edmund Pearson, recognized authority on nonfic-
tional homicide here and abroad, has called the Webster-Parkman case America's classic murder and the one which has lived
longest in books of reminiscences. Certainly in Boston's First
Family Society the aftermath of the case has been hardly less
distinguished than its actual occurrence. To this day no Proper
Bostonian grandfather autobiography is complete without some
reference to the case. The Beacon Hill house at 8 Walnut Street
from which Dr. Parkman started out on his walk that Friday
morning almost a hundred years ago is still standing, and its
present occupant, a prominent Boston lawyer, is still on occasion
plagued by the never-say-die curious.

Among Boston Parkmans the effect was a profound one. For
years certain members of the Family shrank from Society altogether, embarrassed as they were by the grievous result of Dr.
Parkman's financial punctiliousness and all too aware of the
sympathy extended Professor Webster in his budgetary plight.
In the doctor's immediate family it is noteworthy that his widow
headed the subscription list of a fund taken up to care for Webster's wife and children. Dr. Parkman's son, George Francis
Parkman, was five years out of Harvard in 1849. He had been, in
contrast to his father, a rather gay blade as a youth and at college had taken part in Hasty Pudding Club theatricals; at the
time of the murder he was enjoying himself in Paris. He returned to Boston a marred man. He moved his mother and sister from 8 Walnut Street and took a house at 33 Beacon Street.
From the latter house he buried his mother and aunt, and there
he and his sister lived on as Boston Society's most distinguished

recluses. His solitary existence never included even the solace of a job. Describing him as he appeared a full fifty years after the crime a biographer records:

> Past the chain of the bolted door on Beacon Street no strangers, save those who came on easily recognised business, were ever allowed to enter. Here George Francis Parkman and his sister Harriet, neither of whom ever married, practised the utmost frugality, the master of the house going himself to the market every day to purchase their meager provisions, and invariably paying cash for the simple supplies he brought home.
>
> The windows of his house looked out upon the Common but he did not frequent it . . . He always walked slowly and alone, in a stately way, and attracted attention by his distinguished though retiring appearance . . . In cool weather he wore a heavy coat of dark cloth and his shoulders and neck were closely wrapped with a wide scarf, the ends of which were tucked into his coat or under folds. He sheltered himself against the east winds of Boston just as he seemed, by his manner, to shelter his inmost self from contact with the ordinary affairs of men.*

Tremors of the Parkman earthquake continued to be felt by Boston Society often at times when they were least desired. Twenty years later, when Boston was privileged to play proud host to Charles Dickens, there was a particularly intense tremor. Dickens was asked which one of the city's historic landmarks he would like to visit first. "The room where Dr. Parkman was murdered," he replied, and there being no doubt he meant what he said, nothing remained for a wry-faced group of Boston's best but to shepherd the distinguished novelish out to the chemistry laboratory of the Harvard Medical School.

A Webster-Parkman story, vintage of 1880, is still told today by Boston's distinguished author and teacher, Bliss Perry. He recalls that for a meeting of New England college officers at Williamstown, Massachusetts, his mother had been asked to put

* *Famous Families of Massachusetts,* by Mary Caroline Crawford (Boston: Little Brown) © 1930.

up as a guest in her house Boston's First Family poet laureate, diplomat and first editor of the *Atlantic*, James Russell Lowell. Unfortunately Lowell was at that time teaching at Harvard and for all his other accomplishments Mrs. Perry would have none of him. He had to be quartered elsewhere.

"I could not sleep," Mrs. Perry said, "if one of those Harvard professors were in the house."

CHAPTER ELEVEN

CUSTOMS BUT NO MANNERS

The scene is the dining room in the Proper Bostonian home of Judge John Lowell in the suburb of Chestnut Hill. The time is the early morning of half a century ago. The characters are: Mrs. John Lowell, the true Boston dowager type, serene, capable; a maid, also Boston type, ageless, starchy; old Judge John himself—a Lowell.

As the curtain rises, the time is 7:30 by the grandfather clock. The Lowells are at breakfast, Mrs. Lowell at one end of the table, her husband at the other. The judge's face is hidden behind his morning paper. From the pantry the maid enters, comes over close to Mrs. Lowell and says something in a low voice. It is obviously bad news, which Mrs. Lowell is determined to communicate at once to her husband. The cook has burned his cereal. There is no more of such cereal in the house. Lest there be any misunderstanding Mrs. Lowell concludes her speech slowly: "There isn't going to be any oatmeal this morning, John."

This is no minor domestic tragedy. To the best of his wife's knowledge Judge John Lowell has up until this morning had oatmeal every single day of his life. The silence is nerve-racking. Slowly the paper is lowered and the face of the judge appears. Then the reply:

"Frankly, my dear, I never did care for it."

The significance of that story goes beyond the fact that it is gospel truth as handed down in a succeeding generation of the Lowell Family. It is more than the single story of one Lowell going without oatmeal for one morning. It is actually a typical story. Old Judge John Lowell, last of a line of three Judge John Lowells, was a character, but not in the individual sense that, for example, the Father of Clarence Day's *Life With Father* was a character. Day's Father was a breakfast-table tyrant capable of turning every morning repast into a regal ceremony for himself and an ordeal for his wife, children and cook, but one can scarcely imagine his sons or his grandsons carrying on in his tradition. In Boston the tradition of the ceremonial breakfast lives on. At her "Sunrise Farm" home in Westwood, Mrs. Ralph Lowell, wife of Boston's most prominent Lowell today, serves oatmeal every morning. In other Proper Bostonian homes in Chestnut Hill or Dedham or Dover there are also other Lowells or Cabots or Higginsons who eat their oatmeal—and do so, of course, without considering the irrelevant question of whether they like it or not.

Oatmeal is simply a Proper Bostonian custom, and as such it has taken its apparently permanent place alongside such other recognized customs as the morning lecture and the afternoon walk, the trustee meeting and the charity bazaar, the daily tea and the anniversary dinner, the formal call and Friday Symphony. Unfortunately, somewhere along this line, in the Proper Bostonian mind, the mandatory maintenance of all these customs or social conventions would seem to have taken the place of manners or social graces. The poet T. S. Eliot put this in philosophical terms when some years ago he defined Boston Society as "quite uncivilized—but refined beyond the point of civilization." Speaking more specifically, a historian of the Cabot Family summed up his subject briefly. "A strange dynasty," he declared, "with customs but no manners."

Such a phrase, it seems only fair to note, might well have been used for almost any other of Boston's First Families besides the oft-maligned Cabot. Certainly the Forbeses are strange. Their repertoire of customs runs the Boston gamut from bird walking to mahjong. As for their manners, acting what is called "Forbesy" has long been synonymous in Boston with high-hat behavior. The phrase is also applicable to the Adamses. Branded as strange from their insistence on living in Quincy instead of in more socially circumspect territory, they have been practicing their Family customs since 1636. Yet their manners were classified for posterity in the phrase that they alone could say "even a gracious thing in an ungracious way."

It would be possible to go farther down the line. But in the same way that the Lowells' oatmeal stands forth as the typical Proper Bostonian custom it is possible to take the Cabots as typical of Boston Society's lack of manners. The Cabot record of living up to the phrase originally coined for their Family is a strong one. Cabot women, in particular, have been known for their brusque deportment apparently from the time the Family first moved to Boston. An authority on these women, since he himself married one, old Colonel Lee, nineteenth-century lion of Lee, Higginson & Co., was among the first to take cognizance of this. He once declared that not only his Family, but the Lowells, the Jacksons and the Higginsons as well, "came up from Newburyport to Boston, social and kindly people inclined to make acquaintances and mingle with the world pleasantly . . . But they got some Cabot wives who shut them up." In more recent times another Cabot husband has been known to admit that he has often discussed with his wife what he frankly regards as an inherent gracelessness in her Family. Meeting the late Dr. Richard Cabot, he felt free, in view of his wife's kinship, to ask the distinguished doctor and sociologist to dinner. He has never forgotten Dr. Richard's matter-of-fact reply: "Really I have so many people I should like to dine with but never get around to, I should not pretend that I ever would do it."

The redeeming feature of such a remark would seem to lie in its frankness. Cabots are nothing if not forthright. In another

Society a Family occupying the same position as the Cabots in Boston would undoubtedly feel it incumbent upon themselves to make at least a pretense in the direction of social polish. The Cabots make none—and Boston Society cherishes them the more for this. The Cabots are in their way the Great Danes, or the mastiffs, of the Boston social breed, and if a Proper Bostonian, proudly pointing out a Cabot home to a visitor, should be greeted at the gate by a Cabot with an assumed show of friendliness, he would feel as foolish in front of his visitor as if, after expounding on the fierceness of his favorite watchdog, the animal should appear on the scene and behave like a lap dog.

Fortunately his Cabots rarely let him down. Occupying close to two pages in the Boston *Social Register*, the most impressive representation in that volume of any First Family in the city, the Cabots, wherever they may live and no matter how remote their connections with one another, all seem to share a magnificent disregard of the minor amenities of life. "My wife's always telling me," explains Judge Charles Cabot, "I can run a community drive but I don't know how to give a Christmas present." Godfrey Lowell Cabot, present-day Family patriarch, is a charming example of social independence. At various gatherings where he is in attendance, conversation must be tailored to suit his presence. Though he was once active in Boston politics himself, politics under a Democratic administration would never be a fit subject for discussion. So bitterly was the patriarch opposed to the liberal policies of Woodrow Wilson—a man, he once said, "who could not run a peanut stand"—that even his closest friends never cared to find out where he stood on Franklin D. Roosevelt. A young man from Philadelphia tells the story of having been invited to Godfrey Lowell Cabot's house on Beacon Street and, knowing nothing of the man's reputation and indeed little about him except his name, proceeded to josh him on the latter point, asking him how it felt to be both a Lowell and a Cabot in Boston. What followed was a silence of such ominousness that he knew at once he had overstepped his

bounds. "I'm afraid that's a pretty silly question, Mr. Cabot,"
he said sheepishly. "Young man," thundered Cabot, "it's the
damnedest silliest question I've been asked in eighty years."

Ironic as it may seem today, Boston was once America's manners center. In the nineteenth century the city reigned supreme
in the business of publishing books on etiquette. Even the great
Emerson took it upon himself to become a missionary of manners and has been classed by one etiquette historian as the ablest
philosopher of manners this country has produced. "Manners
alone," said Emerson, "get people out of the quadruped state
. . . get them washed, clothed, and set up on end." The philosopher, however, left it to other Boston writers to get down to
specifics. One of the most widely read of all these was Mrs. John
Farrar, who published in 1838 a little volume entitled *The
Young Lady's Friend*. The fact that Mrs. Farrar was the wife of
a Harvard professor undoubtedly lent her work additional
prestige; in any case, she carried her idea of Proper Bostonian
manners into virtually every civilized part of America of her
day. From behavior at the lecture in the morning to the formal
dinner at night, Mrs. Farrar's book was a bible. Her ideal "gen-
tlewoman" she frankly defined as "the daughter of a rich man."
At lectures, such a girl must never "run, jump, scream, scramble,
or push, in order to get a good seat." At the formal, or what Mrs.
Farrar calls the "ceremonious" dinner, her girl's behavior was
carefully outlined from the very moment of entry through her
hostess' door.

"With erect carriage and firm step," Mrs. Farrar advised,
"enter the drawing-room, either with your parents, three together, or following them alone, or on the arm of a friend or
sister." She made clear that there were to be no distractions
until her young lady had properly curtsied to her hostess. Five
suitable topics of conversation were listed to use up the time
until the move to the dining room: "a child, a picture, an animal, a worked ottoman, a bunch of flowers." The dining room

itself was full of perils. The young lady must not play with the cutlery, make pellets of the bread, blow her nose or touch her hair. Something spilled was not to be fussed over, and commended to her attention on this score was the conduct of a "very accomplished gentleman" who, in the carving of a tough goose, had the misfortune to land the bird in the lap of the lady seated next to him. Instead of becoming confused in this situation, he calmly addressed the lady with the words, "Ma'am, I will thank you for that goose." Mrs. Farrar decorously withheld the name of the man but as all of Boston Society knew—since the episode occurred at a large First Family dinner party—her "accomplished gentleman" was none other than Daniel Webster.

In her closing remarks on the ceremonious dinner Mrs. Farrar would seem to have hit the nail on the head, albeit unconsciously, in the matter of the ever-characteristic ennui of Boston Society at play:

> Be sure to get through with your dessert, and have your gloves on, all ready to move, by the time the lady of the house gives the signal . . . the sooner you depart after taking coffee the better . . . A dinner, well performed by all the actors in it, is very fatiguing, and, as it generally occupies three hours or more, most persons are glad to go away when it is fairly done.

A curious trend of Boston etiquette writers was their early antipathy toward New York. In the later days of the Gilded Age there was of course to be a lasting chasm between Boston Society and the Manhattan merry-go-round as headed by the Astors, the Vanderbilts and the Whitneys. But even in Mrs. Farrar's heyday in the middle of the century one notes a brief slur at the upstart Gothamites in her paragraph devoted to "jiggling":

> Some girls have a trick of *jiggling* their bodies (I am obliged to coin a word to describe it); they shake all over, as if they were hung on spiral wires, like the geese in a Dutch toy; than which, nothing can be more ungraceful, or unmeaning. It robs

a lady of all dignity, and makes her appear trifling and insignificant. Some do it only on entering a room, others do it every time they are introduced to anybody, and whenever they begin to talk to anyone. It must have originated in embarrassment, and a desire to do something, without knowing exactly what; and being adopted by some popular belle, it became, at one time, a fashion in New York, and spread thence to other cities.

Mrs. Farrar's "fashion in New York" becomes downright "folly" when Florence Howe Hall, daughter of Boston's revered grande dame Julia Ward Howe, has her say in *The Correct Thing in Good Society*, published in 1888. Flinging down the Proper Bostonian gauntlet she declares:

There is a form of folly quite prevalent in New York which seems to be peculiar to the place. It is for women who are entirely respectable and well-behaved members of Society to imitate the dress of a fast loud class, because they think it is rather knowing to do so. Thus, one will often see a middle-aged, quiet-looking woman resplendent with gold-dyed hair and a very showy costume, the incongruity between the garments and their wearer quite startling.

In many cases these rules of etiquette reach remarkable heights. Mrs. Hall decrees that the mark of a gentleman was his removal of his hat with his left hand; only by so doing could he leave his right hand free for a possible handshake. Mrs. Hall also points to the exemplary upbringing of a First Family girl who, though only three years old, would *never* help herself at table from a dish unless it was one passed from the left side. Another writer cautions the male dinner-table partner of a lady who in the course of the meal may perchance "raise an unmanageable portion to her mouth." The dictum was stern: "Cease all conversation with her, and look steadfastly into the opposite part of the room." Still a third etiquetteer summarizes the visiting-card ordeal. This was "simplified" for persons of high social position who could not be expected to repay all their obligations with actual calls into a matter of leaving cards as follows: For a personal visit, turn down the upper right-hand corner; for congratulation, turn the upper left corner; for condolence, the lower left; adieu, lower right; and for a call on the whole family, turn down the entire left end. Though Boston Society today still sets much store by card-calling, even the vaunted Brahmin mentality appears to have been overtaxed by this dog-earing rigmarole, and the system was ultimately officially dismissed by Maud C. Cooke in her *Social Etiquette*, published in Boston in 1896. "Its disuse," she wrote, "is a satisfaction to all concerned."

As might be expected in a city in which the No. 1 nineteenth-century women's club was composed of a group of unmarried ladies who met once a week for the specific purpose of discussing "the proper attitude to be maintained toward gentlemen," Boston's etiquette books were starchy in their concern over the relationship between the male and the female. Mrs. Farrar was a strong believer in the good influence that sisters could be on brothers:

> I have been told by men, who had passed unharmed through the temptations of youth, that they owed their escape from many dangers to the intimate companionship of affectionate and pure-minded sisters. They have been saved from a hazardous meeting with idle company by some home engagement, of which their sisters were the charm; they have refrained from mixing with the impure, because they would not bring home thoughts and feelings which they could not share with those trusting and loving friends; they have put aside the wine-cup and abstained from stronger potations, because they would not profane with their fumes the holy kiss, with which they were accustomed to bid their sisters good night.

The advent of the waltz in the city coincided with the heyday of the etiquetteers, and virtually all of them warned of its pitfalls. "A gentleman," one counsels, "never encircles the lady's waist until the dance begins and drops his arms as soon as it ends." Another codifier washed her hands of any attempt to tell young things how to behave during such a dance. "The waltz," she declares, "is suitable only for married persons." If they had been left to the manners mentors the Nineties would never have been known as Gay—at least in Boston. The era of the Plush Age man was also the era of what has been called the "antimacassar approach to womanhood," and Mrs. Farrar took firm steps to warn Proper Boston girls against the male animal:

> If the natural feelings of modesty are not sufficient to guard you from all personal familiarity with the young men of your acquaintance, let good breeding, and good taste, aid you in laying down rules for yourself on this head. Never join in any rude plays, that will subject you to being kissed or handled in any way by gentlemen. Do not suffer your hand to be held or squeezed, without showing that it displeases you by instantly withdrawing it. If a finger is put out to touch a chain that is round your neck, or a breast-pin that you are wearing, draw back, and take it off for inspection. Accept not unnecessary assistance in putting on cloaks, shawls, overshoes, or anything of the sort. Be not lifted in and out of carriages, on or off a horse; sit not with another in a place that is too narrow; read not out of the same book; let not your eagerness to see anything induce you to place your head close to another person's. These, and many other little points of delicacy and refinement, deserve to be made fixed habits, and then they will sit easily and gracefully upon you, heightening the respect of all who approach you, and operating as an almost invisible, though a very impenetrable fence, keeping off vulgar familiarity, and that desecration of the person, which has too often led to vice.*

For Boston the cherished Victorian chaperone was not enough. Into the Boston language came the phrase "to matronize," one still heard on occasion in First Family circles and which has always had a sinister meaning indeed for young twosomes.

---

* There is evidence that even inhabitants of the staid Boston Athenaeum have difficulty in swallowing Mrs. Farrar in toto. In the margin of the page opposite this quotation from *The Young Lady's Friend* there appears the notation: "BAH!"

By it the guardian becomes more than a mere third party to the
scene; she becomes an actual mother-on-the-spot and must watch
with motherly intuition, as one writer put it, "the character and
intentions, as well as the actions" of the young man in question.
As the businesswoman emerged in the social picture she alone
would seem to be immune from this sort of matronization. In
one Boston book, however, she is sternly cautioned, evidently by
a disciple of Mrs. Farrar, to avoid "the pretty little airs and
graces, the charming ways which are so delightful in a parlor,
but which are so utterly out of place, nay even dangerous, in the
arena of daily struggle for bread and butter."

There was only one place for a gentleman to propose to a lady
—under her father's roof. Furthermore father must be asked,
and definitely, for his daughter's hand. It is basic to an understanding of Boston Social history to realize how slowly and gingerly these morals maxims, which elsewhere in the country
became rapidly regarded as antediluvian, managed to date
themselves in Boston. Up to the time of World War I a man
who took a young lady to a Boston theatre, even a matinee, was
socially suspect if he did not provide a third ticket for the chaperone or matron for the occasion. Genius was not the only thing
which, in the words of Henry Adams, "dawned slowly on the
Bostonian mind." Sex did, also. When Henry James wrote in his
A London Life of the plight of a young woman who was left
alone and unchaperoned with a young man for a short period in
a box at the opera—and confidently expected the young man to
marry her after having placed her in such a compromising position—he was satirizing the morality of the manners books of the
day. James's readers, however, took the book in all seriousness.
When John Marquand had his Bostonian of Bostonians, George
Apley, become concerned with the propriety of placing a volume
of Freud beside that of Emerson, even this bit of parlor Puritanism was based on stern fact. Boston's book collectors had been
specifically warned against literary uncongeniality in an etiquette pamphlet of the year 1863: "The perfect hostess will see
to it that the works of male and female authors be properly

separated on her bookshelves. Their proximity unless they happen to be married should not be tolerated."

Unfortunately for the history of Boston manners the Proper Bostonian's attention to the etiquette books published in his city would seem to have ended with the advice he found under their sections devoted to morality. One diarist and significantly a Cabot one, Elizabeth Dwight Cabot, went so far as to hold too much morality responsible for this sorry situation. She is doubtful, however, about Continental gallantry:

We are moral over the breakfast table and moral the last thing at night, and moral all the hours between. We moralize in society and at home, and I confess to an unsatisfied longing, occasionally, for a little of the harmless and graceful superficiality of the French. These, however, are the natural sensations of a girl brought up in the most moral of cities and belonging to the most moral family in that city, and I have no doubt that if I tried the superficial system a while, I should seek refuge from a still deeper discontent in morality.*

The Cabots were not alone at fault. Dr. Holmes, in the midst of the era when the etiquette books proclaimed good manners to be the paramount mark of gentility, noted rather wryly that among his own friends it was the exception rather than the rule for one to be "openly pleasant and courteous." Barrett Wendell, last of the Boston Brahmins, went Holmes one better. In a single line which he wrote with evident pride about his father Wendell managed what would seem to be a summary of Boston's First Family mannerlessness. "My father," he declared, "was never the first to seek a friendship." Still another noted commentator who viewed Proper Bostonian manners with distinct disfavor was Julia Ward Howe. In a memorable lecture delivered before

* *Letters of Elizabeth Cabot,* by Elizabeth Cabot (Boston: Privately printed, 1905).

the New England Woman's Club in 1895 entitled "Is Polite Society Polite?" Mrs. Howe concluded in no uncertain terms that it was not—at least, she declared, not "the class [of Boston Society] which assumes to give the rest a standard of taste." Meanwhile Mrs. Howe's etiquetteer daughter Florence, writing her manual on *Hints on How to Acquire Good Table Manners,* advised her customers that Boston's best could not even be trusted with knife and fork:

> Go to . . . Young's in Boston, and bribe the head-waiter to point out to you any "real old families" that may be present and watch their operations. Alas! even then you may be disappointed. There are men of old family and high degree who eat unpleasantly—champing the end of the fork perhaps, as if it were a curb bit.

Boston's "men of high degree," it would seem, have established a wide reputation for their want of social graces. Hearing a friend expound on the virtues of Lawrence Lowell, late president of Harvard, the novelist William Dean Howells was moved to remark, "Ah, but is he a *friendly* person?" The answer was of course obvious. Though Howells was a much older man than Lowell, both had at the time been members not only of Boston's Saturday Club but its Tavern Club as well—and for many years—yet the novelist had never had the high honor of speaking to Lowell. The late Proper Bostonian Rodman Weld was a picture of formal courtesy. Driving down Beacon Street he never failed to salute the traffic policeman with a grave doffing of his hat. Outside the Somerset Club, however, he showed where he stood in the matter of manners when, observing a fellow club member pass him hastily without a greeting, he hailed the man. "William," said he, "do we bow when we meet, or do we not? It is a matter of complete indifference to me, but it is for you to choose." Such bluntness, long accepted in Boston, is often misunderstood in other parts of the country. Even the best-intentioned have been known to be brought up short. Historian M. A. DeWolfe Howe tells the story of a young Proper Bostonian, traveling in the West on a train and chatting with a Westerner, and attempting to stoop to conquer with a remark, unfortunately too obviously patronizing, about the beauty of the countryside. "If Columbus had landed on the West Coast," snapped his companion, "Boston would never have been heard of." A present-day Beacon Streeter, a Cabot husband and charter member of Boston's newly founded Waltz Club, found himself in an equally hopeless position when, dancing with an attractive girl from the South, he was told what a good dancer he was. "I love to dance," was his candid reply. Whereupon the girl left him in a huff. Catching up with her, he endeavored to find out what he had said to offend her. "It's time you Bostonians learned," she said, "that there are places in this country where girls aren't used to giving compliments first—and when they do, the least they expect is one in return!"

In extreme instances, when ruffled or crossed, the Proper Bostonian has been known to be a mannerless man indeed. Afflicted, apparently at birth, with what Henry Adams called "a certain chronic irritability—a sort of Bostonitis," he is no man to trifle with. A Milton Cunningham, entering his driveway and noting a stranger cutting wood on his place, promptly repaired to his house, procured a gun and shot the man dead. He was later freed by the courts. A Chestnut Hill Curtis, involved in a seat-saving altercation with a fellow passenger on a commuting train, twisted the man's nose so violently the man was disfigured for life. For this he was forced to serve a stretch in the Brookline jail, and though his stay was a short one and made pleasant by the solicitude of his First Family friends, who kept him supplied with port wine, tea biscuits, and copies of the Boston *Transcript*, he was so indignant over the handling of his case that, when freed, he promptly left Boston for Europe and never returned. On the North Shore, Boston's millionaire investor Frederick H. Prince lived up to his national classification in *Time* magazine as "testy," "box-jawed," and "spriest of all financial oldsters" when, in 1929, at the age of seventy, in a pick-up polo game at the Myopia Hunt Club, he first warned an opposing player that if he didn't get out of his way he would kill him, and then, when the man did not, came close to making good his threat, splitting the man's head open with his mallet. The man, a Myopia riding teacher, claimed permanent injury to his eyesight, and five years later Prince was forced to pay $15,000 in damages. Even Prince's closest friends did not consider this excessive in view of the fact that, some years before, following a disagreement over the fit of a suit, Prince had been convicted of mauling a tailor to the extent of $10,000. A few of Prince's fellow Myopians— notably Quincy Adams Shaw II, who had taken up the case of the riding teacher—even went so far as to undertake to have Prince expelled from Boston's most exclusive country club. This attempt failed when it was discovered that Prince, as the last surviving member of the four Prince brothers who had founded Myopia—and, all being nearsighted, had given the club its quaint name—enjoyed the kind of life membership immune to such transitory social judgments.

Startling evidence of the Proper Boston merchant's unreconstruction in the manners field can be found in the record of almost all the city's First Families, but the case of the late Frank Higginson of Lee, Higginson & Co. would seem to warrant special mention. Outranking Cabots, Curtises and Cunninghams, Boston Higginsons have always had the reputation of enjoying the lowest boiling point of all of Boston's best, and that of the late Frank was scarcely above room temperature. When a nephew attempting to learn the banking business in his office was one day dilatory in carrying out one of his orders, he seized the lad by the scruff of the neck and, to the consternation of passers-by in the street below, hung him for several perilous moments out of one of the upper windows in the bank building. Out on his boat one day with a lady passenger Higginson ordered his steward to serve tea. The banker's tea was cold and in a rage he threw the cup overboard. Some moments later when he had calmed down and new tea had been procured and quaffed to his satisfaction, he graciously offered to relieve his guest of her cup and return it to the tray. "Oh, don't bother, Frank," she said, and with a smile tossed not only her cup, but her saucer and sandwich plate along with it, into the sea.

But Banker Frank was hardly the man to learn a lesson from such a delicate rebuff. Even when his wife, after years of ducking dishes at the breakfast table, finally despaired of him altogether and ran off with a man named Smith—he still lived on in his charmingly unreformed manner. A trained nurse in Boston, who took care of him during a long illness in his later years, still recalls taking her first paycheck to her local bank to be cashed. The teller looked at the vaunted Higginson signature, even in a branch bank one to conjure with. "Gee," he asked the nurse, "do you know that guy?" "Surely," she replied with some pride, "Mr. Higginson is my patient." The teller bent to the task of cashing the check, then handing her the money looked up. "The Lord help you," he said.

To place the Proper Boston lady in the same class as the Proper Boston gentleman, as a type equally short on manners, is to do her an injustice. Her reputation—as witness the Cabot women known for "shutting their husbands up"—may not be perfect in Boston social history, but it is better than his. From a distance, at least, she appears the height of courtesy. Punctilious in details, she answers her mail promptly, carefully returns invitation for invitation, and usually gives her best businesslike attention to her birthday calendar, her Christmas list, the various obligations which she has always called her "good works," and other matters of social decorum. At her dinner parties she is adept at "turning the table"—or knowing when to cease conversation with the gentleman on her right and begin with the man on her left—and she also knows what to talk about. Boston's nineteenth-century etiquette writers, who usually laid great stress on women fortifying themselves for social functions by studying up in advance on suitable topics of conversation, would have had little fault to find with the First Family lady of either their time or today. A woman who was a "Friend" of Symphony, a member of the Browning Society, a regular attender of Chilton Club lectures, and perhaps a collector of Lowestoft china as well, was not to be confused with the woman so severely reprimanded by the etiquetteers—the type whose mind was "bounded on the North by her servants, on the East by her children, on the South by her ailments, and on the West by her clothes."

It is possible that these etiquette writers made the Proper Boston woman too confident. In any case, she became a manners-mender. She won such a reputation for this that putting people in their places, in public or private, has become known as a sort of blue-plate special of the Boston Society house. In some instances First Family ladies have even achieved a certain finesse in this field—and certainly more than the First Family man. Compare, for example, two cases of ballroom etiquette as handled respectively by a First Family host and a First Family hostess. Faced with a young Harvard gate-crasher at a ball given for his daughter at the Ritz Carlton one First Family host lost his manners bearing completely. He gave the offender such a verbal dressing-down that, though the affair occurred more than ten years ago, his choice of words is still remembered by employees of the hotel. At about the same time, at a debutante ball given at the Copley Plaza, Milton's Mrs. S. Huntington Wolcott carried off without any loss of temper the far more difficult task of ridding her party of a girl who had arrived unbidden. Informed of the presence of the young lady, Mrs. Wolcott gave the girl just time enough to remove her coat and join her friends in the gaiety. Then she moved quickly to the scene, and extending her hand said in her most pleasant voice, "I hear you've been looking for me, my dear—to say good night."

Unfortunately such tact is the exception rather than the rule in the record of the Proper Boston woman's manners-mending. Too many First Family ladies would seem to have followed in the footsteps of the late Mrs. Jack Gardner, in her day the leading exponent of a less progressive school of the art. For more than a quarter of a century Mrs. Gardner was a one-woman vig-

ilante committee of Boston's manners, and many who crossed
her rugged path discovered the fact to their sorrow. A New York
born woman recalls coming to Boston as a bride and, passing the
Gardner house one early spring morning, being startled by a
severe rapping on the pane. At that time she had never met the
great Mrs. Jack and was sorely alarmed. It soon became apparent, however, from the rappings as well as from a beckoning
finger which she was just able to observe between two drawn
curtains, that she was expected to enter the house. Entering,
she was escorted by a maid to the austere and darkened drawing
room whence the tappings had come. Peering through the gloom
she was barely able to make out the figure of Mrs. Gardner, now
facing her but still by the window across the room. Without so
much as a good morning Mrs. Gardner observed tartly that she
had noticed the girl pass by, that she was an unusually tall girl
and like so many tall girls did not carry herself well. That was
all. "Walk erect," Mrs. Gardner concluded, then rang for the
maid to usher the still-dazed and speechless girl once more into
the street.

Mrs. Gardner is amply illustrative of the fact that manners-
mending, a treacherous avocation at best, was hardly suited to
the blunt, unbending approach to life of the Proper Boston
woman. The First Family lady is not one who readily stoops to
conquer, and in the manners field the easygoing trend of the
twentieth century would seem to have passed her by. The story
told of a charter member of Cambridge's Cantabrigia Club who,
asked why she had never in nine years called on former friends
of hers who had rented a house literally next door to her own,
replied, "Why, I *never* call on people in hired houses," may not
be typical but it is by no means of as ancient vintage as might be
suspected. To Proper Bostonians the frozen formality of their
First Family femininity is as accepted a part of the city's social
picture as the fact that there is a right and a wrong side to Commonwealth Avenue. To strangers from more slap-on-the-back
parts of the country, however, it has often proved baffling indeed. There are many variations on this female manners-formal-

ity theme, but one story, authenticated by the senior partner of one of Boston's better-bred law firms, runs as follows:

A young lawyer in the firm, a man from the West who had settled in Boston, was invited to play bridge one winter night some years ago in Brookline. Finding the street on which his hostess lived blocked with snow, he left his car and made his way toward her house on foot. Almost there, he was attracted by the barking of a dog to a snowbank in which he found to his amazement the shivering form of a little girl. The young man picked up the child and rushed to his hostess' door. There the child was recognized as a member of a First Family who lived close by. With his hostess to aid him he took the little girl to her own home and there put her in the charge of a servant who hastened to summon a doctor. Apparently the child had wandered outdoors unnoticed. But the man had arrived in the nick of time; the girl was numb with cold.

The next day the mother of the child came to call on the man's hostess and thanked her for her part in the rescue. "I wish I could thank that young man, too," she added, "but then I've never met him. Would you mind conveying my gratitude to him?" This was done of course, but to this day, to the senior partner's certain knowledge, the young man from the West has not received so much as a personal phone call from the lady whose daughter's life he may well have saved.

No less a manners museum-piece is the tale told by an ex-Boston clergyman now located in Philadelphia. His introduction to the Proper Boston woman's deficiency in social grace occurred one afternoon when he received a call to come immediately to the home of one of his wealthiest parishioners, an elderly First Family widow. On his arrival he found the lady in a state of high distress. She beckoned him to follow her out to her garden and told her servant they were on no condition to be disturbed. Delicately she unfolded a dilemma which, the minister soon discovered, resolved itself into the simple fact that the lady's dentist had just sent her a present of a brace of pheasants. What, she wanted to know, should she do? Her first inclination, she admitted, had been to return the birds, but then, since she had no wish to hurt the man's feelings, she had decided it would be all right to accept them and send a gift in return. This, of course, brought up the problem of what to send. Her first thought on this score had been, typically enough, a book—the all-occasion Proper Bostonian present. If it had been her doctor, she declared, she would have just called her bookstore and had one sent, and not troubled the minister at all. "But a dentist," she concluded hopelessly, "does one send a *book* to a *dentist?*"

What it has lacked in manners, both male and female, the Society of the Proper Bostonian has always made up in customs. These customs are primarily British. "The true Bostonian," Henry Adams once observed, "always knelt in self-abasement before the majesty of English standards," while the late Henry Cabot Lodge, who for all his robust prejudices was certainly no Anglophile, found Boston Society shot through with the Londonesque—all the way from its fashions of dress to its foreign opinion. More recent observers such as the historians Van Wyck Brooks and Dixon Wecter have also taken note of the total effect of Boston's devotion to English customs. Declares Brooks: "The more the center of gravity of the nation shifted toward the West, the more the Boston mind, thrown back on itself, resumed its old colonial allegiance." Wecter is more specific, seeing in Boston Society's Anglophilia of today its "great bulwark against Irish, German and Jewish invasion."

Lesser commentators have taken Boston to task on this matter. In 1882 when the English custom of fox hunting got under way in earnest in Boston Society with the importation of twenty full-blooded English foxhounds for the newly formed Myopia Club, one writer waxed wroth indeed. "All the arrangements and accessories of the club are to be quite too utterly English," he declared, and he found "altogether nauseating" the spectacle of sixty "swell young men of Beacon Street" dressed in scarlet coats and white knee breeches going out to "try to catch up with the anise seed bag or poor devil of a fox." From what to Proper Boston of course was the wilderness of the West came the comment of the Albany *Journal:*

> Anglomania can go no farther than this, and all Yankeedom would look on with applause if the sturdy farmers of Lexington and Concord would repeat a little feat of theirs a hundred years ago and drive the "red coats" back through Cambridge into Boston.

But Boston's British background is made of sterner stuff than twenty foxhounds. Today the whole tone of Boston Society, from oatmeal and Dundee marmalade at dawn on through a day which may well be topped off with a bedtime reading snack of the London *Illustrated News,* is still English. The First Family man, if he pays any attention to his clothes at all, is likely to have his best suits and his shirts tailor-made in England; if he does not break his day with a stop at one of his English-type clubs he will probably choose to pause at one of the typically English "For-Men-Only" spots—the main dining room at Locke Ober's or Thompson's Spa, or the Parker House bar. The First Family lady on her way to shop at such a store as the London Harness Company may choose to stop for refreshment at any one of a half-dozen British-style tearooms. First Family children are brought up strictly, in some cases with English governesses, and when the First Family boy goes out into the world it is usually to the English-type boarding school. First Family girls in Boston are still, in the Victorian tradition, mentally confined and morally sheltered. They early learn their place in a Society which is, on the English model, male-dominated. Men do not usually talk business "after hours" in Boston, but dinner talk is hardly a fifty-fifty proposition between the sexes. Boston debutantes soon learn they must know how to discuss politics, sports and other masculine subjects, or else be still. And even at the more informal kind of supper party they must be conditioned for what is one of the most striking of all Proper Boston's English customs

—the rigid post-meal separation of the sexes. This custom is significantly engineered by the men and not by the women. With the coming of after-dinner coffee the ladies retire, to be rejoined when, and only when, the men see fit—often only shortly before the time when the men also see fit to go home. For many years the suburb of Milton boasted, in its Brush Hill Road section, one of the most engaging of all Proper Bostonian clubs. Known as the Brush Hill Bridge Club, it included just eight couples who met once a month to play bridge, all of the men at two tables in one house, all the women at two tables in another.

The formality of Proper Boston's Victorian conventions has sternly outlasted the relaxation of etiquette rules which took place following World War I in other American cities. Formal calls, for example, ancient history to modern etiquetteers, are still routine in Boston Society, and there are definitely accepted ways in which they must be made. "Calling hours" are between four and six, but the day is also important. Several First Families have their regular reception days or "at-homes," and these must be learned. A prominent blue-blood doctor, entering retirement, recently sent out cards announcing he would henceforth be at home at his Marlboro Street address Friday afternoons; he apparently expects a reasonable attendance—after Symphony, of course—every Friday from now until he either changes his day or dies. Some years ago a girl who married an Appleton paid a heavy price for not establishing such a "calling day." A New Yorker, she had scoffed at such Boston formality on first coming to the city. A year of married life in Boston, however, taught her manners—or rather customs. During that year, she recalls, her father-in-law, a gentleman of the old school, felt free to pay a formal call upon her every single afternoon on the dot of five o'clock.

Time in Boston's businessman's Society is, as it is in England, of the essence. If you are invited for dinner at 7:30 in Boston you are expected to arrive at that hour and not drift in around eight or some time thereafter. There is even a well-recognized leaving time. Ten concludes an informal seven o'clock dinner, ten-thirty a formal seven-thirty affair. This custom carries over to ladies' luncheons as well. Usually held at one o'clock, they break up punctually at 3:30. If your hostess has asked you for 1:30, however, you may feel free to partake of her hospitality until four.

To the Proper Bostonian the British home is the beau ideal. Of late years, under the auspices of the Boston League of Women Voters, he has made it an annual habit each November to exhibit a group of his proudest dwellings to a Boston public interested enough to buy tickets well in advance at $1.50 per head to see how the other half lives on a Beacon Hill that has been called more London than London. Formerly, custom required Beacon Hill's best to hold open house every Christmas Eve in conjunction with the annual caroling and bell-ringing celebration, and admit anyone who came to the door. Gradually this practice had to be abandoned in favor of the more mercenary plan when the holiday celebrators grew to unruly proportions and could no longer be trusted to wander deferentially among Rockingham dessert sets and Derby bisque figures. If a present-day sight-seer remains unconvinced that Proper Boston is basically English, however, he has but to pay his $1.50 some November, and enter the home of Mr. and Mrs. E. Sohier Welch. No. 20 of the homes surrounding the leafy quadrangle of Beacon Hill's Louisburg Square, it boasts a drawing room so authoritatively British that it was used without a change for Becky Sharp's marriage by the Hollywood studio which filmed *Vanity Fair*.

In his suburban habitats the Proper Bostonian cannot live in quite such authentic surroundings. Nonetheless there is an air of old English feudal aristocracy in even the least pretentious of his dwellings. The average First Family house is a collection of antiques which are mixed with catholic impartiality, often the rarest relic of the China trade with the most outmoded Victoriana. As in England, the taste of the owner is immaterial for, generally speaking, everything is either an heirloom or a wedding present. If anything is of exceptional value it will rarely see service unless the occasion is a most extraordinary one. "If there is one bit of porcelain that excels another," Mrs. Harrison Gray Otis once wrote of the Proper Bostonian home, "it is sure never to be forthcoming when it is most required." To the strict Proper Bostonian, to purchase more than an occassional replacement of household furnishings is to cast a reflection on the previous generations of one's Family, and it is not surprising that in extreme instances antique hunting has come to be regarded as a sport for mere social upstarts. It is indulged in, of course, as in other parts of the country, but the Proper Bostonian prefers to do it surreptitiously. The First Family lady on the trail of an antique may well have the feeling that she is a duck hunter out of season. She will see her dealer and make her purchase, then rearrange her room so that it can be made to swallow the new and socially spurious item into a safe anonymity among the genuine inherited articles.

Not so easy is the task of the First Family lady brash enough to set her heart on something modern. Recently Boston's leading Society jewelers displayed in their windows a set of gold-colored flatware for the table. Proper Bostonian disapproval was instant and icy. Not only was the ware brazenly different, it had only been on the market a dozen years or so. A Dedham dowager, seeing it advertised in the paper, made a special trip to the store to tell the floor manager just how she felt about it. "I don't see who would want that," she sniffed. "Anybody would know you had just come in here and *bought* it."

It is ironic that the Proper Bostonian's traditional lack of manners, stemming of course from his rugged individualism, may well have been responsible for his failure to incorporate into his Society, among all his English customs, that most British of institutions, the so-called gentleman's gentleman. Into New York, Chicago and other smart-set American Societies the valet made his way, but it is a rare First Family home in Boston that has ever boasted any manservant in its ménage. The idea of another man around his house is apparently incompatible with the character of the Proper Bostonian—as witness a letter written by William Everett, son of the noted Boston orator, Edward

Everett. The letter, dated January 1, 1908, is in answer to an invitation evidently extended Everett to pass the night in a friend's house. He begins his answer, typically, not with thanks but with an expression of doubt as to his ability to accept. "I shall come," he declares, "if I can do so without an effort." He then proceeds to give full Boston vent to his feelings on the subject of the English valet:

> I do not know how your house is organized: but I pray you do not let me suffer from the officiousness of a body servant or *valet de chambre.* The English servant who seizes your bag, unstraps & opens it, takes out the contents, disposes of them as he thinks proper, comes into your room while you are in the drawing room, carries off half your clothes the Lord knows where—then wakes you up with some horrible bath performances and what not, is in my view a patent engine to make a man thoroughly uncomfortable. I can wait on myself, having done so for fifty odd years, much better than any other man; and I want all such attendants to keep their hands off my property, and their feet out of my room. I don't mind having a rap on the door a reasonable time before breakfast; but otherwise I desire to be let alone.
>
>   Yours very faithfully,
>   WILLIAM EVERETT *

Preserved among virtually all First Families in the Boston alphabet, from Adamses to Wigglesworths, is the custom of afternoon tea. Boston teas come in two sizes, the large or party tea, and the small or daily tea. What the cocktail party is to New York or Washington the large tea is to Boston. Debutantes who for one reason or another have to forego the pleasures of evening balls have their coming outs at large teas. At large teas also post-debutantes usually announce their engagements—indeed for a First Family girl to make her announcement at a cocktail party is considered by strict Proper Bostonians of questionable taste. But the small tea is the real Boston custom. As English

* *Athenaeum Items.* The Boston Athenaeum, November, 1945.

as a puff off Winston Churchill's cigar, it is at the same time thoroughly Bostonian, a sort of Holy Communion of Proper Boston hospitality. It is cozy and intimate, for Family, Family friends and "drop-ins." It is served daily, on the stroke of five, winter and summer, rain or shine.

To the uninitiated in the function of tea as a custom this ritual is likely to prove rather disappointing. The Boston lady's "tea things," the crested silver service and the best of English teacups, are apt to be exactly the same as those preferred by half of the other Society ladies of the city, and the proceedings are apt to be slow indeed. After the hostess has poured several cups of tea there is invariably a pause while the maid—an integral part of the ceremony—is rung for and more hot water procured. The food is wholesome but is, in the Proper Boston tradition, simple. Buttered toast suffices for most occasions, though English muffins with English marmalade are often served. Tea is a rite to be quietly observed, not a party at which to have a high old time. Nothing has arisen to take its place as a happy little oasis on the Boston social desert, and in all probability nothing ever will. One Milton lady boasts that except in the case of illness, in all the years her children were at school, she never missed a day being present to greet them, on their return, from behind her tea table.

As the least common denominator of entertainment effort tea would seem to be made to order for the Proper Boston woman. It is inexpensive, which is by no means unappealing to her, and yet it gives ample evidence of her genteel standard of living without being in the least disruptive of the well-ordered routine of her home. To the outsider whom she asks to tea and who begs her not to go to any trouble, she cannot only say that it will not be any trouble but will actually know that it won't be. Tea will be served anyway, whether the outside guest comes or not. Fifty years ago Boston's noted letter writer, Susan Hale, was undoubtedly thinking of tea when, visiting in the Midwest, she wrote home that she could not understand Chicago Society. To her the pork-baron set of that strange land seemed to be patently in need of some sort of social base, or center, such as of course a quiet Boston tea would have afforded:

> Noise, racket, hurry, bustle, no repose, no particular center, outside people pouring in, the family pouring out, everybody late to meals, the father hurrying on the food, carriage always at the door . . . such is life in Chicago. I can't think the race can stand it more than a hundred years, if so much.*

But even tea pales before that most curious of all Proper Bostonian customs—the love of funerals and funeral going. This custom was in the Boston blood long before the pomp and circumstance of the Victorian death rite reached its height in England. First Family social history starts with funerals and ends with funerals. Ever since the time of Thomas Hancock, uncle of Boston Society's first recognized King and a man of whom it is recorded that "Thomas liked a good funeral and acted as executor with especial relish," the Proper Bostonian has dedicated himself to the funeral art with a devotion he has reserved for no other. Today Boston's First Family men and women plan for their obsequies as eagerly as in other city Societies brides and grooms plan for weddings. Long before there is, from a life insurance point of view, actuarially any risk at all, hymns are chosen, Bible verses selected, pallbearers nominated, and occupants of front-row pews designated. For the funeral and the funeral only the Proper Bostonian throws his Yankee caution to the winds. He forgets the trouble of it, the show of it, even the money involved. For once his motto becomes a shockingly un-Bostonian one. Hang the expense, he baldly declares. After all, you only die once.

Admitting his interest in his own departure, it is still difficult to comprehend the Proper Bostonian's zest for attendance at other people's funerals. Graciousness of manners does not matter at funerals, and funerals are formal enough to suit the most officious side of his social taste, but these facts alone do not ex-

* *Letters of Susan Hale,* by Caroline P. Atkinson (Boston: Marshall Jones Co.) © 1919.

plain his enthusiasm for them. To get out of a Saturday night cocktail party at the home of his best friend and neighbor the Proper Bostonian may plead anything from hay fever to the pressure of business. For the funeral of a mere acquaintance, on the other hand, he will often cheerfully give up an entire business day and even take a trip to New York—an acid test indeed. One prominent Boston businessman admits he attends the funerals of all the members of his Harvard college class held anywhere within one-day range. An avid obituary-column reader, he does not believe he has missed a single one of these funerals in the past ten years and yet he can think of no real reason for his action. "I guess it's a habit," he says, "or a hobby." He goes whether he actually knew his classmate personally or not, ruefully admitting his presence, particularly at the more intimate gatherings, has been known to arouse actual suspicion. "Often nobody knows who I am," he says. One latter-day Boston merchant, asked point blank why he attended funerals with such obvious enjoyment, managed an equally point-blank reply. "Melancholy, Sir," he said, "is the one passion of my life."

Whatever the reason for its popularity, funeral going is undeniably Boston Society's favorite sport. Proper Bostonians mark social eras by noted First Family funerals. "I *love* a good funeral," says one of Chestnut Hill's most prominent socialites, a woman who has at her fingertips names and dates of every important one which has taken place in her lifetime. To her the twenties were the great period of Boston funerals. Ushered in by the gala obsequies surrounding the passing of Major Henry Lee Higginson in the fall of '19, the era moved on with such triumphal, red-letter demises as those of Mrs. Jack Gardner, Henry Cabot Lodge, and Judge Frederick Cabot and Moorfield Storey. "Now *there*," she says feelingly, "were funerals for you."

No detail is overlooked for such an event, and strict attention is always paid to every wish of the deceased, no matter how extreme it may seem. Among the most noted funerals of the thirties was that of Mary Lee Ware, donor of Harvard's famous collection of glass flowers. The only flowers allowed on the Ware casket were those from people actually connected with Harvard. At old Samuel Dexter's funeral, in accordance with the terms of his will, there was no mention of his name in the service. Having expressed the wish that no "men of distinction" but only "poor men" be chosen for pallbearers, Dexter went to his grave on the shoulders of six men chosen at random from the Boston streets and paid five dollars each after the ceremony. Another merchant had desired children for pallbearers, and children he had. He had felt, according to his will, that by so serving they "might better appreciate the brevity and uncertainty of life."

Proper Bostonian obsequies range from high-Episcopal to low-Unitarian, and as might be expected, Mrs. Jack Gardner's funerals reached the ultimate among the "highs." As befitting her position as Boston Society's most spectacular character she had two complete ceremonies, a private one in the Spanish chapel of her Italian palace and a public one at the Church of the Advent. Following the second service her body was taken back to lie in state covered with a purple pall in the palace. Under a huge black crucifix between tall candlesticks were *prie-dieux* where nuns, relieving one another at regular intervals, dwelt in constant supplication for four days and nights. On the other hand, the passing of Ralph Forbes, one of the generally recognized prototypes of Marquand's George Apley and a man who had made a full-time career of serving as tree warden of the suburb of Milton, was a standout among "low" affairs. The funeral was held in the hallway of Forbes' home, the only music being supplied by the chirping of canaries in various rooms through the house, and the service itself including, in the Boston Unitarian tradition, a minute or two of the Bible and a solid half hour of Emerson. At one of the more recent of Boston's great First Family funerals, that of the late Bishop Lawrence, who always desired that his funeral be "as happy as his life," emphasis was placed on the cheerful. With determination to do justice to the Bishop's wishes the congregation joined lustily in reciting the General Thanksgiving and closed with a rousing rendition of the "Battle Hymn of the Republic."

The strength of the Proper Bostonian funeral custom is such that a man's stature as a Boston figure can only be measured with real accuracy by what happens when he dies. The number who attend his services is of course one index to this, but the number inside the church—socially speaking, everybody in Boston is always there—is not of such importance as the number outside. Old-timers declare that to this day no one has ever matched the figure set by Boston's greatest preacher, Phillips Brooks, back in the fall of '92. Outside Trinity Church that day, they say, there were more people gathered in Copley Square than had ever been in the Square before for any reason. Present-day historians, however, point to the funeral of the late Bishop Lawrence as being just as remarkable. The times were inauspicious for a record-breaking attendance—the Bishop having died just a month before Pearl Harbor—yet the Lawrence funeral crowd reached from St. Paul's Church, where the services were held, out across Tremont Street and onto the Boston Common. On the day of such funerals everything in Boston bows its head. At the death of one First Family patriarch the head of Boston's largest Society florist hurried home from his vacation because he felt it would be "more trying" for both Family and friends to order funeral flowers from a mere subordinate. The funeral of First Family Governor Roger Wolcott took place the day before Christmas, 1900, and his biographer, State Street banker Allan Forbes, has painfully recorded his own awe-inspiring tribute: "All stores closed although it was the best day of the year for shopping."

The funeral is one social function at which there is no rigid prescription for behavior. Even ministers have been known to color the proceedings. At the funeral of the merchant David Sears, whose death had been occasioned by a fall from the step of his carriage, the Trinity Church rector, officiating at the service, was unable to resist choosing as his text for the funeral sermon the passage from the First Book of Samuel: "There is

but a step between me and death." Some time later the Sears
Family, apparently resenting this slur on their illustrious Family-founder, established a church of their own in the Longwood
section of Brookline which to this day remains unique among
Proper Bostonian churches being open to Searses alone and for
two purposes only—for weddings and for funerals. The square
box pews of Boston's historic King's Chapel, where occupants
sit face to face, have seen many a famed First Family funeral
in which there has been marked deviation from the norm of
Proper Bostonian churchly behavior. To Edith Forbes Perkins
King's Chapel funerals called to mind the hour when the cows
came home at her Brookline farm. "You know the cows come
to the stalls," she writes, "stop, sniff, back and slide, and finally
go in." But she adds, "If they didn't like the pew they were put
in, they went and took another one." *

The Proper Bostonian funeral custom does not end with the
closing of the funeral service. Great attention is also paid to the
final resting place of the deceased. In Boston's early days Old
Granary, across from the ancient Park Street Church, was a
sort of Proper Bostonian Westminster Abbey. Here First Family
dead lie buried four-deep, with tablets commemorating such
luminaries as Benjamin Franklin's father and mother, Paul
Revere, John Hancock and Samuel Adams. In more recent
times Forest Hills, located on the high road to Milton, and
Mount Auburn, the so-called "Gateway to Heaven" in Cambridge, have risen to positions of high favor. The latter has a
special niche in Boston legend from its commemoration in a
three-part poem written many years ago by a First Family lady
with the assistance of her seamstress. Unfortunately never completed in publishable form, the poem was conceived to tell the
story of the cemetery in its three phases: Mount Auburn As It
Was on the Day of Creation, Mount Auburn As It Is, and
Mount Auburn As It Shall Be on the Day of Resurrection.

The crowding of these graveyards in latter years has proved

---

* *Letters and Journal of Edith Forbes Perkins,* by Edith Perkins Cunningham
(Boston: Privately printed, 1931).

no small impediment to the correct carrying-on of the custom of ancestor worship. Many notable First Family remains have had to be moved several times, the outstanding example being the post-mortem adventures of General Joseph Warren of Bunker Hill fame. Originally buried on the battlefield where he fell, he was moved in 1825 to Old Granary, space having been generously donated by the Boston Minot Family, close friends of the Warrens. But Minots soon needed more room themselves and Warren was forced to move a third time, on this occasion travelling to a branch Warren Family tomb in St. Paul's churchyard. As time went on, however, more immediate Warrens began to look on the General, for all his distinction, as somewhat of an intruder, and still another move was necessitated. This was to Forest Hills, General Warren's fourth, and so far final, resting place.

The moving of General Warren was comparatively easy in view of the fact that he could always be accurately identified by a bullet hole behind the left ear of his skull and by two false teeth that had been wired in place by Paul Revere. But in the moving of other remains mistakes have been made. When England wished the body of their war hero, Major Pitcairn, brought back from Boston for burial in Westminster Abbey, Boston was glad to comply and with Proper Bostonian efficiency sent along a body right on schedule—not, however, the body of the Major which was many years later found to be still in the city. The body of Gilbert Stuart, the painter, in transit from Old Granary to another graveyard, disappeared altogether. More recently social Boston was shocked by what remains today undoubtedly the greatest case of mass grave-juggling in its history —the affair Higginson.

Suspicion had somehow grown up that all was not well with the Higginson Family lot at Old Granary. After some legal complications a Higginson relative finally received permission to have the Granary caretaker dig up the lot and check the matter. The suspicion proved to be well founded when the caretaker, after diligently digging for two days under the lot carefully marked with the names of eleven Higginsons, was unable to find a single body. Other Higginsons now became interested and a thorough investigation was undertaken. After some time it was learned that old George Higginson, a man going on ninety and mindful of his future, had been frightened over a proposed extension of Tremont Street—which he felt might obliterate the Family lot entirely—and had taken it upon himself to order all Higginson occupants of Old Granary moved. He had done this through a third party, however, and an absent-minded man himself had never checked the carrying-out of his orders. He knew only that they had been moved, all eleven of them.

Relatives immediately checked Mount Auburn. But there were no recent Higginson arrivals at the Gateway to Heaven. Forest Hills was combed with equal lack of success. By this time all Proper Boston was interested. Finally, at the little Walnut Hills Cemetery in Brookline, a caretaker solved the riddle. He announced he had recently received a shipment of Higginsons and what was all the fuss about anyway?

The caretaker was as good as his word. He did indeed have the bodies. There was only one trouble. Somewhere along the way there had been two additions in the Higginson Family. The Walnut Hills caretaker had received—and buried—not eleven bodies, but thirteen. Furthermore he was proud of the new lot on his grounds, and as far as he and other authorities of Walnut Hills were concerned there would be no more digging and checking of bodies.

In a way the affair Higginson may be said to be concluded. In another way, however, it is not. It may take a sympathetic understanding of the Proper Bostonian, as well as of the power of First Family customs, to appreciate the fact, but the affair still causes uneasiness of mind among certain present-day Higginsons. Aspiring to their final resting places, they cannot help knowing that the time is coming when they must enter such retirement in the company of, as they or any other Proper Bostonian would put it, two "total strangers."

CHAPTER TWELVE

WINE, WOMEN AND WALTZ

Certain sounds, perfumes, places, always bring associated pictures to mind: Restaurants, Paris! Distinguished audiences, London! The essence of charm in Society, Rome! Beguiling and informal joyousness, San Francisco! Recklessness, Colorado Springs! The delightful afternoon visit, Washington! Hectic and splendid gaiety, New York! Beautiful Balls, Boston! *

With that invocation Mrs. Emily Price Post pays tribute to the Hub in her latest discussion of this country's dance tradition. Furthermore, Mrs. Post gives Boston's First Family Society full credit for making its city what she apparently feels is America's caper capital. Even in these changing times, she finds, this Society—as befitting one which has always maintained "its social walls intact" and has admitted only persons "of birth and breeding"—has never permitted the art of the dance to degenerate as it has in other cities. No jitterbug, Mrs. Post evidently feels that some cities would do better if they would go back and take a leaf from the Boston bluebook. "The extreme reverse of a 'smart' Boston ball," she writes, "is one—no matter where—which has a roomful of people who deport themselves abominably, who greet each other by waving their arms aloft, who dance like Apaches or jiggling music-box figures, and who scarcely suggest an assemblage of even decent—let alone well-bred—people."

Not unknowingly does Mrs. Post use the word "ball" as dis-

* *Etiquette,* by Emily Post (New York: Funk & Wagnalls) © 1942.

tinct from the word "dance." The difference between a ball
and a dance lies not only in the degree of formality but has also
come to be accepted by Society as a matter of age. People of
all ages are asked to a ball; of only one, or approximately one,
age to a dance. This has given Boston a head start in making a
name for itself in the field. Nothing could be more up the Boston social alley than a mixture of ages. Generally speaking, a
dance isn't a dance in Boston Society unless there is a liberal
sprinkling of grandmothers on the floor—which, of course,
makes it a ball to start with. The Proper Bostonian attitude
has always been that young people should be shown the way to
a good time by having the example of their elders in active
participation before them. Today one of Boston's best-beloved
hostesses, Mrs. Fiske Warren, a lady approaching eighty, puts
the matter squarely. "Young people don't know how to have a
good time together," she declares. "It's nonsense for them to
be alone."

Like so many other distinguishing elements of Boston Society the all-age ball has its roots deep in the nineteenth century.
But the father of the Boston ball was no Cabot or Lowell, merchant prince or Family-founder. He wasn't even a Bostonian,
Proper or otherwise. He was a tall, skeleton-thin, fiery tem-
pered Italian count named Lorenzo Papanti. An officer in the
royal guard of the Duke of Tuscany, he was on the wrong side
of a coup against the duke and was forced to flee his native land.
Arriving in Boston with only one suit of clothes to his name—
though it was significantly an outfit of full court regalia—he first
got a job as a violinist in a Boston orchestra and then, in 1827,
went on to set up a dancing academy.

At first Papanti's school had hard sledding. Though his original prospectus was hardly a wild one—the basis of his curric-
ulum consisting of such modest step-livelies as the polka and
the quadrille—dancing in any form was regarded as a gamey
kind of indoor sport for mid-nineteenth-century Boston. Before
Papanti only one dancing school existed in New England. Furthermore, though his title as a count was a genuine one and

though he was in the age-old Proper Bostonian phrase "obviously a gentleman," he had no First Family blessing to go on. Such has always been essential to the establishment of a social institution in Boston, and fortunately for the future of the Boston dance Papanti soon recognized his deficiency. He set his sights high, determined to enlist the support of the then reigning queen of Boston Society, the celebrated widow, Mrs. Harrison Gray Otis. The choice was a happy one. Still referred to even among Boston Otises of today as "the notorious," the widow was the Mrs. Jack Gardner of her times. It amused her to do things other Boston ladies didn't do, and to do them first. She had been to Europe many times in her younger days and had developed a taste for Continental dancing and titled Continental men. The handsome count, with his flossy wig and twinkling pumps, seemed to her almost too good to be true, and in short order she became one of his regular students—the first "real lady," he was fond of saying, who ever entered his academy. The First Family blessing became official when in 1834, at a ball given at her Somerset Street mansion, Mrs. Otis chose Signor Papanti to be her partner for the first waltz ever seen in Boston.

By 1837 Papanti had become so successful that he was able to move his academy to new and palatial quarters on Tremont Street. Here he built a hall with a $1200 chandelier, five enormous gilt-framed mirrors and the first ballroom floor in America to be built on springs. Enemies of Madam Otis always maintained that the count had his floor designed specifically to accommodate his star pupil, who for all her spirit was amply proportioned and none too light on her feet. Whether true or not, it was on Papanti's spring floor that four generations of Boston's best—from 1837 until 1899, when the hall finally closed—were initiated into the art of the Boston ball beautiful. Three of these generations learned under the count himself, the fourth under his son who inherited his father's money only on the condition that he continue the good work.

Actually the count's work in teaching dance steps was of less importance than his work in the instruction of ballroom behavior. A stickler for formality, he laid the foundation for the chaste severity which still characterizes the Boston dance. Each of his pupils upon entering his ballroom was required to give either a bow or a curtsey as the case might be. Standing near the door, Papanti kept his fiddle bow poised to insure that these obeisances were performed to his satisfaction. His quick temper brooked no uncertainty, and a smart rap on the shoulders was the fate of not only a boy whose bow was not waist-deep but also a girl whose curtsey was either hurried or jerky. Not even Papanti, however, confined himself to youth. Each season he gave a series of subscription balls for an older group including the mothers and fathers of his pupils. Being an acute student of the Proper Bostonian nature, he ran these in an equally high-handed way and thus was able to give these elders the comfortable feeling they were back in their dancing-school days.

When the august Boston Assemblies—to which Boston owes perhaps the major part of its country-wide ballroom fame—got under way in 1845, they were off to a good start on Papanti's spring floor. Moving from there to Horticultural Hall, the Mechanics Building, Copley Hall and finally the Hotel Somerset, these balls had a long and illustrious history, reaching their heyday in the early 1900's. Never a pain to the Proper Bostonian purse—fifteen dollars covered a season's subscription for four dances—the Assemblies did not make their name on terrapin suppers or cotillion favors, but they achieved a distinction for selectivity of patronage unmatched by the gaudier balls in other city Societies. New York's Patriarch's Ball might spend as high as $10,000 for an evening's favors, supplying gold cigarette cases to the men and Paris millinery to the ladies, but it was unable to keep its list down to Ward McAllister's sacred Four Hundred. The Boston Assembly, on the other hand, with no such external refinements to offer, held its line. Its Four Hundred was a real four hundred; it meant First Families and only First Families. Ruthlessly the sheep were separated from the goats. A divorced person was immediately removed from the list. Newcomers to Boston, regardless of their native social standing, had to wait a year—a sort of probation period—before being considered for admission. The stand against the invasion of youth was firm. Many a grandmother merrily waltzed her way through season after season of the Assemblies, but fortunate indeed was the debutante invited to attend just one dance. Often no more than two debutantes were selected, and so terrifying was the honor that it was a poised girl indeed who could get through the evening without frequent recourse to her ever-handy vinaigrette and a whiff of smelling salts.

Dignity was the keynote. No gentleman ever attended an Assembly without full dress, and this included not only gloves and a fine linen handkerchief—to be delicately placed 'twixt his gloved hand and his partner's back—but also shoe polish with which to shine his pumps to gleaming perfection in between dances in the men's room. For the ladies "pastes" were unknown. On the morning of an Assembly Boston's First Family femininity trooped to their safe-deposit boxes for their tiaras and sunbursts of diamonds. These jewels would be returned the next day, of course, but for the evening—particularly when worn with the ever-favored black velvet—they made of many a doughty Boston dowager, in that oft-abused Victorian phrase, a "great beauty."

The Proper Bostonian answer to the indispensable "cotillion leader" was S. Hooper Hooper. Tall and graceful on the dance floor and a man of impeccable ancestry—his name indicated that he was "a Hooper" both matrilineally and patrilineally—he was nonetheless never the dandy type of Philadelphia's Williams Carter, Baltimore's Walter De Courcey Poulteney, or even New York's Harry Lehr, with whom he was often compared. Fundamentally he was always the practical, hard-headed merchant, and now nearing eighty he is still capable of a stern display of Yankee wrath when public reference is made to his Society life. Where a lesser man might have taken pleasure from the publicity which came his way in 1936 following his nomination, on the part of the Society journal *Town Topics*,

for national president of the Chisel Chin Club, Mr. Hooper
took none.

Early in life Hooper Hooper chose the Boston Assemblies
as his career. He ran them as a Boston business. Far from content with the glory of being chosen to lead the cotillion's Grand
March at dance after dance, he took care of every detail of the
balls, from the rigorous censoring of invitations to arranging
the receiving line on a red-carpeted dais and dispensing seat
checks. Working on a business-like Assembly budget he made
frequent trips to Europe to see that the Boston balls had, if
not the most elaborate favors, at least genuine European ones
without the discomfort of paying fancy American prices for
them. In 1911, when the Bunny Hug and the Turkey Trot were
sweeping the country, Proper Bostonians looked to Hooper
Hooper, as an earlier generation might have to Papanti, to see
whether these steps would also sweep the Boston Assemblies.
Hooper's verdict was no; they must do their probation like
other foreign influences on Boston Society. A year later he allowed them, and when the Assembly orchestra played its first
fox trot the moment was an unforgettable one. "It was awe-
inspiring," declares Proper Bostonian Francis H. Appleton, himself founder of the Boston Supper Dances. "I remember just
where I was standing."

With the coming of World War I the Assemblies languished,
but Hooper Hooper was quick to revive them afterwards, and
off and on these balls held their stately own until doomed to
final death by the depression. Hooper, a lifelong bachelor
whose only other job besides the Assemblies had been the chairmanship of the Somerset Club wine committee, entered the
wine business on his own and retired from the dance field. Once
in a while this retirement has been broken, though through
no wish of his. One such occasion occurred some years ago when
he was called to the witness stand in a law case involving a complaint made by residents of the select Tennis and Racquet
Club—of which Hooper Hooper was founder and first president
—against the activity of a near-by repair shop. The lawyer for

the repair shop determined to win the judge's favor by showing up Hooper Hooper as typical of the stiff-collared Society drones he felt made up the Club's membership. He asked the cotillion leader several personal questions, all of which Hooper answered with so little apparent irritation that it was the lawyer who finally lost his temper and shouted, "What time do you get up in the morning?" Hooper remained outwardly calm but looked the man squarely in the eye. "That, Sir," he said, "is none of your business." With this the judge so heartily agreed that the case was promptly won by the Racquet Club.

More recently Hooper Hooper was interviewed by a reporter whose curiosity had been aroused by the cotillion leader's claim of having crossed the ocean seventy-nine times. The newspaperman felt that here at last the businesslike Boston socialite had been caught.

"You say seventy-nine?" he checked.

"Yes, seventy-nine."

"But, Mr. Hooper, that would leave you on the other side."

The cotillion leader cleared his throat. "It would," he replied thoughtfully, "had I not been born in Paris."

Only a cut below Hooper Hooper's Assemblies were the Hunt Balls. These were held chiefly under the auspices of the Myopia Hunt Club, long the social redoubt of Boston's North Shore. Of late years the "North Shore crowd," which includes all in-season inhabitants of such areas as Essex, Beverly Farms, Magnolia, Prides Crossing and Manchester-by-the-Sea, has come to be regarded by strict Proper Bostonians as overly uninhibited and a rather rowdy fringe of their Society, but there was little rowdiness in evidence at Myopia's early-day Hunt Balls. They were not held on the North Shore but in the heart of Boston. Paralleling the august Assemblies, the balls also got their start on a spring floor—though this necessitated stooping to rent Boston's Odd Fellows Hall, which, in 1885, the date of the first Hunt Ball, was the only place outside of Papanti's which had such a floor.

Hunt Balls were airtight. As early as 1887 even *Town Topics*, which was New York published and by no means overly charitable to sister cities—bulletins from Chicago being printed under the title of "Skunkville"—admitted that the Myopia Bostonians were "something almost too good for this world" and that to crack a Hunt Ball was a social achievement for anyone. Annual invitations for the balls, which featured foxes and hounds dressed in dinner costumes, were regarded by Proper Bostonian recipients as rigidly as passports, but they bore a huge NOT TRANSFERABLE label—just in case. An elderly member of the Boston police force recalls in his younger days being stationed outside a Hunt Ball and, since the evening was a wintry one, stepping inside the door for a moment to get warm; promptly he was greeted by a Myopian Master of Foxhounds who informed him that he could either get the hell out of the hall or be kicked all the way to Boston Common. Old-line Myopians still delight in a tale told in the Club's early-day history book of the Hunt Ball of 1889 given in honor of the elder J. P. Morgan. An ambitious young Boston banker, it is recorded, anxious to promote himself and apparently unaware of the social strain of both Myopia and Morgan-mixing at the same time, had somehow managed to persuade his shy wife to become a patroness for the affair. "She was so confused and bashful," the historian concludes happily, "she could hardly say a word and finally had to be taken home."

For the "real Myopians" at Hunt Balls up to 1916, standard dress was scarlet coats and white knee breeches. Ladies who wore red dresses which would clash with the male scarlet were frowned upon, and according to Clara Endicott Sears, Boston authoress and herself belle of many a Boston ball, they generally chose soft-colored tulle and looked "like clouds floating through the ballroom"—certainly the Boston woman at her most ethereal. For all their grandeur, however, Hunt Balls bore the ever-

present traces of Proper Boston social astigmatism. In the great
Hunt Ball of 1899 the "beckoning figure" of the cotillion saw a
shocking display of this before it was even under way. Impe-
riously "beckoned" at the start of the dance by a Boston grande
dame who had been chosen to lead the figure, a Myopian obeyed
the summons to join her with some reluctance. Noting his hesitation the lady greeted him, as they stood alone in the center of
the floor, with the phrase, "I'm sure I don't know why I beckoned to you." Replied the Myopian with more truth than
gallantry, "I'm sure I don't know why I came," and forthwith
returned to his seat. Fortunately cooler heads prevailed, and
in the spirit of the famed Myopia Toast, which calls for "stout
hearts in adversity," the dance proceeded. Drinking at Hunt
Balls was on occasion heavy enough to have done justice to one
of Ward McAllister's champagne picnics at Newport, but no
Proper Bostonian would ever tell on another as having been,
even for one evening, the worse for wear. Recently a former
Hunt Ball patroness, asked if she could not remember an instance when one of the gentlemen present had imbibed too
freely, said she recalled only one—when a man crossed the hall
on his hands and knees and asked her for a dance. "A visitor,"
she explained, "from out of town."

In recent years the outstanding development in the Boston
Society dance tradition has been the revival of the waltz. This
dance, while it was of course the staple diet of the Assemblies
and the Hunt Balls, did not catch the Proper Boston fancy as
soon as might have been expected. Despite its introduction by
Madam Otis and Signor Papanti in 1834, it was regarded as
risqué in some instances as late as the Civil War. Mrs. Otis' own
father-in-law had set himself against it, and so had the Boston
etiquette books. One man seeing his daughter dancing the waltz
at a private ball dragged her forcibly from the floor. He later
wrote to a friend of how "humiliated" he had been on first
perceiving his daughter and her partner among the dancers.

"I can only describe the position they were in," he wrote, "as the very reverse of back-to-back." Much of this kind of ice was apparently broken by the visit of Waltz King Johann Strauss to Boston in 1872. Even Boston's silk-stocking set went bobby-sox berserk over the romantic figure with his cropped beard and handle-bar mustache. Many of Boston's best were in the crowd that daily besieged Strauss during his stay in the city and that even went to such un-Proper Bostonian extremes as to push its way into his house and beg his servant for a lock of hair. According to the music magazine *The Étude*, however, Strauss' servant was equal to the occasion. He had, the magazine records, thought up a trick that "enabled him to satisfy the women—even if a certain Newfoundland dog began to look somewhat mangy." Later it was in Boston, at an outdoor concert commemorating the hundredth anniversary of the signing of the Declaration of Independence, that Strauss conducted an orchestra before an audience of an estimated 100,000 people. He had a hundred sub-conductors and a huge chorus to assist him, and according to a Boston *Globe* reporter the spectacle was such a success that New York "could not conceal its jealousy and promptly hired Strauss for its Academy of Music."

After World War I waltz enthusiasm in the country at large waned rapidly before the frolicking fox trots of the Jazz Age. To the latter-day Proper Bostonians, whose pulse still beat loyally in three-four time, this seemed an unfortunate development. When the one-step tide of the twenties had even swept aside their beloved "Boston"—a sort of modified version of the Viennese waltz in which couples swooped rather than swirled and stayed in one spot instead of circling the floor—they were ready with characteristic Proper Bostonian resolve to do something about it. In 1934, a hundred years after Mrs. Otis had first introduced the dance, they began a waltz-revival movement which has made such headway that it is today one of Boston Society's sharpest answers to those prone to maintain that Boston is socially played out.

From its beginning the movement has been handled with

all the public privacy and well-heeled simplicity so characteristic of Boston Society on the march. Only ten couples were present at its birth, which took place at a party given by Mrs. E. Sohier Welch in her historic Louisburg Square home. Trim, blue-eyed and energetic, wife of one of State Street's leading First Family trustees and herself an able crusader in causes ranging from rat extermination to birth control, Mrs. Welch is nonetheless sometimes accused of "playing the social game" from the fact that her name has long been a Society-page fixture. To the strictest elements of Boston Society this is a cardinal sin. Fortunately for the future of the waltz movement Mrs. Welch recognized this fact. She was careful to surround her early efforts on behalf of the movement with just the right air of mystery. Privately everyone talked about her parties; publicly no one had ever heard of them. By the time the Boston newspapers were "allowed" to print a word of the Beacon Hill goings-on, Mrs. Welch had tucked four long winters of parties under her belt, had initiated the majority of Boston's social leaders in the magic rites, and had personally seen to it that Boston's waltz revival had all but reached the proportions of an underground movement in an occupied country.

The salient features of all these parties were the same. There were never more than ten couples invited at one time. The parties started at 9 and ended at 12. Though the only music supplied was by phonograph record—albeit records especially imported from Europe for the occasion—both men and women came in full dress, the women in their most bouffant gowns. No one was allowed to smoke or drink which, since Mrs. Welch's husband ranks as Boston's leading wine connoisseur and has a collection of madeiras dating to the Revolution, alone bears testimony to the deadly seriousness of the occasions. Today Mrs. Welch recalls that even at her first party the ages of her guests ranged from seventeen to seventy. "Nobody cared about age or sex," she says briefly. "It was a pure passion for the waltz."

By 1937 Mrs. Welch, ably seconded by Mrs. Chilton Cabot and a patroness list featuring such names as Mrs. T. Jefferson

Coolidge, Mrs. F. Murray Forbes and Mrs. Gurdon Saltonstall Worcester, was ready to take her Waltz Evenings, as they came to be called, to the Hotel Somerset. Here, and later at the Copley Plaza, where they soon became as desirable as any events on the Boston social calendar, they were launched in the best Proper Bostonian tradition, as balls given for charity and open to the public. The public of these Evenings, however, was never intended to be confused with the general public. Admission is still today by invitation only and, while ostensibly handled by the patronesses, actually boils down to the socially sure touch of Mrs. Russell Howell, capable secretary of the Waltz Evenings Committee and adviser to the social stationers who print the invitations. Even a First Family hostess, reserving a table for a Waltz Evening, must submit to Mrs. Howell in advance the list of people she intends to bring with her to the party. Mrs. Howell is not unwilling to invite such Waltz Evening "strangers"; at the same time she likes to make a mental note of what table they are going to sit at so that she can keep a weather eye on their ballroom behavior in case they should want to come again. If a person who is not a table guest or on one of Mrs. Howell's own lists applies to her over the telephone for an invitation, she makes her decision, she admits, largely by "the sound of the voice" and by her ever-ready Proper Bostonian question, "Whom do you know?" As a specific example of how she handles a difficult case, Mrs. Howell likes to cite a hypothetical "Texas boy." "If he should call me," she declares, "I should ask him not only whom he knew in Boston but also what sort of parties he's been to before—in Texas."

Ballroom behavior is important at Waltz Evenings. Dress is white tie for men and preferably fluffy bouffant dresses for the women. The Evenings feature the strict Viennese version of the waltz, and while the committee in charge feels that one or two polkas are admissible—as being old-fashioned enough to keep from marring the affair's *éclat*—they are so dead set against the introduction of any other type of dance that a supremely exclusive "Waltz Club" has been formed in addition to the Waltz Evenings to hold the line against the younger generation, which has on occasion expressed a plaintive desire for a fox trot or even a rumba every third dance. This is a mere jurisdictional dispute, however, and has in no way affected the Proper Bostonian zeal for the waltz in general. On January 18, 1945, Boston's waltz revival reached its apogee when a cordon of First Family fans, led by Mrs. Welch and Mrs. Howell with the beloved Proper Bostonian orchestra Ruby Newman in tow, invaded New York's Ritz Carlton Hotel and held a Waltz Evening in the heart of Manhattan. When New Yorkers afterwards made plans to hold such evenings on their own, all of Proper Boston rejoiced that it had at last been able to introduce something which had caught the fancy of the jaded Gothamites. As might be expected, Society editors in the two cities disagreed as to the lasting effect of the invasion, with one alien critic swinging below the belt and noting that some of the most enthusiastic Manhattan support for Boston's waltzes had come from such "New Yorkers" as Mr. and Mrs. James Russell Lowell of Park Avenue. On one point there was general agreement. This was that New Yorkers, even when waltzing to the strains of a Boston orchestra, could never be Bostonian. The Society editor of the Boston *Herald*, having made out a case for a certain similarity of ballroom behavior on the part of the two traditional social rivals, at length concluded:

> But there was a difference. Bostonians take their pleasure seriously and go about the business of finding their tables and settling themselves with a determined air. New Yorkers arrive with a smile, and soon champagne corks are popping and the evening is merry . . . Boston keeps it rarest jewels in the safe-deposit vault, but New York wears its best proudly . . . Boston wraps itself in mink, but New York is swathed in sables, chinchilla, and snowy ermine.

The dignity, formality, exclusiveness and age-mixing—all qualities which distinguished Boston's early-day Assemblies and Hunt Balls, and its latter-day Waltz Evenings—have had a less satisfactory relationship with the history of the Boston debutante party or coming-out ball. Whether the Proper Bostonian could have gone on, in the mad days of the twentieth century, launching his debutante daughter in the social security of his own home as he did in the nineteenth—when "a small dance" really meant a small dance and the presence of grandmother dowagers and other elements of cold Boston formality were deftly mulled, like wine, by the personal warmth of the surroundings—is an unanswerable "if" of social history. For the bare fact is that he did not. There have been exceptions of course, notable among these being the case of the doughty social warrior Godfrey Lowell Cabot who, after entering the lists with one granddaughter at a gala prewar St. Valentine's Day Ball at the Hotel Somerset and winning no special laurels, returned to the fray in 1945 to score the admitted hit of Boston's first postwar debutante season when he launched his second granddaughter direct from his Beacon Street home with all the time-tested coziness of an ultra-select Christmas holiday party. By and large, however, the Proper Bostonian has refused to admit he could not change with the times, and in launching his daughter outside his own home, as on other occasions when he has rashly attempted twentieth-century conformity, he has all too often proved himself a fish out of water. Try as he will, he neither likes nor understands the modern hotel-type debutante ball and Boston's great dance tradition has suffered accordingly. Of late years the intercity collegiate stag line, the tweedy Princetonian and the pipe-smoking Yale man, accustomed to judge their coming-out balls by the name size of the orchestra, the glamor quotient of the femininity, and the per capita allowance of champagne, have all but ruled Boston off their regular debutante circuit. To them Boston Society seems frankly stuffy, and as debutante territory they are quite content to leave the city to the tender mercies of the Harvard sophomore.

Young Proper Bostonians might of course reply that they never wanted such outsiders at their balls. Traditional is the story of two First Family debutantes preparing their invitations for a joint coming-out ball, with one nominating a boy from New Haven for inclusion and the other snapping in some irritation, "But we already *have* a Yale man on the list." The fact remains, however, that even the Harvard sophomore has recently begun to sniff at Boston's vaunted ball beautiful. As the dominant feature of the stag line he has always been regarded as essential to the success of any Proper Bostonian coming-out party, but no longer does he seem entirely content to chant, in the words of Harvard's Hasty Pudding Club theatrical of 1910:

> For of many ways you can enjoy your days
> A gentle Boston dance is best.

Instead, he has begun to plan his fall season with a view toward making an appearance in some less inhibited territory where hostesses make up for what they may lack in Bostonian refinement by their ability to give him his idea of a good time. Observers have attached some social significance to the fact that certain up-and-coming Boston hostesses have moved with the trend and have gone A.W.O.L. to launch their daughters. The most outstanding recent example of this was Mrs. George Tyson, wife of Boston's millionaire banker. Oklahoma born and a woman who can take her Boston Society or leave it alone, Mrs. Tyson journeyed to Newport to give the first really lush post-World War II debut in which she presented her eighteen-year-old daughter, Harriet Elizabeth Tyson, to a 600-guest Newport Society. Mrs. Tyson's guests included only a modest ratio of age to youth, and in place of the usual rows of lorgnetted elders her Family friends were largely made up of the kind that even the teen-agers were glad to have there—the Douglas Fairbanks, Jrs., Mrs. Cornelius Vanderbilt, Jim Farley, etc. The ball cost $40,000, most of this sum going into the hiring of two orchestras, the maintenance of a continuous flow of champagne, and the building of an outdoor tent ballroom with a canopy draped in pink and silver to match Miss Tyson's gown. At 6 A.M. the playing of "Good Night, Ladies" was not the signal for the guests to leave but merely for all present who so desired to take a rousing dip in the ocean and return to what was described as a gourmet's breakfast.

At about the same time as the Tyson ball in Newport, Boston's First Family Society was making merry at home in a postwar revival of the Boston Supper Dances at the Copley Plaza. Originated in the twenties by Proper Bostonians Francis H. Appleton and Ronald T. Lyman as a sort of bulwark against the flaming youth of the F. Scott Fitzgerald era, they have remained a bulwark against the younger generation of today. Currently sponsored by such names as the Henry Cabots, the Lawrence Coolidges, the Allan Forbeses, the George Higginsons, the Hollis Hunnewells, the Robert Saltonstalls and the Richard Searses, these dances admit no debutantes or collegians and boast a hand-picked clientele "from young marrieds to grandparents." In comparison with the Tyson affair the Copley Ball was the essence of Boston social gravity. Described in a Society page report as sartorial standouts on the floor were a "hoopskirted yellow gown that swayed gracefully," a "pale lilac taffeta with a perky bustle," an "orchid organza with violets," and a "pair of lace mitts." The high point of the evening's entertainment was reserved for the witching hour of 10:30, at which time all frivolity ceased and guests listened attentively to a loud-speaker broadcast of one of ex-Prime Minister Winston Churchill's addresses.

There is a sameness to Boston's twentieth-century debutante balls that in happier days the individuality of the Proper Bostonian home would have prevented. Most typical are those given at the Brookline Country Club. Never called by that name but simply "The" Country Club, under the impression that it is the oldest of such organizations in America—though Charleston, S. C. had a golf club eighty-seven years before its founding—it has long been the favored runway for First Family debutante launching. The majority of Boston's best have always held family membership in the club, but even those who do not belong can present their daughters within its precincts provided they are able to team up with a member and give a joint coming-out; the club asks only that a member's name appear on the invitation. Year after year, fall Friday after fall Friday, First Family debutantes come out at balls so identical that they have almost no individuality at all. The size of the dances always ranges from 250 to 300—the club limit—and since a three-to-one boy-girl ratio is considered axiomatic for a Boston debut the proportions are almost invariably divided on the order of from 50 to 60 debutantes, 150 to 180 stags, the remainder being made up by the ever-present "Family friends." Club decorations vary little from week to week, the orchestra is almost always Ruby Newman, and even the man at the door, a husky recruit from the office of the Harvard Athletic Association, has become practically a permanent accessory and is now working on his second generation of would-be gate crashers.

It is significant that in recent years the balls which stand out in the minds of their younger participants as most memorable were not only far cries from this Country Club type but also, judged by the strictest Boston Society standards, extremely outlandish affairs. These would include the two balls given by Mrs. Francis P. Sears for her daughters Elizabeth and Sarah, the balls given by Mrs. Dudley L. Pickman for her daughters Nancy and Lucy Cochrane, and the ball given by Mrs. Albert Cameron Burrage for her granddaughter Elizabeth Burrage Chalifoux. Mrs. Sears presented her daughters in successive years from her North Shore home and studiously avoided all Proper Bostonian dance inhibitions. She had a huge ballroom addition built off her drawing room, and for her second party invited almost 2000 people to dance until sunup to the tunes of two orchestras, one white and one colored. Mrs. Pickman gave her balls right on Commonwealth Avenue, but her version of the Boston at-home debut was some distance from the traditional. For Nancy's ball the Pickman home was entirely transformed into a Paris street scene, complete with sidewalk cafés, lampposts and twinkling stars. For Lucy's ball two years later the home became almost equally unrecognizable, the entrance hall being transformed by a vigorous array of potted trees and plants into a garden scene and the dining room being hung from top to bottom with gold satin looped up with mountain laurel and hemlock boughs. "Home" for the famed Burrage ball of 1938 was Proper Boston's tradition-deep Louis XIV ballroom of the Hotel Somerset, but Mrs. Burrage had some very definite ideas of her own. She had the entire room decorated with orchids, and she and her granddaughter boldly received their guests in front of a jungle-thick display of rare blooms which were being kept fresh by an artificial waterfall running from ceiling to floor.

If three Proper Bostonian hostesses had given such extravaganzas it would be difficult to avoid the conclusion that Boston Society had abdicated in favor of the modern debutante ball. Upon analysis, however, not a single one of these hostesses rates, in the strict sense, as Proper Bostonian at all. Mrs. Sears is a Chicagoan, Mrs. Pickman a New Yorker. Mrs. Burrage is Bostonian; at the same time she represents the new rather than the old in the Boston social hierarchy, her husband having had the misfortune to amass his wealth—which he did by some remarkably astute investments in Chilean copper mines—too late to place her in the "right" era of Boston's First Familyland. Her so-called Orchid Ball, while a landmark on the social scene, stands as no more typical of the Proper Bostonian debutante party than the lavish receptions of ex-Governor and Mrs. Alvan T. Fuller—who are also representatives of a twentieth-century fortune—stand as typical of Beacon Street at-homes.

The most serious charge levelled against the more typical Boston debuts is that there is often a feeling in the air that the fiscal corners are being cut. This is no new indictment. In 1909 when Boston was beginning to follow the trend of moving debuts out of the homes into the hotels and clubs and the textile machinery Drapers gave Dorothy Draper her coming-out ball at the Hotel Somerset, serving 1100 guests a four-course seated supper and spending over $2000 on the evening's champagne, they won a reputation for extravagance that has to some extent plagued them ever since. Yet in New York the Draper ball would have been regarded as mild indeed compared to the high fashion of the day. Lavishness was the order of an era which had been ushered in by the 1897 Bradley Martin masquerade ball at the Waldorf—for which August Belmont paid a cool $10,000 for his costume—and was moving on through such triumphs as James Hazen Hyde's $200,000 ball at Sherry's and Harry Lehr's dog dinner at Newport, when four figures' worth of imported *pâté* went down the collected gullets of his friends' canines. Newport revelled in this kind of largesse, but the true Proper Bostonian watched the era blow itself out with great increase to his peace of mind. He saw another of such eras in the twenties, and he sees one today—but he still stands firm. His Yankee affection not only for his dollar but also for his dollar value has always been strong enough to withstand the charge that his hospitality is on the nigh side. The matter of champagne at his debutante balls is revealing. To the Proper Bostonian champagne is more than a matter of the seven dollars and up per bottle. Whether he can afford it or not he cannot bear to keep it "turned on" all evening. He looks at the matter practically. He has made an investment, and as on all of his investments, he wishes a reasonable return. He cannot get such a return by continuously pouring champagne down the throats of those members of his stag line who insist upon hanging around his punch bowl instead of doing a fair share of what he has, in effect, invited them to do—which is, of course, to dance with his daughter and his daughter's debutante friends. When he sees such a group gathered he is inclined, much to the wrath of those affected, to order the champagne "off" until such a time when it can be more fairly distributed. When desperate he has even been known to turn to milk. At the Boston debut held several years ago of the daughter of William Tudor Gardiner, ex-Governor of Maine, a New York cousin was amazed at the over-all picture of the liquid consumption for the evening. "There was plenty of champagne around," she recalls, "but the only thing that flowed like water was the milk. There was gallons and gallons of the stuff."

Champagne is the No. 1 item of the modern debutante ball budget, and the Proper Bostonian attitude toward it is a large reason for the fact that the typical First Family debut in Boston rarely costs more than half the price for giving such affairs in comparable cities. A recent survey of a hundred representative New York debuts revealed the average price—which varied considerably from year to year—ranged from $5000 to $10,000. Compared with this, Brookline Country Club's average charge for a debut runs around $2500, a sum which includes both an ushers' dinner for up to 65 guests and what the manager of the club considers an "adequate" supply of champagne for a total of 300 guests for the evening. The orchestra and the decorations are extra, but a Country Club dance rarely runs much over $3000 altogether, which, in view of the fact that many of these debuts are joint affairs, is considered, Society-wise, dirt cheap. At the last ultra-select First Family ball given before the late war, a ball which occupied the entire second floor of Boston's Ritz-Carlton Hotel and was correct in every detail, the total bill for the evening came to exactly $3000. The ushers' dinner was given in a friend's home, and while keeping her hotel expenses to the $3000 mark necessitated, the hostess admitted, not only vigilance in the matter of the champagne but also careful clock watching of the orchestra to avoid overtime, she had obviously enjoyed these measures of economy as much as anything else about her party. "I stopped the orchestra myself," she said in characteristic Proper Boston style, "at one minute to four."

Not the least distinctive feature of the Boston debutante ball is the Boston debutante. When some years ago on his radio program Charlie McCarthy likened the Boston girl making her bow to Society to the groundhog in spring—"who comes

out," said Charlie, "sees her shadow, and goes back in again"—
he was merely one in a long line of outsiders who have been
known to make uncharitable comments on Boston's First Family
buds in bloom. As far back as 1889 Oscar Wilde, visiting Boston
and attending a debutante ball, found the status of feminine
pulchritude so low that he wrote following the affair that for
the first time he understood why it was that Boston artists were
reduced "to painting only Niagara Falls and millionaires."
More than one visitor to a Boston coming-out ball of today has
expressed surprise to learn that before a ball the head usher
will give to each of his assistants a list on which will be written
the names of the girls for whom the individual usher must be
personally responsible during the evening and who must be
provided with as many cut-ins as can be arranged. Since there
are usually a dozen ushers for a dance of no more than sixty
debutantes and each list generally includes three and sometimes even four girls, it is plain that a high proportion of Boston debutantes are regarded as slow movers on the market. In
actual practice, of course, many of these girls can take care of
themselves without attention on the part of their ushers. But
the head usher, usually a prominent Bostonian socialite in his
junior or senior year at Harvard, has invariably had unfortunate
experience with the "sticky" type of Boston ball and is generally
determined to be safe rather than sorry. A perennial head
usher at Boston coming-out parties during the thirties, who
married a Boston debutante and is now an architect in New
York, recently reminisced of his lists: "Darn few of those girls
were real wallflowers. But we seemed to have a lot of what we
used to call the 'good eggs'—you know, the tag football type.
Sunday afternoons the guys would break their necks to get out
to their houses, all the way to Dedham or Milton, but Friday
nights they wouldn't know them."

If the Boston debutante is rarely a siren, there is a reason for
it. Her opportunities to learn the role are limited. She is known
for maturing slowly. Her mother, inclined to look down a
Proper Boston nose on sophistication in general and "clothes-

horse" women in particular, has usually raised her at home to regard the cultivation of external glamor as cheap artifice and hardly the way in which a self-respecting girl should wish to attract a man. At school her Proper Boston life is Spartan-strict. Brookline's Beaver Country Day School, for example, has the reputation of being Boston's "charm school" largely through the fact that it permits its older girls to don lipstick before leaving school at 4:30 on Monday through Thursday and at 1 o'clock on Friday. In-town Winsor, on the other hand, forbids the wearing of cosmetics until a girl has actually left the school grounds, and its catalogue states severely that the school requires all pupils at all times to wear "low heeled shoes and sensible, simple clothing." A recent addition to Winsor's staff from Washington D. C.'s Cathedral School was surprised at such beauty bans as they related to the immaturity of Boston girls. At Cathedral she had apparently had experience with girls, mostly from the deep South, who had been wearing high heels and lipstick and going out with boys—some of them from the time they were thirteen years old. At Winsor she found most of the girls, even at sixteen or seventeen, relatively unaware of the existence of boys.

How easily a Proper Boston girl may win the reputation for being "wild" and the drastic consequences that may follow was demonstrated some years ago by two Beaver School girls who were not invited to join Boston's Junior League in their debutante year. They were the only First Family girls who failed to make the League on schedule, although the mothers of both had been League members in their day and one mother had even been an officer of the organization. It soon became common knowledge among Boston social circles that the reason the girls were not passed as provisional members by the League's admissions committee was that they had broken two of the many unwritten laws of Proper Boston conduct; they had worn black dresses and they had been seen in a night club prior to their official coming-out. One offender, after a year of scarlet-letter humiliation, was taken into the League with the debutantes of the following year. The other has never been asked to join. Similarly hidebound is Boston's Chilton Club which, though primarily a club for older women, is a recognized social step for First Family post-debutantes. As recently as World War II the club blackballed a girl who, in her debutante year, had the audacity to dye her hair. Reviewing the case, an officer of the club ruefully admitted. "It's too bad. —— has such charming manners. But she's a *naughty* little girl."

Curiously symbolic of the regimentation of the First Family girl is the grand climax each year of the show put on by Boston's Vincent Club. A socio-charitable organization which shares the swank office of the Boston Junior League at Zero Marlboro Street and which admits only what is considered the cream of Boston's annual crop of 175 or more debutantes, the club was formed in 1892 by a group of sedate Back Bay ladies who annually staged what were called *tableaux vivants* to make money for a local hospital. While never uninhibited—up until 1916 the only males who were allowed to view a Vincent Show were firemen whose presence in the club was required by law but who wore masks so that members would not be embarrassed by recognizing them outside—the shows have gradually succumbed to the times and now allow a mixed audience and include kicking routines and torch songs. For all club members, however, the greatest honor is to make the Vincent Drill. This is the show's highlight, a marching routine which takes months of daily practice to master and is today performed almost exactly as it was in the club's first show more than half a century ago. Tradition is so strong in the Vincent that all members willingly forego the more flattering costumes of the song-and-dance numbers for a chance to wear the time-honored Drill dress. The fact that this is always soldierly—the British grenadier uniform is a perennial favorite—and seems almost expressly designed to hide not only the identity but even the sex of the wearer bothers the true Vincent clubber not at all. To her the sixteen members chosen—most of whom, since selection is based on "good height and proper carriage," are likely to be Amazons of five feet eight and over—are Boston's glamor queens of the year.

In the security of her Vincent Drill regimentals the Boston First Family debutante would seem to be in her element—much more so than when she stands bared to the merciless stare of modern Society in her traditional off-the-shoulder white gown at her coming-out ball. Her mother, at any rate, seems to see the picture this way. To this mother, the Drill stands as the one true constant in the changing social world into which she must send her daughter. The modern debutante ball, on the other hand, is far from this. First Family mothers look back longingly to "their day" when there was no cutting-in and no champagne problem and apparently none of the other terrors that beset their hapless daughters today. One went to a dinner before a dance and enjoyed oneself with one's maid and one's carriage waiting to take one on to the ball. One's mealtime pleasure was never overshadowed by the pressing necessity of wheedling the all-important ride to the party out of a callow Harvard sophomore seated on one's right or left. Instead there was the ever awe-inspiring prospect of sitting down beside an elderly businessman of twenty-five or so, a man of the world obviously.

The fact that this mother is inclined to lump into "her day" stories of the delectable pleasures of all Boston balls which preceded the era of her daughter merely adds to the charm of her swan song. She makes just two divisions in the history of the Boston coming-out party, a yesterday and a today, blithely ignoring the fact that the biggest change of all in these parties came in the days of her own youth with the advent of the out-of-home ball, when for the first time a "nice girl" was allowed out after dark. Her particular bane is present-day Society reporting. In all previous Boston days, apparently, Society editors knew their place—and kept it. The public relations of the Assemblies, for example, were handled by Cotillion Leader Hooper Hooper himself. He met the problem squarely, never allowing a reporter to darken the door of one of his balls. In 1885 only the ever-delicate *Transcript* was permitted to give an on-the-spot account of the first of the Hunt Balls. At a later Hunt Ball one *Globe* man was allowed to observe the hallowed scene and promptly showed his appreciation by a glowing account of the ball's "seductive waltzes." At the debutante balls of the early 1900's old Colonel William Sohier, self-appointed major-domo for all First Family debuts, was the all-time terror of the Boston press. Colonel Sohier permitted coverage of the parties only by the *Transcript* and by Boston's best-known Society editor, Mrs. Caroline Hall Washburn of the *Herald*—the latter not in deference to her reputation but only because, as he used to say, "her mother was a Parkman." On one noted occasion, however, Colonel Sohier was foiled. This was when Mrs. Washburn, ill, had sent her secretary to report a coming-out ball held at the old Hotel Tuileries. Colonel Sohier, meeting her at the door, told her to go home, making Boston-clear that it was a private party and that the entire lower floor of the hotel had been hired for the evening. Biding her time, the secretary managed to attract the attention of the manager of the hotel and told him her plight. "Well," said the manager cheerfully, "the old——hasn't hired my office. You can sit in there." The office was located close to the main entrance and all evening, while Colonel Sohier raged in helplessness, Mrs. Washburn's efficient secretary sat at the manager's desk with the door to the hallway open, leisurely jotting down names and costumes as they passed in review before her. It was the outstanding social scoop of its time, and shortly afterwards the young secretary was rewarded by being named Boston correspondent for the New York edited *Social Register*—a position which she holds to this day.

Actually the proper Boston mother of today would seem to have rather little to complain about in launching a debutante daughter in her city—and there is probably no better example of this than in the question of Society reporting as handled in Boston's modern era. Of late years certain individual Boston debutantes have been known to receive some attention in the press, but it is notable that these have usually been the daughters of mothers not representative of the true anti-publicity Proper

Boston school, and as in the cases of the Cochranes and the Searses, for example, have often been the daughters of mothers who have already bucked Proper Boston tradition in the matter of coming-out balls. In recent years there is only one piece of evidence to show that the great debutante ballyhoo, which began in the twenties and has swept on, interrupted only by World War II, in full fury in other cities, ever really hit the heart of Proper Boston at all. This came significantly not through the Boston newspapers but through an outside medium.

It occurred during the winter of 1932-33 when, after several milder stabs in the direction of Boston in previous years, *The Tatler*, a national Society journal, chose to publish a complete rating of the 170 debutantes of the season. Taking its cue from Miss Juliana Cutting, long New York's social arbiter who used to mark her debutantes by Family standing as A, B, or C, *The Tatler* used not only those three classifications but also went on to lump 56 of the 170 girls under the heading Grade E-Z. In the manner of a racing-form sheet there were individual comments after each girl's name. The author of the article, apparently aware of Boston's social sensitivity, wisely chose to remain anonymous but managed a restrained foreword to his blunt exposé:

> Boston this year, as last, and the year before that, welcomes into its sacrosanct social sphere a list of debutantes not only noteworthy but numerous. If my gradings do not always seem to please certain of those making their bows, they must remember that in all instances the family background of the girl is taken into consideration, not the characteristics, charm or personality of the buds themselves. I trust I make myself perfectly clear upon this all-important point.

A large proportion of Boston's First Families apparently had entries in the debutante field of that year, and virtually all won Grade-A rating with varying individual comments. Moving alphabetically, an Appleton girl was "overflowing in values," a Coolidge had "a galaxy of notables in background," and a Cunningham was shown to be "here by right of heritage." From there the list went on to include an "azure blood" Fay, through a Hallowell, a Holmes and a Jackson to a Lawrence who was classed as "cloistered and conservative." Peabody was "a name to conjure with," Richardson, "of the ultra-conservatives," and Saltonstall, "a name that counts." A Sears was "to manor born," a Shaw had recognition as "prominence without pretense," and of a Thayer it was stated, "none better connected." The list concluded with a Weld, a Whitman and a Winthrop, one of the final comments reading, "Could one desire more?" Two of Boston's First Families, the Dexters and the Pierces, had to be content with B ratings for their daughters though both girls received flattering mentions, the former being noted as "of THE Dexters" and the latter a "family great in values." Not so charitable were the comments opposite the E-Z listings. One girl was "just percolating," while another was "merely pelf." In the various instances where the author encountered two girls of the same Family name he made his distinctions ruthlessly, but few could say that he was drawing his lines very differently from the way in which the Proper Boston mother, scanning the debutante list for her daughter's coming-out ball, might well draw hers. The Lawrence girl whose grandfather was Bishop Lawrence, for example, was Grade A; her second cousin, while still "a Lawrence," was, apparently because of a less distinguished grandsire, Grade B. The Crocker who was Grade A was evidently, in the Proper Boston vernacular, a "Fitchburg Crocker"; her cousin from an offshoot of the select Fitchburg branch, Grade C. Faced with two Emersons, the author apparently traced one direct to the Ralph Waldo, or Concord, Emersons and gave her Grade B; unable to establish a clear Concord connection with another Emerson, he summarily reduced her to E-Z.

Happily for the Proper Bostonian peace of mind no other national publication has ever honored Boston with such a painstaking scrutiny of its debutante Society, and *The Tatler* ceased publication shortly after its Boston bombshell. In recent years the Boston newspapers have not only failed to follow the move-

ment toward increased attention to debutantes, but they have
actually attempted to reverse the trend. The lone Hearst representative in the Boston field, the *American*, formerly published a mild chit-chat column about debutantes, but now combined with the *Record* it has no such feature and treats the
subject so gingerly that judging from his Boston performance it
would seem that Mr. Hearst has forgotten that it was he who
originally broke down the Society-page barriers and decreed the
calling of socialites by their first name.

It is not always easy for Boston's papers to be as deferential to
the debutantes and their coming-outs as they are apparently
determined to be. At the very first of each season's debutante
doings they are annually faced with a problem which might
strain the patience of a less amiable press. This is the problem of
the advance publicity for the Empire Junior Dance, a traditional affair held the first Saturday in May in the Empire Room
of the old Hotel Vendome, when the debutantes of Boston's
coming season, arrayed in hoop skirts and portrait gowns, are
each year formally introduced by the debutantes of the past
season to a severe array of Proper Bostonian patronesses. The
Empire Dance, like so many Boston balls of today, is given for
charity, to benefit the New England Regional Scholarships of
Bryn Mawr College, and the Society editors find themselves in a
most unenviable position. On the one hand, the Bryn Mawr
committee demands publicity—a patent necessity for attracting
paying customers to a party which is non-alcoholic begins at 9,
and ends at 12. On the other hand, since the dance is held in
May and the debutantes to be are still schoolgirls, the Proper
Boston schools demand no publicity. Both groups are stern. The
Bryn Mawr alumnae include some of Boston's most militant
women, and the Proper Boston school authorities have been
known to expel a girl whose picture appeared in a paper prior
to graduation. Caught between these two fires, a Society editor
from such a city as New York might well abdicate responsibility
to either group. No Boston editor would think of indulging in
such a weak-kneed out. Almost invariably, in the days preceding

the Empire, they manage a journalistic tightrope walk which is not only a pleasure to read but which would do credit to the Society-page propriety of the old *Transcript* itself.

No one can foresee the future of Boston Society's great dance tradition. At present this tradition rests, as it always has, in the hands of its dance academies. From the make-up of Boston's First Family Society there can never, of course, be more than one of these at a time—one which is "the" place to go—and hence the individual teacher at such an institution is of paramount importance. Following the great days of Papanti Boston's dance tradition suffered something of a setback at the hands of the Hotel Somerset's noted "Mr. Foster." A short stocky Frenchman who looked like Napoleon III and was highly acceptable socially, he spent a quarter of a century at the Somerset before anyone apparently realized that, despite his assumed American name, he had never quite mastered the American dance. Mr. Foster taught his boys, in the French manner, to start each dance with their right foot and his girls to follow with the left, in contrast to the accepted American practice which has always called for the reverse. To his dying day, Mr. Foster never changed this system, and it is a tribute to the provinciality of Boston Society that before Boston itself changed to the left-foot-first method, an entire generation of Boston's best had cavorted happily around their ballrooms oblivious of the fact that they were out of step with the rest of the country.

Overlapping Mr. Foster's era and succeeding him on her own, has been a woman who for close to forty years has boasted a name familiar to all Proper Bostonians. Operating in Eliot Hall in suburban Jamaica Plain, Miss Marguerite Souther, a former basketball coach, fits far better than her predecessor into the Boston dance tradition. Bostonian to the core, a woman whose merchant grandfather invented the steam shovel, she has never had to cull favor, not even from Cabots and Lowells. Today her dancing classes have become the recognized first essential in the regimental march of Proper Boston's younger Society. "If you send your daughter to the wrong dancing school at the age of six," wryly warned the Boston *Globe* as recently as 1938, "you don't recover for three generations." Even more recently an eleven-year-old Beacon Hill girl, whose mother had been dilatory in taking the social steps necessary to enter her daughter in Miss Souther's first class, brought her mother up sharply on this point. "If I don't get to Miss Souther's first class," she exclaimed, "I won't get to her other classes. If I don't get to her other classes I won't get to her dances. If I don't get to her dances I won't get to the Junior Holidays. If I don't get to the Holidays I won't get to either the Saturday Evenings or the Friday Evenings and frankly, mother, I might just as well not try to come out at all."

Few can deny that there is truth in this remark. For Boston Society to begin in Miss Souther's Eliot Hall is not, however, an altogether happy commentary. An ancient, dingy building, the hall is still today—though through no fault of hers—exactly as it was when Miss Souther held her first class in it in 1912. As for Miss Souther herself, she is a woman by no means without charm, but she is extremely firm. Now in her sixties, she has through the years stood like a rock against the Charleston and the Big Apple, the cheek-to-cheek and the rumba, and all other crazes which have come her way. In the rigid tradition of the Boston formal she wears an evening gown for her afternoon classes as well as those at night. Stories of the severity with which she manages the college-age crowd at her older dances show that she has by no means mellowed in recent times. On one occasion, when a Boston Shaw arrived at Eliot Hall in a dress which Miss Souther felt was too décolleté in back, she stopped the party until the girl, whose mother was an Eliot Hall patroness, agreed to go home and pin enough lace on her gown to pass the inspection. On another occasion Miss Souther caught sight of a flask protruding from the hip pocket of a Harvard boy. Warned by a friend, the boy quickly thought of the men's room and made for it on the run. Entering, he closed the door in relief—only to have it promptly opened by Miss Souther who charged in, took the flask, and charged out again, all before he had a chance to realize what was happening.

In a city with a less well-developed dance tradition such firmness in matters of ballroom etiquette might be considered essential. In Boston it may be doubted if this firmness is the kind of thing which is needed to remedy the defects which, to youthful outsiders at least, have for some time been apparent in the Boston version of the ball beautiful. No Proper Bostonian, for example, would like to think that the last word on the Boston dance was spoken some time ago by a young man from the University of Alabama who, when a graduate student at Harvard, was prevailed upon by a group of his Boston friends to accompany them to one of Cambridge's noted Brattle Hall parties. During the evening the young man appeared to be having a good time, and on the way home his friends joshed him about the conquests he had made and asked him what he thought of his first Boston ball. To their surprise the Alabamian spoke at some length. He had been rather startled, he admitted, by the wide mixture of age and youth at the ball, and he laid particular emphasis on the subject of the more elderly of the Boston mothers who, while denied the floor, had apparently maintained a ceaseless vigil over their daughters from the balcony of the ancient hall. He didn't mean to sound ungrateful and with Southern tact he declared he had indeed had a good time. But his conclusion was firm.

"Ah've never in all mah life," he said, "been to such a sexless affayuh!"

CHAPTER THIRTEEN

HARVARD AND ITS CLUBS

One of the most charming characteristics of the Proper Bostonian is his regard for something which is not located in Boston at all but a few miles up the Charles River in Cambridge, and which he calls Hahvud. The brevity of this pronunciation gives scant indication of the high degree of respect he has for this place. Harvard is Harvard, and since it has been in existence for well over three hundred years—only six less than Boston itself —he believes it is time everyone, not excepting the Deity, should be cognizant of its importance. Some sign of this was given on the final day of Harvard's Tercentenary Celebration in 1936 by the late Bishop Lawrence. It was pouring rain that day and the Bishop, then at the age of eighty-six, was observed by a friend in an automobile to be splashing his way on foot across Harvard Square without even the protection of an umbrella. Shocked the friend begged him to enter his car and avoid such unnecessary exposure. The Bishop refused. "The Lord," he said sharply, "will not allow me to take cold on Harvard's three hundredth birthday."

Boston First Family statistics do not alone tell the story of Harvard and its interrelationship with the Proper Bostonian. Sixty-one members of the Proper Bostonian's two ranking Families, the Cabots and the Lowells, have beaten a path to Harvard's door in the past hundred years, but even this figure falls far short in explaining the extent of his connection with the place. Harvard is actually a major part of the Proper Bostonian's total existence, of his adult life in some respects even more than his college life. Not only has he always shared personally in the many honors which have come Harvard's way throughout its history, but he has also manfully shouldered a full share of the blame for the occasional vicissitudes which have befallen it— when through no fault of his a man of dangerous political tendencies has been tolerated on its faculty or when its football team has suffered a reverse at the hands of a team which would not have dared take the field against the eleven of his day. Furthermore, this feeling has never limited itself to the male members of his Family. In September of 1881, for example, a rather inauspicious opening of Harvard's sixth regular football season coincided with the death by assassination of President Garfield. In her diary for the day Elizabeth Dwight Cabot wrote feelingly of the assassination, closing her entry with the line: "Of course I could think of little else, and coming on top of the Harvard defeat I went blundering around doing my shopping and found myself so tired that I had to stop and go for some dinner."

Socially speaking, Harvard and Boston could hardly be anything but inseparable. The nineteenth-century Proper Bostonian Edmund Quincy laid down First Family law memorably on this point, and as the son of a man who was at one time Mayor of Boston and at another President of Harvard, he knew what he was talking about. "If a man's in there," he used to say, tapping his Harvard Triennial Catalogue, containing a complete list of Harvard graduates, "that's who he is. If he isn't, who is he?"

To this day the Proper Bostonian never ceases to wonder at the large number of young men who, apparently happily, attend colleges other than Harvard. Western institutions he can dismiss with a wave of his hand, but close by, as he sees a score of other colleges within a few miles of his home, he is often curious why it is that he so rarely meets any of the graduates of these colleges—not at dinner, perhaps, but at least on some sort of social footing. He is willing to concede that in other city Societies— New York for one—a certain cachet of social prestige derives

from colleges like Yale or Princeton, but he attributes this to
the fact that it stems from the kind of boy who really belonged
at Harvard and went afield through wanderlust or youthful
indiscretion. Major Henry Lee Higginson, dedicating his gift
of Harvard's present-day athletic field, drew this line of con-
descension as delicately as he could. "Princeton is not wicked,"
he reminded his audience in what was described as one of his
simple, manly addresses, "Yale is not base . . . Mates, the
Princeton and Yale fellows are our brothers. Let us beat them
fairly if we can, and believe they will play the game just as we
do."

A curious example of the strength of the Boston Society stamp
on Harvard is the fact that Midwesterners, traditionally accorded the shortest social shrift of all "foreigners" to enter the
Proper Bostonian sphere, have come to prefer almost any other
Eastern college to Harvard and still come to Cambridge with
marked reluctance. Socially ambitious boys from other parts of
the country have also been known to be repelled by stories they
have heard of the provincialism of Harvard Society. It took just
one of Boston's blue-blood Families to win for Harvard the label "a Lowell monopoly," and Harvard's so-called Corporation,
which has sole control of the institution's two-hundred-mil-
lion-dollar endowment fund, is run in many respects as if Harvard were merely one more in the long line of First Family
trusts. Samuel Eliot Morison, official historian of Harvard, has
taken a stern stand on the matter of the college's Boston stamp.
A First Family man who lives on Beacon Hill and has launched
no less than three debutante daughters in the Boston-Harvard
social swim, he has nonetheless kept an objective approach to
the problem. "Boston," he records in his *Three Centuries of
Harvard*, "has been a social leech of Harvard College." Taking
to task for their interest in Harvard's "appetizing young men"
even those among his own Beacon Hill set—he describes them as
"Boston mammas"—Morison declares that these hostesses have
"baulked all attempts" to make a "social democracy" of the college. "In vain are freshmen tossed onto the same heap," he

writes. "Freshman fellowship, brisk enough in the opening days of college and the first elections of committees, blows away in a whiff of invitations to dances and week-end house parties." *

In its early days Harvard was admirably trained for its role of playing social slide-rule to Boston Society. In the seventeenth and eighteenth centuries, when that Society was dominated by ministers and magistrates, Harvard was primarily a minister-and-magistrate sons' proposition. As the merchant era began in Boston Society so the merchant, or rather his sons, rose to prominence in the college. In these formative years the college was as academically inbred as the Society beside it was biologically so. With the exception of a few language instructors the college did not have a single teacher who was not a Harvard graduate until the nineteenth century. The provincialism of its student body was entirely in character with the ever self-sufficient Proper Bostonian. In all the years between 1737 and 1790 not a single New Yorker entered the college, and not until 1865 were there enough Harvard graduates to make the formation of a New York Harvard Club a paying proposition.

From the first Harvard's presidents were extremely concerned with keeping up the social tone of their college. By the nineteenth century this had become a tradition, and Harvard's leaders—almost invariable recruited from the ranks of Boston's now stabilized First Family Society—were apparently determined to keep the tradition alive. The "heart's desire" of President Quincy, who led Harvard from 1829 to 1845, his own son wrote, "was to make the College a nursery of high-minded, high-principled, well-taught, well-conducted, well-bred gentlemen." When the noted orator Edward Everett succeeded Quincy as president, he was apparently unable to forget that as minister to England he had once been a house guest of Queen Victoria. One morning in chapel, confronted with a group of students all

* *Three Centuries of Harvard,* by Samuel Eliot Morison (Cambridge: Harvard University Press) © 1936.

of whom seemed to have colds, Everett was silent for several moments, then solemnly remarked: "In England, boys, gentlemen never blow their noses. They sometimes use their handkerchiefs but they do not blow their noses." Even such recent Harvard executives as Presidents Eliot and Lowell, though they did their best to make Harvard a national institution, seem to have been conscious of the fact that they also bore a sacred social trust. Eliot, a man of impeccable dignity, insisted that whatever else Harvard might be it should always exert "a unifying social influence" and be "a school of good manners," while the frosty Lowell was once described by a New York newspaperman as "genial enough when he wanted something such as endowment" but who "from all persons less important than himself . . . exacted the most rigid conformance to propriety." This latter may seem harsh, but was scarcely more gently phrased by Harvard's own *Lampoon*, when that publication suggested that a place in Harvard Yard be commemorated by a monument to mark the spot where Lowell spoke to a freshman.

The student body at Harvard had by the middle of the eighteenth century a system of caste that not even Boston Society of that day could match. By 1749 all students were, upon entering, ranked by the president according to their social standing. The ranking was strictly official; students were listed in the catalogue by it, and it determined not only the order of chapel seating and marching in college processions but also precedence for classroom reciting and serving oneself at table. While all ranking was done in what was to become the great Boston Society tradition—according, it was recorded, "to the Dignity of the Familie whereto the students severally belonged"—there can be no doubt that it caused a certain amount of hard feeling. In a noted essay on the subject the late New England historian, Franklin Bowditch Dexter, a Yale man, put the matter of these early-day Harvard rankings as tactfully as possible but made clear that it was usually some time before each newly ranked class was "settled down to an acquiescence in their allotment," and that often the parents of the young men were "enraged beyond bounds." Dexter blamed most of the trouble on the "intermediate" members of the class, claiming that the highest and the lowest rankings were more "comfortably ascertained" than theirs. He cited the case of one Bostonian who, piqued to note his son was ranked fourteenth in a class of thirty-five while he had been tenth in a class of thirty-seven, went off and tried unsuccessfully to found a new college in western Massachusetts.

The most notable case of dissatisfaction with the rankings was no matter of the "intermediates" or Harvard bourgeoisie, however, but concerned the distinguished Phillips Family, noted for their connection with Andover and Exeter Academies. It took place in the summer of 1769 with the publication of the rank list for the following fall. Searching the list Samuel Phillips, wealthy merchant, discovered that his son Samuel, Jr., later founder of Andover Academy, was well down the line, and in time-honored Proper Bostonian manner he complained directly to Harvard's president. He felt particularly strongly about his son's being placed below a boy named Daniel Murray, but it is worth noting that he did not make his complaint on the grounds that he was a wealthy merchant and that Murray's father was not. The merchant era had not yet come into its nineteenth-century own in Boston Society; this was the magistrate era, and Phillips rested his case solely on the point that while both he and Murray, Sr. were Justices of the Peace, he had been a Justice longer than Mr. Murray, and therefor Phillips, Jr. deserved precedence over Murray, Jr.

Harvard's president was a man named Edward Holyoke, distinguished in the college's social history largely through the fact that it was in his reign—1759—that an edict was passed forbidding the wearing of nightgowns by students. At the time of Phillips' complaint he was in the last of his thirty-two years on Harvard's throne and had apparently little stomach for a quarrel over the point. In any case, he promptly re-ranked his entire student body, elevating young Phillips not only the number of notches demanded by his parent but also a few extra ones for good measure. Phillips never troubled to thank Holyoke for this, but upon noting the new ratings, under date of 29 August 1769 he wrote his son a letter which remains—more for what it does not say than for what it says—a sharp commentary on Proper Bostonian father-to-son protocol:

You are now in the most difficult situation & the eyes of all, above and below you, will be upon you, & I wish it might be that you could be at home till the talk about the change was a little over. Every word, action, and even your countenance, will be watched, particularly by those who envy you, and perhaps by those who do not. If any difficulties should arise with any of your classmates that now fall below you, treat them with all possible tenderness. If Murray is uneasy and manifests it to you, say nothing to irritate him. On the whole say as little as possible.

It is significant that Harvard's presidents finally abandoned official social ranking, not in deference to democratic ideals, but simply because, as highlighted by the Phillips case, it had begun to cause them a great deal of trouble in their public relations. Unofficially the practice was continued well into the nineteenth century. A historian writing of the year 1820 notes no outward evidence of social ranking but records that President Kirkland was, on his own hook, still finding it convenient to keep up a method of placing his students "other than alphabetically." President Eliot refused to have anything to do with such listing, but by his time it was completely unnecessary. Harvard's clubs had already taken over where Harvard's early presidents had left off, and as more than one historian has pointed out these clubs have with notable aplomb carried the tradition of social ranking forward to the present day. For seventy-five years the powerful "Hasty Pudding," core of Harvard's present-day club system, has reigned supreme as a sophomore sifter, and though it no longer publishes its elections in the Boston newspapers— as it did up to 1905, in the exact order of their choice—the Pudding order of sophomores is still, to Boston Society at least, an index of social seniority almost as authoritative as the old colonial rating.

Today, for example, noting in the Society columns the marriage of a Harvard man, the Proper Bostonian looks to his listed clubs and refers to the man's Pudding rating as confidently as a credit bureau turns to Dun & Bradstreet. If the man is listed as "Hasty Pudding—Institute of 1770" followed by the letters "D.K.E.," the Proper Bostonian knows that he was a "Dickey" or one of the first forty-five sophomores elected to the club and hence very definitely a social somebody. If there is "Hasty Pudding—Institute of 1770" but no D.K.E., then the man ranked somewhere between Nos. 46 and 150—the latter figure being the average Pudding membership for each Harvard class of about 1000—and is at least "in Society." If there is no mention of Hasty Pudding at all, the Proper Bostonian probably will not know the man but his social conscience can be clear; the man is obviously, to his way of thinking, a person of "humble" origin.

As currently constituted Harvard's club system is probably the most exclusive of that in any college in America. The Hasty Pudding organization, with its well-defined ratings, is one indication of this. But the Pudding, despite the fact that it has its own clubhouse and stages a musical comedy each Easter—which to Boston Society is a male counterpart of the debutantes' annual Vincent Show—is not a club at all in the sense of one of Harvard's so-called "final" clubs. These clubs, for which the Pudding acts as a sort of proving ground, are the real be-alls and end-alls of Harvard social existence, and since there are but ten of them and in lean social years some have been known to take as few as four members, it is not a life for everyone.

To have a chance for membership in a final club a boy must be, to start with, what is called "club material." Being such material covers a multitude of sins but in the main usually means that early in his freshman year—by which time he will be watched by upper-class club spotters and, if distinguished, surreptitiously feted at Boston Society Sunday lunches in Dedham or Brookline where by coincidence all males present will have the same pattern on their necktie—a boy must show that he has a healthy respect for the observation of Harvard's social taboos. These taboos have always included, among other things, over-careful dress, undue athletic exertion, serious literary endeavor, rah-rah spirit, long hair, grades above C, and Radcliffe girls.

Since the ability to recognize such taboos must be second nature to a club man, and since such instincts are best developed in a boy's more formative years, the question of being club material at Harvard boils down to a boy's having graduated from one of a small number of socially correct Eastern private schools. Of the five hundred or so public-school graduates—half of each class—entering Harvard each year, rare indeed is the boy who manages to break into the purple pale of its club Society. If the school is "wrong," even "right" ancestry is usually of no avail. Graduates of such venerable private institutions as Exeter, Andover and Roxbury Latin may make clubs but far more often do not; as their social standing has declined in Boston's Society, so it has in Harvard's. Graduates of Milton Academy, Noble & Greenough, Pomfret, a few select country day schools and some new boarding schools have a better chance, but still by no means a good one. Only the top-ranking émigrés of New England's elite Episcopal Church schools—Groton, St. Mark's, St. Paul's, St. George's and Middlesex—can be positive from the start that they are club material with no questions asked. Even these, the "St. Grottlesexers" as they have been called, find themselves in the position of waiting anxiously for the call to Harvard clubdom at the same time knowing that more than a third of them, as sophomores, will never make it. As juniors, or even late in their senior year, a few more will be chosen, but the latter is a dubious honor, since such boys sometimes go through life with the feeling that while judged socially presentable enough to be seen on the occasions when they may as graduates return to club dinners, they were deemed hardly worthy of close fellowship during their undergraduate years.

The acid test of a club's standing is its ability to keep in line its "legacies" or boys who have had grandfathers, fathers or brothers in the club, and conversely its power to ferret the more desirable of other clubs' legacies away from them. Based on this, the social rank of Harvard's ten clubs with appropriate spacing, may be indicated as follows:

Porcellian
A.D.

Fly
Spee
Delphic (Gas)
Owl

Fox
D.U.
Phoenix
Iroquois

At the time of their founding most of these clubs were chapters of national fraternities, but the Harvard chapters always felt their obligations to their brothers from other colleges rather burdensome and were only too delighted, when the opportunity presented itself, to surrender their charters and become local independent clubs. They have remained local in respect to Harvard, but their independence in respect to Boston—or Boston Society—is a matter of opinion. The Porcellian, Gas, Spee, and particularly the Fly, have always numbered in their memberships each year a fair proportion of New Yorkers, and there is no specific exclusion of Philadelphians, Chicagoans, or indeed youthful members of any other recognized Societies. By and large, however, Harvard's clubs range themselves almost exactly in accordance with the Boston social standing of the Families which have long dominated them. Porcellian men are Boston's best, A.D. men Boston's next best, and so on down the line. To go a step farther, it would even be possible to draw a close paral-

lel between the accepted ranking of Boston's leading clubs and
what would, roughly, correspond to their Cambridge chapters.
Thus, Somerset would be substituted for Porcellian, Union for
A.D., Tennis and Racquet for Fly, and so forth. Certainly few
would deny that Proper Bostonians are inclined to rate one
another socially as much by what club they made at Harvard as
by what club they may later belong to in Boston. The graduate
presidents of every one of Harvard's clubs today are Bostonians,
the majority of them in the investment business and all men of
high distinction in Boston Society. The Proper Bostonian's interest in the affairs of his Harvard club is sternly enduring—one
First Family man was still regularly attending graduate luncheons of the A.D. Club in his ninety-seventh year—and it is also
one which is remarkably compelling. In February of 1942 Leverett Saltonstall was offered the position of Grand Marshal of
Porcellian and, though already occupied as Governor of Massachusetts and warned by more than one of his advisers that the
club Grand Marshalship was of extremely doubtful political
value, he eagerly embraced the post. He served until September
of 1945, only resigning when it became apparent to him that, as
a Senator living in Washington, he was no longer able to discharge his Porcellian duties faithfully.

Harvard's clubs are modeled on the Proper Bostonian idea of
a gentleman's club. Though the Hasty Pudding still puts its
first forty-five members through a three-day hazing period, the
final clubs avoid Lost Weekend initiations and any semblance
of the jack-o'-lantern type of ritual beloved by most college
fraternities. Generally speaking, the clubhouses are not elaborate and dues not excessive. Since under Harvard's "House
Plan" boys have to pay for twenty-one meals a week in their dor-
mitories, club members rarely eat in their club and, since there
are no bedrooms in any of the clubs, never sleep there. The
exclusiveness of the clubs is notably evident in their treatment
of female guests. Once a year the latter are invited to a tea party
in a guest room always entirely separate from the main part of
the club; otherwise they are shunned completely—so much so

that following the Yale or Princeton game each year, both undergraduate and graduate club members invariably leave their dates or wives to shift for themselves and attend a lengthy, formal-dress club dinner which occupies the entire evening. Exclusiveness is also evident in the clubs' treatment of male guests. By what is called the "Unwritten Law" of Harvard's clubs members of one club are allowed in the guest room of another; non-club men, however, are not admitted to any part of a Harvard club until they have been out of Harvard for ten years.

Appropriately enough, Harvard's hierarchy is headed by the Porcellian, which is the only one of the college's ten final clubs to date from the very beginning of Boston's days of First Family-founding. Born in 1791, it was once known as the Pig Club from the fondness of two of its first members, Francis Cabot Lowell and Robert Treat Paine, for that delicacy in roasted form. As the organization grew in social stature, however, it became incumbent upon these men and others to refine their name to the present one. In recent years the A.D. has the reputation for culling a slightly more genial type of club man than the Porcellian, but from the simon-pure social standpoint the latter has always reigned supreme. Whatever other clubs have the Porcellian has also, and it usually has more besides. In the Roosevelt Family, for example, the Fly has the Hyde Park or Franklin Roosevelts, but the Porcellian has the even more socially august Long Island or Theodore Roosevelts. The Porcellian's record for unbroken Family dynasties is one that no other club can come close to matching. For the better half of Boston-Harvard history the club has enjoyed generation after generation of Cabots and Cutlers, Lowells and Lymans, Gardners and Gardiners, Hallowells and Hunnewells, Saltonstalls and Searses, Warrens and Welds. Nepotism, prevalent in all Harvard clubs, hangs so heavy over the Porcellian that its present membership includes no less than six Cutler brothers directly descended from the club's first Grand Marshal, Charles Cutler, who served from 1792 to 1794, and even the present club steward prides himself on being a second-generation "P.C. man," his father having held the same position before him.

Of such a club might be expected a million-dollar clubhouse and an initiation fee in four figures. Actually, in the Proper Bostonian tradition, the Porcellian is located directly over a corner cafeteria in a rather shabby building on Cambridge's busy Massachusetts Avenue, and its initiation fee is ten dollars. Annual dues are forty dollars. The outer door of the Porcellian is never locked, but so great is the awe in which the club is held that few ineligibles have ever bothered to try it. Inside there is what passes for the Porcellian guest room. This is a vestibule which contains a number of bicycle racks dating from the 1890's, six cane chairs always piled forbiddingly one on top of another, and reading matter in the form of a sign which says that booksellers, peddlers and solicitors are at no time allowed in the building. There is also a button which, when pushed, brings forth a sternly inquiring voice through a loud-speaker tube. Only a handful of men unprivileged to wear the green, pig-studded P.C. necktie have ever gotten beyond this speaking tube to the inner sanctum upstairs. One of these was the late Al Smith whose curiosity had been so aroused by tales of the Porcellian that, on coming to Harvard, he prevailed upon his Porcellian friend, New York's patrician lawyer Grenville Clark, to extend him the honor of seeing the place. When during the late war, however, amenable Clark also took a second guest, General Eisenhower, on a whirlwind tour of the premises, he was sternly reminded by other members that he had then had more visitors than any other man in Porcellian history.

Actually Clark's friends saw little of the Harvard high life they undoubtedly expected. The Porcellian prides itself on being the simplest of all Harvard clubs, and its upstairs sights consist chiefly of a library, a dining room, a bar, a large variety of pig figurines in various poses, and a number of ageing leather armchairs endowed by P.C. Families and suitably engraved with P.C. Family names. So strict is the Puritan tradition in the Porcellian that there is not even a game room, standard equipment for other Harvard clubs. Card playing or gambling of any sort has never been permitted. One of the most striking features of the club is a mirror attached out of a second-floor window at such an angle that members seated inside the main room of the club may look down on the Massachusetts Avenue life passing beneath them without troubling to leave their chairs. This mirror, typically enough, cost the Porcellian nothing, having been designed and installed in 1901 by a mechanically inclined son of the club steward. Through the years, however, it has come to stand as a sort of symbol of Porcellian social *laissez faire* and has taken its proud place in Boston-Harvard legend beside the story of the Porcellian stroke of the Harvard crew of whom it was said: "He's democratic all right—he knows all but the three up front."

While members of each of Harvard's clubs maintain close connections in after years and stand ready to help clubmates out at every turn, the affiliation between Porcellian graduates is proverbial. The late novelist Owen Wister, in an interview which took place in 1936, fifty-seven years after his election to the club, patiently tried to describe to a reporter his affection for the place. Nothing, he stated, not even the national distinction which came to him following the success of his novel *The Virginian*, had ever meant so much to him. It was a bond, he declared, which could be "felt but not analyzed." It was in this same spirit that Theodore Roosevelt, informing Kaiser Wilhelm of Germany of the engagement of his daughter Alice to Nicholas Longworth, volunteered the line: "Nick and I are both members of the Porc, you know." Expressed in terms of the Boston debutante Porcellian prestige is awe-inspiring. Since time immemorial Boston's belles have been adjusting their caps for the prize catch among Harvard husbands, a Porcellian man. In the Cabot Family the story is told of a Cabot girl who, seated on the front porch of her Beverly home shelling peas one fall morning in the year 1810, looked up to see coming into her driveway a chaise driven by Charles Jackson, a man who enjoyed Boston-wide prestige as one of Porcellian's original founders. He was an acquaintance of hers, a widower whose first wife had died only a few months before. Alighting, he asked, in the direct Boston manner, for her hand in marriage. Miss Cabot accepted. Some time later a member of her family, who knew that she must have been taken by almost complete surprise, asked her how she had been able to make up her mind so quickly. "My dear," came the quiet reply, "*not* marry Mr. Jackson?"

Porcellian power was amply illustrated in more recent times when, in the election of its annual group of sophomores in the carefree days of the twenties, the club chose to include in the number a boy from a small town in western Massachusetts. He was a young man of unusual charm but one about whom, in contrast with the rest of the group which had in customary fashion banded together since early school days, little else was known. As an undergraduate member he was a success, and upon his graduation his well-connected Porcellian friends saw to it that their adopted brother had an opportunity to marry well and take a good position in an old-line Boston firm. This dizzy rise was continued until the depression. Then it stopped short. Finding himself involved in a large financial deal at an inopportune moment, the man appropriated some of the firm's money. He had intended to pay it back but was caught red-handed. He wished to make a clean breast of the affair.

The club was in no mood for this. Not only had the man figuratively bitten the hand that had fed him, he had literally done so. He had been elected a graduate officer of the Porcellian and among the funds he had misappropriated had been some of the club's own. Stern measures were also indicated for another reason. Already two Porcellian men, a prominent New York investment counsellor and stock exchange head Richard Whitney, were in Sing Sing prison for similar fiscal irregularities. In the case of these two New Yorkers—particularly Whitney, who had been photographed by *Life* magazine on his way to jail with his gold Porcellian pig prominently displayed on his watchchain —it had been impossible to avoid scandal. In the case of the Boston man it was not. The offense did not reach the newspapers at all. Porcellian men simply hushed the matter of their own deficit, quietly paid off the firm and prevailed upon it not to prefer charges, and finally chartering a plane for the occasion took the man on a "vacation." The spot chosen is known to have been a ranch in Arizona, but further details of the affair have never been aired, and it remains to this day, to all participants, a closed book.

Harvard's authorities do not defend Harvard's club system. Many of them are inclined to look upon the sophomore club man, the beau ideal of Boston Society, as a necessary evil in their Cambridge community, and some have even gone so far as to wonder why it is necessary to have even such a relatively insignificant number of Harvard's total student body made up of boys who, in the words of a recent *Town and Country* author, "dress alike, look alike, walk alike, talk alike, and, if pressed, think alike." Nonetheless, it would be out of character with Harvard's age-old position as Boston's social annex if its authorities had ever openly condemned the system. Even Harvard's current leader, James B. Conant, who, while a member of the D.U. club, probably ranks as the most socially elastic president in the college's history, has not advanced a plan to level the social sights. For the most part official Harvard prefers to ignore the clubs in the same manner that the columns of the *Crimson*, undergraduate newspaper, take no notice of their existence. A Harvard professor recently declared that having been a faithful attender at faculty meetings for twenty-five years he has yet to hear the clubs brought up for discussion. A Harvard historian goes further and states that to his knowledge in all the sixty-four years of college history under Presidents Eliot and Lowell—Porcellian and Fly men, respectively—he believes there was only one faculty-meeting mention of them. That was when Lowell, engaged in promoting Harvard's House Plan whereby undergraduates would live in an atmosphere of social equality, was asked if he did not intend to go further and abolish the clubs. Lowell replied that he had no such intention, that Harvard's clubs represented the college's most influential graduates, and that he had no wish to lose his job on their account—"like Wilson did down at Princeton."

The Proper Bostonian finds himself in a position where he can hardly do other than stand up for Harvard's club system. Not only is Harvard's Society, in which there are so very few sheep and so very many goats, an almost exact counterpart of his own First Family Society, but Harvard's clubs are actually vital to his Society. As far back as 1892 the Madrid-born Boston-bred philosopher, George Santayana, noted the sharp line which divided the majority of Harvard boys from the so-called "club crowd" among which he found "the most conspicuous masculine contingent of Boston Society." As Harvard has expanded the importance of this line has grown. The Proper Boston woman who in the nineteenth century might have been satisfied with a Harvard man as dancing partner for her debutante daughter now demands a Harvard club man. For hostesses lacking first-hand Harvard connections one of Boston's leading social stationers are happy to supply, at a rental charge of twenty-five dollars for three days, their "Harvard list," the basis of which is an up-to-date membership of Harvard's clubs. The same stationers keep up a "date book" in which hostesses sign up in advance for their parties so that the coveted stag line of sophomore club men will not be overtaxed. Invitations pour into the Porcellian, A.D., Fly and other clubs in such profusion that the Fly maintains a social secretary for the purpose of answering them and the Porcellian, in keeping with its proud position, makes a practice of sending a scout out to reconnoitre a debutante party early in the evening and report back to his clubmates on the charm of the girls present, the quality and quantity of the champagne being served, and whether in his considered opinion the party is worth the trouble of dressing up and going to.

Since defend Harvard's system he must, the Proper Bostonian makes a valiant attempt at it. His first point is that it is wrong to regard wealth as the basis of the selective process of Harvard's clubs. He is likely to choose some such example for this as the case of one of New York's wealthiest men who, arriving in Cambridge as a freshman in 1911 and setting himself up in style in an apartment complete with a valet, is said to have waited confidently for the attention of club spotters for close to a year. Finally, feeling himself totally ignored, he withdrew from Harvard altogether.

In making such a point, of course, the Proper Bostonian has to convince the sceptic that there is a very definite distinction between the kind of Family wealth which is admittedly a recognized club criterion—in other words, Boston Family wealth —and Family wealth as it is understood in New York or other parts of the country. In making his usual point No. 2 about Harvard's club system the Proper Bostonian has an even more difficult task. This is to convince outsiders that Harvard's club system is so constituted that anyone who doesn't make a club is perfectly free to go out and start another club on his own. The classic example for this is the Delphic, a club which was founded by a New Yorker, who was, like the freshman of 1911, slighted by his fellow Harvardians. Nonetheless, certain additional facts belong in this story about the Delphic. For one thing, the date was 1889 and there has not been another club in Harvard's history started in this manner. For another, the club is still today known as the "Gas" from the fact that it had such hard going in its early days that the club steward used to keep the lights on all night to prove a good time was being had inside. And finally, the New Yorker who founded the Delphic, or Gas, was not the sort of man who undertook anything he didn't intend to finish; his name was J. P. Morgan.

There is still a third point the Proper Bostonian is fond of making about Harvard's club system, and the one on which he rests his case. This is that a system whereby 15 percent of the students make clubs and 85 percent do not is preferable to the average college fraternity system in which these proportions are reversed and a mere 10 or 15 percent of students are left to a life of social solitude. Stop the first Harvard boy you see on the street in Cambridge, says the Proper Bostonian, and ask him where the Porcellian Club is, and the chances are he will not know and furthermore will not care. So small is the group affected by Harvard's system that more than three quarters of Harvard's undergraduates are able to lead happy lives oblivious of it.

That there is something to be said for this line of reasoning few observers of the Harvard scene would deny. It is noteworthy, however, that when the Proper Bostonian finds that his own son has failed to make a club and thus becomes a member of that large and happy 85 percent, he is the first to stand up and be counted against the whole system. A club man of the class of 1905, for example, whose son failed to make a club, declared unhesitatingly that Harvard's clubs never choose the boys who become the outstanding men in their class in later years but go after only the social playboys whose graduation, he felt, involved little more than a move "from armchair at the Porcellian to armchair at the Somerset." From his own class he proudly pointed to such non-club men as Walter S. Gifford, president of the American Telephone Company, Clarence Dillon, head of New York's Dillon, Reed banking firm, and Edward E. Brown, chairman of the board of Chicago's First National Bank, and named them as the three most successful men in the class. A club man of the class of 1912, a member of whose Family was also ignored by Harvard's system, nominated as the outstanding successes in his class ex-Ambassador Joseph P. Kennedy, author Frederick Lewis Allen, and the late Robert Benchley—all non-club men. He further declared that Benchley, though a member of the Hasty Pudding, always felt strongly about having been excluded from a final club, and on being asked to come back to a class reunion once replied, "Why should I? No one paid any attention to me when I was there."

From the emphasis placed by Boston Society on the Harvard clubs it is fortunate for the Proper Bostonian that instances of his sons failing to make a club are relatively rare. Tight though Harvard's social squeeze is, connections which begin at the Family-conscious club-feeder schools and continue through the important freshman year usually take care of the First Family boy's being fitted into the club mold by the time of sophomore elections. When these connections fail and a boy is fated to go through Boston social life with some such whispered label as "He didn't make the A.D., you know," the results have been known to prove almost disastrous.

One such case is recalled by a Boston lawyer who, though he failed to make a Harvard club, managed to bear up so well that he won a Boston-wide reputation for being able to do so. Attending Harvard Law School he was approached one evening by a member of the Porcellian Club whose brother-in-law had not been able to make a club. The Porcellian man asked for his advice in mapping out the most satisfactory college life possible for a non-club man, stating frankly that he knew nothing of such things himself and that his brother-in-law had been so affected by his misfortune that he was on the verge of leaving Harvard. Many times the two had serious discussions on the subject of the extra-club activities which might help the boy. Today the lawyer enjoys telling on himself the conclusion to which they came.

"After two months," he says, "we decided that if by any chance the boy could manage to become interested in his studies, his Harvard education might still be worth while."

CHAPTER FOURTEEN

THE OLD GUARD ON GUARD

Visitors to the Hub of the universe rarely leave the city without being impressed by the profound awe in which First Family leaders are held. There may be some question as to how far down the line this respect goes on the part of Boston's total population, but among the socially elect and socially ambitious, there is nothing quite like a genuine First Family patriarch, a Cabot or a Lowell, a Higginson or a Peabody, on the face of the Boston earth. Not long ago a wealthy widow in the city, not strictly a First Family lady but one far enough up the social scale to be listed in the Boston *Social Register,* began to have brief periods of mental aberration. In between times she was quite normal, but her doctor felt it would be best for her to go to a sanitarium for proper care. Knowing the woman's distrust of psychiatry in general, he waited until she was entirely capable of making her own decision before broaching the subject. The woman heard him out and then named her condition; she would go if the step should be declared necessary not by a single psychiatrist but by a committee of two psychiatrists, one to be appointed by Lawrence Lowell, then president of Harvard, and the other by Godfrey Lowell Cabot, long a First Family stand-by. The fact that the doctor met this condition, brought Mr. Lowell and Mr. Cabot into the case, and that on the advice of the Lowell and Cabot appointed committee the woman went happily off to the sanitarium, is interesting enough. But it is at least equally interesting that neither her doctor, nor the psychiatric committee, nor Messrs. Lowell and Cabot were ever particularly surprised at the affair. The lady had never met either of the two gentlemen in her life, but that too was unimportant. She knew they were Boston's best, and that was that.

Such men, in Boston's curious social oligarchy, are not mere men; they are institutions. When on October 5, 1933, the late Bishop William Lawrence was given a "day," it was a social landmark in many respects similar to a day of the Harvard Tercentenary celebration. It began with a church service by invitation only in St. Paul's Cathedral, went on through a large luncheon in the Cathedral rooms, and continued with a rally at Symphony Hall for which tickets were engraved in landmark style "The Fortieth Anniversary of Bishop Lawrence." Actually Lawrence was no longer bishop of the diocese, having retired six years before, but no successor could challenge his right to reign supreme over Boston Society. He was still called Bishop Lawrence, and he took part in the ceremonies commemorating him in a modest yet notably objective manner.

Major Henry Lee Higginson, whose celebration was set for November 18, 1914, on his eightieth birthday, had to do even more. Since it was planned that the affair would begin with a dinner at the Tavern Club, of which he was president, proceed with a dinner at the Boston Harvard Club, of which he was also president, and end with a dinner at the Copley-Plaza to the accompaniment of the Symphony Orchestra, which he had personally founded, Higginson had to take an executive hand in all the advance preparations for his honoring. Fortunately there was no occasion for embarrassment; the Major had for some time given unmistakable evidence that he accepted himself as an institution. "He always seemed to me," declared Joseph Lee, writing his distinguished cousin's obituary for the Saturday Club, "like the old knight of the castle—a part he played in some theatricals—giving sympathetic, spirited advice and inspiration of high example to the apprentice squires." Among Higginson's squires were Presidents Roosevelt, Taft and Wilson. Actually he had no platform position; he never held public office and even his Majority had expired as of the formal ending of hostilities in the Civil War. But he was senior partner of Lee, Higginson & Co. and a Boston Society institution man, and he did not hesitate to correct such mere elected mortals as the temporary occupants of the White House.

The Major saw it as an obligation. "Any well-trained businessman," he was fond of saying, "is wiser than the Congress and the Executive." Certainly he was not just any businessman. When Theodore Roosevelt began speaking harshly about monopolies, Higginson told him to stop his nonsense. "Cease all hard words," he wrote briskly, "about corporations and capitalists." The Major was fond of "Teddy" but apparently Roosevelt did not stop his hard words soon enough. When Charles W. Eliot was about to resign as president of Harvard, Higginson was considering Roosevelt—entirely irrespective of his being occupied in Washington—for what would soon be the supreme earthly vacancy. But though Roosevelt seemed to him "generally satisfactory" as President of the United States, he felt that he lacked the necessary "judgment" to be President of Harvard. After the trust-busting campaign, Higginson was sure of it. "I give him up!" he wrote a friend tersely. President Wilson gave him, as he used to admit, even more trouble, but he generously noted that he invariably received "very pleasant replies" about his directives as to the war leader's proper course. If Wilson found the correspondence onerous he was too tactful a man to give any indication of the fact. Only once did he ever chide the Boston institution, and then so delicately that he could be sure the Major would not be aware of it. "I think I realize," he wrote Higginson from the White House on December 10, 1914, "that there are two sides to every question, and sometimes two of almost equal weight."

Bishop Lawrence, unlike Higginson, left the Presidents and Congress alone but his power was nonetheless a wondrous one. It was felt in Geneva, Switzerland—he was a stern opponent of the League of Nations—and it was felt in Milton, Massachusetts. The Bishop had three homes: a winter home on Commonwealth Avenue, a summer home at Bar Harbor, Maine, and a fall-and-spring home in Milton. Near this last residence a family of Boston Hallowells possessed a large and none too even-tempered dog. The animal had long been the bane of the neighborhood. At one time or another he had bitten the postman, the milkman, the garbage man and several children. But all complaints were in vain. He was recognized as a bad dog but he was a Hallowell dog living in the suburb of Milton, and he enjoyed on a canine scale a life of First Family privilege that made him immune to ordinary neighborhood dissatisfaction. One day, however, the animal, which had always shown a catholic impartiality in his nippings, observed Bishop Lawrence taking a short cut across Hallowell soil onto Lawrence property. In a twinkling he was on the spot, and before the trespasser could make a getaway he had between his teeth a sizeable portion of the back of the Bishop's trousers. That evening Bishop Lawrence paid a call on the Hallowells. In comparison with the many previous complaints the Hallowells had had of their dog's behavior the Bishop's was a mild one, but the next day the dog was gone. Even the Hallowells had no use for a dog which could not distinguish between the biting of a postman and the biting of a Boston institution.

Endicott Peabody of Groton was another of Boston's lords of creation, the third in a recognized triumvirate which included Harvard's Lowell and Bishop Lawrence. Operating thirty miles from Boston and as much or more concerned with New York scions of privilege as with the sons of Boston's First Families, he was nonetheless a city "First Citizen" and stood, with or without Groton behind him, as a Proper Bostonian institution. It was to Peabody that Boston fathers sent their sons, not just to Groton. Peabody stood for Proper Bostonian manhood and he, like Higginson, was all wool and a yard wide. Higginson corrected Theodore Roosevelt, Peabody corrected Franklin Roosevelt. It has been said that Boston fathers would have sent their sons to him whether he had been engaged in building a school or a railroad. For generations boys who have attended Groton School have gone out into the world as Peabody's personal product. They never lost their respect for him or their awe of him. At the time of his death in November, 1944, he had, in his capacity as an Episcopal minister, married over one third of the school's twelve hundred living graduates. One graduate, ten years out of Groton with a wife and two children, was leaving Hamilton harbor aboard the *Monarch of Bermuda* and had climbed out to the end of a lifeboat to wave good-bye to his Bermudian acquaintances. At the moment he reached his post Peabody, returning from a vacation on the same boat, came striding down the deck. "Come down off that davit, boy," boomed a stern voice. With a smart "Yes, Sir" down came the "boy" and Peabody continued his walk without a word.

This sort of awe made more than one father or mother feel that Peabody was almost too much of an institution. One Boston mother complained to him. "The trouble with your school, Mr. Peabody," she said, "is that it makes boys despise their parents." "No," said Peabody, "it makes boys anxious about them." Tributes to the Boston Colossus were never lacking during his lifetime or after his death, but Yale conferring an honorary degree on him as far back as 1904 left no doubt that here was something more than human clay:

> What strength is to weakness, what experience is to ignorance or blind confidence, what light and faith are to darkness and doubt, what courage is to trembling fear, what the spiritual potter is to the pliant clay of youthful character, what Paul was to Timothy—that, all that, is the Head Master of Groton School to the young manhood blessed with his devoted instruction and companionship.

To the Proper Bostonian such praise would not seem excessive. Loyal to a fault with the men he has elevated to the position of institutions, he recognizes no limitations in them. He follows them blindly because he knows they rose to the top naturally. No amount of playing the game, either the social game or the political game, ever made a Henry Lee Higginson, an Abbott

Lawrence Lowell, a William Lawrence or an Endicott Peabody of yesterday—or for that matter a Godfrey Lowell Cabot or a Charles Francis Adams of today. The late Henry Cabot Lodge did a great many things in his lifetime, but he never became a First Family institution. Nor can his grandson, the present Henry Cabot Lodge, or Leverett Saltonstall ever aspire to that honor. As Senators they are too political; they cannot maintain the severe attitude toward personal publicity, which is perhaps the first requisite for a man's becoming an institution in Boston. Certainly in all of the men who have so risen this quality has been noticeable. Reporters have been creatures of the devil.

Even their friends take no liberties beyond those parcelled out within the secluded radii of home and club. Boston institutions are not called by their nicknames. It was a close friend indeed who dared recall to Major Higginson's face in later years the name by which the Major had always been known by his schoolmates, "Bully Hig." As for Lowell, when Proper Boston's prodigal son Lucius Beebe returned from New York in 1935 to write a book about his native land, he chanced to mention Harvard's president with the parenthetical note, "Cousin Larry, to half of Boston." Though Proper Boston did indeed crawl with Lowell's cousins—his wife had been one and his first law partner another—Beebe was promptly brought to task. Even Mrs. Lowell had never called her husband anything but Lawrence in her life. When Bishop Lawrence retired from the office of Bishop in 1927, he surprised a younger friend by telling him, "No more 'Bishop,' boy, call me Bill." But the line "Call me Bill" died in its tracks. "Needless to say," notes a biographer of Lawrence, "this was not done or meant to be done." Even as a young man leaving Harvard to attend the Andover Seminary, Lawrence had feared close contact with his fellows. In his *Memoirs* he writes:

> The students were compelled to chum. The only person whom I knew was a Harvard classmate by the name of Harry Nichols, whom I had seen something of at college but had not been inti-

mate with. Frankly, I dreaded the experience and shrank from
chumming. However, Harry Nichols turned out to be the best
of chums. He got up early, lighted the fire in the Franklin
stove, cleaned the study lamp, dusted the room, and kept everything in perfect order. All that I had to do was make my bed.*

College acquaintances of Lawrence Lowell remember that
as a young man he had a habit during the mile run, at which
he was adept, of constantly looking back over his shoulder at
those behind him and yet never being able to realize how exasperating this was to his competitors. A Yale man who had run
against him went up, still panting, to congratulate him at the
conclusion of one event. "Sorry I didn't give you a better race,"
he said. Replied Lowell: "Well, I would have made it in better
time if I'd been pushed." Such men as Lowell and Bishop
Lawrence were never designed to be trapped in the give-and-
take of mortal life; at the same time they were eminently fitted
for rising briskly through Boston First Family Society to the
exalted heights of institutionalism. Once in that position there
was no more need for familiarity, and since there is life tenure
in the office, no more need to cater to anybody. Surely there
was no occasion for modesty. Major Higginson took with good
grace the fact that Harvard waited until he was almost fifty to
give him an honorary degree, but his cousin, Colonel Higginson,
could not fail to observe that his degree which did not come to
him until he was seventy-five was handled "somewhat tardily."
Lowell's self-assurance was as formidable as his full red cheeks
and bushy brown mustache. When Bishop Lawrence died, Harvard's president was nominated to write his epitaph and he
proceeded to do so. "Only genius," he wrote, "has the scope to
write an epitaph for such a man."

As with so many other elements of Boston Society there is a
purpose underlying its making of men into institutions. In Boston's early days such men would have had little place, but as
the political complexion of the city changed and the very foun-

* *Memories of a Happy Life*, by William Lawrence (Boston: Houghton
Mifflin) © 1926.

dation of the Proper Bostonians' social system became threatened by the peaceful penetration of the Irish Catholic and foreign-born groups into positions of high influence, these institution men became essential. They stood as the Old Guard and there was nothing pathetic about their stand. To the naked eye their power was almost invisible—as far back as 1900 when Major Higginson had become an institution less than a quarter of Boston's population was Anglo-Saxon Yankee—but these men were never supposed to be looked at by the naked eye. They had to be looked at through a telescope with lenses graduated to show the city's tightly controlled wealth, its huge Family trusts and its interlocking bank directorates, and then it was possible to arrive at something like the correct perspective. These institution men did not themselves necessarily run the mills and the railroads and the banks and the insurance companies, but they ran the men who did. To a somewhat smaller extent, but still to a considerable one, the inheritors of their positions continue to do so and thus continue to give Boston Society its appearance of permanence.

The men themselves have always known their power, but being benevolent men they have rarely wielded it in unseemly fashion. Only when clearly oppressed have they stooped to bare their teeth and the results have been what might be expected. Informed by a master that the Boston and Maine Railroad had failed to provide proper heat in two special cars for Groton boys leaving the school for their vacations, Endicott Peabody wrote the president of the line direct. He wanted assurance it would not happen again. "The parents of many of our boys," he wrote pointedly, "are prominent railroad people, and I am quite sure they would bitterly resent such neglect on the part of your road." Peabody of course got his assurance. When Bishop Lawrence moved into his winter home on Commonwealth Avenue late one fall he noted that the public mailbox on the sidewalk outside had disappeared. The Bishop had a large correspondence and he liked his letters to be on their way without delay; he had long regarded the mailbox as his personal property. That afternoon he called the post office department. He was told that the department was economizing and that all unnecessary boxes had been removed. These were hard words to use to Bishop Lawrence. Placing his derby hat on his head, he strode over to look at the home of an acquaintance of his by the name of William Cardinal O'Connell. The public mailbox in front of the Cardinal's home had not been moved. The Bishop returned and called the department once more. Boston might be three-quarters Catholic, its city government even more so, and Cardinal O'Connell might be the most august member of America's Catholic hierarchy, but the next morning the mailbox of Episcopal Bishop Lawrence was back in its place.

The indefinable power of Boston's First Family institutions might well have continued to be a mere local phenomenon, of little interest to the world outside the Hub, but for a certain event that happened one early spring afternoon of 1920 in the humble Boston suburb of South Braintree, Massachusetts. On April 15th of that year at 3 P.M. a paymaster and his guard, carrying two tin boxes containing the sum of $15,766, the payroll of a small shoe factory, were robbed and killed. At first there was nothing startling about the event. The crime had been committed by men who had made their getaway in an automobile, but the details were not sensational to a country in the midst of a crime wave. The affair was of such local character that it was not even reported in *The New York Times*. Two weeks later two Italians of avowed radical sentiments were arrested and a year later tried and found guilty. Their trial was reported on the back pages of the Boston newspapers—and so, presumably, would have been their scheduled execution.

This execution, however, did not come off according to schedule. For ever since the men had been arrested three of their acquaintances, a Spanish carpenter, an Italian newspaperman and a young Jewish boy, had been busy working on their behalf. Racing against time they had been writing about the men and what they felt had been an unfair trial to various left-wing organizations all over the world. They won the race. Before the execution could take place two bombs had gone off in Paris, anti-American demonstrations had taken place in Rome and Mexico, and a general strike had been called in Montevideo. One of the bombs in Paris had gone off in the home of Ambassador Myron T. Herrick, and Herrick made inquiries to the State Department about two Bostonians who to him seemed to be the cause of all the trouble. A shoemaker and a fish peddler, respectively, their names were Nicola Sacco and Bartolomeo Vanzetti.

If Sacco and Vanzetti were a trouble to Ambassador Herrick they were something more than that to Boston. As the case dragged on year after year, public opinion began to side more and more with the men. Baited in court they retained remarkable poise. Vanzetti's followers became legion. He advocated his political creed more like a philosopher than a payroll killer and, anarchist or not, it was apparent that he was behaving with rather more dignity than the convicting jurist Webster Thayer, who, busily denying appeal after appeal and repeatedly refusing the admission of new evidence, took time off to boast on the first tee of a local golf course of what he was doing to those "anarchist bastards." Finally, after six years, Boston and Massachusetts justice moved. It was decided the case should be reviewed. To the world watching and hitherto unfamiliar with Boston Society, the *modus operandi* of this decision was startling. It was not caused by the injudicial conduct of Judge Thayer. It was not caused by the able defense of lawyer Herbert Ehrmann. It was not caused by the declaration of Felix Frankfurter that the men had had less than a fair trial. It was not caused by the State House "pickets" or the pilgrimages to Boston on behalf of the defendants by such celebrities as Dorothy Parker and Robert Benchley. It was not even caused by the press—though the powerful Springfield *Republican* had pleaded the men's cause for years and even the staunchly conservative Boston *Herald* had reversed its original position and won a Pulitzer prize for an editorial beginning, "As the months have merged into years . . . our doubts have solidified into convictions." It was caused by a group of Boston's social leaders, under the aegis of Bishop Lawrence and including Dr. Richard C. Cabot, who took it upon themselves to "venture to speak" for the public and ask Governor Alvan T. Fuller to appoint a board to review the case.

Fuller acted. Having been prodded by one Boston institution, Bishop Lawrence, he promptly appointed another, in the person of Harvard's Lawrence Lowell, to his board. The other two men on Fuller's board of three were also eminently satisfactory to Boston Society—Robert T. Grant, a blue-blood judge of the probate court, and Samuel W. Stratton who, while a Westerner, was head of a university second only to Harvard in Proper Bostonian affection, the Massachusetts Institute of Technology. Outsiders had their own opinions, but everyone waited breathlessly while for weeks the committee read testimony, sifted evidence, and interviewed half a hundred persons, including Sacco and Vanzetti themselves. Then the committee made its report; they saw no grounds for a retrial or for clemency. There would be no pardon. On August 22, 1927, this time definitely, the men would be executed.

The Boston institutions had proved their power for all the world to see, but cold roast Boston never seemed any colder to a great many observers than it did in the aftermath of the Sacco-Vanzetti case. The city was aired from all directions. The Paris Soir spoke of the "dry hearts" of Yankees who could be unmoved by the "barbarous" and "monstrous" decision. "Is there no Christ," it asked, "above American courtrooms?" The financing of the entire record of the case in six volumes was undertaken by none other than the Rockefellers. Upton Sinclair came from California to write a novel called Boston and tell what he thought about the workings of Boston Society, which was not a great deal, and his book was promptly banned. Lowell, in particular, was bludgeoned. The picture of Harvard's president with his coldly virtuous face and frosty manner, personally sending to the electric chair two Italian "dreamers of the broth-erhood of man," as they were called, was not a pretty one. Har-vard's "White House" had to be guarded day and night, and a delivery man who came to the back door on such a peaceful mission as to fill an order of aluminum pots and pans was knocked cold by a waiting policeman. It was said that Lowell regularly looked for Communists under his bed each night be-fore retiring and that he had made up his mind about the guilt of the men before he ever read a line of the evidence. It was also said that he had assumed leadership of the board by the fact that he had in customary fashion—though a man of seventy-one—run up the stairs and reached the committee room in ample time to make sure he would be firmly seated in the chair-man's chair before Grant and Stratton, who had waited docilely for the elevator, could be there to argue with him about it.

Such stories were of course exaggerated. Lowell had a sister who did indeed have Communism on the brain, and though Governor Fuller today admits his board was set up to be a com-mittee of three without a chairman, there is no question but that Lowell did assume the chairmanship. But he was not the sort of man who would send men to the electric chair without giving them what he at any rate thought was a fair hearing. On the other hand, what Lowell thought was a fair hearing was merely one man's idea of this—and the idea of a man who was not only a novice at criminal law but whose authority to make such a life-and-death legal decision rested on no stronger ground than the quaint mechanics of Boston Society. It was his mis-fortune to have been a Boston institution at a time when it was necessary to stand up and be counted not just before an admir-ing group of Proper Bostonians but before the pitiless scrutiny of a world which appeared to be more interested in a fish peddler named Bartolomeo Vanzetti than it was in a Harvard president named Lawrence Lowell.

It is curious that the same Proper Bostonians, who will admit when pressed that if they were men of avowed radical senti-ments they would not particularly care to have their lives in the hands of a man like Lowell, will vigorously point to Lowell's record as a liberal. At Harvard he had fired a law professor when he discovered the man had been receiving a secret retainer from the New Haven Railroad to make speeches opposing the regulation of public utilities, and he had backed Harold Laski, at that time instructing at the college, to the extent of telling Harvard's Corporation that if they dismissed the leftist Englishman he would resign himself. But as more than one biographer has demonstrated, Boston's institution men have always conscientiously made their bows to liberalism. Major Higginson was fond of saying that "the workmen ought to have a bigger share of pie," biographer Bliss Perry notes—and then adds that the Major was at the same time "disinclined to pass the knife and ask the workman to help himself." Groton's Endicott Peabody wanted very much to be a progressive and even kept a picture of the most illustrious member of the Peabody Family, Franklin D. Roosevelt, in his study—but, declares Grotonian George W. Martin in *Harper's:* "He was determined to be a liberal—if it killed him. And so, of course, he was not liberal, he was only determined."

Lowell was, it would seem, no worse and no better. Boston's institution men fit into a remarkably simple behavior pattern. There have been minor differences of course. Major Higginson voted for Wilson; Godfrey Lowell Cabot didn't think he could operate a peanut stand. Bishop Lawrence opposed the League of Nations; Lowell was for it. By and large, however, these institutions have stood shoulder to shoulder. By the very nature of their position they have had to stand on guard against all threats to the social system they are called on to represent. Lowell may have fired a law professor because of irregularities with the New Haven Railroad but he fought to the last ditch against federal child labor legislation, which of course struck directly at Boston's First Family textile fortunes. He backed Laski, but when the man who made the highest marks ever attained by any member of Harvard Law School came up for appointment to the U. S. Supreme Court, he signed a petition opposing his nomination. Louis D. Brandeis, said Lowell, lacked "judicial temperament and capacity" and had a reputation "such that he has not the confidence of the people." Sydney Winslow of Boston's United Shoe Machinery Corp. was more direct about the famous jurist who made his name in a Boston law firm and went on to become the city's most celebrated gift to the Court since Oliver Wendell Holmes. "Mr. Brandeis," Winslow testified in Washington, "has persistently sought to injure our business."

Lowell's position in the Brandeis controversy was in its way as striking an illustration of the power of institution men as the Sacco-Vanzetti case. There were fifty-five Bostonians who signed the petition against the Wilson nominee, but it was Lowell's name which gave it such prestige that a second petition opposing the first made extremely slow headway in getting the necessary signatures. Even such men as Moorfield Storey, regarded as extremely progressive as Boston First Family lawyers go, and Charles Francis Adams, then no institution himself, obediently sided with Lowell. Brandeis, who throughout the struggle maintained a calm reserve, could not forbear after his victory to single out Lowell as the symbol of men who, he wrote, had been "blinded by privilege, who have no evil purpose, and many of whom have distinct public spirit, but whose environment—or innate narrowness—has obscured all vision and sympathy with the masses." Walter Lippmann was not so calm. With bitter irony he called Brandeis a "rebellious and troublesome member of the most homogeneous, self-centered, and self-complacent community in the United States."

If Boston's Old Guard have stood shoulder to shoulder in political crises they have been equally steadfast in maintaining a gentlemanly standard of morality in their city. It is noteworthy that Bishop Lawrence neither smoked nor drank during his lifetime and that, to date, neither have Godfrey Lowell Cabot or Charles Francis Adams, both men in their eighties. Lawrence Lowell smoked, but he did not believe a pipe should be enjoyed in the presence of a woman and did not touch his until five o'clock, which was a signal between him and his secretary for her to leave for home. He wore a boiled shirt to work every day and never removed his coat, even on a hot May day when he had two thousand Harvard diplomas to sign. But these men did more than look after their own morality. They also recognized an obligation to watch over those more prone to let down the bars. Bishop Lawrence would never call at the homes of those whose "way of life," as he used to say, he disapproved of. He was no dogmatist but he was a firm believer in what he defined as "the deep tide of quiet, self-controlled habits." He took sharp issue with the attitude which he found even among clergymen that to hold one's position in certain circles of Society necessitated a tolerant attitude toward alcohol. "I leave it to the physicians," he declared, "to tell of the effect of hard liquor upon the digestion of anyone, especially the young, even in small quantities."

Endicott Peabody left such instruction to no one. As a watchdog of what his wife called the "minor morals," he had few peers. Groton boys toed a narrow line, and no Peabody product has ever forgotten his "Nails and notebook, boy!" the war cry with which he opened his class in Sacred Studies, and which was the signal for a boy to demonstrate that his fingernails were clean and his copybook ready for the recitation. Peabody's range of guardian activity at Groton was a wide one, running in the field of literature from *Tom Jones* to *Life* magazine, and in other fields from vacation movies to the injudicious wearing of raccoon coats. Of major morals his particular bane was divorce, which he called the "natural climax of self-indulgence." A letter answering a Groton graduate who, at the age of forty-five, had written his headmaster from Bermuda that he had taken the liberty of marrying a divorcée, stands as a testimony of Peabody's Yankee firmness in such things:

March 8, 1916

My dear ———,

You are right in believing that anything that concerns you is of interest to me, for I have cared for you ever since you came to Groton in 1884.

I feel obliged to tell you that the contents of your letter from Bermuda have brought me great distress. I have been informed that Mrs. ——— obtained a decree of divorce from her husband for some reason other than that of unfaithfulness on his part. This being the case, she was not in my judgment free to contract another marriage.

The step is directly contrary to the teaching of Christ and strikes at the very foundations of family life.

I am of course ready to believe that you take a different view of the matter. To me it is not a question of error but of actual wrong.

I wish I could write differently. Indeed it hurts me, my dear ———, to withhold my blessing—but I am compelled to do so under the circumstances.

I shall always hold you as a friend and follow your course with affectionate interest and stand ready as I have ever done to do any service for you that lies in my power.

Aff yr friend,
ENDICOTT PEABODY*

It is not necessary to probe deeply into the Boston locale to discover that the work of the institution men as morals mentors did not fall on fallow ground. A casual reading of the letters to the editors in the Boston newspapers shows that the city does not lack for self-appointed vigilantes in a day and age which, to Boston at least, is moving in an extremely dangerous direction. How many of the writers are Proper Bostonians as opposed to other Bostonians is conjectural as Proper Bostonians signed letters only to the Boston *Transcript;* in regard to other journals they have always preferred to travel under pseudonyms. But the Proper Boston hand is held responsible, as witness the

---

* *Peabody of Groton,* by Frank D. Ashburn (New York: Coward McCann) © 1944.

following letter recently published in the Boston *Herald*. After complimenting General Joseph T. McNarney on his stand against the association of American troops with German women, the author surveyed the local scene with obvious sarcasm:

> I am shocked constantly as I walk through Boston Common, by the number of men and women, usually not mature, who stroll wantonly hand in hand. I have also noticed men sitting on the benches with their arms over the shoulders of their female companions. In two or three instances I have noticed that the latter reciprocated.
>
> Can't something be done about these unseemly manifestations of sexuality? . . . There was a time, I believe, when persons were put into the stocks on Boston Common for offences no graver than those to which I advert. I would not go that far, in these days of broader conception of personal freedom, but something certainly should be done by the press, the clergy, the police authorities, or all, to repress this flouting of our sense of decency. We have a very large police force in Boston, but I am not sure that these guardians would be effective. Indeed, I have seen policemen look in the opposite direction when passing couples who are walking hand in hand.
>
> The present phenomena are not quite so shocking as the bathing of practically nude children in the Frog Pond was some years ago. I notice that most of the children there are less scantily clad than formerly, but unless we exercise vigilance over the Common and the Public Garden, I fear for the moral safety of the coming generation.
>
> BEACON HILL

The gentlemanly attitude toward vice is in evidence in the matter of Boston's book banning. Although many a Proper Bostonian has an understandable desire to pass the buck somewhere else—to the Catholic Church, to Mayor Curley, to "middle-class morality"—the fact remains that the Old Guard cannot disown a large measure of the responsibility for something which has made Boston world infamous. Richard F. Fuller, head of Boston's venerable Old Corner Book Store, for thirty years president of the Board of Boston Booksellers and a man who had been offered as high as $1000 cash by a publicity-minded New York publisher to get a book banned, states the blue-blood stand on the question: "They don't like the notoriety it has brought Boston, but on the other hand they don't like the kind of books being published nowadays. They don't believe in censorship, but they believe such and such a book ought to be stopped."

For such a position the New England Watch and Ward Society, an organization which describes itself as "a quasi-governmental law enforcement agency" and which is dedicated to "the protection of the family life in New England," was virtually made to order. Boston's institution men have taken to it wholeheartedly. Phillips Brooks, beloved First Family preacher, was one of its first guiding lights and one of his assistants founded it. Bishop Lawrence was an officer, and so was Endicott Peabody; Godfrey Lowell Cabot was long its treasurer and is still its honorary president. Operating in a Beacon Hill office with an endowment fund of over a quarter of a million dollars, the Society has never been solely interested in books but has always maintained a militant inhospitality to sex stimuli of all sorts. Its quarterly magazine entitled *On Guard* is witness to the fact that it regularly reconnoitres state fairs, beano games, horse and dog tracks, night clubs, stag parties and other more remote fields where indecency could conceivably occur. In the beginning, however, it was primarily concerned with belleslettres, and it is from this field that it still derives most of its prestige. In the words of the *American Mercury*, the Watch and Ward has "kept the Puritans pure," and from its ban against Walt Whitman's *Leaves of Grass* in 1878, the year of its founding, to its suppression of Kathleen Winsor's *Forever Amber* in October, 1945—so rapidly that not even Miss Winsor, who had come to Boston to address the Boston Book Fair on the day her novel went on sale, had any idea that almost as she was speaking her volume was being retired from the bookstore windows—the Society has always done its best to live up to the reputation. Its banner year was 1927 when Boston saw no less than sixty-eight volumes impaled, including works by such authors as H. G. Wells, Sinclair Lewis, Ernest Hemingway, John Dos Passos, Sherwood Anderson and Thorne Smith. In reference to such wholesale slaughter and addressing a judge of the Massachusetts Supreme Court which had, despite a notable defense by Clarence Darrow, convicted the New York publisher of Theodore Dreiser's *American Tragedy,* an anonymous poet felt that the jurists had overlooked another dangerous volume:

> Your Honor, this book is a bucket of swill:
>   It portrays a young couple alone on a hill,
> And a woman who lived in a shoe as a house
>   With her brood, but not once does it mention her spouse.
> I submit that this volume's obscene, lewd and loose
>   And demand its suppression. Its name? Mother Goose.

Such a poem may have had something to do with the fact that the Massachusetts obscenity law was changed in 1930 to forbid the public sale not of any book *containing* obscene, indecent language but only of any book which *is* obscene—thus limiting the authority of a zealous police force to ban a book for one or two minor passages in the text. In 1945 the Board of Boston Booksellers were also able to engineer the passage of a law which provides for action against a book in civil court rather than against a bookseller in criminal court, as heretofore, and declares that before any ban, a book must be judged obscene by due legal process. Such changes may help. But the Watch and Ward Society, like so many other features of Boston's social system, is not necessarily tied down by legal responsibility. Though it has admittedly tried since 1930 to "cooperate" with local police and though it has usually been in high favor with the Catholic potentates in Boston's city government, it still remains as charmingly independent in its work as its patron saint and impeccable institution man, Godfrey Lowell Cabot.

Cabot is nothing if not independent. Now nearing ninety he saw service for more than half a century as a Watch and Ward officer, always making up any annual operating deficit, and he still makes it a practice to contribute the sum of $2500 each year toward its support. What Peabody was to Groton, Cabot is to Boston, and when even his Watch and Ward fails him he is perfectly willing to defend morality on his own. An example of this occurred many years ago when for a brief period a black-mail ring began terrorizing Boston blue bloods by luring them into compromising positions in Back Bay apartments with women of ill repute. The ring appeared to be headed by two men named Dan Coakley and Joe Pelletier, and Godfrey Lowell Cabot was the Proper Bostonian answer to Dan and Joe. Believ-ing his life to be in danger, he undertook the struggle only after changing his will to leave half a million dollars for the continu-ance of his work if he should be done to death before he saw it through. The city was treated to a spectacular battle, the climax of which came when Godfrey, feeling that Dan, as the lawyer behind the blackmailers, was bribing Joe, as district attorney, determined to get a witness of this by hiring a spy to get himself hired by Dan and go to Joe—only to find himself back where he started when it was revealed that it was Dan who had hired the spy to get himself hired by Godfrey to come to Dan and go to Joe.

In the end, though it cost him $78,000, Cabot won his fight; and his Watch and Ward has the same staying power. Only in the theatrical field has it given any evidence of infirmity. Eu-gene O'Neill's *Strange Interlude* was banned in Boston but played to packed houses when the Theatre Guild removed the production to the suburb of Quincy. A Russian war picture de-picting the Nazi persecution of a Jewish doctor was banned for Sunday showing as an "incite to riot" but permitted on weekdays. *Strange Fruit* was banned as a book but allowed as a play. *Hellzapoppin* was given such a going-over that the firing of cap pistols was forbidden and Chic Johnson was denied the privilege of throwing his trousers into the audience, but Bos-ton's Old Howard which daily exhibits as profusely illustrated burlesque shows as exist this side of Paris has rarely been mo-

lested. Individual instances of delicate linedrawing behind the
Boston footlights have been equally striking. In *Life With Father* after 270 performances Father was persuaded to cry "Oh,
heavens!" instead of "Oh, God!" and finally settled for "Oh,
Gad!" Playwright Ben Hecht proved less amenable. He washed
his hands of Boston altogether when, in his play *To Quito and
Back,* he found his "bitch" and "bastard" had been tailored
respectively to "dame" and "buzzard."

Attacked for such activity, the Watch and Ward declares that
it serves the theatre only in an advisory capacity, and that if
fault there be criticism should be at least equally directed at
the office of the city licensing division. Even in the book-banning
field, it is sometimes accused of accomplishments in which it
was only an innocent bystander—as, for instance, the case of
Strange Fruit which it left to the police department and the
Massachusetts courts. Basically it feels its work is sound. It classes
all those who feel there should be more books in the Athens of
America as "longhairs," and though one Boston institution,
Bishop Lawrence, deserted its fold after an exposure of its methods in 1929, it wants all those who attack it to bear in mind the
fact that they are at the same time attacking not only the institution Godfrey Lowell Cabot but two other Cabots and a Lowell
and a Forbes and a Sears and a Weld, etc. "The Brahmins,"
says its secretary with reasonable pride, "are our main support,"
and in each year's annual report of the agency are written the
stirring words: "Our honored list of Officers and Directors is,
we believe, a guarantee that our work has the confidence of
some of New England's foremost citizens and is directed by men
of social experience and ability."

Before this line it is a brash Bostonian who does not care to
bend the knee. At the Boston Public Library, however, there
is a record of one First Family lady who did not care to do so.
One day not long ago the lady approached the main desk of the
library in determined fashion. She wished a copy of *Lady
Chatterley's Lover.* The girl at the desk was horrified. Did not
the lady know that of course such a book had been banned? The

lady did, but she had heard a great deal about the book, and she wished to read it before she died. Looking the lady over the girl decided that since she obviously would never see sixty again, the case called for special handling. She took the woman to the chief of the reference division and explained the situation to him. The chief of the reference division decided in favor of the lady and ordered the volume procured from the non-circulating rare-book room. After some delay the book arrived and the librarian gave it to the lady with the warning that she would have to look at it right in his office; she could on no condition take it home.

The lady sat down and read. She could not finish and at closing time relinquished the book, only to return the next day and continue her task. At length she completed the book and handed it back to the librarian. But as she got up to leave she told him candidly that she could not see anything wrong with it. "I don't even see why it was banned," she said.

"Ah," said the librarian, tapping the volume gently, "but remember, Madam, this isn't the original version. This is the expurgated edition."

It is doubtful if Boston's institution men would ever have achieved such prominence in their city if they had not had a voice to carry their "way of life" to the Proper Bostonian masses. They found this voice in one of the all-time curiosities of American journalism, the Boston *Evening Transcript*. Daily except Sunday, just at tea-time—when the Proper Bostonian mind is traditionally at its most receptive stage—the *Transcript* was quietly laid, never tossed, on the doorsteps of the best people in Boston. Not to read the *Transcript* was unthinkable. It was never a newspaper in the vulgar sense of the word. The story of three representatives of the press who were received into a Beacon Hill home with a servant's announcement, "Two reporters from the papers, Sir, and a gentleman from the *Transcript*," was actually a legend once removed from the London

Times, but it became the Boston paper's trademark. The loyalty of its readers was proverbial. In the wind of its editoral opinion they swayed, said the poet T. S. Eliot, "like a field of ripe corn."

Employees served the *Transcript;* they did not work for it. The sign at the bottom of its six-story granite building at Milk and Washington Streets read: "Editors two flights, reporters three flights," but in spite of this evidence of the caste system even the paper's copyboys spoke with Harvard accents. One First Family man, Harry D. Eustis, was listed as an employee of the press department. Though he came to work in a chauffeur-driven limousine and dressed in a stiff collar, he promptly changed to overalls and worked a full eight-hour day doing such tasks as baling waste paper in the basement. He did so for fifty years, until he retired in the 1930's. To ask for a raise on the paper was tantamount to an attempt to make change out of the Trinity Church plate. William Durant, a seventy-year man who rose from office boy to treasurer and controlled *Transcript* finances as well as a large measure of the editorial policy of the paper, believed that the permanent salary of a newspaperman should be twenty dollars a week. In connection with a case where he had consented to a five-dollar-a-week raise for a man he was quoted as having remarked that the added five dollars meant nothing to the recipient except the development of hurtful extravagance. "What does he do with that five dollars? He moves into a house that costs him that much more in rent or he buys a piano for his daughter." On the question of women on his paper Durant was adamant. He once hired a girl only on the condition that she agree that her salary should never exceed ten dollars a week. Since she remained close to forty years and became one of the most valuable members of the *Transcript* staff, the agreement was regarded as a landmark in Yankee bargaining.

All parts of this paper were must reading for Proper Bostonians, but the Wednesday evening genealogical columns and the Saturday obituaries were the week's highlights. At one time an attempt was made to prove that the mortality records of blue bloods showed a marked increase on Friday over all other days due to the desire of the socially elect to make their last bows on the Saturday page—and when this failed there was always the legend of two Beacon Hill spinsters who each week fought so determinedly for the honor of being the first to read the Saturday columns that they gave the paper its Proper Bostonian war cry, "Who nice in the *Transcript* died tonight?" Niceness was ever the paper's keynote. It won for it deserved praise when in 1930 the *Transcript* was found, in an exhaustive study, to be one of only eight newspapers in the country free from any advertisements condemned by the American Medical Association. But *Transcript* delicacy was carried to such extremes that the result was not always so felicitous. On one occasion the paper's standing injunction against any reference to anatomy in its columns was ignored by a reporter who used the word "navel" in an article he was writing. It passed the copy desk and the edition was already running before the managing editor spotted it. He stopped the presses with a stern order to chisel out the offensive word. Unhappily he had not had time to read the full context. The reporter had used the word in a descriptive sense about the calm of a concert musician, and the *Transcript* appeared on the Boston streets that evening with the sinister information that the musician had been "in a state of repose as complete as that of a Buddhist regarding his   ."

The late Henry Cabot Lodge, John P. Marquand and Brooks Atkinson were among those who got their start on this remarkable journal, but no reporter ever lived so long in Boston newspaper annals as the late H. T. Parker. The "H.T.P." reviews of Symphony were so erudite that it was claimed they were written in Latin and translated for the benefit of lesser minds. They were not, but as Lucius Beebe recalls two typographers had to be retained in the paper's composing room to decipher Parker's original copy. Often Parker could not wait until his review to criticize the performance of the orchestra but in the midst of a number of which he disapproved would give an inkling of what was coming the next day by pounding Symphony's floor with his thick knotted cane. If anyone made a sound, he would use the same cane to rap them into silence. Among Boston's First Familyites he showed great favoritism for Mrs. Jack Gardner and was fond of attending social events with her. Visitors often stared in amazement seeing the two together—Mrs. Jack short and plain-faced and Parker even shorter with a beetle face and a square apelike body—but they were Boston's best, and no mistake.

Throughout its history the paper stood like a rock for Boston's Old Guard. The *Transcript* was sound. Never giving an inch to Bennett sensationalism, to Hearst sensationalism, or even to pictures—it rejected "illustrations" until World War I—it was just the sort of sturdy support the Proper Bostonians needed in a time which saw the steady encroachment of the new and different on their sacred soil. Its genteel tub-thumping for the blue bloods began with its first edition on July 24, 1830, with a front page devoted to column after column of free advertising for Boston merchants—of which one historian notes that "one will search the columns in vain for other than a good Yankee name"—and continued unabated for more than a hundred years through every test of Proper Bostonian standards. In May, 1846, the quasi-Bostonian Edgar Allan Poe was giving trouble and the *Transcript* editor was firm:

He is a wandering specimen of the Literary Snob, continually obtruding himself upon public notice; today in the gutter, tomorrow in some milliner's magazine; but in all places, and at all times, magnificently snobbish and dirty, who seems to invite the Punchy writers among us to take up their pens and impale him for public amusement. Mrs. Louisa Godey has lately taken this snob into her service in a neighboring city, where he is doing his best to prove his title to the distinction of being one of the lowest of his class at present infesting the literary world. Whenever seen in print his falsehoods are ever met by the reader with the simple exclamation—pooh!—Poe!

The paper reserved its most telling anti-Poeism for the poet's death in 1849. Leaping at the chance to disown the man entirely, it printed his obituary word for word from the New York *Express* and baldly refused to correct the misstatement made that the poet had been born in Richmond instead of in Boston. Even on the question of Emerson, who in his early days was by no means a Proper Bostonian stand-by, the *Transcript* maintained firm reservations. "Original thinkers," it warned, "are not always practical men, and they are sometimes led into unsupportable theories." In the great Boston fire of November, 1872, the paper first encouraged the city as a whole—"I thought for a while," said its editor, "that we couldn't stand up under it, but—well, we had the *Transcript* left"—and then went on to give advice to the ladies of Boston to sleep with loaded pistols at their bedside in the wake of the murder and rapine that they felt convinced must be stalking the Boston streets. Major Higginson was pushed a long way on his path to institutionalism by the paper's citation of his valiant vigil at the Lee, Higginson safe-deposit vaults—a vigil which, it later became clear, was not at all concerned with the thwarting of robbers but only with attempting to keep back an aggressive group of First Family depositors, including several Higginsons, who wished to remove their securities to their own homes.

Bostonians, the late Philip Hale of the Boston *Herald* once said, are "hell on facts," and the *Transcript* did its little part to make them more so. In the Boston police strike of 1919 it rose to its greatest heights. The pay of Boston's constabulary was based on a minimum of $1100 a year, out of which they had to buy their own uniforms, and in the inflation year of 1919 they asked for more. The strike, which the astute Boston merchant Frank Stearns used to make a national figure of Calvin Coolidge, was actually settled by the paying of new policemen the same increased salary that the strikers had been refused— but to the *Transcript* the issue was as clear-cut as an Irish rebellion. "Boston's black night" the paper called the evening before the state guard was called out, and the unofficial police force made up of "General" Francis Peabody, T. Jefferson Coolidge and S. Huntington Wolcott, etc. were "Minute Men of 1919." Even after an ignorant guard lieutenant had fired on a crowd in Boston's South End and killed two men, and after other Minute Men had bayoneted several members of another crowd which had given way to a long-suppressed desire to shoot craps on the sacred Boston Common, the *Transcript* found words to make rousing editorial comment. "It is good to know," it said, "that many of Boston's blue coats are true blue."

In the Sacco-Vanzetti case the *Transcript* showed a mettle reminiscent of the days when it had called on Shakespeare to sum up the murder of Dr. George Parkman. A reporter from the paper who had come to the conclusion that the men deserved a new trial and said as much was summarily taken from the case, and even after the Boston *Herald* had reversed its original position the *Transcript* never wavered. When Felix Frankfurter came out in defense of the men, the paper reached all the way to Northwestern Law School to answer the Harvard professor in its very next edition. The name of the professor was John H. Wigmore, and the paper gave Wigmore's lusty disavowal of Frankfurter its largest headline since the Armistice.

Finally, on July 24, 1930, the *Transcript* was ready in its centennial edition to compliment not just Proper Boston but all of Boston. "We do not believe," it declared editorially, "that there is a city in the United States where the young men and minors are so little prone to heedless extravagance as in Boston." In this same issue the paper laid down its creed for the future:

> Quick to sense new currents in life and thought, the *Transcript* marches in the van of progress without sacrifice of dignity and self-respect. To the flapper, male or female, it makes no appeal. To men and women in all walks of life who are earnest in their work, clean in their play, and thoughtful in the hours between, it is, as of old, counsellor and friend. It differentiates solids from froth, the permanent from the passing,

substance from shadow. In a yeasty newspaper generation plagued by real and imitation yellow journalism it affords abundant proof that enterprise and serious purpose may go hand in hand to ever new prosperity and success.

Unfortunately the proof remained in the pudding. Eleven years later the *Transcript* was dead. In its last illness, however, the paper showed the dignity that had made it, apart from its arrant Old Guardism, Boston's outstanding newspaper. All Proper Bostonian hearts felt a tug when its advertisers, particularly Jay's clothing store—which had long alternated with such fiscal stand-bys as the New England Trust Co., Brown Brothers, Harriman, Kidder Peabody and Harris Forbes for the honor of displaying its wares on the left-hand corner of the front page— bid the paper a fond farewell. Its circulation, down to 15,788 daily, seemed to prove that there were not very many Proper Bostonians left and to Proper Bostonians at least this was sad. In one of its last editorials, on Saturday, April 26, the *Transcript* did not ask for money but stated that "it has been suggested" that those who believed in its principles should send $500 to the National Shawmut Bank. One thousand such offerings were needed but only nine were received at the Shawmut Bank by the following Wednesday, and the next day "Today's Truth— Tomorrow's Trend" became a Boston yesterday.

A more durable custodian of the city's Old Guard tradition has been the Boston Athenaeum. There are a number of other private libraries in operation in the country, but all have made at least slight obeisances to modernity and admit the public to certain privileges. The Athenaeum, however, has never let its hair down. Founded in 1807 it was the only library in Boston for almost half a century, but aside from a temporary order permitting the entrance of Harvard professors it operated in complete privacy through the period. It still operates so today. Located in a grimly archaic building at 10½ Beacon Street overlooking the Old Granary Burial Grounds, it is strictly a library for its proprietors or shareholders. A few of the 1049 Athenaeum shares change hands from time to time at prices which have ranged from a low of $152.50 to a high of $900, but the majority of them come down among Boston's best like Family silver from generation to generation. Shareholders who want to take books out may pay ten dollars a year and do so, and also may give two guest permissions. But the Proper Bostonian is not by nature a library inhabitant; new books he likes to buy and as for old, he has a library of his own that he intends to get around to reading before he dies. The result is that the Athenaeum is sparsely settled—so much so that guest ticket holders who use the place usually have the feeling they are not in a library at all but rather unwanted visitors in a shrine whose primary purpose is to preside over the last rites of Brahminism.

There are those who feel that from the standpoint of culture this is a pity and that the library's able staff and its assortment of 360,000 books, including most of the personal library of George Washington and the best collection of Confederate history in existence, might well be put to better use. From the standpoint of a study of Old Guardism, however, the Athe-naeum is Mecca itself. The library fairly bristles with reaction. Its vigilance in the matter of fiction is striking. Novels which the library purchases by authors not tested by time contain criticism slips at their backs which read: "Readers who care to express an opinion of this book for the guidance of others may do so below. An opinion should contain not more than five words and should be followed by the initials of the reader." By such critiques the Athenaeum has long felt it can assess the value of current volumes which, if unfavorably reviewed, will then be disposed of rather than allowed to occupy permanent shelf space. It is a rare detective story which survives—the recent thriller *Poison, Poker and Pistols,* for example, received the words "monotonously ill-tempered. M.P.B."—and in the long run it would appear that the majority of these reviews have been unfavorable. In contrast with other libraries of its size, which devote in some cases as much as half of their total book population to novels, the Athenaeum has five floors and a basement, with only part of one floor devoted to any kind of fiction.

No list of Athenaeum shareholders has been published since 1907, it having been decided at the time that the listing of such prominent people was a nuisance to them from the publicity angle. Trustees' names are published, however, and to be elected to the board of the library has always been considered an honor in Boston Society second only to membership on the Harvard Corporation. In 1946 a working quorum of the board was over seventy, and the library's president and secretary were both over eighty. These men set Athenaeum tone—together with such Athenaeum legends as that of Sam, the janitor, who used to sweep the floors of the building but who held a degree from Oxford University, and that of an anonymous ghost, an elderly bluestocking who is supposed to have lost her way in the stacks one late afternoon in the last century and met with foul play in the rare-book department. But there are also Old Guard features of the place which need no legends to support them. One is its morality. For the first twelve years of its history no woman was ever allowed in the library. Finally permission was granted to historian Hannah Adams of the royal Adams Family, but when the "new" Athenaeum was built in 1849 the bars went up again. The narrow galleries and steep staircases of the building were adjudged by the trustees "an insuperable objection which should cause any decent female to shrink," and their report made on the situation concluded: "Nor is it desirable that a modest young woman should have anything to do with the corrupter portions of polite literature. A considerable proportion of a general library should be to her a closed book."

It is not surprising that almost a century later the Athenaeum should still boast what it calls its "scruple room," probably the strictest of such book departments in any library in America. It is invariably locked and to get a book from it permission must be obtained from the head librarian, with the additional stipulation that the book desired must be named in advance; no one may enter and make a choice from what he finds there.

Even lifelong Athenaeumites have been known to quail at this protocol, among them an ex-Morgan partner and current Grand Marshal of Harvard's Porcellian Club, who not long ago started to go through the process to get out a French book he was interested in, only to blurt out to the librarian at the last minute, "Aw, the hell with it" and give up. In recent years under the influence of Boston book banning this room has increased out of all proportion to the rest of the library, but even in years of comparative liberalism it has stocked such volumes as *All Quiet on the Western Front, The Postman Always Rings Twice* and *What Makes Sammy Run.*

Not the least of Athenaeum features is its penury. Though it is handsomely endowed, like other First Family charities in the city, it does not believe in throwing its money around. During World War II a visitor to the library overheard its librarian, Mrs. K. D. Metcalf, explaining to a trustee some matters which had been brought up for discussion at a meeting of the previous night which he had apparently been unable to attend. "We did not make any decisions on new books," she assured him, "but we did decide to go ahead and order a pamphlet. We do hope it meets with your approval. The cost is five cents and we feel it will be a real addition to the library." Mrs. Metcalf was not being humorous. The Athenaeum is proud of its reputation for economy, and its afternoon tea served daily at 4 P.M. on the fourth floor to all inhabitants of the building is in its little way perhaps the most militant stand against inflation that can be found anywhere in the country today. The menu reads:

TEA or BOUILLON

with 3 crackers plain	.03
with 3 crackers & cheese	.05
with 1 cracker plain, 1 sweet	.03
with 1 cracker & cheese, 1 sweet	.04
Each sweet cracker extra	.01
Each 2 plain crackers extra	.01

For at least one of its workers this menu is a lifesaver. Miss Sophia Elizabeth Haven joined the Athenaeum staff in the spring of 1880 as a girl of sixteen. Her cousin's husband was librarian and procured her position for her. Her initial wages were 12½ cents an hour, which were increased to 15 cents when she was able to do shorthand and typing. She once reorganized the library of Oliver Wendell Holmes, not the "young one," as she refers to the late Justice, but the elder Dr. Holmes. She got a brief glimpse of Ralph Waldo Emerson on one of his last trips to the Athenaeum in 1882. In 1901 she began typing, on the typewriter she still uses today, a complete list of Athenaeum books. She finished the list in 1921, and since then she has been constantly recopying it as well as attending to other library duties. Although Athenaeum employees are allowed six days of sickness leave each year, she never took hers and once went fifteen years without missing a single day. She has lived at the same lodging house for forty-five years. Her current salary is $24 a week.

Looking over her career Miss Haven is philosophical. "It's pretty monotonous work," she says, "but after all, a lot of people pay good money to be able to get in here."

CHAPTER FIFTEEN

CHANGE AND STATUS QUO

It has for some time been the opinion of many people that Boston Society ain't what she used to be. Old Boston is dead. The *Transcript* is dead. Beacon Hill is tottering and the heart has been cut out of the Back Bay. The home of the late Mr. and Mrs. Walter Cabot Baylies is the Boston Center for Adult Education. The home of Mr. and Mrs. J. Montgomery Sears is a recreation center for members of the Armed Forces—people from "dear knows where," Mrs. Sears would say if she were alive today. If you want to get in touch with such Boston institutions as Charles Francis Adams or Godfrey Lowell Cabot, all you have to do is to look them up in the phone book and buzz them direct. But if you wish to call such comparative newcomers as Mrs. Alvan T. Fuller, wife of the ex-governor of Sacco-Vanzetti days, or Mrs. Vincent Greene, president of the League of Catholic Women, you are faced with the problem of an unlisted number. The Boston of Lever Bros. and the Raytheon Mfg. Co. is a far cry from the Boston of American Telephone and United Shoe—and even these were Johnny-come-latelys to Perkins & Co., Bryant & Sturgis, Calumet & Hecla and Lee, Higginson. In the select suburban areas the once extremely private homes of Hallowells, Searses and Horatio Slaters have been bought by the Catholic Church and turned into monasteries and convents, and some of the most impressive estates are owned by such men as Howard Johnson of roadstand-restaurant fame, Judge John C. Pappas, a partner of the "Golden Greek" of Boston's Suffolk Downs race track, and Elias M. Loew of Loew's Boston Theatres. Mr. Loew in particular has caused arched eyebrows in the Brush Hill Road section of Milton by decorating the avenue of his place, a home formerly owned by the late "General" Francis Peabody, brother of Groton's Endicott, with two large stone Metro-Goldwyn-Mayer lions.

Meanwhile what Upton Sinclair called Boston First Families' "technique of self-suppression" has been making heavy weather. No longer are Proper Bostonians entirely content to choose their life partners from among the ranks of their cousins. A Cabot girl found her husband at a Fireman's Ball and a Frothingham located hers in the brass section of a local band. A Fitchburg Crocker eloped with a cowboy, a Saltonstall paired off with her chauffeur, and an elderly Ayer was dropped from the *Social Register* for marrying his secretary. One midsummer night in 1942 four impeccable First Family debutantes, hailed as "Boston's American Beauties," made their debut as floor-show stars on the Ritz Roof with their mothers, sisters, aunts and, as a reporter noted, "even a governess" on hand to admire the proceedings. Francis H. Appleton III, who married a girl from Santa Barbara and now makes his home outside of Hollywood, declares he was "born the day I left Boston," and Crosby Hodgkins, head of Beaver Country Day, looking toward the future says candidly that he has no interest in running "a stable for debutantes."

In the face of all this few Proper Bostonians have risen to meet the challenge as they surely would have in happier days. A First Family lady like Mrs. Horatio A. Lamb finds herself the exception rather than the rule. Particularly concerned with the youth movement, Mrs. Lamb, now in her eighties, has all her life been collecting books with what she calls "moral uplift" to them and recently presented these to Harvard University to combat the trend. "I am a Victorian and a Puritan," she says, "and I'll never be anything else until I die. I was brought up on books that held me accountable for every act I did. Their responsibility haunts me, but I believe in them." Too many other

First Family leaders have all but abdicated. Commenting on Boston's present-day Society pages, Mrs. Robert F. Herrick declares, "It's all Greek to me," and S. Hooper Hooper says darkly from his black leather chair in the Somerset Club, "I don't know any of these people. I don't know who they are." An officer of the Tavern Club apologizes for the fact his club has the reputation of having let down the bars. "Some awfully nice fellows get elected, I guess, simply because they're awfully nice fellows." And the Rev. Palfrey Perkins, D.D., of King's Chapel, tops the group. "We might as well admit it. We're just a drop in the bucket."

The case is, on the surface, a good one. Certainly a blue blood of today might well have qualms about noting in his diary such a line as that of Family-founder T. Jefferson Coolidge. Visiting Montserrat in the West Indies he exhibited the old George Apley prejudice by writing, "We were tormented on landing by the negroes. They are coarse and seem to have an Irish accent." But the over-all picture is hardly as desperate as the Proper Bostonian would have one believe. The Proper Bostonian maintains, for example, that he has lost all political influence. "Look at Mayor Curley," he says. The outsider looks and he sees Mayor Curley, but he also notices Governor Robert P. Bradford of *Mayflower* ancestry, two Senators by the names of Leverett Saltonstall and Henry Cabot Lodge, and a battery of Coolidges, Codmans, Curtises, Parkmans and Wigglesworths, all of whom have been extremely successful in the political line for men who are "drops" in a bucket. The Proper Bostonian declares that his lack of influence is indicated by the fact that weddings of the Smiths and the Joneses take place on the Society pages side by side with those of the Cabots and the Lowells. He points out that Mrs. Alvan T. Fuller and Mr. Joseph P. Kennedy receive more attention in the local press than any comparable Mrs. Cabot or Mr. Lowell. But the outsider, questioning these potentates, gets a different picture impression. "Oh," says Mrs. Fuller, "A.T. and I were born and brought up here, but we aren't what you mean by Bostonians at all." Ex-Ambassador Kennedy has no illusions about being a Proper Bostonian. He would settle for the privilege of not being referred to in the Boston press as an Irishman. "I was born here," he says. "My children were born here. What the hell do I have to do to be an American?"

The Proper Bostonian also maintains he no longer has any financial control over his city. Ever a genius at talking poor he does his best to convince the outsider that his "clipper-ship money" has disappeared or that it came down in the "other branch" of the Family. The outsider, overcome with such a tale of woe, buys the Bostonian's lunch for him and then later hears that the man's chief occupation is serving as trustee of a Family trust fund which runs to six or perhaps to seven figures. The outsider looks at the names of Boston's interlocking bank and insurance directorates and notes group after group which may not reach the nominal tone pitch of a State Street law firm or the real-estate organization of Cabot, Cabot & Forbes but which are nonetheless hardly to be confused with the membership of the local Elks Club. He observes that Charles Francis Adams, with his affiliation with fifty-six different boards, spread-eagles the Boston financial field more than any other man, that Godfrey Lowell Cabot is rated as Boston's wealthiest individual citizen, and that in the matter of the Provident Institute for Savings, which was founded in 1816 largely through the efforts of a Catholic archbishop and which has always had a preponderance of Irish Catholic depositors, it was not until 1945 that an Irish Catholic man became a member of its board of directors. When all other arguments fail, the Proper Bostonian states flatly that his First Families are dying out. But it does not take an outsider to answer that one. It was answered by Godfrey Lowell Cabot's own brother-in-law when, on November 28, 1946, one hundred and sixty-one members of the Boston Cabot Family assembled in their patriarch's Beacon Street home to partake of their Thanksgiving dinner. "Godfrey," said Arthur W. Moors sternly, "this doesn't look like race suicide to me."

To the outsider the youth movement seems the most convincing sign of change. There is as yet no large-scale revolt of the masses among younger Proper Bostonians, but the insurrection of late years cannot be dismissed simply because so many of its leaders have fallen by the wayside. At first glance the record may seem discouraging. The Fitchburg Crocker left her cowboy and the Frothingham girl dismissed her saxophonist in favor of a Harvard man. John Lodge, brother of Henry Cabot Lodge, Jr., married dancer Francesca Braggiotti, took a determined fling at Hollywood and British motion pictures, but now has settled among the Connecticut station-wagon set. Groton's Charles Devens, who started a promising athletic career pitching for the New York Yankees, tossed it up to marry a Boston Wolcott, sign off with the Yankees and on with the State Street Trust Co., of which he is now assistant treasurer. Julia Barbour, daughter of the late Harvard naturalist Thomas A. Barbour, started out bravely burning the candle at both ends; she would begin her day riding to hounds at her Beverly Farms home, would then travel to Boston to write, for $35 a week, a Society column for Hearst's tabloid *Daily Record*, and end her day fulfilling a $150-a-week engagement singing in a local night club. Finally Julia gave in, became president of the Boston Junior League, and in the spring of 1946 married Samuel H. Hallowell in Boston Society's biggest postwar wedding, an affair which was topped off by a reception for over 1000 guests at the Chilton Club. Lucy Cochrane, who went from the Vincent Club to the Ziegfeld Follies of 1944, also made a good start and was even described by a fellow showgirl as "game as they come." After three years, however, never having had enough success to achieve her ambition—which she had announced as to have enough theatrical prominence to get herself dropped from the *Social Register*— Lucy settled for an extremely Social Register alliance with Long Island's millionaire polo player, Mr. Winston Frederick Churchill Guest. In the same manner Miss Sarah Pickering Pratt Lyman Sears, though she had a brief go at torch singing under the name of Sally, recently retired in good order to marry the son of a Virginia Master of Foxhounds and become Mrs. Richard Hunter Dulaney Randolph of "Old Wellborne," Upperville, Virginia.

But the whole movement should not be judged by these individual instances of failure. In spite of its stumblers the revolt has made good headway, or at least it has made more than those which have from time to time preceded it in the Hub of the social universe. Leaders of other rebellions, Mrs. Harrison Gray Otis, Jr. and Mrs. Jack Gardner, have come and gone, but in retrospect their revolutions seem only parlor pink. A more recent example of this is still at hand on the Boston scene. Called by her friends "Eleo" and occasionally by the newspapers—to her utter infuriation—"Eleanor," her name is Eleonora Sears. An outstanding beauty in her day, blue-eyed and blonde, Miss Sears wowed Back Baydom in the 1900's, danced the meanest Portland Fancy in town, and was at various times rumored engaged to a number of people. She made a wide reputation as a walker, once hiked 110 miles non-stop, and as recently as 1940 made 47 miles in one day, leaving Boston at 4 A.M. and swinging into Providence trailed by her faithful chauffeur in a large limousine at 8:30 that evening. On a national scale, adept not only at ambulation but also at polo, tennis, skating, squash and backgammon, Miss Sears figured prominently in the emancipation of American womanhood in the field of athletics, but even at this she has moved cautiously; she has always walked in a skirt and would not be seen dead in slacks. On the local scene her record of un-Bostonianisms may bring a blush to the cheek of her upstairs maid, who has been with her for over fifty years, but they have not been of lasting significance. She has been guilty of such extravagances as buying an extra seat at the theatre so members of her party may have somewhere to put their coats, and she has given entertainments at her palatial Beacon Hill studio in which members of the cast of the Ice Follies have rubbed shoulders with such impressionables as the members of

Harvard's Porcellian Club. But Miss Sears is still welcome in the ladies' dining room of the strait-laced Somerset Club, and she is a member in good standing of the Chilton. Even in her younger days she was never engaged to anyone but a gentleman—the foremost of whom, according to the papers of the day, was Harold Vanderbilt—and today Miss Sears has no desire to be an outcast. Questioned about Boston she says reassuringly that people are always writing stupid things about it, that it is no different from any other city, that she has never met a George Apley in her life, that she doesn't like walking and walks only because it is good for her soul, and so on.

The current revolt seems made of sterner stuff. The Appleton who was "born the day I left Boston" has come a country mile from the days of his grandfather whose oft-expressed ambition was to become the oldest living graduate of Harvard and who, failing to make it, took pride in the lesser distinction of being the oldest living graduate of St. Paul's School. Furthermore the present movement had come at a time when the very pillars of the Proper Bostonian world are undergoing some marked alterations. Harvard University under President Conant, who has preached the doctrine of a classless Society and issued a call in the *Atlantic Monthly* for "American radicals," is not the Harvard of the late Lawrence Lowell. Its enrollment shows a decided change from the time when the class of 1929 could in their ten-year report state that the average unearned income of each member of their class was $1890 a year. The Groton School which currently numbers among its outstanding undergraduate leaders the son of the postmaster of Lincoln, Nebraska, is not the Groton from which the late Endicott Peabody wired a parent in Indianapolis that there was an unexpected vacancy available in the admissions set aside for boys living west of the Mississippi. Even Symphony Hall which now regularly rents its premises to such jazz bands as Woody Herman and Eddie Condon is hardly the Hall it was as little as a decade ago. At that time the Hall was host to Benny Goodman and his orchestra, and a Boston music critic reviewed the performance by stating in his column that it would have been better if a baseball reporter had been sent to cover the event.

Bishop Norman Nash may never attain the institutionalism enjoyed by the late Bishop Lawrence but he, too, represents change. A severe critic of the social atmosphere he found in his previous position as headmaster of St. Paul's School, he is a challenge to some of the more rock-ribbed elements to be found among the prayer cushions of Trinity and Emmanuel. At the Massachusetts General Hospital an order has revoked a long-standing injunction against internes having pockets in their pants, and at the Athenaeum there have been revolutionary undercurrents. A new librarian, taking office in 1946, failed to find sufficient reason for the only smoking room to be located in a cubbyhole off the fifth floor—a floor on which no talking is allowed—and has ordered smoking to be permitted in a more convenient location. He is also considering putting *All Quiet on the Western Front*, which has been under lock and key in the "scruple room" since the time of its appearance in 1929, back into general circulation. Even the Boston Junior League, second oldest and often regarded as the stuffiest of Junior Leagues, has seen change. During World War II the girls became so distressed with their liquorless dining room that they initiated a system whereby each girl could keep a bottle marked with her name in a secret closet. To date this system is still in operation.

In short it appears as if something of a new age may be dawning in Boston Society, and in this age the question of being a blue blood is at least open to public analysis. Governor Robert B. Bradford gave some indication of this when, taking office as Governor at the beginning of 1947, he declined to be entertained on his inauguration day at the Somerset Club and chose the far more plebeian Hotel Statler. He was promptly backed in his stand by his wife, who in her first interview on the following day could not be shaken from her insistence that the favorite

dish of the entire Bradford family was Irish stew. Senator
Leverett Saltonstall has come to view the question entirely
dispassionately. A man who takes four hours to consume one
highball, he is not given to snap judgments. "Being a blue
blood works both ways," he says quietly. "When they don't like
what you do they say it's because you had a narrow and sheltered
upbringing. When they like what you do they say it's because
you have had the advantage of education and breeding."

Along with the change there is status quo in the picture. Boston Society, founded on the basis of nineteenth-century wealth
and First Familyhood, was never designed to be a fluid one. A
refugee doctor, whose introduction to this Society began with
an unsuccessful attempt to procure accommodations at Brookline's Longwood Towers, familiarly known as the home of the
newly wed and the nearly dead, was brought up short on this
score by a doctor acquaintance of his. The man had come from
what he admitted to be an aristocratic background in Pennsylvania fifty years before and had attained much eminence in his
field in Boston. "You may have all the best people for your
patients before you're through," he said, "but don't ever expect
to be asked to their homes socially. It won't be because you are
Jewish either. It'll be because you can never be anything but an
outsider." A Boston Society editor feels that there is still much
to be said for the adage of Boston's inner circle—that "money
can't get you in, but lack of it sure can get you out." Her mother
had always wanted her to be "conventional Boston" and after a
brief fling at the New York stage she returned to do her best.
When her husband lost his money it became necessary for her
to work—"Not for myself," she says, "I don't really believe in
'Society,' but for my daughter. She had to go to the right
schools." She concludes wistfully, "I always feel I'm doing pen-
ance writing up weddings and things." Another lady of rebellious social nature admits she considered giving up the idea of

sending her daughter to Winsor School. "I could have been a pioneer and sent her to public school," she says, "but who wants to be a pioneer with their own children?"

A few years ago New York's Frank Crowninshield came to the conclusion that the playing of the big-league social game in Manhattan was a matter of spending something around $60,000 a year for the maintenance of appearances and for compulsory entertaining. In Yankee Boston Society such a figure is unheard of. The simple fact of the matter is that there is not that much of a game to play. The opera, once called by Henry James "the great vessel of social salvation," has never achieved such formidable standing as this in Boston, and first nighting at theatres is regarded with some suspicion. The funeral of a First Family leader is perhaps the closest approach to a place where one really must "be seen," but beyond such an occasion Boston Society moves on from year to year without a single mandatory event on the social calendar. There is little doubt that this peculiarity of Boston Society, combined with the absence of any semblance of Café Society, has served the First Families well in their maintenance of the city's unchanging standard of social stratification.

One of Boston's most indefatigable social organizers exhibits a striking example of this stratification in her copy of the *Social Register*. She has marked the volume in three colors to indicate what she calls "ball-y" people, the "workers" and the "sponsors." The first classification includes the correct young marrieds and those among the elders who are known for liking to go out and have a good time, the second is a small group of those who have proved by previous performances that they are willing to do actual work on the dance committee, and the third are the "name" people. This latter group is subdivided to include one long list of possible sponsors of events of which the primary object is to make money, and a short list of sponsors for events in which the monetary consideration is secondary to pure social succulence. Such listing may seem elaborate, but it has apparently always been necessary in the routing out of the First Family desirables. A Southern war veteran who recently rented Symphony Hall and hired an orchestra as a money-making venture, was blocked at every turn in his attempts to interest what he called the "nice people" in his concert. Finally he learned through a Boston Society underground channel that he should telephone Mrs. Ronald T. Lyman. "Who the hell's she?" the young man wanted to know. "Never mind," he was told, "just call her." The man did, explaining his proposition to Mrs. Lyman who not only agreed to sponsor the concert but also enlisted the support of such of her friends as Mrs. George Saltonstall West and Mrs. Bayard Warren, and the concert was a success.

The social reticence of the Proper Bostonian seems almost purposeful. Boston's First Families operate in exact reversal of the Hollywood idea of publicity, and from their own social standpoint have been equally successful. In 1932 when blonde Mrs. Powell M. Cabot and red-haired Mrs. John Gardner Coolidge II stooped to accept nomination by the makers of Camel cigarettes to endorse their product in the public press, the strictest elements of Boston Society regarded the decision as an intolerable act of social nudism. Mrs. Cabot herself had qualms about the affair and went to her father-in-law, Henry B. Cabot, to get his view. The depression was on and Mr. Cabot, at first reluctant, was won over by the idea of the sum of $1500 plus expenses. "Times are changing," he told her. "It's no worse than what other people are doing. Go ahead." Since Mrs. Cabot and Mrs. Coolidge have also received a carton of cigarettes every week since their testimonial, even during the war shortage, they have never regretted their work but admit that it has made them marked women in Boston Society. Another Cabot wife, Mrs. Hugh, Jr., also caused a flurry on the local scene as recently as the summer of 1946 when she appeared on a radio program with the director of the Massachusetts Society for Social Hygiene and plumped for sex education for children. It was part of a series sponsored by the Community Fund and there was no money involved, but the fact that a Cabot wife had publicly recognized the existence of sex was regarded of such social significance that *Time* magazine chortled nationally over Mrs. Cabot's remark: "I've been interested for a long, long time in the whole subject."

The core of the Boston social system is clubdom, and here the status quo remains awe-inspiring. In the feminine field a girl may become a debutante in Boston simply by applying to the secretary of the Parents League for Debutantes and asking for an admission blank. No questions will be asked beyond those on a simple form to be filled out. The fact that she will be on the social stationers' official debutante list, and will have her name in the newspapers as such, does not, however, mean that she will in her debutante year be favored with an invitation to join the Vincent Club or to become a provisional member of the Junior League. Nor does it mean that she will in later years enjoy the elite feminine fellowship inherent in such quaint organizations as the Mah Jong Monday Club or a Sewing Circle. Boston's Sewing Circles are a unique feature among present-day city Societies. In other cities these Circles have all but died out; in Boston such Circles as the "97" and the "99"—both of which are named from their founding dates, 1897 and 1899—still go merrily on their way.

Sewing Circle 97 is particularly swank. Limited to sixty members with three blackballs being sufficient to keep out any proposed candidate, it meets once a week for lunch from November through May and costs just $2.00 a year. Members no longer sew for charity as they did in bygone days but instead are asked to contribute two articles of clothing to some charity each season. They meet on Wednesdays, rotating from dining room to dining room in members' houses. A rule of the Circle states severely the terms of this meal: "Luncheon shall be served promptly at 1 P.M. and shall consist of two solids, a sweet, bread, cake, tea, coffee or chocolate." At the fiftieth-anniversary meeting of this Circle, held on January 15, 1947, at the Chilton Club and given by Mrs. Robert H. Saltonstall, an article from the Boston *Evening Transcript* of fifty years before was read. To many of the assembled members the article seemed dated, but more than one left the meeting impressed with the fact that here was stern proof that Boston Society had changed little in fifty years. In part the article read:

> The Sewing Circle is as old as Boston Society. It began so far back that only tradition keeps green the memory. Old as it is, it is ever young, for each season is marked with a new circle whose members have but recently acquired the art of doing up their tresses, and gracefully accepting an occasional bouquet from a young man—Harvard preferred. Debutantes are hardly aware that there are young men other than Harvard men. Outside of Scotland there is no more clanish clan on the face of the earth than this Boston Sewing Circle. In order to belong to this conservative organization a maid must have been born into the Sewing Circle set or else be able to prove that she had at least one grandmother or great grandmother or some relative who once had that honor.
>
> When they reach their last year of school, they join the Saturday evening class. Out of this class the Sewing Circle is formed, with possibly a few additions and a few omissions.
>
> Those girls who make their debut that same year and, perhaps, attend the same dancing class, who do not sew with the rest, are never able to enter the fold of the select few. They may occasionally be tea'd and dined and danced but they never will be admitted into the full swing.
>
> The girl may be handsome, she may be rich, she may be well bred and well born, but all avails nothing of any consequence unless she has the right to make little flannel petticoats and "nighties" when the rest do.

In the male field one way of measuring the status quo of the Proper Bostonians' clubs lies in the service records of their chief employees. The Somerset had a James for a full fifty years and now has a Joseph who recently celebrated his twenty-fifth year of stewardship. The Union had Max for twenty-five years and still has two Pats who have divided desk duty for over forty years. The Tennis and Racquet has had Touhey in its locker room since the club was founded in 1904, and the Tavern's Bernard died after thirty years on the job. The City Club Corporation has a Joseph of thirty-five years' standing, and even the Club of Odd Volumes, an organization devoted to some genteel camaraderie as well as to the sampling of rare books, has its John of equal vintage. At the Brookline Country Club Mr. Sleeper served so faithfully and long that he was finally rewarded with membership in the club, and at the Somerset not only the late James but also the present James and Joseph have made permanent places for themselves in Boston Society.

Joseph won unusual recognition on January 4, 1945. On that date, at 7:30 in the evening, when the monthly dinner of the Somerset was in progress, a fire started in the flue of the charcoal broiler of the kitchen. It was four hours before the blaze, which extended to other parts of the club, was totally extinguished, but Joseph's behavior throughout the crisis was exemplary. When the firemen arrived at the club's front door at 42 Beacon Street Joseph promptly barred the way and ordered them to the service entrance. This action caused some delay in the fire-fighting operations, but members were spared the pain of seeing strangers enter by the front door. Dinner for thirty-one members was already in progress when Joseph first received word of the fire, and he saw to it that all thirty-one were allowed to consume the major part of their meal without being disturbed. Finally, after all main courses had been served, Joseph went from table to table with the advice, still remembered by all present: "There will be no dessert this evening, gentlemen. The kitchen is on fire."

Even the Boston Harvard Club, membership in which is not merely a matter of a man's having attended Harvard but which also involves being proposed and seconded and voted on as in the case of any other Proper Bostonian inner group, is a bulwark of Boston Society. The importance of it and other clubs on the Boston scene is difficult to overemphasize. A startling example of this occurred some years ago when the eminent Harvard historian Samuel Eliot Morison confided to an editorial writer of the Boston *Herald* that he attached deep significance to the fact that the founding of the Brookline Country Club in 1882 coincided with the closing of the American frontier. The *Herald* man, who later wrote an editorial on the subject, did not feel that Mr. Morison was attempting to be humorous, and "closed" is the word for Boston's clubs. "What this city needs," declares John F. Fitzgerald who was Boston's first native-born Irish Catholic mayor and who has been observing the ways of his city for close to ninety years, "is a lunch club where the blue bloods will eat with the rest of us." Mr. Fitzgerald is not likely to get his wish. The Proper Bostonians' clubs are far more than lunch clubs and they dominate the social life of Boston so thoroughly that even the city's No. 1 Society restaurateur, Monsieur Josef, has always used the word "club" for his restaurants to attract those whom he feels are the right people. Josef, who had some twenty years' service at the Copley-Plaza and the Ritz before branching out on his own, has long enjoyed a high reputation for his ability to tell the right people from the wrong people, and though this ability appears to rest on his readily offered opinion that when the right people gather at dinner they will agree on the same choice of food and that the wrong people will all order differently he has had outstanding success in his field. So too has the Proper Bostonian. In 1941, when it became necessary for the Boston Symphony Orchestra to make a deal with James Caesar Petrillo, President Henry B. Cabot and Treasurer Richard C. Paine handled the negotiations with such delicate finesse that, although the Boston Symphony had fought Petrillo for years and was the last important organization to give in to him, the union changed its by-laws to meet Boston's demand that it be allowed to hire musicians outside the Boston area without permission from the local union. It later appeared that the chief feature of these negotiations had been an exclusive dinner tendered Petrillo and his men at the Boston Harvard Club, and their welcome into the bosom of Boston Society and princely treatment by Mr. Cabot and Mr. Paine is generally credited with having had much to do with the unexpected amiability of Mr. Petrillo.

So severe are Boston's leading clubs that even blue bloods have had to watch their step to gain admission. The late Rodman Weld made a habit of entering his nephews in the Somerset at birth so that they would be ready for their election immediately upon their graduation from Harvard. One nephew, Rodman Peabody, has recalled in his diary protesting that he would rather wait a few years after his graduation until he could better afford the dues. Upon which he was told by the shrewd Mr. Weld: "Young man, some day you may do something. Whatever you do some member of the Somerset Club will disapprove of it. I will pay your dues until the time when you tell me you would like to." At the City Club Corporation First Family sons have been known to stand in line as long as fifteen years to get under the wire of its steady 180 limit; and to become a Family member of the Myopia Hunt Club, which has long had a 100-maximum rule, is still a feat of such magnitude that it was accomplished by the president of the State Street Trust Co. only after he had spent the better part of two years writing the early history of Myopia. That the majesty of these organizations does not end with a man's election is evidenced by such haughty house rules as the City Club Corporation's ban against smoking during lunch, the Union Club's reading-room sign "Only Low Talk Permitted," and the curious note over the only basement-floor toilet in the Somerset: "This lavatory is to be used only in the case of emergency."

Even buttressed by such apparently unassailable redoubts the Proper Bostonian is taking no chances on the future. Clubs within clubs have sprung up as an answer to possible increased membership, notable among which is the Bridge and Badinage within Myopia. The Somerset, in keeping with its august position as probably the only club in America in which members never have to stoop to such vulgarity as the signing of checks for services rendered, has several of these inner sanctums, some of which number as few as four members who meet once a week during the afternoon and evening in one of the upstairs rooms of the building. That such groups are the last word in the status quo of Boston Society was perhaps best indicated on April 12, 1945, when four members of one gathered at the club for their usual lunch before their cards. Afterwards they withdrew, only to come down again at dinnertime, eat together, and go upstairs once more. Late that night they retired to their respective homes. The next morning all four heard for the first time of the death of President Franklin D. Roosevelt—news of importance to these estimable gentlemen—which had occurred at almost the exact moment they had entered the club some twenty hours before.

These were all elderly men, however, and to draw the conclusion that when the world of the Proper Bostonian does come to an end, there will be at least four First Family men who will not know about it until the next day, would not be warranted unless there is also clear evidence that the Proper Bostonian breed is still firmly extant in younger form. Fortunately this evidence was conclusively given to a large number of men who underwent their training for World War II during the period from November, 1942, to March, 1943, at Camp Forrest, Tennessee. Among their buddies in camp was a Boston lawyer named Charles Gaston Smith, Jr., of Commonwealth Avenue. Smith was forty-four years old when drafted and had never been away from Boston except for a few vacations and an eight-year tour of Harvard and Harvard Law School. He looked forward to his first adventure in life and wrote letters home of the experience. His family thought so much of these they had them bound as a permanent record of their Minute Man son. With or without this permanence, however, Private Smith was fated to be a Tennessee legend before his career was cut short by the operation of the Army's policy to release men over thirty-eight.

At the beginning Bostonian Smith, who is not only a successful lawyer but whose previous field of activity had included membership in both the Union Club and the Brookline Country Club and who was classed by the Society journal *Town Topics* in 1936 as among the nine most eligible bachelors of Boston's "400," determined to remain as incognito as possible. This policy proved to be a wise one when, on his way to camp, a Long Island chauffeur in a philosophical mood told him that he knew for a fact that "the rich aren't any happier than we are." Once at camp, however, Private Smith had trouble keeping his background to himself. When his supply sergeant asked him what size underwear he wore, he replied without thinking, "I don't know. My mother's always bought them for me." His secret out, Bostonian Smith never again resorted to posed anonymity. Recognizing his helplessness, his buddies became fond of him, called him variously "Pop" and "Reverend," carried his barracks bag for him when he was unable to lift it, and generally made his army life a happy one. In return for this, at the approach of Christmas, Smith was nominated to write his companions' thank-you letters. The men copied the more personal of these, and one at least was impressed with Boston Brahminism. "You know," he told Smith, as he copied away diligently, "when this is read to the Women's Auxiliary of Salem, New Hampshire, my wife is going to ask me why in hell I don't write parlor stuff like this to her."

Finally one evening, shortly before he was to return to Boston and private life, the test came. A bull session was in progress in Camp Forrest that night, and the talk had turned to schooling. The men came from various sections of the country and the schools named ran an interesting gamut. Then it was Smith's turn. "Say, Pop," asked a two-hundred-pound Maine lumberman, "what school did you go to?"

Charles Gaston Smith, Jr., remembered the code of the Proper Bostonian. He prefaced no apology and he gave it to the men straight. "I started my career," he said, "at Miss Pierce's School for Little Boys and Girls in Brookline, Massachusetts."

ACKNOWLEDGMENTS AND BIBLIOGRAPHY

Since the bulk of the material for this book was manufactured from interviews with Bostonians, by far the majority of whom have expressed a keen desire to remain anonymous, the author has no alternative but to attempt to express herewith his thanks, and to hope that some hundred or more persons will themselves be able to see from the text, far better than he could tell them, just how much help they have been.

Special thanks go to the editors of *Harper's* and of *Town and Country*, who gave the author the opportunity to discuss this material with them and who have used portions of the book in their magazines; to Daniel K. Wallingford, whose map is reproduced between these covers; to George Peabody Gardner and the other trustees of the estate of Mrs. John Lowell Gardner for rescinding, at their annual meeting on February 10th last, the hitherto permanent ban on pictures of Mrs. Jack and thus permitting the book's frontispiece; to Augustus Hemenway who, as trustee of the estate of William Caleb Loring, executor of the estate of Susan M. Loring, has graciously permitted quotations from the diary of William Appleton; to James Truslow Adams, Frank D. Ashburn, Lucius Beebe, Eleanor Early and Mrs. Price Post, as well as Houghton Mifflin, Little Brown, Scribner's and the Massachusetts Historical Society, for other lengthy quotations; to Leonore Amory Sawyers for a special study of the Adams Family; to Mrs. James B. Ayer (Hannah Palfrey) for special information about her three aunts, Cambridge's illustrious Palfrey sisters; to Marjorie Crandall, assistant librarian of the Boston Athenaeum, for generous library help; and finally to Maude Parker Pavenstedt for much-needed encouragement to take on the job at the outset.

For those wishing to pursue the subject of Boston Society further the author wishes to recommend two books above all others —*The Saga of American Society,* by Dixon Wecter, and *Famous Families of Massachusetts,* by the late Mary Caroline Crawford. Of individual Family histories the two outstanding would seem to be *The Adams Family,* by James Truslow Adams, and the recently published *The Lowells and Their Seven Worlds,* by Ferris Greenslet. Lucius Beebe's *Boston and the Boston Legend* is first-rate reading on the subject of the Hub as a whole, while from the cultural standpoint Boston as the Athens of America is perhaps best recorded in the manifold works of M. A. De-Wolfe Howe, for several decades the acknowledged archduke of the Boston archives. For an understanding of the Proper Bostonian and how he grew, however, the pamphlets compiled under the able direction of Allan Forbes, president of the State Street Trust Co., in which are recorded the lives of the early-day shipping merchants and Family founders, and the files of the late Boston *Evening Transcript,* now enshrined in microfilm in the Public Library, are two sources which this author at least has found invaluable.

The following is a list of books, pamphlets and magazine articles consulted:

Adams, Charles Francis. *An Autobiography.* Boston: Houghton Mifflin, 1916.

Adams, Henry. *The Education of Henry Adams.* Boston: Massachusetts Historical Society, 1918. New York: Modern Library, 1931.

Adams, James Truslow. *The Adams Family.* Boston: Little Brown, 1930.

Alexander, Jack. "The Cardinal and Cold Roast Boston." *Saturday Evening Post,* October 4, 1941.

Appleton, William. *Selections from the Diaries of William Appleton.* Boston: Privately printed, Susan M. Loring, 1922.

Ashburn, Frank D. *Peabody of Groton*. New York: Coward McCann, 1944.

Atkinson, Caroline P. *Letters of Susan Hale*. Boston: Marshall Jones Co., 1919.

Baxter, W. T. *The House of Hancock*. Cambridge: Harvard University Press, 1945.

Beebe, Lucius. *Boston and the Boston Legend*. New York: Appleton Century, 1935.

"Boston." *Fortune*, February, 1933.

Brooks, Van Wyck. *The Flowering of New England*. New York: E. P. Dutton & Co., Inc., 1936.

———. *New England Indian Summer*. New York: E. P. Dutton & Co., Inc., 1940.

Cabot, Elizabeth. *Letters of Elizabeth Cabot*. 2 vols. Boston: Privately printed, 1905.

Carter, Morris. *Isabella Stewart Gardner and Fenway Court*. Boston: Houghton Mifflin, 1925.

Cary, Thomas G. *Memoir of Thomas Handasyd Perkins*. Boston: Little Brown, 1856.

Chamberlain, Allen. *Beacon Hill*. Boston: Houghton Mifflin, 1925.

Chamberlin, Joseph Edgar. *The Boston Transcript*. Boston: Houghton Mifflin, 1930.

Coolidge, Alice B. *My Early Reminiscences*. Manuscript, Boston Athenaeum.

Coolidge, T. Jefferson. *The Autobiography of T. Jefferson Coolidge*. Boston: Houghton Mifflin, 1923.

Crawford, Mary Caroline. *Famous Families of Massachusetts*. 2 vols. Boston: Little Brown, 1930.

———. *Romantic Days in Old Boston*. Boston: Little Brown, 1922.

———. *St. Botolph's Town*. Boston: L. C. Page, 1908.

Cullen, James Bernard. *The Story of the Irish in Boston*. Boston: James B. Cullen & Co., 1889.

Cunningham, Edith Perkins. *Letters and Journal of Edith Forbes Perkins*. 4 vols. Boston: Privately printed, 1931.

Davis, Elmer. "Boston: Notes on a Barbarian Invasion." *Harper's*, January, 1928.

Dempewolff, Richard. *Famous Old New England Murders*. Brattleboro, Vermont: Stephen Daye Press, 1942.

Dinneen, Joseph F. "Brahmin From Boston." *New Republic*, February 24, 1947.

Drake, Samuel G. *The History and Antiquities of the City of Boston.* Boston: Luther Stevens, 1854.

Drown, Paulina Cony. *Mrs. Bell.* Boston: Houghton Mifflin, 1931.

Early, Eleanor. *And This Is Boston!* Boston: Houghton Mifflin, 1938.

Familiar Letters of John Adams and His Wife Abigail Adams. New York: Hurd & Houghton, 1876.

(Farrar, Mrs. John). *The Young Lady's Friend.* Boston: American Stationers' Co., 1836.

Fifty Years of Boston. Boston Tercentenary Committee, 1932.

Forbes, Allan. *Early Myopia.* Boston: Privately printed, 1942.

Forbes, A. and Greene, J. W. *The Rich Men of Massachusetts.* Boston: Fetridge and Co., 1851.

Forbes, Esther. *Paul Revere and the World He Lived In.* Boston: Houghton Mifflin, 1942.

Forbes, Robert S. *Personal Reminiscences.* Boston: Little Brown, 1882.

Frothingham, O. B. *Boston Unitarianism.* New York: Putnam, 1890.

Gilman, Arthur. *The Story of Boston.* New York: Putnam, 1889.

Greenslet, Ferris. *The Lowells and Their Seven Worlds.* Boston: Houghton Mifflin, 1946.

Hall, Florence Howe. *The Correct Thing in Good Society.* Boston: Estes and Lauriat, 1888.

———. *Social Customs.* Boston: Estes and Lauriat, 1887.

Harlow, Alvin F. *Steelways of New England.* New York: Creative Age Press, 1946.

Higginson, Henry Lee. "A Word to the Rich." *Atlantic*, March, 1911.

———. "Justice to the Corporations." *Atlantic*, January, 1908.

Higginson, Mary Thacher. *Thomas Wentworth Higginson.* Boston: Houghton Mifflin, 1914.

Holbrook, Stewart. "Murder at Harvard." *The American Scholar*, 1945.

Howe, Julia Ward. "Social Boston, Past and Present." *Harper's Bazaar*, February, 1909.

Howe, M. A. DeWolfe. *Barrett Wendell and His Letters.* Boston: Atlantic Monthly Press, 1922.

————. *The Boston Symphony Orchestra.* Boston: Houghton Mifflin, 1931.

————. *Boston, The Place and The People.* New York: Macmillan, 1903.

————. *Holmes of the Breakfast-Table.* New York: Oxford University Press, 1939.

————. *The Humane Society of the Commonwealth of Massachusetts.* Boston: Humane Society, 1918.

————. *Later Years of the Saturday Club.* Boston: Houghton Mifflin, 1921.

————. *Memories of a Hostess.* Boston: Atlantic Monthly Press, 1922.

————. *Portrait of an Independent: Moorfield Storey.* Boston: Houghton Mifflin, 1932.

————. *A Venture in Remembrance.* Boston: Little Brown, 1941.

Hughes, Sarah Forbes. *Letters and Recollections of John Murray Forbes.* 2 vols. Boston: Houghton Mifflin, 1899.

Hunnewell, Mary B. *The Glades.* Boston: Privately printed, 1914.

Hunt, Freeman. *Lives of American Merchants.* New York: Hunt's Merchants Magazine, 1856.

The Influence in History of the Boston Athenaeum. Boston: Boston Athenaeum, 1907.

Jarman, Rufus. "You Can't Beat A Lodge." *Saturday Evening Post,* March 15, 1947.

Lawrence, William. "An Invigorating Avocation." *Atlantic,* September, 1923.

————. *Life of Amos A. Lawrence.* Boston: Houghton Mifflin, 1888.

————. *Memories of a Happy Life.* Boston: Houghton Mifflin, 1926.

Lee, Mary. *A History of the Chestnut Hill Chapel.* History Committee of the First Church of Chestnut Hill, 1937.

Lodge, Henry Cabot. *Early Memories.* New York: Scribner's, 1913.

Lowell, A. Lawrence. *What a University President Has Learned.* New York: Macmillan, 1938.

Lundberg, Ferdinand. *America's 60 Families.* New York: Vanguard Press, 1937.

Marcosson, Isa F. "The Millionaire Yield of Boston." *Munsey's Magazine.* Vol. 47, No. 5, 1912.

Martin, George W. "Preface to the Biography of a Headmaster." *Harper's,* January, 1944.

Martin, Pete. "The George Apleys Banked Here." *Saturday Evening Post*, March 15, 1947.

Mason, Alpheus Thomas. *Brandeis*. New York: The Viking Press, 1946.

Minnigerode, Meade. *Some American Ladies*. New York: Putnam, 1926.

Morison, Samuel Eliot. *Builders of the Bay Colony*. Boston: Houghton Mifflin, 1930.

———. *Maritime History of Massachusetts, 1783-1860*. Boston: Houghton Mifflin, 1921.

———. *Three Centuries of Harvard*. Cambridge: Harvard University Press, 1936.

Morse, John T., Jr. *Memoir of Colonel Henry Lee*. Boston: Little Brown, 1905.

Our First Men. A Calendar of Wealth, Fashion & Gentility. Boston: Privately printed, 1846.

Parker, Maude. "Boston's Best." *Saturday Evening Post*, March 19, 1927.

Pearson, Edmund. "America's Classic Murder." *Murder at Smutty Nose*. New York: Doubleday Doran, 1926.

Perry, Bliss. *And Gladly Teach*. Boston: Houghton Mifflin, 1935.

———. *Life and Letters of Henry Lee Higginson*. Boston: Atlantic Monthly Press, 1921.

Perry, George Sessions. "Boston." *Saturday Evening Post*, September 15, 1945.

Pier, Arthur Stanwood. *St. Paul's School*. New York: Scribner's, 1934.

Post, Emily. *Etiquette*. New York: Funk and Wagnalls, 1942.

Regan, Mary Jane. *Echoes from the Past*. Boston: Boston Athenaeum, 1927.

Robbins, Rev. Chandler. *Memoir of Hon. William Appleton*. Boston: John Wilson & Son, 1863.

Rossiter, William S. *Days and Ways in Old Boston*. Boston: R. H. Stearns, 1915.

Schlesinger, Arthur M. "Learning How to Behave." A Study of Manners. *Bulletins of Boston Public Library*, February, March, and April, 1946.

Sedgwick, Ellery. *The Happy Profession*. Boston: Little Brown, 1946.

Shackleton, Robert. *The Book of Boston.* Philadelphia: The Penn Publishing Co., 1917.

Sherrill, Rev. Henry Knox. *William Lawrence—Later Years of a Happy Life.* Cambridge: Harvard University Press, 1943.

Singer, Kent and Bergen, Clarence Q. "Who Bans the Books in Boston." *This Month,* October, 1945.

Snow, Edward Rowe. *The Romance of Boston Bay.* Boston: The Yankee Publishing Co., 1944.

Spring, James W. *Boston and the Parker House.* Boston: J. R. Whipple, 1927.

State Street Trust Company. *Old Shipping Days in Boston.* Boston: 1918.

———. *Other Merchants and Sea Captains of Old Boston.* Boston: 1919.

———. *Some Merchants and Sea Captains.* Boston: 1918.

———. *Some Statues of Boston.* Boston: 1946.

Thwing, Annie Haven. *The Crooked and Narrow Streets of Boston.* Boston: Marshall Jones Co., 1920.

Ticknor, Caroline. *Dr. Holmes's Boston.* Boston: Houghton Mifflin, 1915.

Train, Arthur. "The Puritan Shadow." *Scribner's,* September, 1930.

Washburn, Frederick A. *The Massachusetts General Hospital.* Boston: Houghton Mifflin, 1939.

Wecter, Dixon. *The Hero in History.* New York: Scribner's, 1941.

———. *The Saga of American Society.* New York: Scribner's, 1937.

Welles, Benjamin. "Harvard Has Class." *Town and Country,* December, 1939.

Whiting, Lillian. *Boston Days.* Boston: Little Brown, 1902.

Willison, George F. *Saints and Strangers.* New York: Reynal and Hitchcock, 1945.

Wilson, Fred A. *Some Annals of Nahant.* Boston: Old Corner Book Store, 1928.

(Wilson, Thomas L. V.). *The Aristocracy of Boston. By One Who Knows Them.* Boston: Privately printed, 1848.

Winsor, Justin (Ed.). *The Memorial History of Boston, 1630-1880.* 5 vols. Boston: Ticknor & Co., 1880.

Winthrop, Robert C. *Memoir of Hon. Nathan Appleton.* Boston: John Wilson & Son, 1861.

INDEX

INDEX